Two Timely Issues

Two Timely Issues

*The New Mass and the Possibility
of a Heretical Pope*

ARNALDO VIDIGAL XAVIER DA SILVEIRA
TRANSLATED BY JOHN RUSSELL SPANN AND JOSÉ ALOISIO SCHELINI

*The Foundation for a Christian Civilization, Inc.
Spring Grove, Penn.*

FIRST PUBLISHED IN PORTUGUESE AS
Considerações sobre o "Ordo missae" de Paulo VI
© Copyright 1970
Self-published by author, São Paulo

PUBLISHED IN SPANISH AS
Implicaciones teologicas y morales del nuevo "Ordo missae": Elementos para un diálogo que se va generalizando en todo el orbe catolico
© Copyright 1971
Self-published by author, São Paulo

PUBLISHED IN FRENCH AS
La nouvelle messe de Paul VI: Qu'en penser?
© Copyright 1975
Diffusion de la Pensée Française, Chiré-en-Montreuil, 86190 Vouillé, France

PUBLISHED IN ENGLISH AS
Theological and Moral Implications of the "Novus Ordo Missae"
© Copyright 1976
Lumen Mariae Publications,
Cleveland, Ohio 44199

PART TWO PUBLISHED IN ITALIAN AS
Ipotesi teologica di un papa eretico
© Copyright 2016
Edizioni Solfanelli, Chieti, 66100 Italy

REVISED PART TWO PUBLISHED IN ENGLISH AS
Can a Pope Be . . . a Heretic? The Theological Hypothesis of a Heretical Pope
© Copyright 2018
Caminhos Romanos, Porto, Portugal

Printed in the United States of America

Hardcover: 979-8-9863093-0-9
Paperback: 979-8-9863093-1-6
Ebook: 979-8-9863093-2-3

Library of Congress Control Number: 2022945238

Contents

Abbreviations

1917 CIC—*The 1917 or Pio-Benedictine Code of Canon Law in English Translation With Extensive Scholarly Apparatus*, edited by Edward N. Peters (San Francisco: Ignatius Press, 2001).

AXS.pt—*Considerações sobre o 'Ordo missae' de Paulo VI* (São Paulo: self-published, 1970).

AXS.fr—*La nouvelle messe de Paul VI: Qu'en penser?* (Chiré-en-Montreuil, France: Diffusion de la Pensée Française, 1975).

AXS.it—*Ipotesi teologica di un papa eretico* (Chieti, Italy: Ed. Solfanelli, 2016).

Denz.-Hün.—Heinrich Denzinger, *Compendium of Creeds, Definitions, and Declarations on Matters of Faith and Morals*, ed. Peter Hünermann, English ed. Robert Fastiggi and Anne Englund Nash, 43rd ed. (San Francisco: Ignatius Press, 2012).

Denz.-R—*The Sources of Catholic Dogma*, ed. Karl Rahner, S.J., trans. Roy J. Deferrari (St. Louis: B. Herder Book Co., 1957).

Denz.-Sch.— Heinrich Denzinger, *Enchiridion symbolorum*, ed. Adolfus Schoenmetzer, S.J.

D.T.C.—*Dictionnaire de théologie catholique*, edited by Jean Michel Alfred Vacant, Eugène Mangenot, and Émile Amann, 30 vols. (Paris: Letouzey et Ané, 1902–1950).

E.C.—*Enciclopedia cattolica*, 12 vols. (Vatican: Ente per l'Enciclopedia Cattolica e per i Libro Cattolico, Soc. p.a., 1948–1954).

I.C.E.L.—International Commission on English in the Liturgy.

P.L.—*Patrologia cursus completus: Series latina* (Paris: J.P. Migne, 1841–1865), 221 vols.

Publisher's Note

This book compiles three independent studies published in Portuguese: *Considerations on the Ordo Missae of Paul VI*,[1] "Modifications Introduced in the 1969 Ordo,"[2] and "The Infallibility of Ecclesiastical Laws."[3]

The author assembled these three studies into a single work. Chapter 4 contains the "Modifications" study, while Chapter 6 presents the "Infallibility" one. The author updated his work in 1974 and again in 2017.

After his last update, the author kept abreast of developments in the new Mass debate and believed that his work needed no further changes. He died in September 2018.

This is the first edition, in any language, compiling all initial studies and their updates. Accordingly, it was slightly restructured, turning the two original appendices into chapters and numbering chapters sequentially across the two parts. The appendix to Part One became Chapter 6, while that of Part Two became Chapter 17. The original final chapter of Part Two was turned into the book's final one, becoming Chapter 18. The author made no changes to the Conclusion in 2017.

Because the base studies were written in the 1970s, all Canon Law references are to the 1917 Pio-Benedictine Code of Canon Law, abbreviated as 1917 CIC (*Codex iuris canonicis*).

In this revised second English edition, the translators assume responsibility for the English translations from the 1969 *Institutio*'s Latin original.

Scriptural references are from the Douay-Rheims version unless otherwise noted.

In quotations from very old sources (e.g., Torquemada, *Summa de Ecclesia*, Venice: 1561), the translators have taken the liberty to insert some paragraph breaks.

When provided, access dates and hyperlinks to online sources are shown only in the bibliography.

The 10,000-word essay by Mr. José A. Ureta, titled "A Brief Study of Theological Deviations in *Desiderio Desideravi*," is being added by the Publisher as an Appendix.

---

1. See Arnaldo Vidigal Xavier da Silveira, *Considerações sobre o* Ordo missae *de Paulo VI* (São Paulo: self-published, June 1970).
2. See Arnaldo Xavier da Silveira, "Modificações introduzidas no Ordo de 1969" (São Paulo, Aug. 1970).
3. See Arnaldo Xavier da Silveira, "A infalibilidade das leis eclesiásticas" (São Paulo, Jan. 1971).

You Are Holding a Forbidden Book

On June 14, 1966, the Sacred Congregation for the Doctrine of the Faith abolished the *Index librorum prohibitorum*. Yet, seven years later, on September 24, 1973, Pope Paul VI did not hesitate to forbid the publication of this book. Vicente Cardinal Scherer, archbishop of Porto Alegre, Brazil, transmitted the pope's verbal order to Most Rev. Antônio de Castro Mayer, bishop of Campos. They had studied together at the Gregorian University in Rome.[4]

Two months earlier, in separate mailings and with cover letters from the then-bishop of Campos, the entire Brazilian episcopate had received a mimeographed copy of two of the studies that make up this book. They were titled "Considerations on the New *Ordo Missae* of Paul VI" and "Modifications Introduced Into the 1969 *Ordo*."

A third study titled "The Infallibility of Ecclesiastical Laws," written in January 1971, was added in a new mimeographed edition in Portuguese, Spanish, and English. The two translations had a limited circulation among traditionalist-oriented priests and laity in their respective linguistic areas.

In 1975, as the first print edition intended for the general public was coming off the press, the author was obliged to stop its distribution and buy the complete print run. He could not help but bow to a request from Bishop Mayer, who sought to avoid a frontal clash with Paul VI. This French edition was prepared by the well-known publisher Diffusion de la Pensée Française (Chiré-en-Montreuil, France).

This explains why the first part of the present work, which studies the *Novus ordo missae* in detail, is practically unknown to the general Catholic public and is rarely cited by authors who have dealt with this subject, despite its substantive analyses.

The book's second part—on the theological possibility of a heretical pope—is better known, albeit dealing with a topic no modern scholar had systematically studied. It stirred up renewed interest during debates about heterodox statements

---

4. See "O Leão de Campos (VI): O bispo de Campos e o magistério de Paulo VI," FratresInUnum.com, June 27, 2010.

in the post-synodal apostolic exhortation *Amoris laetitia* and was published separately in Italian[5] and English.[6]

Interest in this new English edition of all three studies is not merely historical. In seeking to ultimately eliminate the immemorial rite of the Holy Mass, Pope Francis's July 16, 2021, motu proprio *Traditionis custodes* reopened the liturgical war. John Paul II and Benedict XVI had sought to quell that conflict, the first with the apostolic letter *Ecclesia Dei afflicta* and the second with the motu proprio *Summorum pontificum.*

However, many priests and faithful are determined not to renounce a liturgy that has enriched their faith and spiritual life. They feel compelled to explain their fidelity to the traditional rite to themselves and their opponents. They know it stems from important theological motives, not from a sentimental or cultural attachment to old liturgical forms.

The desire to know the profound reasons for fidelity to the ancient Mass is especially evident among younger people who did not live through the troubled period of Paul VI's implacable application of the liturgical reform, participating in the ensuing debates.

That desire became more acute as controversy swirled on social media on the delicate subject of concelebration with the bishop at Maundy Thursday's Chrism Mass. Pope Francis wants to impose concelebration on priests wishing to say the traditional Latin Mass as a *conditio sine qua non* to benefit from the meager permissions granted by *Traditionis custodes*. Any answer to the theological, canonical, and strategic questions raised by this requirement depends on the greater or lesser gravity of the deficiencies and deviations of the *Ordo missae* of Paul VI. Hence, in many Catholic circles, there is a renewed desire to study this issue in depth.

Since 1969, when Paul VI's new Ordinary of the Mass came into effect, several studies analyzed those failings. The best known are *The Ottaviani Intervention: Short Critical Study of the New Order of Mass*, written by a group of theologians and delivered to Paul VI by Cardinals Ottaviani and Bacci, and *The Reform of the Roman Liturgy: Its Problems and Background,* by Msgr. Klaus Gamber, whose French edition received an introduction by then-Cardinal Joseph Ratzinger. Michael Davies's three volumes on the liturgical revolution—*Cranmer's Godly Order, Pope John's Council,* and *Pope Paul VI's New Mass*—were widely disseminated in the English-speaking world.

Nevertheless, two particularities distinguish Arnaldo Vidigal Xavier da Silveira's book from these and later books on various aspects of the New Ordinary of the Mass.

First, he courageously dealt with and exhaustively resolved two objections that had paralyzed many minds. People wondered whether it was legitimate to raise doubts about the orthodoxy of the New Mass for two reasons:

---

5. See Arnaldo Xavier da Silveira, *Ipotesi teologica di un papa eretico* (Chieti: Edizioni Solfanelli, 2016).

6. See Arnaldo Xavier da Silveira, *Can a Pope Be . . . a Heretic? The Theological Hypothesis of a Heretical Pope* (Porto: Caminhos Romanos, 2018).

(1) most theologians consider infallible a universal ecclesiastical law, such as the New Mass, ordered as it was for the entire Latin rite; and

(2) most Catholics think a pope cannot lapse into heresy.

The author painstakingly resolves the first stumbling block in Chapter 6 and the second in Part Two.

Secondly, the work not only provides an overall view of the shortcomings of the New Mass, giving illustrative examples, but also makes a thorough analysis of the *Institutio generalis missalis romani* and the 1969 *Ordo missae*, as well as the modifications made in 1970.

After more than fifty years since its original mimeographed publication, an updated edition might have been envisaged with contributions to the theological debate from the progressive and traditional camps, or even of high-ranking prelates, such as the severe criticisms from then-Cardinal Joseph Ratzinger. He wrote of "falsification" and "a fabricated liturgy," which resulted in "devastation."[7] Some passages that might seem obsolete to contemporary readers could also have been updated. For example, the author illustrates the 1969 *Institutio's* heterodox character as interpreted by *Nuevas normas de la misa* (New Norms for the Mass), a work published in 1969 by *Biblioteca de Autores Cristianos,* the important publishing house of the Spanish Dominican Fathers. More radical interpretations have emerged since then.

One could also have considered enhancing the author's arguments with later revelations by the architects of the New Mass themselves, for example, Fr. Joseph Gelineau, S.J. He gloated over the reforms, stating, "Indeed, it is another liturgy of the Mass. It must be said bluntly: the Roman Rite as we knew it no longer exists; it has been destroyed."[8] This confession is even more compelling as he was one of the *Consilium's* leading specialists, and he and his team are said to have written the Fourth Eucharistic Prayer from scratch in a single night.[9]

However, this revised English edition preserves the original work with no additions except those made by the author to Part Two in 2017. For one, including later developments could alter the balance of the work's original analyses by placing greater emphasis on some points or changing the final assessment concerning the New Mass. On the other hand, updates could obscure that it was a *war manual* of sorts. Some of its chapters were written in the heat of battle, shortly after Paul VI's New Mass went into effect. It aimed to provide some first elements of reflection to priests and laypeople disoriented or perplexed by the radical nature of the reforms.

---

7. Joseph Ratzinger, "L'intrépidité d'un vrai témoin," introduction to *La réforme liturgique en question*, by Klaus Gamber, trans. Simone Wallon (Le Barroux, France: Éditions Sainte-Madeleine 1992), 6–8.

8. Joseph Gelineau, *Demain la liturgie: Essai sur l'évolution des assemblées chrétiennes* (Paris: Les Éditions du Cerf, 1977), 10.

9. See Claire Lesegretain, "Le missel de Paul VI fête ses trente ans," *La Croix*, Apr. 28, 1999, 19.

As the author recounts, Part Two of his book, dealing with the theological possibility of a heretical pope, benefited from having been the object of four years of research and reflections, starting in 1965. The work took shape after a small symposium held in São Paulo, July 28–30, 1966, with the participation of Most Rev. Geraldo de Proença Sigaud, archbishop of Diamantina (1909–1999); Bishop Mayer, then-ordinary of Campos; Brazilian TFP founder Prof. Plinio Corrêa de Oliveira (1908–1995); and the author. They concluded that the studies should continue and eventually lead to taking a stand on the issue. These more leisurely studies resulted in a series of articles on the infallibility of ecclesiastical teaching and related topics, which the author published in the monthly *Catolicismo* in the last three months of 1967.[10] They helped him to delve deeper into the subject.

On the contrary, Part One of the book, analyzing the New Mass, had to be put together very quickly, starting in October 1969, when the first materials reached the author's hands. Just a month later, a symposium was held November 24–29 in Serra Negra, state of São Paulo, with the participation of Bishop Mayer, Prof. Corrêa de Oliveira, Prof. Paulo Corrêa de Brito Filho, and Atty. Gregorio Vivanco Lopes, who acted as secretary. After examining the author's material, they decided that he would write a first draft on the liturgical issues under Bishop Mayer's guidance.

The same individuals met again, in a new symposium, in early 1970, on a farm in Amparo, in the state of São Paulo. The author presented a first draft, which was carefully examined.

The final version of *Considerations on the 'Ordo Missae' of Paul VI* was ready by the end of June 1970. Mimeographed copies were mailed to the Brazilian bishops on July 16. However, in that same month, the magazine *Notitiae*, of the Congregation for Divine Worship, reported that Paul VI had introduced changes in the rite in response to the *Short Critical Study of the Novus Ordo Missae* presented by Cardinals Ottaviani and Bacci. That forced Xavier da Silveira to write, in just two weeks, the study *Modifications Introduced in the 'Ordo' of 1969*. Like the previous work, it was reviewed by the larger commission and mailed to the Brazilian bishops in early August 1970.

Despite the short lead time and the psychological pressure of writing a "combat" text in a highly contentious context, the author's study is serene, in-depth, well-documented, and cautious. In its conclusion, he avoided making a specific theological censure to the *Novus ordo missae*. Still, he bluntly stated that "the New Mass cannot be accepted either in its 1969 or 1970 versions."

A final consideration can be made on this book's relevance. Between 1991 and 1996, a work to revise and update the *Missale romanum* resulted in a new, third edition, on March 22, 2002. According to Jorge Cardinal Medina Estévez, then-prefect of the Congregation for Divine Worship, it was not a mere *reimpres-*

---

10. See Arnaldo Xavier da Silveira, "*Can Documents of the Magisterium of the Church Contain Errors? Can the Catholic Faithful Resist Them?* trans. John R. Spann and José Aloisio A. Schelini (Spring Grove, Penn.: The American Society for the Defense of Tradition, Family, and Property, 2015). All of the articles are listed by the author in footnote 17.

sio amendata (amended reprint) but a genuine *editio typica* that should serve as a paradigm for translations into vernacular languages.[11]

In those same years, then-Cardinal Joseph Ratzinger called for a "reform of the reform" that would incorporate elements of the ancient rite into the new one. Accordingly, some hoped that the *editio typica tertia* in preparation would correct the more serious defects of the 1970 missal. That hope was all the more significant as Cardinal Medina was known to be intellectually close to and a personal friend of the then-prefect of the Congregation for the Doctrine of the Faith.

However, such hopes never materialized. Except for the happy return of the word "soul" in some prayers and prefaces for the dead, the New Mass remained unchanged. Some feasts and prayers were added, and adjustments were made on how to celebrate the Easter Triduum.

The major addition was the insertion of new Eucharistic Prayers: two for reconciliation, four for particular circumstances, and three for assemblies with children (but in 2008, when the missal was reprinted, the particularly inconsistent prayers for celebrations with children were relegated to an offprint).

The General Instruction also remained substantially the same as in 1970 except for making a few initial clarifications, developing some theological explanations, and specifying the exclusive gestures of clergy and faithful.[12]

In addition to the foreword's incorporation into the body of the Instruction, another novelty was a new section on accommodations and adaptations to make the liturgy more "pastorally effective" in culturally diverse communities. A new chapter was added on the competence of bishops and episcopal conferences to introduce such adaptations.

The Instruction went further than previous ones on the question of Communion under both species by significantly extending the cases in which the practice is allowed. A few conservative priests took advantage of the extension to administer Communion under both species by intinction, thus avoiding giving Communion in the hand. However, being progressive, a much larger number of parishes turned reception under both species, sharing the chalice, into the common way of giving Communion, thereby diminishing the difference between the faithful and the celebrant.

The 1970 Instruction contained a section detailing the participation of women in the liturgy. It stated that they should exert their ministry outside the sanctuary at the discretion of the parish priest. In any case, it barred them from approaching the altar. Except for the celebrant, the 2002 Instruction eliminated any reference

---

11. See Congregation for Divine Worship and the Discipline of the Sacraments, "Presentazione del nuovo messale romano: Intervento del Cardinale Jorge Arturo Medina Estévez," Vatican.va, Mar. 18, 2002.

12. For a synthesis of the origin and peculiarities of the new typical edition, see Giovanni di Napoli, "Terza edizione italiana del messale romano: Dono e *kairos* per riscoprire il linguagio, la forza e la grazia del celebrare," *Rassegna di Teologia* 61 (2020): 357–75; for an exhaustive analysis from a progressive perspective, see Edward Foley, Nathan D. Mitchell, and Joanne M. Pierce, eds., *A Commentary on the General Instruction of the Roman Missal* (Collegeville, Minn.: Liturgical Press, 2007).

to the sex of those helping with the liturgy inside the sanctuary. Thus, it remotely paved the way for the motu proprio *Spiritus Domini,* in which Pope Francis formally opened the ministries of reader and acolyte to women.

In short, one can safely say that the structure of the rite and the overall way of celebrating the New Mass remained practically unchanged despite the expectations of conservatives for the 2002 typical edition. Therefore, the Roman Missal's most recent edition, whose vernacular translations are universally used, continues to merit the observations made by Xavier da Silveira about Paul VI's modifications in the 1970 edition. Those were that the *Institutio generalis* only had the effect of "making the errors less evident, without, however, eliminating them," and "the dispositions which marked a profound and violent rupture with the ritual tradition of the Catholic liturgy continue unaltered" in the *Ordo missae* itself.

Reading *Two Timely Issues: The New Mass and the Possibility of a Heretical Pope* is necessary and opportune.

José Antonio Ureta

General Introduction

Careful consideration of contemporary events obliges one to recognize that Pope John XXIII was entirely right in saying that an antidecalogue directs the action of men and societies in our days.[13] The most serious aspect of this situation is that now, as in the time of Modernism, condemned by Saint Pius X, "the partisans of error are to be sought not only among the Church's open enemies: they lie hid . . . in her very bosom and heart."[14] This is what Paul VI pointed out in a pithy expression that immediately became famous, that the Holy Church seems to be involved in a process of "self-demolition" carried out by her own children.[15]

Amid this generalized disintegration, faithful souls turn to the Chair of Peter, as if instinctively, in search of the clear and energetic direction that will end the follies spreading in Catholic circles. To him who is the "sweet Christ on Earth"[16] and apart from whom there are no words of eternal life, Catholics direct the appeal with which the chosen people implored Jephte to lead them in the fight against the Ammonites: "Come thou and be our prince" (Judg. 11:6).

However, disturbing surprises and perplexities seem to cloud the hope which animates those who, like us, are unconditionally devoted to the papacy. For example, on the occasion of the implementation of the new *Ordo missae*, most eminent figures among the hierarchy, theologians, and laity declared that the new liturgy of the Eucharistic Sacrifice was unacceptable. These pronouncements not only became public but were even reported on in major media. The new *Ordo missae* polemic takes on an immediate and transcendental interest in that the Holy Mass is related to the everyday piety of the fervent Catholic and is representative of everything that is most sacred in the Church. The issue is fraught with dramatic consequences for every son of the Church.

Concerned with clearing up the anguishing doubts on the principle of authority in the Church that in recent years have troubled numerous faithful, we have been studying doctrinal questions related to the present-day crisis for a long time.

---

13. See John XXIII, "Christmas Radio Message" (Dec. 22, 1960).
14. St. Pius X, encyclical Pascendi Domenici Gregis (Sept. 8, 1907), no. 2.
15. Paul VI, "Allocution to the Students of the Pontifical Lombard Seminary" (Dec. 7, 1968).
16. St. Catherine of Siena, "Letter 196 to Gregory XI," in Saint Catherine of Siena As Seen in Her Letters, trans. and ed. Vida Dutton Scudder (New York: E.P.Dutton, 1905), 120.

Thus, we wrote in *Catolicismo*—a cultural monthly published under the auspices of the eminent bishop of Campos, Most Rev. Antonio de Castro Mayer—several articles about the ecclesiastical Magisterium and other themes of a dogmatic, moral, and canonical nature.[17]

Since the promulgation of the New Mass, we have been studying it in detail and feel compelled to express in writing some conclusions from this study—they are the reason for this volume.

In presenting an analysis of the *Ordo missae* of Paul VI, it seemed indispensable to examine an objection that could be formulated against anyone who wished to question the orthodoxy of a pontifical act. The objection would be the following: Given the divine promises made to Saint Peter and his successors, it is absurd to even raise the hypothesis that a papal act can be susceptible to reservations, in any degree, as to its orthodoxy.

Therefore, it becomes indispensable to present here after examining the New Mass (Part One), an analysis of another problem discussed abundantly by theologians and canonists over the centuries. We have been studying it for some years. It is the theological hypothesis of a pope falling into heresy (Part Two). Together with this question, we shall consider some others connected to it: the hypotheses of a dubious pope and a schismatic one, the possibility of error and heresy in documents of the Magisterium, and the right of public resistance to iniquitous decisions handed down by ecclesiastical authority.

We wish to emphasize that we do not write these lines in a spirit of *contestation*. We are not moved, in any way, by any intent of questioning the principle of authority in Holy Mother Church. On the contrary, it is in defense of Catholic unity itself and of the supreme authority of the Church—Jesus Christ—Whose vicar on earth is the pope, that we offer the present considerations on the new *Ordo missae*, as well as on the hypothesis of the defection of a pope from the Faith.

In addition, we feel perfectly willing to analyze—in scientific and always respectful terms—what is the measure in which, *according to theology and canon law*, specific papal acts effectively oblige. Defending the principle of authority was always one of the supreme guiding rules for the action of *Catolicismo* (with which we have collaborated since its early years) and the Brazilian Society for the Defense of Tradition, Family, and Property, to whose National Council we have the honor to belong.

---

17. Our essays published in *Catolicismo* are: "Qual a autoridade doutrinária dos documentos pontifícios e conciliares?" ("What Is the Doctrinal Authority of Pontifical and Conciliar Documents?"), *Catolicismo*, no. 202 (Oct. 1967); "Não só a heresia pode ser condenada pela autoridade eclesiástica" ("Not Only Heresy Can Be Condemned By Ecclesiastical Authority"), *Catolicismo*, no. 203 (Nov. 1967); "Atos, gestos, atitudes e omissões podem caracterizar o herege" ("Acts, Gestures, Attitudes, and Omissions Can Characterize the Heretic"), *Catolicismo*, no. 204 (Dec. 1967); "Respondendo a objeções de um imaginário leitor progressista" ("Answering the Objections of an Imaginary Progressivist Reader"), *Catolicismo*, no. 206 (Feb. 1968); "Pode um católico rejeitar a *Humanae Vitae*?" ("Can a Catholic Reject *Humanae Vitae*?"), *Catolicismo*, nos. 212/214 (Aug.–Oct. 1968); "Pode haver êrro em documentos do magisterio?" ("Can There Be Error in Documents of the Magisterium?"), *Catolicismo*, no. 223 (July 1969); "Resistência pública a decisões da autoridade eclesiástica" ("Public Resistance to Decisions of Ecclesiastical Authority"), *Catolicismo*, no. 224 (Aug. 1969).

In other words, if one understands by contestation the action whereby an inferior refuses due obedience to a superior, offending against the principle of authority in any of its aspects, then we find ourselves at the extreme opposite. We have the fieriest love and most ardent enthusiasm for papal primacy and the principle of authority in general. We would never have raised the problems studied herein had we not the sure precedent of saints and doctors such as Saints Paul, Leo II, Ivo of Chartres, Bruno of Segni, Godfrey of Amiens, Hugh of Grenoble, Thomas Aquinas, Robert Bellarmine, and so many others. They have taught us, by word and deed, that one must not accompany an authority if it should happen to depart from the right path. Therefore, following in the steps of so many and such great doctors, we do not contest ecclesiastical authority in any sense. Rather, we are trying to determine in what measure one can or must, *according to the most genuine teachings of the Church*, accept the new *Ordo missae*.[18]

---

18. **Author's note for the 1976 English edition:** In writing the present book during the years 1969 and 1970, we had a very limited intention: To investigate up to what point the Latin text of the new *Ordo missae* keeps within the tradition of pure orthodoxy inherent to all Catholic liturgy until that day, or whether, on the contrary, it showed the influence of heterodox theologians, such as Protestants, for example. Thus, a question of great importance, arising *not from the 1969 Latin text* but rather from gravely incorrect vernacular translations of the *Ordo missae* of St. Pius V appearing around 1967, was not treated by us. We are referring to the problem of the validity or nullity of the Mass in the face of the expression "for all," introduced into the formula of the Consecration of the wine. For the same reason, a study of the canonical consequences of the "*in perpetuum*" clause with which St. Pius V promulgated the bull "*Quo primum*" is likewise beyond the scope of the present book.

Therefore, our readers will not find here a reference to these two questions—about which traditionalist North American theologians have produced abundant and valuable studies. Eventually, we shall take up these questions in another edition of this work or in special monographs.

PART ONE

The New Mass

On April 3, 1969, Paul VI published the apostolic constitution *Missale romanum,*[19] which promulgated two important documents related to the reform of the rite of the Mass.

Those documents are the *Institutio generalis missalis romani* (General Order of the Roman Missal) and the new *Ordo missae* proper,[20] that is, the new text of the Mass with its accompanying rubrics.

The apostolic constitution explains that the traditional Mass of the Roman rite dates from Saint Gregory the Great, having been modified in accidental points by Saint Pius V, in 1570, following the decrees of the Council of Trent. It recounts the recent alterations introduced into the liturgy and declares that the reform of the Mass now established has in view the fulfillment of the decisions of the Second Vatican Council. That reform—says Pope Paul VI—was not improvised but resulted from long and careful study. The apostolic constitution further indicates the principal alterations introduced and, finally, promulgates the *Institutio generalis* and the new *Ordo missae,* giving them papal authority. These two documents came into effect on the First Sunday of Advent, November 30, 1969.

The *Institutio generalis missalis romani*[21] was prepared by the Pontifical Commission for the Implementation of the Constitution on the Sacred Liturgy.[22] As indicated, the pope gave that 1969 *Institutio* the character and authority of a pontifical document. It consists of 341 items in which the new rites are minutely explained, and theoretical and practical principles are established for the Eucharistic celebration.

Concerning the liturgical movement which developed during the pontificate of Pius XII, Paul VI writes in *Missale romanum,* "Since that time there has grown and spread among the Christian people the liturgical renewal which, according to Pius XII, Our predecessor of venerable memory, seems to show the signs of God's providence in the present time, a salvific action of the Holy Spirit in His Church. This renewal has also shown clearly that the formulas of the Roman Missal ought to be revised and enriched. The beginning of this renewal was the work of Our predecessor, this same Pius XII."[23]

---

19. The citations of the documents promulgated by this apostolic constitution in 1969 will be made from the typical edition.

20. In its broad sense, *Ordo missae* signifies "the ordering of the Mass." In this acceptation, it includes the fixed parts of the Mass, the variable ones, and all the laws and rubrics referring to the celebration. In its narrow sense, the expression is generally used only to indicate the fixed parts of the Mass. We refer to the *Ordo missae* only in this narrow acceptation.

On the other hand, since the Latin formula has always been current among us—as in all of the West—we shall use the expression *Ordo missae* and its vernacular translation "Ordinary of the Mass" interchangeably. We shall also use the abbreviated Latin form *Ordo.*

21. Consilium Pontificium ad Exsequendam Constitutionem de Sacra Liturgia, *Institutio generalis missalis romani,* in *Ordo missae,* editio typica (Vatican: Typis Polyglottis Vaticanis: 1969). **Translator's Note**: We shall call this document the 1969 *Institutio.* In this revised English edition, the translators assume responsibility for the English translations from the 1969 *Institutio*'s Latin original.

22. "Consilium Pontificium ad Exsequendam Constitutionem de Sacra Liturgia." As its name reveals, this is an organ of the Holy See in charge of establishing norms for the implementation of the constitution *Sacrosanctum concilium* (on the Sacred Liturgy) of the Second Vatican Council.

23. Paul VI, apostolic constitution *Missale romanum* (Apr. 3, 1969).

It seems noteworthy that Paul VI, when referring to the liturgical movement of the time of Pius XII, said absolutely nothing about the very grave doctrinal errors infecting large sectors of that movement. Indeed, the magnificent liturgical revival initiated in the nineteenth century by the Benedictine abbot of Solesmes, Dom Prosper Guéranger (d. 1875), was later derailed from its true goals in many of its followers, meriting, for this reason, various censures from Pius XII. The most grave of these was the encyclical *Mediator Dei,* which proscribed precisely many of the errors that have now become official legislation through the new *Ordo missae.*[24]

It is also to be noted that the very document of Pius XII mentioned here by Paul VI[25] warns the faithful once more against various liturgical deviations. Pius XII had denounced these errors previously.[26]

The text of the New Mass, promulgated on April 3, 1969, underwent various modifications on the occasion of the publication of the new Missal in May 1970.

We shall study the 1969 text and the 1970 modifications in separate chapters.[27] We do this because we firmly believe that only someone who knows the original 1969 text can comment on the 1970 text of the New Mass. We will detail our reasons for thinking this way during our exposition.[28]

In Chapter 1, we shall study the 1969 *Institutio,* referring whenever necessary or advisable to the places in subsequent chapters where 1970 changes are discussed.

In Chapter 2, we shall take up a possible objection: that the *Institutio* also affirms traditional doctrine, so our criticisms in Chapter 1 have no solid foundation.

In Chapter 3, we shall consider the 1969 *Ordo missae,* also referring, when appropriate, to the passages in which we study the 1970 modifications.

---

24. On the condemnations contained in the encyclical *Mediator Dei* see also Antonio de Castro Mayer, "Carta pastoral sobre problemas do apostolado moderno" [*Pastoral Letter on Problems of the Modern Apostolate*] (Jan. 6, 1953), in *Por um cristianismo autêntico,* 17–118 (São Paulo: Editora Vera Cruz, 1971).

25. See Pius XII, "Allocution to the Participants of the International Congress on Pastoral Liturgy, Held in Assisi" (Sept. 22, 1956).

26. See Pius XII, encyclical *Mediator Dei* (Nov. 20, 1947); Allocution (Nov. 1, 1954); and Instruction of the Holy Office on Sacred Art (June 30, 1952).

27. The 1970 texts of the *Institutio* and the *Ordo* will be cited directly from the *Missale romanum* (Vatican: Typis Polyglottis Vaticanis, 1970). **Translator's Note:** For the English translation of the 1970 *Institutio,* the version used is that of Clifford Howell, trans., *Apostolic Constitution (Missale romanum) of Pope Paul VI and General Instruction on the Roman Missal* (London: Catholic Truth Society, 1973).

28. See our observations about the efforts made by official bodies of the Sacred Congregation for Divine Worship to deny the existence of doctrinal deviations in the 1969 *Institutio* and *Ordo*—chap. 4, sec. 8 (*The 1970 Revision of the* Institutio); their care in sustaining that the 1970 modifications did not correct anything in the previous text but only further elucidated what was already doctrinally beyond reproach—see the text supported by footnotes 321 and 322; Luther's temporizations and strategic retreats—see chap. 5, secs. 1 (*A Slow and Cautious Reform*) and 2 (*Luther's Temporizations*); the tendencies of the Protestant liturgy in recent decades—see chap. 5, sec. 3 (*A Lutheran Work on the Liturgy*); the contradictions which characterized the heterodox movements of every age—see chap. 2, sec. 2 (*Second Answer: The Contradictory Character of All Heresies*); and so forth.

In Chapter 4, we shall briefly study the 1970 modifications.[29]

In Chapter 5, we shall analyze some salient features of the Lutheran liturgy.

In Chapter 6, we shall consider another possible objection: Given that the Church is always infallible in the promulgation of universal laws, it is *a priori* absurd to doubt the orthodoxy of the text of the New Mass.

---

29. **Publisher's note:** Chapter 4 of *Considerações sobre o Ordo missae de Paulo VI* contains a study of the translation errors in the Portuguese version of the New Mass, many of them of very grave doctrinal consequence. We suppress that chapter in this English revised edition as not being of interest to the English-speaking reader. We cannot fail to observe, however, that the Portuguese translation of the New Mass is not the only one that frequently falls into deviations meriting grave doctrinal censure. To our knowledge, no systematic comparative study of the various vernacular texts of the New Mass has been done. Such a study is most desirable and would certainly reveal a general tendency meriting serious reservations.

CHAPTER ONE

The 1969 *Institutio Generalis Missalis Romani*

In analyzing some items of the 1969 *Institutio generalis missalis romani*,[30] we do not intend to study the document exhaustively. We shall make only those observations necessary for the reader to form a judgment about it in the light of traditional Catholic doctrine.[31]

Together with our observations, we shall present some commentaries on the *Institutio* made by four Spanish authors in their work *Nuevas normas de la misa*.[32] It was the first systematic explanation of the new *Ordo missae* to appear among us. For this reason, it has received wide distribution, all the more so since the book is part of the well-known collection Biblioteca de Autores Cristianos—B.A.C. (Library of Christian Authors), organized by eminent figures among Spain's theologians.

This work, inspired by the most extreme neomodernism, contains affirmations that depart completely from Catholic doctrine, as we shall demonstrate. That such publications are permitted to spread reveals that there is no intention to forbid such interpretations of the new *Ordo*.

---

30. In this chapter, we shall study some aspects of this document that have, above all, a doctrinal character, leaving to be analyzed together with the *Ordo* of 1969, in Chapter 3, certain practical dispositions of the 1969 *Institutio* which constitute true rubrics.

31. We want to note here that the promulgation of the New Ordinary of the Mass does not involve the infallibility of the Church. As this question has complex and delicate aspects, we shall discuss the problem of the infallibility of the Church in her liturgical laws *ex professo* in Chapter 6.

32. See J.M. Martín Patino, A. Pardo, A. Iniesta, and P. Farnes, *Nuevas normas de la misa: Ordenación general del misal romano* (Madrid: Biblioteca de Autores Cristianos, 1969). This work's first printing is dated June 1969. By November, it was already in its eighth. Fr. José María Martín Patino, S.J., whose name heads the list of authors, is a consultor to the "Consilium ad Exsequendam Constitutionem de Sacra Liturgia" and secretary of both the Spanish Liturgical Commission and the Mixed Episcopal Commission, Celam-Spain (C.E.M.), in charge of preparing the Spanish translations of the liturgical texts. See *Notitiae*, 1966, 200; 1967, 26. As for the other three authors of the *Nuevas normas de la misa*, we could not ascertain if they were consultors of the *Consilium* at the time because of the difficulty in obtaining a complete list of such consultors, who numbered two hundred in 1966. See *Notitiae*, 1966, 345.

For greater convenience, we shall indicate this book as the "B.A.C. commentary" on the *Institutio*, and its authors as "the B.A.C. commentators."

Publisher's Note: Fr. Martín Patino was also named consultor of the Sacred Congregation for Divine Worship.

This being the case, we shall occupy ourselves with the above book published by the B.A.C. not only on account of the evil it can do but, above all, because its free and broad distribution in Catholic circles shows how the 1969 *Institutio* and new *Ordo* are being interpreted.

1. The 1969 *Institutio* and the Dogma of Transubstantiation

One does not find the word *transubstantiation* a single time in the entire document. Nor does the 1969 *Institutio* refer to the *Real Presence* of Christ in the Eucharist even once.[33] There are, undoubtedly, many references to the "presence" of Our Lord. Various terms and expressions are used for this. However, the *Institutio* uses them indiscriminately to indicate Jesus's presence in the words of Scripture, the Eucharist, among those who are gathered in His name, and so forth. Here are some significant texts:[34]

> 1. ... (In the Mass) the mysteries of the Redemption are remembered in the course of the year, in such a way that they are recalled in the PRESENT. ...
>
> 9. When the Sacred Scriptures are read in the church, God Himself speaks to His people, and Christ, PRESENT IN HIS WORD, announces the Gospel. ...
>
> 28. The entrance hymn finished, the priest and all the assembly make the Sign of the Cross. Immediately afterward, through a salutation, the priest manifests to the united assembly the PRESENCE of the Lord. ...
>
> 33. ...In the readings, which the homily explains, God speaks to His people, reveals the mystery of redemption and salvation, and offers spiritual nourishment; and Christ Himself, by His word, is personally PRESENT amid the faithful. ...
>
> 35. The liturgy itself teaches [that] the greatest reverence should be paid to the reading of the Gospel since it surrounds it with special honor in comparison with the other readings, whether on the part of the minister ... or on the part of the faithful, who, with acclamations, recognize and profess Christ PRESENT WHO SPEAKS TO THEM, and listen to the reading standing; or from those acts of reverence given to the book of the Gospels. ...
>
> 48. The Last Supper, in which Christ instituted the memorial of His death and resurrection, IS CONTINUOUSLY EFFECTED PRESENTLY IN THE CHURCH when the priest, representing Christ the Lord, does the same as the Lord Himself did and handed down to His disciples that they do. ...

---

33. On the manner in which the expressions *transubstantiation* and *Real Presence* appear in the new 1970 text of the *Institutio*, see chap. 4, secs. 1 (*The Principal Features of the Foreword in the 1970* Institutio), 4 (*Do These Errors No Longer Exist Today?*), 9 (*Number 7 of the 1970* Institutio), and the Conclusion (*The New Mass and the Catholic Conscience*) *infra*.

34. Unless otherwise noted, the use of ALL CAPS for emphasis in quotations is always ours.

(2) In the eucharistic prayer, thanks are given to God for the whole work of salvation, and THE OFFERINGS BECOME THE BODY AND BLOOD OF CHRIST.[35]

(3) ...by communion the faithful receive the Body and Blood of the Lord in the same manner as the apostles from the hands of Christ Himself. ...[36]

60. ...When [the priest] celebrates the Eucharist, he ought to serve God and the people with dignity and humility, and REPRESENT TO THE FAITHFUL THE LIVING PRESENCE OF CHRIST, in his comportment and manner of saying the divine words.[37]

In number 241, the only item in which the 1969 *Institutio* refers to the Council of Trent, we read, "Above all, [the sacred pastors] should instruct the followers of Christ that the Catholic faith teaches that CHRIST, WHOLE AND ENTIRE and the true sacrament, is equally received under either of the two species."[38]

Number 55 of the *Institutio* explains the various parts of the Canon—now called the "Eucharistic Prayer." In respect to the Consecration (item "d"), we read the following: "The narrative of the institution: In this part, with words and actions of Christ, that Last Supper is represented again (*repraesentatur*) in which Christ the Lord Himself instituted the sacrament of His Passion and Resurrection, and gave to the apostles His Body and Blood to eat and drink under the appearances of bread and wine, commanding them to perpetuate the same mystery."[39]

The Latin term *repraesentatur* is translated, in the Brazilian Editora Vozes version,[40] as "He becomes present again." Without a doubt, the word also has this sense, but it also has another, as the translator knew, for this reason putting the Latin term in parentheses. This other sense would be "is represented," and it would give the text a very strong Protestant flavor, for the Mass is not a simple representation. Rather it is a true renewal of Our Lord's sacrifice.

---

35. As we shall show further on, the affirmation that "the offerings become the Body and Blood of Christ" is also admitted by Protestants since it does not necessarily involve the Catholic doctrine of transubstantiation—see the text supported by footnote 42; chap. 5, sec. 3, item C (*The Lutheran Canon*); and the text supported by footnote 467. Similar expressions appear various times in the *Institutio*. See, for example, *Institutio*, nos. 49, 55, 56.

36. This item of the 1969 *Institutio* was modified in 1970; see chap. 4, sec. 10 (*The Other Numbers That Have Been Changed*), where we point out and comment on the new text.

37. 1969 *Institutio*, nos. 1, 9, 28, 33, 35, 48, 60, 241, pp. 13, 15, 20–22, 24, 29, 55. Although no. 60 was modified in the 1970 *Institutio*, the portion quoted here was not—see chap. 4, sec. 10 (*The Other Numbers That Have Been Changed*).

38. 1969 *Institutio*, no. 241, p. 55.

39. 1969 *Institutio*, no. 55, p. 26. This number of the 1969 *Institutio* was modified in 1970; we comment upon the new text in chap. 4, sec. 10 (*The Other Numbers That Have Been Changed*).

40. *O novo Ordo missae* (Petrópolis, R.J.: *Vozes*, 1969). **Publisher's Note:** The publishing house *Vozes* to which the author refers, is one of the main Catholic Brazilian publishing houses. The booklet cited here, *O novo Ordo missae*, was the first and largest Brazilian edition of the *Institutio*, having had at least four printings in 1969 alone.

Furthermore, note that the 1969 *Institutio* does not say, in this item, that *Christ* becomes present again *(repraesentatur)*, but it says that the *Last Supper* is represented in this part of the Mass.[41]

On the other hand, the affirmation which follows, that Our Lord gives his Body and Blood to eat, under the appearances of bread and wine, strictly speaking, is acceptable to Protestants. *They deny transubstantiation*—that is true—*and here is the true watershed between Catholics and Protestants.*[42]

The absence of the term *transubstantiation* in the 1969 *Institutio* is incomprehensible.[43] In 1786, a Jansenist synod met in Pistoia, Italy. It approved various propositions concerning the Eucharist. In these, they even spoke of the "Real Presence" and admitted the full cessation of the substances of bread and wine in the consecrated species, but they did not use the word "transubstantiation." Pius VI condemned this omission in 1794 as "dangerous, derogatory to the exposition of Catholic truth about the dogma of transubstantiation, favorable to heretics."[44] Pius VI declared further that one could not consider the word *transubstantiation* "a merely scholastic question" but that it absolutely must be used to expound on the mystery of the Real Presence.[45]

Now, if the omission of the word transubstantiation was an error favoring heresy at the end of the eighteenth century, this same omission would merit even graver censure today. Indeed, there are those today who try to replace the notion of transubstantiation with theologically unacceptable concepts such as "transfiguration," "transignification," and "transfinalization."[46] The silence of the 1969 *Institutio* regarding transubstantiation deserves serious censure. *Transubstantiation* is a term which, using its infallibility, the Council of Trent declared very suitable

---

41. One cannot object that the Council of Trent (Denz.-Sch., 1740) also taught that Our Lord instituted a sacrifice by which the sacrifice of the Cross would be represented *(repraesentaretur)*, for, in the context of the Tridentine definition—in opposition to the *Institutio*—it becomes clear that it is not a question of a mere symbolic representation. It is enough to consider, for example, the first canon on the Mass: "If anyone says that in the Mass a true and real sacrifice is not offered to God; or that to be offered is nothing else than that Christ is given to us to eat, let him be anathema." *Canons and Decrees of the Council of Trent*, trans. J. Schroeder, O.P. (St. Louis: B. Herder Book Co., 1941), 149, sess. 22, can. 1.

42. On the position of Protestants regarding this, see the texts supported by footnotes 350, 359, and 463–71.

43. In defense of the *Institutio*, one cannot allege that the introductory documents of the traditional Missal did not use the word *transubstantiation* either. For those documents are mere expositions of the rubrics, with no doctrinal character whatever, while the *Institutio* is unquestionably a doctrinal document, despite the declarations to the contrary made by Fr. Bugnini, secretary of the Commission charged with the implementation of the Constitution on the Liturgy of the Second Vatican Council. We cite and comment upon these declarations in chap. 1, sec. 2 (*Number 7 of the 1969 Institutio*). Indeed, a summary comparison between the introductory documents of the traditional Missal and the *Institutio* is enough to verify the doctrinal character of the latter and the merely normative character of the former. In this respect, see also the declaration made by the semi-official magazine of the Liturgical Commission, *Notitiae* (1968, p. 181), which we cite in footnote 51.

44. Denz.-Sch., 2629, Denz.-Rahner, 1529.

45. Denz.-Sch., 2629, Denz.-Rahner, 1529.

46. See, for example, Edward Schillebeeckx, "Transubstantiation, Transfinalization, and Transignification," in *Living Bread, Saving Cup*, ed. R. Kevin Seasoltz (Collegeville, Minn.: The Liturgical Press, 1982), 175–89; refuted by Francis Clark, S.J., *Adiumenta ad tractatum de SS. eucharistiae sacramento* (Rome: Gregorian University, 1966).

to indicate the conversion of the substances of bread and wine into the substances of the Body and Blood of Our Lord.[47]

Note that the 1969 *Institutio* was especially drawn up to explain the Mass. Unlike the synod of Pistoia, though, it does not declare the Real Presence of Our Lord in the Eucharist nor that the substances of bread and wine cease to exist in the Consecration.

2. Number 7 of the 1969 *Institutio*

Even in a merely descriptive definition of the Mass, it is impossible, under any circumstances, for its principal element—the notion of sacrifice—to be absent.[48]

Now, the item of the 1969 *Institutio* dealing with the "General Structure of the Mass" begins with a phrase to which it is difficult to deny the character of a Mass definition. However, the term *sacrifice* is unmentioned: "The Supper of the Lord or Mass is the sacred synaxis or gathered assembly of the people of God, with the priest presiding, to celebrate the memorial of the Lord whereby the promise of Christ is meaningful in an altogether special way for the local meeting of the holy Church: 'Where two or more are together in my name there am I in the midst of them' (Matt. 18:20)."[49]

We shall leave aside this new ambiguity regarding the notion of the *presence* of Christ, according to which the principal presence of Our Lord in the Mass would appear to be of the spiritual order and not the substantial presence under the consecrated species.

We shall also set aside the attempt made repeatedly throughout the 1969 *Institutio* to introduce expressions that weaken the opposition to Protestantism or the sacrificial significance of the Mass, such as "Supper of the Lord," "assembly," "People of God," and "Memorial of the Lord."

Furthermore, we shall leave aside, for now, the affirmation that the priest "presides" over the assembly. This notion is agreeable to Protestants because it insinuates that the priest is primarily the delegate of the people, or the *primus inter pares* (a first among equals), and not the sacred minister, selected by God, who acts in place of Christ (*in persona Christi*). This question will be analyzed further on.[50]

We shall consider here only the point in focus at the moment—the Mass definition seemingly contained in this item. A reference to sacrifice would be missing from this definition. Above all, it would be lacking any reference to propitiation, that is, the atonement Jesus Christ makes in the Mass for the sins of men. Then, if what is here pretends to be a *definition of the Mass, it is a false one, contrary to the Council of Trent.*

---

47. See Denz.-Sch., 1642, 1652.
48. See Council of Trent, Denz.-Sch., 1751 (we cite this canon in footnote 41). In connection with the modified text of the *Institutio*, referring to the notion of sacrifice, see chap. 4, sec. 9 (*Number 7 of the 1970* Institutio).
49. 1969 *Institutio*, no. 7, p. 15.
50. See chap. 1, sec. 5 (*The President of the Assembly*).

However, the authors of the 1969 *Institutio* try to evade such accusations by denying that this item contains a *definition* proper. See how Father Annibale Bugnini, secretary of the commission for the reform of the liturgy, related the conclusions of the twelfth plenary session of this official body, in which the objections made to item no. 7 of the 1969 *Institutio* were considered:

> The Fathers (cardinals and bishops, members of the Commission) considered difficulties manifested recently concerning certain points of the *Institutio generalis missalis romani*. They recalled that the *Institutio generalis* is not a dogmatic text but rather a pure and simple exposition of the rules which order the eucharistic celebration;[51] it does not seek to define the Mass but only to present a description of the rite.[52] From the theological point of view, what the Mass is can be deduced from certain *Institutio*

---

51. This affirmation is false. The 1969 *Institutio* is filled with doctrinal affirmations. No one would dare to say, for example, that the following assertion of number 1 does not have a doctrinal character: "In it [the Mass] occurs the high point of the action whereby God, in Christ, sanctifies the world, and of the worship which men offer to the Father, adoring Him through Christ the Son of God." Would this be "a pure and simple exposition of the rules which order the Eucharistic celebration"? 1969 *Institutio*, no. 1, p. 13. Such doctrinal concepts are found repeatedly throughout the document.

One must say the same thing about number 7 cited above. How can one deny that that text has an affirmation about dogmatic material? How can one hold that all it contains is a mere "exposition of the rules which order the Eucharistic celebration"? What are the "rules" which that item contains? If we want to avoid sophisms, we absolutely must recognize that number 7 of the 1969 *Institutio* contains a doctrinal assertion that gives the basis of the "rules which order the Eucharistic celebration" that subsequently appear in the document.

The traditional Roman Missal, it is true, contains various introductory documents which are not "dogmatic text[s]," but rather "pure and simple exposition[s] of the rules which order the Eucharistic celebration." As we have observed (see footnote 43), even a summary comparison between the documents alluded to and the recent *Institutio* reveal unequivocally the doctrinal character of the latter and the merely practical character of the former.

Furthermore, when the 1969 *Institutio* was in preparation, the Liturgical Commission itself said that the document ought to contain "THEOLOGICAL PRINCIPLES, pastoral and rubrical norms for the celebration of the Mass." "Decima sessio plenaria 'Consilii'," *Notitiae* 40 (May-June 1968), 181. In a report made to the Second General Conference of the Latin-American Episcopate, in Medellín, on August 30, 1968, Father Bugnini even declared that the 1969 *Institutio* is "an ample THEOLOGICAL, pastoral, CATECHETICAL and rubrical exposition, that it is an introduction to the COMPREHENSION and celebration of the Mass." A. Bugnini, "Exposição na II Conferência Geral do Episcopado Latino-Americano, em Medellin," *Revista Eclesiástica Brasileira*, 28 (1968), 628.

52. As can be seen, Father Bugnini himself recognizes that number 7 of the 1969 *Institutio*, if it contains a definition of the Mass, is liable to the criticisms that were being made of it.

paragraphs[53] and, as well-known by all, from the treatises of theology and pontifical documents of a doctrinal character.[54]

Even though one takes number 7 of the 1969 *Institutio as a nonessential definition*,[55] it is impossible to accept it. In any case, it is a clause that presents to the faithful an assertion on the Mass that is at least insidious while simultaneously leading them to think that something has changed, as far as the traditional concept of the Mass as a sacrifice is concerned.

3. A Propitiatory Sacrifice

Concerning what we have just said about the absence of the notion of sacrifice in the apparent or real definition of the Mass in the abovementioned number 7, it can be alleged that, even in its 1969 edition, the *Institutio* affirms various times that the Mass is a sacrifice, namely in numbers 2, 48, 54, 56h, 60, 62, 153, 259, 335, and 339.

Now, the 1969 *Institutio* defenders have alleged that there are no grounds to censure the absence of the notion of sacrifice in number 7 when it appears so often in others.

We do not wish to insist, but given the nature of number 7's assertion, the notion of *sacrifice* had to be included. This point has been seen.

Instead, we would like to show that all allusions to sacrifice in the 1969 *Institutio* are insufficient to distinguish the Catholic notion of the Mass from the Protestant concept of the Lord's Supper.

---

53. Would the aforementioned text of number 7 of the 1969 *Institutio* be one of those paragraphs from which one deduces what the Mass is? If it is, then we fall again into a heterodox definition of the Mass. If it is not, what is the objective of this paragraph of the *Institutio*, which can only confuse the faithful, leading them to form an erroneous idea about the Eucharistic sacrifice?

The observation of Fr. Bugnini would, it is true, hold for the introductory documents of the traditional Roman Missal. Indeed, practically all of its paragraphs help the faithful to comprehend "what the Mass is, from the theological point of view." The numerous genuflections indicate the littleness of men and the grandeur of the sacrifice which is realized there; the use of the Latin language expresses the unfathomable mystery which is celebrated; the priest, facing the altar, makes it clear that he acts as a minister of God and not as a delegate of the people; and the great care with which the sacred species are treated reveals our faith in the Real Presence.

54. A. Bugnini, "Les travaux de la XIIeme session plenière de la comission pour la réforme de la liturgie," *L'Osservatore Romano*, weekly edition in the French language, Nov. 28, 1969, p. 12.

To say that the definition of the Mass is already known and that it can be found in treatises and pontifical documents is to evade the question. The issue is whether the new *Ordo missae truly* agrees with Tridentine and traditional theology.

55. Father C. Vagaggini, O.S.B., one of the experts of the Liturgical Commission, presents it this way. See "O novo *Ordo missae* e a ortodoxia," *Revista Eclesiástica Brasileira*, 30 (1970) 93–101.

Indeed, as is known, the sacrifice of the Mass has four ends: adoration, thanksgiving, propitiation, and petition.[56] What is in question in the age-old dispute of Catholics and Protestants over this matter is not, properly speaking, the sacrificial character of the Mass. Rather, it is its propitiatory character. In other words, Catholics and Protestants admit that the Mass is a sacrifice of praise and thanksgiving, but the Protestants deny—and here is their heresy in this matter—that the Mass constitutes a *propitiatory sacrifice.*[57]

Thus, it is very important to verify if the 1969 *Institutio* admitted the notion of propitiation or merely mentioned *sacrifice* while silencing its propitiatory character.

This importance is all the greater since the Council of Trent defined the Mass as a "truly propitiatory"[58] sacrifice. It established the following anathema: "If anyone says that the sacrifice of the Mass is only one of praise and thanksgiving, or that it is a mere commemoration of the sacrifice consummated on the Cross, but not one of propitiation . . . let him be anathema."[59]

Now, in analyzing the various passages of the 1969 *Institutio* which speak of sacrifice, we see that in none of them is the propitiatory character of the Mass affirmed.[60] On the contrary, at every moment, they refer to the Mass as a sacrifice of praise, thanksgiving, and commemoration of the sacrifice of the Cross. All of these are true aspects, but the Council of Trent declared them insufficient for the Catholic conception of the Mass. For emphasis, in the 1969 *Institutio* texts we cite below, we show these non-propitiatory aspects of the Mass in all caps.

[Referring to the fruits of the Mass, number 2 states:] . . . for the obtaining of which Christ the Lord instituted the EUCHARISTIC SACRIFICE[61] of His Body and Blood and confided it to His beloved bride, the Church, AS A MEMORIAL OF HIS PASSION AND RESURRECTION. . . .

48. The Last Supper, in which Christ instituted the MEMORIAL OF HIS DEATH AND RESURRECTION, is continuously effected presently in the Church when the priest, representing Christ the Lord,

---

56. *Adoration* is the honor offered to God because of His infinite and absolute excellence. *Thanksgiving* is the manifestation of our gratitude to God for the benefits received from Him. "A sacrifice is said to be *propitiation* inasmuch as it is an act placating the offense given to God by the sinner. This placation takes place through the satisfaction which is a recompense for the inflicted injury according to the proportion of equality; therefore it pertains to the virtue of justice." Joseph A. de Aldama, S.J., *On the Sacrament of Christian Unity or On the Most Holy Eucharist*, Treatise 3 of *On the Sacraments in General*, vol. 4 of *Sacrae theologiae summa*, trans. Kenneth Baker, S.J. ([Saddle River, N.J.:] Keep the Faith, Inc., 2015), 367. Through *impetration*, we ask for new benefits from God.
57. See the text supported by footnotes 402 and 437. See also the paragraph following footnote 193; we show that Protestants are consistent with their errors when they deny to the Mass its character of a *propitiatory* sacrifice.
58. Denz.-Sch., 1743.
59. Denz.-Sch., 1753.
60. On how the notion of propitiation figures in the 1970 *Institutio*, see the paragraph after footnote 278, the first several paragraphs of chap. 4, sec. 10 (*The Other Numbers That Have Been Changed*), and the Conclusion (*The New Mass and the Catholic Conscience*) infra.
61. In its etymological and technical sense, "eucharist" signifies "giving thanks."

DOES THE SAME AS THE LORD HIMSELF DID AND HANDED DOWN TO HIS DISCIPLES THAT THEY DO IN HIS MEMORY, instituting the SACRIFICE and paschal banquet. . . .[62]

54. And now begins the center and high point of the whole celebration, that is, the EUCHARISTIC PRAYER itself, a PRAYER OF THANKS-GIVING AND SANCTIFICATION. . . . Now, the sense of this prayer is that all the congregation of the faithful unite itself with Christ in the PROCLAMATION OF THE MARVELS OF GOD and in the OFFER-ING OF THE SACRIFICE. . . .

335. The Church offers the EUCHARISTIC PASCHAL SACRIFICE of Christ for the dead so that, [with] all members of Christ communicating among themselves, that which OBTAINS SPIRITUAL ASSISTANCE for some, GIVES THE COMFORT OF HOPE to others.[63]

Numbers 56h, 60, 62, 153, and 339 refer to the sacrifice celebrated in the Mass, without, however, presenting major explanations about its nature. The same thing occurs with number 259, which only indirectly relates the idea of sacrifice with "the table of the Lord" and "thanksgiving."[64]

On the other hand, the 1969 *Institutio* uses expressions with sacrificial content numerous times, such as "host." None of these passages, however, affirms the propitiatory character of the sacrifice of the Mass.

Expressions tending to relegate the sacrificial and propitiatory character of the Mass to the shadows also occur in the *Institutio*. This is the case of the exaggerated insistence on the principle—which is incontestable in itself—that there is a banquet in the Mass since Jesus Christ gives us His Body and His Blood as food. This aspect of the Mass is undoubtedly true. Still, it must be subordinated to the sacrificial and propitiatory elements. This is especially needed because Protestants try to reduce the Eucharistic Sacrifice to a banquet. We see this in the already mentioned condemnation handed down at Trent: "If anyone says that in the Mass a true and real sacrifice is not offered to God, or that the act of offering IS NOTHING ELSE THAN CHRIST BEING GIVEN TO US TO EAT, let him be anathema."[65]

Now, the 1969 *Institutio*, which refers to the sacrifice in only ten passages, uses expressions relating to the Eucharistic agape innumerable times. Examples include "spiritual food," "supper," "table of the Lord," "banquet" ("convivium"), and "refection" (meal). Again, for example, see numbers 2, 7, 8, 33, 34, 41, 48, 49, 55d, 56, 56g, 62, 240, 241, 259, 268, 281, 283, and 316.

*   *   *

---

62. See the text of this paragraph in the 1970 *Institutio* in chap. 4, sec. 10 (*The Other Numbers That Have Been Changed*).
63. 1969 *Institutio*, nos. 2, 48, 54, 335, pp. 13, 24, 25, 76.
64. 1969 *Institutio*, no. 259, p. 61.
65. Denz.-Sch., 1751.

Proceeding from the 1969 *Institutio* to the B.A.C. commentary,[66] we shall see that, in the latter, the omissions and ambiguities tending to relegate the sacrificial and propitiatory character of the Mass to the shadows are even more numerous.

Among the 171 titles of the analytical index of the work, the words "sacrifice" and "propitiation" do not even appear.

In discussing the places where the Mass must be celebrated—according to traditional practice, these are the churches—the B.A.C. commentators say: "If we are allowed to make the comparison, such places have something of the character of a great banquet hall; a conference room, where the wisdom of God is heard; a theater where one assists at the great spectacle of theophany; a room for conversation, where one dialogues with God; and something of a salon for parties, where believers celebrate their joys."[67]

Note how the authors speak of everything except a church proper, that is, a sacred place in which Our Lord, really present, immolates Himself upon the altar in propitiation for the sins of men. Later on, they lapse again into the same unjustifiable omission. After making the dubious affirmation that the faithful ought to "offer a spiritual sacrifice everywhere,"[68] they continue: "This idea of a Christian meeting ought to be at the root of every structure of a church: An assembly of Jesus Christ with his brothers to hear the word of God, to respond to those words with their gratitude, songs, and supplications, as also to express to one another the love which Christ asked for in the Supper as that which characterizes his disciples. Everything which helps to express this reality and in the measure it expresses it[69] will be praiseworthy; everything which disturbs and hinders this will be deplorable."[70]

In explaining the new concept of the altar, the B.A.C. commentators underline the same idea once more:

> As stated several times in the *Institutio*, the altar is, above all, the table of the Lord (nos. 49, 259, etc.). It should appear as such in its ornamentation, cloths, the form of construction, the catechesis made from it to the people, and the motives given to justify its veneration. If later, as time passed,[71] the altar *also* took on the character of a sepulcher of martyrs and altar of sacrifice, these aspects can be complementary. Still, they are by no means what ought to stand out most for the persons gathered to celebrate the memorial of the Lord. For this reason, the *Institutio*, which seeks that the

---

66. We refer to the book *Nuevas normas de la misa*. We explain at the very beginning of Chapter 1 why we use it for special commentary.

67. Martín Patino, *Nuevas normas*, 61.

68. Martín Patino, 61.

69. Therefore, churches should not have for their principal inspiration the notions of the Cross, suffering, sacrifice, propitiation, or repentance for our sins. The measure of everything is the "word of God," giving thanks, mutual love, joy, and the like.

70. Martín Patino, *Nuevas normas*, 61.

71. Note the insinuation that Our Lord did not institute the Mass as a sacrifice.

altar be always presented as the table of the Lord, is not so categorical in the detail of the relics.[72]

4. The "Narrative of the Institution"

Another doctrinally censurable passage of the 1969 *Institutio* is the cited item "d" of number 55.[73] It treats *ex professo* of the Consecration.

The item is introduced with the title *narratio institutionis*—that is, "narrative of the institution." According to Catholic doctrine, the priest who consecrates does not merely "narrate" what Our Lord did in the Last Supper but acts "in persona Christi," in place of Christ, lending Him his own lips and voice.

For Protestants, however, in the Consecration, the minister only narrates what is in the Gospels. He only repeats the words of Christ, thus *recalling* the Last Supper. Since there is no transubstantiation, according to them, this *narration* is enough. They claim that it is not necessary nor possible for the words of Christ to be pronounced *affirmatively and imperatively* by the priest.[74]

Note then the gravity of the subtitle *narratio institutionis*.[75] In addition, this passage becomes even more suspect because of the previously pointed out silence of the 1969 document regarding the concepts of Real Presence and transubstantiation.[76]

*   *   *

The same ambiguity about the nature of the Consecration is present in the B.A.C. commentary.[77] In explaining this central part of the Mass, the B.A.C. commentators adopt a position fully consonant with Protestant principles: "(The Eucharistic Prayer) is a consecratory action because the sanctification of the gifts is effected by its means."[78]

---

72. Martín Patino, *Nuevas normas*, 246.
73. See no. 55d in the text supported by footnote 39. In chap. 4, sec. 10 (*The Other Numbers That Have Been Changed*), we show the changes made to this no. 55d in the 1970 *Institutio*.
74. According to certain Protestants, the words of Christ are not pronounced *merely* narratively. However, they do not admit in any way that the celebrant utters them *affirmatively and impera-tively* in the name of Our Lord Himself. Instead, they maintain that a theatrical representation is essential to the ceremony in addition to the verbal narration. As can be seen, this detail—which we shall discuss *ex professo* in chap. 4, sec. 10 (*The Other Numbers That Have Been Changed*)—has nothing to do with the question we are analyzing here.
75. As is obvious, we do not censure the use of the expression *narratio institutionis*, which is even classical in Catholic theology. See, for example, Ludovicus Lercher, *Institutiones theologicae dogmat-icae* (Barcelona-Innsbruck: Herder-Rauch, 1948), 4-2-1:330n303. What is censurable is that the very words of the Consecration, which ought to be said imperatively, not narratively, are presented under the subtitle "narrative of the institution" *without further explanations*.
76. See chap. 1, sec. 1 (*The 1969* Institutio *and the Dogma of Transubstantiation*). Sometimes, the 1969 *Institutio* uses expressions like *in persona Christi*, but it does so in a context in which they lose the precise sense that the scholastics attribute to them. We show this in chap. 1, sec. 5 (*The President of the Assembly*).
77. See our explanation on this B.A.C. commentary at the very beginning of Chapter 1.
78. Martín Patino, *Nuevas normas*, 128. On the Protestant character of this affirmation, see chap. 5, sec. 3, item C (*The Lutheran Canon*) *infra*.

Other passages in which this work conveys Protestant concepts about the Consecration are indicated further on. For example, it insinuates that the presence of Our Lord in the Eucharist is equivalent to His "Real Presence" in the scriptural reading made during the Mass,[79] and it gives one to understand that the transubstantiation is not realized at the precise moment in which the priest pronounces the words of the Consecration.[80]

5. The President of the Assembly

As the Council of Trent defined, the priesthood "was instituted by that same Lord our Savior, and that to the apostles and their successors in the priesthood was handed down the power of consecrating, to offering and administering His body and blood, and also of forgiving and retaining sins."[81]

Therefore, the power of consecrating belongs to the priest, not the people. If the Scriptures and Catholic theology speak of the priesthood of the faithful, it is in the broad sense of the term, which indicates only the consecration of all the baptized to the divine worship, in union with Our Lord, the supreme and eternal Priest.[82]

To conflate this priesthood of the people with that of the priest would be to adopt a Protestant principle again. Indeed, according to the sixteenth-century pseudo-Reformers, the celebrant is not a priest in a sense different from that of the people. Rather, he only presides over the Eucharistic assembly as a delegate of those present.

Also concerning this point, the 1969 *Institutio* has some expressions found in traditional doctrine, but, beside these, it places notions and principles that insinuate or contain the Protestant thesis.

Thus, one reads in number 10 that the priest "presides over the assembly representing Christ" (*personam Christi gerens*). And, in number 60, one is told that "the priest . . . presides over the united assembly, acting in place of Christ" (*in persona Christi praeest*).[83] Number 48 says that the priest "represent[s] Christ" (*Christum Dominum repraesentans*).[84]

As can be seen, these expressions have an altogether traditional tone, being even the technical terms that designate how the celebrant acts in place of Our Lord.

---

79. See Martín Patino, 31, 85. We comment on these passages in chap. 1, sec. 7 (*A Tendency to Make the "Liturgy of the Word" Equal to the "Eucharistic Liturgy"*). The Lutherans accept the expression "real presence," as we show in chap. 5, sec. 3, item C (*The Lutheran Canon*) *infra*.
80. See Martín Patino, 123–24. We comment on this in chap. 5, sec. 3, item C (*The Lutheran Canon*) *infra*.
81. Denz.-Sch., 1764.
82. On this point, one may consult Franciscus a P. Solá, S.J., *De sacramentis vitae socialis christianae seu de sacramentis ordinis et matrimonii*, in *Sacrae theologiae summa* (Madrid: B.A.C., 1962), 587–88; as well as the documents cited there from the Council of Trent, the *Roman Catechism*, Pius XII, and Saint Augustine.
83. In connection with this item in the 1970 *Institutio*, see chap. 4, sec. 10 (*The Other Numbers That Have Been Changed*) *infra*.
84. 1969 *Institutio*, nos. 10, 60, and 48, pp. 16, 29, 24.

Such expressions appear in the 1969 *Institutio,* however, in a context that causes a certain perplexity. On the one hand, it is not said what "taking the place of Christ" and "representing Him" mean *exactly*. On the other, the 1969 *Institutio* contains numerous passages which insinuate that the celebrant is a mere president of the assembly and that his *principal function* in the Mass consists in *representing the faithful* united there.

Such facts open the way for the "representation" of Christ to be understood in a broad sense—for example, that every Christian is another Christ—and not in the strict and precise meaning of a hierarchical and visible priesthood, on account of which the priest lends his own lips and voice to Our Lord at the moment of Consecration. This is what we shall see in the analyses that follow.

A. We have indicated that, according to number 7 of the 1969 *Institutio*, the priest's only distinguishing characteristic is being president of the "assembly of the people of God."[85] This topic is of the greatest importance for, even though it is not understood as a Mass definition, it is undoubtedly destined to orient the faithful toward a better comprehension of the Mass.[86]

B. In number 10, immediately after affirming that the priest presides over the assembly representing Christ, the 1969 *Institutio* declares that the Eucharistic Prayer constitutes a "presidential prayer." The same number defines "presidential prayers" as those that "are directed to God, IN THE NAME OF ALL OF THE HOLY PEOPLE AND OF ALL THE PEOPLE THERE PRESENT."[87] Any reader will be led by this passage to think that, in the Consecration, the priest speaks principally in the name of the people.

Undoubtedly, parts of the Eucharistic Prayer are directed to God also in the name of the people, but its principal one, the Consecration, is said by the priest exclusively in the name of Our Lord. No Catholic can admit any ambiguity regarding this point. Thus, number 10 of the *Institutio* is one of the most censurable in the entire document.[88]

C. The principle we find in number 12 is particularly strange: "THE NATURE of the 'presidential' parts demands that they be pronounced in a loud and clear voice, and be heard attentively by all. Therefore, when the priest is pronouncing them, let there be no other prayers or hymns; let the organ and any other musical instruments be silent."[89]

Therefore, the words of the Consecration ought to be pronounced under those conditions as well. This insinuates once more that the priest acts specifically as a delegate of the people at that moment.

---

85. See chap. 1, sec. 2 (*Number 7 of the 1969* Institutio).
86. See Fr. Bugnini's presentation in Medellín, which we cite in footnote 51.
87. 1969 *Institutio*, no. 10. p. 16.
88. Despite the gravity of the censures it merits, this item 10 was not modified in the 1970 *Institutio*.
89. 1969 *Institutio*, no. 12 p. 16.

Furthermore, that item of the 1969 *Institutio* evidently contains a grave reprimand of the rubric of the traditional *Ordo*, according to which the Canon is not said in a "loud and clear" voice. This is particularly noteworthy because of the anathema established by the Council of Trent: "If anyone says that the rite of the Roman Church, according to which a part of the canon and the words of consecration are pronounced in a low tone, is to be condemned . . . let him be anathema."[90]

When declaring that the *nature* of the presidential parts—which include the Eucharistic Prayer and Consecration—*demands* that they be pronounced in a loud and clear voice, the 1969 *Institutio* establishes a principle valid for all times. Thus, it contains the implicit affirmation that the Council of Trent erred on that point.[91]

D. Number 271 formulates a new criticism of the traditional Mass, also based upon the false notion of the presidential function of the celebrant: "The seat of the celebrant ought to signify his function of presiding over the assembly and directing prayer. For this reason, its most suitable position is facing the people in the center rear of the sanctuary."[92]

According to the Roman *Ordo,* the priest normally faces the altar because, above all, he is a sacrificer who presents himself before the Eternal Father in the name of the Word Incarnate.[93] The introduced change is based upon a notion of a *presidency* of the *assembly,* which conflicts with traditional doctrine.

* * *

We find in the B.A.C. commentary an important confirmation of the fact that the 1969 *Ordo* introduced a new notion, which recalls the Protestant idea of the celebrant being the *president* of the *assembly:*[94]

> It is the people of God who properly celebrates, not the minister.[95]

> The assembly is the work of all. All are baptized and participate in the unique priesthood of Christ. All are filled with the Holy Spirit.[96]

> This rhythm of harmony and structure makes it possible for the mystery to be celebrated by the entire assembly, not just by the clergymen or a sector of the people.

---

90. Denz.-Sch., 1759.
91. Number 12 of the 1969 *Institutio* was not altered in 1970 either.
92. 1969 *Institutio*, no. 271, p. 63.
93. Note that, according to the traditional practice of the Church, there is no exclusivism about this matter. In numerous rites, for example, the Mass is celebrated *versus populum*. What causes perplexity is that the new *Ordo* proscribes the Mass which is not celebrated *versus populum*, as a less apt way, as not expressing the "presidential" function of the priest appropriately.
94. See Martín Patino, *Nuevas normas.*
95. Martín Patino, 77.
96. Martín Patino, 91.

In numerous items of the *Institutio,* we can perceive an artistic spirit and tone of celebration which involve all the celebrating people.[97]

When those who are baptized meet, they all go to exercise their baptismal priesthood. After centuries in which only the action of the ministers appeared in the celebration, we can put things again on their true foundation. The people of God is, all of it, a priestly people. . . .

From the people of God, in general, arise the ministers: From the bishop, the priest, and the deacon, ordained for that end by a sacrament, to the acolytes, musicians, ushers, etc. . . . All should collaborate for a better exercise of the common priesthood.[98]

* * *

As seen, the 1969 *Institutio* insinuates that erroneous notion of the ministerial priesthood of the faithful. Further, the prestigious B.A.C. collection publishes a commentary on the 1969 *Institutio* in which this notion is explicitly defended as being that of the document. The impunity with which that work circulates leads the faithful to understand that it correctly interprets and develops the 1969 *Institutio*. Furthermore, the wide distribution of this work, now in its eighth printing, shows how deeply a false concept of the priesthood is taking root in the people.

6. Jesus Christ, the Principal Priest (*Sacerdos*)

As the Council of Trent defined, in the Holy Mass, Jesus Christ "Himself [is] immolated under visible signs by the Church through the priests."[99] For this reason, it is said that Our Lord is the principal *sacerdos* of all Masses, while the priest is a secondary, ministerial, or instrumental one. On the other hand, as observed, the priesthood of the celebrant is essentially distinct from that of the people.[100] Therefore, the people do not take part in the Mass in the same way as the priest. To deny any of these truths is to fall into a Protestant error.

The 1969 *Institutio* is not explicit in this matter. For if, on the one hand, it contains expressions that can be interpreted as affirmations of traditional doctrine,[101] on the other, considered overall, it leaves the way open for plainly erroneous interpretations. Indeed, not once does the document affirm clearly that Our Lord is the *principal sacerdos* and that the celebrant exercises a *secondary and ministerial priesthood*, but one that is essentially distinct from the priesthood of the people.[102]

---

97. Martín Patino, 54.
98. Martín Patino, 142–43.
99. Denz.-Sch., 1741.
100. See chap. 1, sec. 5 (*The President of the Assembly*).
101. In addition to nos. 10, 48, and 50 of the 1969 *Institutio* already cited in footnote 84, see no. 1, according to which the celebration of the Mass is "an action of Christ and of the people of God hierarchically organized"; and no. 4, where one reads that the Eucharistic celebration is "an act of Christ and of the Church."
102. In connection with the modifications which, in respect to this, were introduced in the 1970 *Institutio*, see chap. 4, sec. 2 (*The Priesthood of the People*) *infra*.

*   *   *

Commenting on the already mentioned numbers 1 and 4, the B.A.C. commentators take advantage of these imprecisions and silences of the 1969 *Institutio* to expound again on a theory about the priesthood—of Christ, the priest, and the people—which disagrees fundamentally with Church doctrine. In connection with the principle that the Eucharist is the "action of Christ," we read in the B.A.C. commentary, "Christ acts personally in every celebration. He is the only priest of the Christian people . . . to such a point that Christian Revelation very intentionally avoided giving the name of priest to those presiding at the Christian liturgical meetings. Rather, it called them bishop or presbyter (elder) or simply 'ministers (instruments, servants) of Christ.'103. . . This is what this first affirmation, theologically so profound, of the *Institutio* signifies: The Eucharist is an action of Christ."104

Continuing to expound on the assertion that the Eucharist is an "action of the people of God hierarchically organized," the B.A.C. commentators write:

> Concerning the Eucharist . . . it is not said that it is the action of the priest to whom the people unite themselves—as the Mass was frequently presented until recently. Rather, it is said, more exactly, that it is the action of this people served by the ministers who precisely give the people the sacramental presence of their Lord through their ministry. One could repeat here what was said in the Council on rejecting the outline proposed for the Constitution of the Church. Indeed, it is known that in the draft of the mentioned Constitution . . . the Church was presented as a "pyramid." It started with the pope and the bishops and continued down to the last of the faithful. It is known further that that schema, which corresponded to the classic theology of the previous centuries,105 was rejected because it placed what is relative and of service (the hierarchy) over that which is ontological and absolute (the people of God).
>
> Similarly, and undoubtedly already as a mature fruit of this new and more exact vision of the Church, the Eucharist is presented here not as an action of the celebrant, to whom the people unite themselves, but as an action of the people of God. It is important, then, that the pastoral guidance emphasize this affirmation and thus not fall into the danger of presenting the participation of the faithful in the Mass as being less import-

---

103. In this passage, the B.A.C. commentators pass over one of the condemnations of Trent: "If anyone says that there is not in the New Testament a visible and external priesthood . . . but only the office and bare ministry of preaching the Gospel . . . let him be anathema." Denz.-Sch., 1771.
104. Martín Patino, *Nuevas normas*, 68–70.
105. The B.A.C. commentators err if they think this conception is a mere opinion of the "classic theology of the last centuries." In reality, it is a dogma of the Holy Church. See Council of Trent, Denz.-Sch., 1767–1768, 1777, Denz.-Umb., 960, 967; J.M. Hervé, *Manuale theologiae dogmaticae* (Paris: Berche et Pagis, 1952), 1:290, 303, 307, 321; Adolphe Tanquerey, *Synopsis theologiae dogmaticae* (Paris–Tournai–Rome: Desclée, 1959), 1:434, 454; Ioachim Salaverri, *De ecclesia Christi*, vol. 1 of *Sacrae theologiae summa* (Madrid: B.A.C., 1958) 548, 604; Serapius de Iragui, *Theologia fundamentalis*, vol. 1 of *Manuale theologiae dogmaticae*, by Iragui and Abarzuza (Madrid: Studium, 1959), 1:278.

ant than that of the minister. Indeed, the participation of the people is not in the same line as that of the celebrant. It is a question of two different realities: the participation of the people is something that belongs to them because the whole Church is the body of Christ which unites itself to its head in the celebration; on the other hand, in turn, the ministry of the celebrant in as much as the latter is distinguished from the faithful, has only a ministerial function: through it, the faithful are united to Christ and with Christ, they celebrate the Eucharist. Thus it is affirmed that the Eucharist is an action of Christ and an action of the people of God.[106]

It is interesting to emphasize also in this topic the explicit mention of how the people of God celebrate the Eucharist: Indeed, they celebrate it as a *hierarchically organized* assembly. With this phrase, it is not a question, in any way, of indicating that among the members of the people of God, some have greater or lesser dignity. We should not speak of diversity of dignity but rather of an interchange of services among the disciples of Him, Who wished that the greatest be the servant of all.[107]

This egalitarian and *horizontal* conception of the Church is unacceptable to Catholics.

7. A Tendency to Make the "Liturgy of the Word" Equal to the "Eucharistic Liturgy"

Heresies always tend to overestimate the importance of Scripture, to the detriment of both the liturgical formulae of ecclesiastical origin and the Eucharistic celebration proper. They try to silence the voice of Tradition in this way and propagate their false dogmas, saying that they are based on Revelation.[108]

The 1969 *Institutio* has, without doubt, passages that appear to affirm the primacy of the "eucharistic liturgy" over the biblical readings. This is the case in number 54, which says that the Eucharistic Prayer is the "center and high point of the whole celebration."[109]

However, other parts of the 1969 *Institutio* that have not been modified in the new 1970 edition seem to overestimate the importance of scriptural readings, at times causing the impression that their importance is equal to that of the worship of Our Sacramental Lord.

---

106. The concept of the Mass introduced here by the B.A.C. commentators is absolutely false. Before being the representative and minister of the people, the celebrant is Christ's representative and minister. For this reason, he is a true *sacerdos*. To say that the participation of the faithful in the Mass is not less than that of the minister is to deny the dogma of a hierarchical and visible priesthood instituted by Our Lord in the Church. See Council of Trent, Denz.-Sch., 1764, 1767, 1771, 1777, Denz.-Umb., 957, 960, 961, 967.
107. Martín Patino, *Nuevas normas*, 70–71.
108. See Dom Prosper Guéranger, *Institutions liturgiques* (Paris: Débécourt Libraire, 1840), 1:415–16.
109. 1969 *Institutio*, no. 54, p. 25.

In number 8, for example, we read, "The Mass consists in a certain sense of two parts, that is to say: the liturgy of the word and that of the Eucharist, which are closely joined to each other so as to constitute one single act of worship. Accordingly, in the Mass, the table of the word of God is prepared as well as that of the Body of Christ to instruct and nourish the faithful. Now, a certain rite opens and closes the celebration."[110]

According to number 9, "when the Sacred Scriptures are read in the church," then "Christ, present in His word, announces the Gospel," and the biblical readings "supply to the liturgy an element of the greatest importance."[111]

Undoubtedly the expression "of the greatest importance" can be understood as an absolute superlative and not relative—that is, it does not necessarily indicate that the biblical readings constitute the most important element of the Mass. However, such an interpretation is not excluded, thereby giving an occasion to fall into the Protestant error of overestimating the value of Scripture in relation to the Real Presence in the Eucharist.

In addition, more than once, the 1969 *Institutio* declares that "Christ Himself, by His word, is personally present amid the faithful."[112]

Considered, then, in their context, the dispositions of the 1969 *Institutio* permit a dangerous equivocation to surround the true importance of the biblical readings in the Mass.

The B.A.C. commentators, always agile in detecting ambiguities in the 1969 *Institutio* to explain them in a neomodernist and Protestant sense, write, "Ordinarily, the privileged location to hear the word of God is in the assembly (to be understood: the Mass). All ought to go to it as they go to the eucharistic communion: prepared not to lose even a fragment through their own fault, for in all of them Christ is equally present."[113]

In another passage, the B.A.C. commentators establish a new comparison between the "liturgy of the word" and the Eucharist, in terms which tend to attribute equal dignity to them: "Both the constitution *Sacrosanctum concilium* (no. 7) as well as the encyclical *Mysterium fidei* emphasize the REAL PRESENCE of Christ in his Church, IN THE ASSEMBLY OF PRAYER, when the SACRED SCRIPTURE is read or is announced or when the SACRAMENT OF THE EUCHARIST is offered or administered."[114]

As we see, it is difficult to imagine a more radical or more daring theory to make the biblical readings and the Holy Eucharist equal.

*　*　*

Furthermore, in connection with the readings of the Bible in the Mass, the 1969 *Institutio* declares, in the same number 9:

---

110. 1969 *Institutio*, no. 8, p. 15.
111. 1969 *Institutio*, no. 9, p. 15.
112. 1969 *Institutio*, no. 33, p. 21. Analogous expressions are found in nos. 9 and 35.
113. Martín Patino, *Nuevas normas*, 85.
114. Martín Patino, 31.

When the Sacred Scriptures are read in the church, GOD HIMSELF SPEAKS to His people, and Christ, PRESENT IN HIS WORD, announces the Gospel....

... But, however much, in the readings of Sacred Scripture, the Divine Word is directed to all men of whatever epoch and IS UNDERSTOOD BY THEM, its efficacy is increased by the living exposition, that is, the homily, a part of the liturgical action.[115]

It is easy to see how much this formulation favors the Protestant error according to which the Holy Spirit illuminates each of the faithful who reads the Bible directly, thus dispensing with the living Magisterium of the Church. Protestants only admit an explanation of the minister destined to "increase" the fruits of the individual reading.

Drawing the consequences of this *Institutio* item, the B.A.C. commentators write:

When a believer reads it (Sacred Scripture), and especially if he does it in a communal atmosphere, which is as it were the normal broth for its cultivation, THE SPIRIT RAISES in the hearts of the faithful, with his grace, AN ATTITUDE WHICH MAKES IT POSSIBLE FOR THE ANCIENT WORDS TO PRODUCE NEW LIFE. Thus, in the same way that the historical Christ continues to be completed in the mystical Christ, to prolong the incarnation of God among men, so also THE SCRIPTURE CONTINUES TO BE COMPLETED IN OUR LIVES UNTIL CHRIST RETURNS, AND ALL OF US WILL HAVE BECOME THE WORD OF GOD MADE FLESH, MADE HUMAN LIFE, to his image and likeness.[116]

Such affirmations from the B.A.C. commentators need no commentary.

8. Memorial of the Resurrection and Ascension

Today's heretics dissimulate the sacrificial and propitiatory character of the Mass by emphasizing excessively the fact that the Mass recalls not only the death of Our Lord but also His Resurrection and Ascension. This is a true but subordinated fact.

We say that the Mass recalls the Resurrection and Ascension only in a subordinate way because in its sacrificial and propitiatory reality, in its principal symbolic elements, the Mass is primarily and directly the renewal of the sacrifice of the Cross. Therefore, it calls to mind, above all, the death of Our Lord. Since, however, the Mystery of Calvary, which worked our redemption, also included all the other mysteries and events in Christ's life, one can and must say that the Mass

---

115. 1969 *Institutio*, no. 9, p. 15.
116. Martín Patino, *Nuevas normas*, 84–85.

also recalls—albeit subordinately—His Resurrection,[117] Ascension, and sitting at the right hand of the Eternal Father.

The 1969 *Institutio* seems to ignore this distinction giving rise to confusion about the concepts.

Thus it is that:

—in number 2, the Mass is called "a memorial of [Christ's] passion and resurrection";

—in number 48, we read that in the Last Supper, "Christ instituted the memorial of His death and resurrection";[118]

—in number 55e, it is said that immediately after the Consecration, "the Church celebrates the memorial of Christ, recalling principally his blessed Passion, glorious resurrection, and ascension into heaven";

—in number 55d, it is affirmed that at the Last Supper, Our Lord "instituted the sacrament of His Passion and Resurrection";[119]

—number 335 calls the Mass "the eucharistic paschal sacrifice of Christ";

—and numbers 7 and 268 declare that, in the Mass, we celebrate the "memorial of the Lord."[120]

The B.A.C. commentators confirm the fear which we express above. They manifest a particular aversion to the tone of sacred and sacrificial sorrow that characterizes the traditional Mass, even on feast days. This tendency to reduce the Eucharist to a joyful celebration expressing only mirth becomes evident in the following paragraph of their work: "The exhortation that the singing is to be given great importance in the celebration could not be more opportune [no. 19 of the 1969 *Institutio*]. The Eucharist is indeed the sacrament of the Lord's Passover, a hope of his glorious coming, and a joyful celebration of Christ's triumph, which has already happened and is awaited by the whole Church. The singing is the natural expression of this joy."[121]

---

117. On this matter, see also chap. 4, sec. 10 (*The Other Numbers That Have Been Changed*) *infra*.
118. In the 1970 *Institutio* version of this paragraph, the explicit reference to the Resurrection was suppressed. See chap. 4, sec. 10 (*The Other Numbers That Have Been Changed*) *infra*.
119. This paragraph was also modified in 1970, the reference to the Resurrection being then suppressed, see chap. 4, sec. 10 (*The Other Numbers That Have Been Changed*) *infra*.
120. 1969 *Institutio*, nos. 2, 48, 55e, 55d, 335, 7, 268, pp. 13, 24, 26, 76, 15, 63.
121. Martín Patino, *Nuevas normas*, 95.

CHAPTER TWO

An Objection: The 1969 *Institutio* Also Affirms Traditional Doctrine

Before analyzing the new *Ordo missae*, it behooves us to refute an objection that has been made frequently against those who in various countries have been pointing out that the recent reform of the Mass is unacceptable. This objection appears, at first sight, to be so important that we would like to consider it here with full attention, dedicating a special chapter to it.

The defenders of the New Mass argue that in the 1969 *Institutio* and, above all, the 1970 one, there are parts that affirm the traditional principles regarding the very points of doctrine deemed by some to be expounded there insufficiently or in a suspect manner. The confusing texts ought to be interpreted, however, in the light of the clear ones, they say, those seemingly heterodox through those that are orthodox. Therefore, the document considered as a whole cannot be classified as suspect.

In support of this reasoning, the followers of the New Mass allege that:

— although the 1969 *Institutio* does not speak of transubstantiation, it does say several times that, during the Eucharistic Prayer, the Body and Blood of Our Lord become present;
— though the term *propitiation* is not used, the expressions *Redemption*, *salvation*, and *purification of sins* are;
— though the presidential function of the priest is emphasized, that he celebrates as Christ's representative is also highlighted;
— though the biblical readings are valued highly, it is clear that the center of the Mass is the Eucharistic Prayer; and so forth.

Moreover, the same defenders of the new *Ordo missae* allege that the 1970 *Institutio* expresses even more clearly these traditional theses, though there are still dubious passages in it.

1. First Answer: A Rule of Hermeneutics

In the face of this objection, we will not consider the particular cases alleged here. In all of them, the traditional affirmation is pushed aside as it were by what is opposed to it. We have demonstrated this in the previous chapter and shall show this further in those that follow.

What we shall consider, in the abstract, is the principle that the objection enunciates: The obscure and suspect-sounding passages of a document do not become suspect when, in the same document, there are also orthodox ones dealing with the same topics.

It behooves us to give a first answer of a hermeneutical order, which we expound here in outline form:

A. In principle, the rule according to which the confused and obscure texts of a document should be interpreted by those that are clear is true.

B. This rule, however—according to which suspect and heterodox texts must be interpreted by orthodox ones—requires a distinction:

1. The rule is applicable when the suspect or heterodox passages occur only one or another time, by mistake as it were;

2. but the rule does not hold when the suspect or heterodox passages are numerous (for that which happens by mistake is, by its nature, occasional and infrequent); in such cases, one should have recourse to other rules and means of interpretation;

3. when, in addition to being numerous, the confused, suspect, and heterodox passages form, one linked to another, a *system of thought*, the above rule of interpretation does not hold. Instead, the *opposite rule applies*: it is necessary then to ask if it is not the orthodox texts which should be interpreted in the light of confused, suspect, and heterodox passages. Let us explain this principle in greater detail.

* * *

Lapses are *not usually frequent* and, above all, *cannot constitute a system*. Therefore, in the hypothesis which has been explained, it is not legitimate to interpret the non-orthodox passages by the orthodox ones. Although the latter passages point to orthodoxy in the document, it is impossible to eliminate or lessen the suspicion of heterodoxy due to the context.[122]

Furthermore, considering the situation only in the abstract, it is not licit to forget that, at least until breaking with the Church, heretics usually present their

---

122. In connection with the caution with which one must apply the principle *"in dubio pro reo,"* see our essay "Respondendo a objeções de um imaginário leitor progressista," *Catolicismo*, no. 206 (Feb. 1968).

doctrine by alternating orthodox passages with confused, ambiguous, suspect, and heterodox ones. Accordingly, in the hypothesis being analyzed, in addition to losing much of their favorable significance, the orthodox texts raise one more reason for grave suspicion. We desire to abstract from persons and ponder the matter with all scientific rigor. It is necessary, therefore, to ask if it is not in the obscure and suspect passages that one will find the true key to the full comprehension of the text, including the real meaning of the seemingly orthodox parts. In other words, it behooves us to ask if, in reality, one should not interpret the orthodox passages through those which disagree with good doctrine.

This leads us to a second answer to be given to the objection we formulated.

2. Second Answer: The Contradictory Character of All Heresies

In addition to the above rule of hermeneutics and contributing to making it more explicit, we must also consider arguments of another order. It is impossible to treat seriously on the scientific plane matters such as those now before us without recourse to the assistance of history. Thus, it seems indispensable to present some observations founded upon the *modus operandi* of heretics over the centuries.

A superficial study of the history of heresies is enough for us to see that all of them tried to disguise their real intentions, at least until their definitive break with the Catholic Church. Bishop Antonio de Castro Mayer writes:

> This tendency to reconcile irreconcilable extremes, to find a middle line between truth and error, manifested itself from the beginnings of the Church. . . . When Arianism was condemned, that tendency gave birth to semi-Arianism. When Pelagianism was condemned, it engendered semi-Pelagianism. When Protestantism was condemned at Trent, it morphed into Jansenism. And from it was born in the same way the Modernism condemned by Blessed Pius X, that monstrous confluence of atheism, rationalism, evolutionism, and pantheism, in a school that desires to stab the Church from behind. The objective of the modernist sect was always to remain within the Church and falsify true doctrine (which it exteriorly pretended to accept) through sophisms, inferences, and reservations.
>
> This tendency has not ceased yet; one could even say it forms part of Church history.[123]

Strictly speaking, an attentive consideration of this magnificent statement of the illustrious bishop of Campos would be enough for us to comprehend how much caution and suspicion are necessary in reading the traditional or seemingly traditional passages that the progressives place right beside their obscure and suspect affirmations.

Such a strange coexistence of opposing assertions leads us to focus on yet another aspect of the history of heresies. In addition to disguising themselves,

---

123. Mayer, "Problemas do apostolado moderno," 20.

heretics have the habit of admitting, when necessary, *openly contradictory* principles. Frequently they place, alongside an error, a truth that is opposed to it. With that tactic, they can always allege, if questioned, that the heterodox passage should be understood according to the orthodox one. To their proselytes, however, they teach that, in reality, the erroneous thesis prevails.

History furnishes us with many examples of such contradictions of heretics. Let us analyze some of them briefly:

A. Arianism

It is not rare to see contradictions among heresiarchs reach the point of lying. The false oath of fidelity to the Catholic faith made by Arius before Emperor Constantine is well-known.[124]

B. Pelagianism

The Pelagians frequently referred to the Redemption. Whoever reads them without remembering that heretics usually use contradiction to dupe their adversaries could believe that they accepted the idea of Redemption. Nothing is falser. In *Dictionnaire de théologie catholique*, R. Hedde and E. Amann explain that Pelagianism was about "abolishing the Christian idea of Redemption. Undoubtedly, the Pelagians spoke very much about the Redemption; they kept the word, not the thing. They referred to the remission of sins founded on the death of Christ, but their manner of comprehending sin and its effect on man obliged them to interpret this remission in the nominalist sense of *non-imputation* of the sins committed; it is nothing more than an *exterior* justification."[125]

Many other contradictions among the Pelagians constituted true lies. In 415, a Synod was convened in Diospolis to judge the heretics Pelagius and Celestius. After careful examination of the writings of Celestius, the Synod condemned him. The works of Pelagius were not analyzed; the Fathers judged him based only on his declarations at the Synod, and they absolved him. After reproducing Saint Augustine's observations about this episode, Hedde and Amann write, "The charity of Saint Augustine makes him add that he did not wish to affirm that Pelagius had lied in denying his doctrines. This, however, is the conclusion one must accept. Pelagius could not have been absolved by the Synod of Diospolis, except thanks to omissions that are strangely similar to lies."[126]

---

124. Doubting the sincerity of Arius, Constantine allegedly said to him, "If your faith is truly orthodox, you did well in making this oath; if it is impious, then may God judge you for your oath." X. Le Bachelet, "Arianisme," *D.T.C.*, 1–2e.:1805. Saint Alexander, the old bishop of the imperial city, begged God to either take him from this world or prevent the rehabilitation of Arius. That same day, when he was crossing the city accompanied by a numerous retinue, Arius suffered an abominable death, so that the ancient historians applied to him the words of Scripture about Judas: *diffusa sunt viscera eius* (Acts 1:18). See Le Bachelet, *D.T.C.*, 1–2e.:1805–1806.
125. R. Hedde and E. Amann, "Pélagianisme," *D.T.C.*, 12–1e.:684.
126. Hedde and Amann, "Pélagianisme," *D.T.C.*, 12–1e.:693.

Later, the same perfidy of Pelagius and his followers deceived Pope Saint Zosimus. Having convoked a Synod in Rome in 417, especially to judge the Pelagians, and immediately proceeding to a careful examination of his errors, the pope ended up absolving Pelagius and some of his defenders. In a September 21, 417, letter to the bishops of Africa, Saint Zosimus reproached them for having believed the accusations against Pelagius. After describing the joy that the professions of faith of the Pelagians had caused "to the holy men there present," the pope added that "some were scarcely able to control their sighs and tears, on seeing how men of such perfect faith could have been so calumniated." Saint Zosimus attached certain writings of Pelagius to that letter and said to the bishops of Africa, "The reading of these texts will probably bring you as much joy as it did to us."[127]

Lies were really frequent among the Pelagians. Saint Augustine, "always so moderate"—observe Hedde and Amann—said of another of them, Julianus de Eclana, that he was "untruthful" in his professions of faith.[128]

C. Monothelitism

Regarding Monothelitism, M. Jugie writes, "It is the chameleon heresy *par excellence*. In the measure in which it was unmasked and met resistance, it retreated and made concessions so that its point of arrival was in perfect contradiction with that of its departure."[129]

D. Protestantism

Luther's contradictions are patent in his liturgical reform and in the doctrines with which he pretended to justify it.

Studying the Lutheran theory about the Real Presence, J. Paquier wrote,[130] "When is Jesus Christ present in the bread and wine? Generally, Luther tells us that He is present only at the moment of the Consecration and Communion. But on this point, as in others, his contradictions are abundant."[131]

Luther never got to the point of implementing his true concepts about the liturgy: "However, the changes were made timidly. It is what was required by a certain good sense of Luther and the falsity of his attitudes. It was necessary to put people to sleep."[132]

Despite his violent attacks against the Roman Mass, Luther nevertheless permitted his followers to celebrate it when necessary, as long as they interpreted

---

127. Hedde, 12–1e.:698. Later, Saint Zosimus found out that he had been deceived by the Pelagians and condemned them.
128. "'In disputatione loquacissimus, in contentione calumniosissimus, in professione mendacissiumus.' (The most eloquent in debate, slanderous in disputes, and untruthful in professions [of faith].) (*Op. imp.*, 4:52)." Hedde, 12–1e.:702.
129. M. Jugie, "Monothélisme," in *D.T.C.*, 10–2e.:2307.
130. We cite this passage integrally in the quotation supported by footnote 359.
131. J. Paquier, "Luther," *D.T.C.*, 9–1e.:1305.
132. Paquier, 9–1e.:1306.

the formulae of the Missal according to their new concepts.[133] In addition, in many places, he maintained the traditional ceremonies he vituperated so furiously. "However, [these] were now no more than mere appearances emptied of their content."[134]

See then how gravely deceived would be anyone who, in assisting at Lutheran liturgical ceremonies, deemed it impossible that true heretics were celebrating them because they match or almost match the Catholic ones.

Saint Robert Bellarmine gives another characteristic example of Protestant contradiction in preaching: "It is noted by Frederick Staphilus that, in the beginning the Lutherans made the Church invisible, then at length, when they saw the absurdity which followed thence, by a secret counsel, they established that the Church may be said to be visible, but still by this name of visible, they mean really invisible."[135]

E. Jansenism

One of the principal errors the Holy See condemned in Jansen was his notion of liberty.[136] In the final analysis, his heretical thesis was the denial of human liberty. However, in his principal work, *Augustinus*, this thesis, while it was there, was continuously disguised in ambiguous propositions, specious distinctions, and deceptive formulations. In this, nothing merits special mention, for it is known that the heretics have always sought to dissemble their heresies to better deceive the incautious.

In addition to ambiguities and sophisms, though, Jansen fell into direct and open contradictions on this and other points. After exposing Jansen's error about human liberty, J. Carreyre writes in the *Dictionnaire de théologie catholique*, "At times Jansen appears to modify his mode of expression: thus, he says that to be free is 'to be master of oneself, to have in one's power one's own acts' (*Aug.*, book 6, chap. 3), and concludes that the indeliberate movements which precede the reason are not free (Ibid., chaps. 36, 38)."[137]

An ingenuous spirit eager to prove Jansen (bishop of Ypres) innocent of the accusation of heresy would see in these passages a complete proof of his orthodoxy. That was the interpretation that his disciples gave to the work of the master,

---

133. See J. Rivière, "La messe durant la période de la réforme et du Concile de Trente," in *D.T.C.*, 10–1e.:1087. We quote extensive passages of this text of Rivière in chap. 5, sec. 2 (*Luther's Temporizations*).
134. Rivière, "La messe," in *D.T.C.*, 10–1e.:1089.
135. St. Robert Bellarmine, *On Councils; On the Church Militant; On the Marks of the Church*, vol. 1 in *De controversiis: On the Church*, trans. Ryan Grant (Post Falls, Id.: Mediatrix Press, 2017), 308. The affirmation is based on the declaration of a Protestant theologian who converted to Catholicism, Friedrich Staphylus.
136. The third proposition condemned by Innocent X in 1653: "In order to merit or demerit in the state of fallen nature, freedom from necessity is not required in man, but freedom from external compulsion is sufficient." Denz.-Sch., 2003.
137. J. Carreyre, "Jansénisme," in *D.T.C.*, 8–1e.:488.

denying that it contained the errors condemned by Innocent X.[138] Carreyre gives us the real explanation of these texts:

> However, in these passages and other similar ones, Jansen interprets the previously mentioned expressions in an altogether special sense. It is commonly said that an act is *in our power* when it depends on us to practice it or not, when we can select between two actions so that our will is not determined to that act.
>
> According to Jansen, it is enough that the will not be constrained by coercion or exterior violence for one to be able to say that the act is in our power (*Aug.* book 8, chaps. 4, 6, 8, 35, 38)....
>
> For Jansen, the power to select good or evil consists only in the fact of the will desiring or acting spontaneously and with delight, not under constraint, violence, or coercion.... Therefore, it is only a question of power without coercion and violence and not a faculty which, freely and on its own, can select this or that.[139]

It is not only in their directly doctrinal declarations that heretics do not hesitate, when necessary, to contradict their own ideas head-on.

An example of this is the approval given by Jansen to the book *Grandeurs de Jésus* by Cardinal de Bérulle. Since this book contains affirmations opposed to certain Jansenist doctrines, an unwary observer could believe that, in giving such approval, the bishop of Ypres was expressing his authentic thinking concerning those doctrines. However, the truth is that Jansen approved the work only to gain Cardinal de Bérulle's sympathy, and it is known that he deliberately did not read the book before approving it because he was afraid to find passages contrary to his own ideas.[140]

F. Modernism

Concerning the flagrant contradictions of modernists, Saint Pius X wrote:

> This becomes still clearer to anybody who studies the conduct of modernists, which is in perfect harmony with their teachings. IN THE WRITINGS AND ADDRESSES, THEY SEEM NOT UNFREQUENTLY TO ADVOCATE NOW ONE DOCTRINE NOW ANOTHER SO THAT ONE WOULD BE DISPOSED TO REGARD THEM AS VAGUE AND DOUBTFUL. BUT THERE IS A REASON FOR THIS, and it is to be found in their ideas as to the mutual separation of science and faith. Hence in their books you find some things which might well be expressed by a Catholic, but in the next page,

---

138. It was even necessary for Alexander VII to define that those errors were found in *Augustinus*. See Denz.-Sch., 2010–2012.
139. Carreyre, "Jansénisme," in *D.T.C.*, 8–1e.:488–89.
140. See, Carreyre, 8–1e.:324.

you find other things which might have been dictated by a rationalist. When they write history, they make no mention of the divinity of Christ, but when they are in the pulpit, they profess it clearly; again, when they write history, they pay no heed to the Fathers and the Councils, but when they catechize the people, they cite them respectfully. In the same way, they draw their distinctions between theological and pastoral exegesis and scientific and historical exegesis.[141]

G. The "Anti-liturgical Heresy"

In his *Institutions liturgiques*, Dom Guéranger highlights the contradiction proper to heretics in the matter of worship. He enunciates fourteen principles that govern what he calls the "anti-liturgical heresy,"[142] that is to say, the common substrate of the liturgical innovations of all heresies.

We reproduce here the fourth principle enunciated by Dom Guéranger, which, from certain points of view, bears on the matter being treated. After referring incidentally in the first three points to various contradictions of the heretics, he writes:

> 4. We should not be surprised at the contradiction heresy presents in its works when we consider the fourth principle, or, if you wish, the fourth necessity imposed on the sectarians by the very nature of their state of revolt: *an habitual contradiction with their own principles.* It must be so, for their own confusion on the great day, which sooner or later has to come, in which God shall reveal the nakedness of heretics before the eyes of the people whom they have deceived, and also because it is not proper to men to be consistent: only the truth can be so. Thus, without exception, all the sectarians begin by crying out for the rights of *antiquity*; they want to purge Christianity of all that is false and unworthy of God, which the errors and passions of men have introduced. They desire nothing but the ancient and seek to take up the Christian institution in its crib once again. For this reason, they mutilate, destroy, and cut. Everything falls before their blows. And when one expects to see the divine worship reappear in its first purity, behold it is filled with new formulae, which date from no earlier than yesterday, and are incontestably human, for those who have written them are still alive. All the sects are subject to this necessity. We see this in the monophysites and Nestorians, and we shall encounter the same thing in all branches of Protestantism. The ostentation with which they preach *antiquity* does nothing more than position them to attack everything of the past. Afterward, they go before the people who have been seduced and swear that everything is good, that the papal excrescences have disappeared, and that the divine worship has returned to its ancient sanctity. We shall

---

141. St. Pius X, *Pascendi*, no. 18.
142. See Guéranger, *Institutions liturgiques*, 1:405–25. See also the concept of "anti-liturgical heresy" at 1:405–14.

note something else characteristic of liturgical modifications made by heretics. In their fury of innovations, they are not content with mutilating the formulae of ecclesiastical style, stigmatized by them as *human* words. Rather, they extend their reprobation to the very readings and Prayers that the Church has taken from Scripture. They change them, replace them, not wishing to pray with the Church, excommunicating themselves in this way, fearing even the least bit of orthodoxy that presided over the selection of those passages.[143]

3. The Third Answer: Neomodernist Metaphysics

The cited passage of Saint Pius X about the contradictions of modernists is particularly illuminating. It reveals that it is *not only because of tactics* that they are not ashamed to affirm on one page what they have just denied on the previous one. *It follows a system.*

Something analogous occurs with progressives, who recycle Modernism into terms adapted to our days.

Indeed, in addition to the enumerated tactical reasons, the progressives have another motive to defend seemingly traditional positions, side by side with heterodox ones. The phenomenology they subscribe to in the philosophical domain leads to extreme relativist metaphysics. This eclectic paroxysm amalgamates all past and present philosophies: Hegelianism, Existentialism, Personalism, the Gnostic doctrines of East and West, Liberalism, Marxism, and the like. How could they fail to include Thomism? But how could they add it if Thomism is the very denial of this relativist syncretism?

This difficulty is easy to resolve in phenomenological terms. It is enough, for example, "to put into parentheses"[144] the foundational objectivism of Thomism; or to invite it to reinterpret or "rethink itself" on a Hegelian or neo-Hegelian base.[145] Thomism thus becomes one more diner at the neomodernist smorgasbord.

One may affirm, for example, that the celebration of the Mass is an "action of Christ and of the people of God hierarchically organized,"[146] but one gives a new meaning to the term *hierarchically organized*—as the B.A.C. commentators do[147]—affirming that it does not involve higher and lower degrees of dignity.

In another example furnished by the B.A.C. commentators,[148] one can admit that there is a real presence of Christ in the sacrament of the Eucharist,

---

143. Guéranger, 1:417–18.
144. On the sense of this expression in Husserl, see Andre Lalande, "Parentesis," in *Vocabulario tecnico y critico de la filosofía* (Buenos Aires: El Ateneo, 1953); Paul Foulquié and Raymond Saint-Jean, "Epoché," "Parenthèses," "Reduction phénoménologique" in *Dictionnaire de la langue philosophique*, Paris: Presses Universitaires de France, 1962.
145. See Plinio Corrêa de Oliveira, *Unperceived Ideological Transshipment and Dialogue.*
146. 1969 *Institutio*, no. 1, p. 13.
147. We cite this text in chap. 1, sec. 6 (*Jesus Christ, the Principal Priest [Sacerdos]*) *supra.*
148. We cite this text in chap. 1, sec. 7 (*A Tendency to Make the "Liturgy of the Word" Equal to the "Eucharistic Liturgy"*).

but this "real presence" is considered equal to the presence of Christ in the "praying assembly."

In summary, the preoccupation with disguising themselves is particularly acute among the progressives, who know very well that the faithful would immediately repudiate them if they knew their real designs. Thus, affirming the traditional doctrine and then relativizing it to the point of concluding the contrary of what was just said is a characteristic tactic of progressive neomodernism. It was one of Modernism. However, in addition to being a tactic, this way of proceeding expresses a basic element of neomodernist metaphysics. Or, rather, it forms part of the dialectical, Hegelian, and phenomenological anti-metaphysics of the neomodernists.[149]

*   *   *

Here are *some examples* taken from the new theories about the indissolubility of matrimony—a point of doctrine very different from those we have been discussing. They will show how broadly progressives take advantage of dialectical contradiction:

(1) In his book *Marriage in the Modern World*,[150] Fr. Bernard Häring—a Second Vatican Council *peritus* considered by the progressives as the best moral theologian of our days—proposes surreptitiously that Catholics accept divorce. For example, referring to divorced persons who are re-'married,' he writes:

> Quite often such [divorced and re-'married'] people have built up an *erroneous conscience*:
>
> Since they live together in peace and harmony, they become day by day more and more convinced that God blesses their union. They probably admit that divorce and remarriage should not be, but for some reason (or none) they are subjectively convinced that in their case the first marriage was invalid, and conclude from this that the new union, even though it cannot be made in church, is a true marriage in the sight of God. In this connection, one must also consider the frequent insufficiency of instruction in such matters. It quite often happens that such people, without mentioning their invalid marriage, go to a church where they are not known, or where at least nothing is known about their invalid marriage, and there sincerely confess their sins and make a devout Communion. There is always the possibility that in recognition of their subjective good intentions, God will pardon them, even though, in spite of everything, their marriage remains invalid.[151]

---

149. For identical reasons, the employment of ambiguous and deceitful expressions, euphemisms, and so forth is not merely a neomodernist propaganda tactic but a metaphysically indispensable means of promoting the "friction" of contradictory ideas capable of generating the redemptive synthesis. On this notion of the Hegelian "friction" of ideas, see Corrêa de Oliveira, *Unperceived Ideological Transshipment*.

150. Bernard Häring, *Marriage in the Modern World*, trans. Geoffrey Stevens (Westminster, Md.: The Newman Press, 1966).

151. Häring, *Marriage*, 302.

Further on, dealing with the case of youthful divorced persons who have re-'married,' he expresses the following ideas:

> Even if they have not entirely succeeded in living together as brother and sister, their constant upholding of the indissolubility of marriage and their efforts to save others from such a situation, associated with a genuine effort on their part, are a kind of preparation for and anticipation of a later sacramental confession. If, after every failure, their love of God leads them to contrition, and they pray together, go to church together, and fight every inch of the way to live a Christian life, they are on the way towards the light and perhaps, too, most of the time, in the state of grace.[152]

Already in these texts of Father Häring, several contradictions appear. It is particularly significant, however, that, in one of the first paragraphs of the item in which he discusses the matter, he declares, "Naturally the Church's principle remains firm that divorced persons whose first marriage was valid in the sight of God and their conscience HAVE NO RIGHT TO REMARRY and that a civil marriage is no true marriage."[153]

(2) On September 29, 1965, the Melkite patriarchal vicar for the See of Alexandria, Cairo, and the Sudan, Bishop Elias Zoghby, made a speech in the Council that caused a sensation, advocating divorce in the case of a young person abandoned, without any fault of his own, by his spouse.[154] Some days later, however, trying to undo the scandal caused by his previous speech, Bishop Zoghby spoke again. He defended the same thesis of divorce but also made some affirmations, apparently unequivocal, that he adhered to traditional doctrine about marriage, such as the following:

> 2. I affirmed clearly in my speech [September 29] the immutable principle of the indissolubility of matrimony. . . .
> 3. This indissolubility of matrimony is so anchored in the tradition of the Churches of East and West, both Orthodox and Catholic, that a Council speech cannot question it. The Orthodox tradition, in fact, always considered matrimony as indissoluble as the union of Christ and the Church, His bride.[155]

(3) In an article about divorce published in the *Revista Eclesiástica Brasileira* in 1968, Fr. Eduardo Hoornaert writes at the beginning, "Catholic thinking regarding marriage has always repeated the basic, fundamental affirmation that the sacrament of matrimony is indissoluble. This affirmation is based on the legitimate

---

152. Häring, 303.
153. Häring, 301.
154. See Fr. Boaventura Kloppenburg, *Concílio Vaticano II* (Petrópolis, R.J.: Editora Vozes, Ltda., 1962–1966), 5:149–51.
155. Kloppenburg, *Concílio Vaticano II*, 5:188.

interpretation of Revelation, whose most clear expression is found in the famous text at Matt. 19:1–12."[156]

In the following pages, however, the author declares that the apostles and their successors did not exactly understand the evangelical message on the indissolubility of matrimony.[157] He sustains that the erroneous interpretation of this message has reached its apex today.[158] He insinuates that Protestants have something in their favor in their attacks on the Catholic doctrine about the sacrament of matrimony.[159] He ends the article proposing "a revision of the rigoristic discipline" on marriage since people are "still incapable of living according to the evangelical requirements."[160]

As we see, this position of Father Hoornaert is the fruit either of real cynicism or crass error. In either case, he falls into flagrant contradiction.

4. Conclusion

Given what has been said, it will be understood that the existence of orthodox passages in the 1969 *Institutio* cannot be alleged as a sufficient reason to exempt it from censure. On the contrary, that opposing doctrines are found there side by side increases the gravity of the criticism that must be made.[161]

---

156. Eduardo Hoornaert, "A indissolubilidade do matrimônio na reflexão católica após Trento," *Revista Eclesiástica Brasileira* 28 (1968): 99.
157. See Hoornaert, "A indissolubilidade," 100.
158. See Hoornaert, 100.
159. See Hoornaert, 102–103.
160. Hoornaert, 106.
161. It is necessary to establish a general principle here. When one really and sincerely wishes to dissipate the suspicions hanging over a text showing traces of neomodernism, one should not merely put an orthodox declaration beside it. Such a measure would only aggravate the ambiguity and cause more confusion among souls. *Rather, rectifying the obscure, equivocal, and heterodox passages would be absolutely indispensable.* It would be *absolutely necessary* to undo the spurious unions between truth and error which characterize Hegelianism, phenomenology, and neomodernism, in addition to teaching good doctrine in its integrity. Not acting this way is to give to one's own children bread mixed with stones and fish mixed with serpents (see Matt. 7:9–10).

CHAPTER THREE

The New Text and Rubrics of the Mass in the 1969 *Ordo*

As noted,[162] we shall study in this chapter the new *Ordo missae*, that is, the new text of the Mass and the rubrics accompanying it. We will also analyze certain instructions in the *Institutio generalis missalis romani,* which constitute true rubrics, although they are not called this in the document.[163]

The new *Ordo*'s translation into Portuguese is characterized by innumerable infidelities, many of which offend against dogma. For this reason, some think that only the Portuguese version is unacceptable, not the Latin original. Such thinking seems unfounded. Consequently, in the present chapter, we shall study only the Latin text of the new Ordinary of the Mass,[164] reserving some observations about the Portuguese translation for the following chapter.[165]

1. Suppressed and Altered Prayers

In the *Ordo* of Saint Pius V, the initial *Confiteor* is said first by the priest and then by the altar server, in the name of the people. This distinction marks the difference between the celebrant and the people. In the new *Ordo,* the *Confiteor* is said together by the priest and the people. Such a modification tends to insinuate equality between the priesthood of the celebrant and that of the laity.

---

162. See footnote 30. As previously stated, we will devote the greater part of our analysis in this chapter to the 1969 *Ordo*, indicating, however, when necessary, the modifications introduced in 1970. These will be studied *ex professo* in Chapter 4. As the reader will see, practically no changes were made in 1970 to the parts we expressed reservations toward in the 1969 *Ordo*.

163. Here, too, we do not pretend to examine the matter exhaustively but only to analyze the most significant aspects of the New Mass, which indicate the spirit it naturally instills into the faithful.

164. When necessary, we shall present the Latin expressions themselves for the reader's convenience. Normally, though, we shall only provide a literal translation of the Latin texts.
Translator's Note: As mentioned in the publisher's note at the beginning of the book and footnote 21, the translators assume responsibility for the English translation from the 1969 *Institutio*'s Latin original.

165. **Publisher's Note:** as mentioned (footnote 29), the chapter in which the author studied the infidelities of the Portuguese translation of the new *Ordo* is suppressed in this revised English edition.

The absolution given by the priest at the end of the *Confiteor*[166] was suppressed. This is another innovation rendering less precise the distinction between the hierarchical priesthood and the condition of the simple faithful.[167]

In the new *Ordo,* various prayers of the traditional Roman Rite emphasizing the notions of humility, sorrow for one's sins, propitiation, and the idea that, without grace, there is no perseverance in virtue, were removed. Thus, both the just-mentioned absolution and its subsequent invocations disappeared.[168] Gone, too, are the prayer *Aufer a nobis,*[169] said by the priest when he kisses the altar,[170] part of the prayer *Munda cor meum,*[171] almost all of the Offertory,[172] part of the prayer *Perceptio corporis tui,* which precedes Communion,[173] two prayers after

---

166. The traditional formula, eliminated in the new *Ordo* of the Mass, is: "May the almighty and merciful Lord grant us pardon, absolution, and remission of our sins." **Translator's Note:** The traditional Roman Rite prayers cited in English are from *The New Marian Missal for Daily Mass* by Sylvester P. Juergens, S.M. (New York: Regina Press, 1963), 1445 pp, and the *Daily Missal With Vespers for Sundays & Feasts*, by Dom Gaspar Lefebvre, O.S.B., of the Abbey of Saint André (St. Paul, Minn.: The E.M. Lohmann Co., 1925). The Canon is from J.S.M. Lynch, *The Rite of Ordination According to the Roman Pontifical,* 2nd rev. ed. (New York: The Cathedral Library Association, 1892), 76–78.

167. In Chapter 5, in the analysis of the Lutheran supper, other observations about the new *Confiteor* will be made.

168. "V. – O God, Thou wilt turn again and quicken us.
   R. – And Thy people shall rejoice in Thee.
   V. – Show us, O Lord, Thy mercy.
   R. – And grant us Thy salvation.
   V. – O Lord, hear my prayer.
   R. – And let my cry come unto Thee.
   V. – The Lord be with you.
   R. – And with thy spirit."

169. This prayer is said when the priest goes up to the altar. Its original formula is: "Take away from us our iniquities, we beseech Thee, O Lord, that we may be worthy to enter with pure minds into the Holy of Holies, through Christ, our Lord. Amen."

170. This prayer is especially directed to the saints whose relics are in the altar: "We beseech Thee, O Lord, by the merits of Thy Saints, whose relics are here, and of all the Saints, that Thou wouldst vouchsafe to forgive me all my sins. Amen."

171. This prayer is said before the Gospel. From its text, which we present below, the new *Ordo* suppressed everything presented here in parentheses: "Cleanse my heart and my lips, O almighty God, (who didst cleanse the lips of the prophet Isaias with a burning coal, and vouchsafe, through Thy gracious mercy, so to purify me,) that I may worthily announce thy holy Gospel. (Through Christ, Our Lord. Amen)."

172. As we shall indicate further on—see chap. 3, sec. 2 (*The New Concept of the Offertory*) *infra*— the new *Ordo* eliminated the traditional Offertory, replacing it with a simple "preparation of the gifts," which moves it closer to the Protestant liturgy—see chap. 3, sec. 2, especially item (3), contrasting the Offertories of the traditional Latin and New Masses. Almost all the suppressed prayers highlight the notion of forgiveness of sins.

173. In the traditional text of this prayer, whose beginning we transcribe below, everything in parentheses was suppressed in the new *Ordo*: "Let not the partaking of Thy Body, O Lord, Jesus Christ, (which I, though unworthy, presume to receive), turn to my judgment and condemnation."

Communion—*Quod ore sumpsimus*[174] and *Corpus tuum, Domine*[175]—and also the supplication *Placeat tibi,* which closes the sacrifice.[176]

Perhaps the suppression of these prayers would not tend to attenuate the expressions of humility, contrition, and propitiation if they had been replaced by others manifesting the same dispositions of soul; or if new and more numerous signs of repentance and adoration such as genuflections and prostrations had been added; or even if the *Institutio* had presented valid explanations for these suppressions that would have dissipated the fears they engendered. None of this was done. On the contrary, these magnificent prayers were not replaced by others expressing the same ideas, and almost all the genuflections, bows, and kisses of the altar were eliminated. The *Institutio* does not give substantive reasons to justify what was done and even omits the idea of propitiation.[177]

Thus, the suppression of these prayers diminishes in the liturgy—in Catholic life, therefore—the expressions of humility, sorrow for sins committed, and our need for grace to persevere in virtue. Consequently, it weakens or at least helps move to the shadows, the propitiatory character of the Mass. Now, besides showing some dissonance with Catholic doctrine, all of this recalls the ways of thinking and acting common in Protestant and modernist circles.

The reference to the Holy Trinity disappeared from various passages,[178] tending to debilitate faith in the central mystery of Revelation.[179]

In the traditional *Kyrie,* each person of the Holy Trinity is invoked three times. Thus, the Trinitarian character of the divine relations is affirmed with particular insistence. This affirmation was also weakened in the *Kyrie* of the new *Ordo missae,* where each Divine Person is invoked only twice.[180]

2. The New Concept of the Offertory

The Offertory of Pope Saint Pius V, which always constituted one of the principal elements distinguishing the Catholic Mass from the Protestant Supper, was

174. "Grant, O Lord, that what we have taken with our mouth, we may receive with a pure mind; and from a temporal gift may it become to us an eternal remedy." In the 1970 text of the new *Ordo,* this prayer was reintroduced, as mentioned in chap. 4, sec. 11 (*Modifications in the Fixed Parts of the Mass*) *infra.*
175. "May Thy Body, O Lord, which I have received, and Thy Blood, which I have drunk, cling to my inmost being; and grant that no stain of sin may remain in me, who have been fed with this pure and holy Sacrament; Who livest and reignest for ever and ever. Amen."
176. "May the performance of my homage be pleasing to Thee, O holy Trinity: and grant that the Sacrifice which I, though unworthy, have offered up in the sight of Thy Majesty, may be acceptable to Thee, and through Thy mercy, be a propitiation for me, and for all those for whom I have offered it. Through Christ our Lord. Amen."
177. See chap. 1, sec. 3 (*A Propitiatory Sacrifice*).
178. In addition to the prayers *Suscipe Sancta Trinitas* and *Placeat tibi,* directed to the Holy Trinity, the trinitarian invocations which close numerous prayers of the traditional *Ordo* have disappeared: "*Deus, qui humanae substantiae,*" "*Libera nos, quaesumus,*" "*Domine Jesu Christe, Fili Dei vivi,*" "*Perceptio corporis.*"
179. As is obvious, this tendency not to insist on the mystery of the Trinity has dangerous repercussions in ecumenism, favoring a modernist-flavored syncretism with non-Christian religions.
180. See chap. 5, sec. 3, item D (*Other Aspects of the Lutheran Supper*) on how this modification of the number of invocations in the *Kyrie* pleases certain Protestants.

suppressed in its specific characteristics.[181] Let us see why one can and must affirm that such suppression occurred.

The true sacrificial oblation realized in the Mass is not in the Offertory but rather in the offering which Jesus Christ, at the moment of Consecration, makes of Himself to the Holy Trinity. The true victim in the sacrifice of the Mass is not the bread and wine or the faithful present, but Jesus Christ Himself.

This being so, why does the Offertory exist?

In carrying out a sacrifice, we offer God a victim in place of ourselves, that is, as a symbol of the offering of our own persons to God. This is a fundamental element of every sacrifice. In the Mass, it is Jesus Christ who immolates Himself for us. Uniting ourselves to Him, we ought to offer Him in place of ourselves and offer ourselves with Him.

However, Our Lord's oblation of Himself is not visible to us since He does not show Himself in a manner perceptible to the senses.

Therefore, it would be well to carry out before the Consecration some sensible expression of the nature of the sacrifice and various offerings to be made. Such are the purposes of the Roman Offertory.

The Offertory, therefore, contains a declaration of what the sacrificial oblation proper consists of and the offering of ourselves to God. It also affirms the propitiatory purpose of the Mass.

It behooves us, then, to make these three elements evident. In addition to constituting fundamental features of the Roman Offertory, they distinguish the Catholic Mass from the Protestant Supper beyond the shadow of a doubt.

(1) The oblation of Our Lord really takes place at the moment of the Consecration; but, for the nature of the sacrifice to become manifest from the beginning, there are in the Offertory of the Roman Missal a group of prayers that already disclose Who the true Victim will be, and offer that Victim to the Holy Trinity in anticipation.

(2) The oblation of ourselves to God, through Jesus Christ, is symbolized by the offering of bread and wine. Secondarily, it is also symbolized through the eventual offering of other material goods. Note that such symbolism becomes effective only if the bread and wine, when *placed on the altar*, are not only *presented* to God

---

181. See chap. 5, sec. 3, item B (*The Lutheran Offertory*), where we analyze in greater detail the position of Protestants in this matter.

but are *offered in a sacrificial spirit*. In other words, the abovementioned gifts are *consecrated* to God.[182]

---

182. St. Robert Bellarmine: "It should not be denied that the bread and wine are offered in some manner during Mass, and hence pertain to the thing which is sacrificed." St. Robert Bellarmine, *On the Most Holy Sacrifice of the Mass*, trans. Ryan Grant (Post Falls, Id.: Mediatrix Press, 2020), book 1, chap. 27, 151. "In the Mass bread is not offered as a perfect sacrifice, but as an *inchoate* sacrifice and *to be perfected*." Bellarmine, *On the Mass*, 152. "The oblation of bread and wine preceding the consecration pertains to the integrity and fullness of the sacrifice." Bellarmine, 152.

Francisco Suárez: "Christ instituted and offered this sacrifice as high priest according to the order of Melchisedech; then, in a certain manner, He offered the bread and wine, not merely as the matter, but also as the term of the oblation, for such was the sacrifice of Melchisedech." Franciscus Suárez, *In tertiam partem D. Thomae*, in vol. 21 of *Opera omnia* (Paris: Vivès, 1877), disp. 75, sect. 1, no. 9, 652. "The bread and wine are offered here (in the Mass) in a certain manner; they are not, however, merely offered in regard to the accidents, but also in regard to the substance; therefore, in respect to both, they pertain to what is offered." Suárez, *In tertiam partem*, disp. 75, no 11, 653. "We here affirm. . . . that the thing which is offered is not merely Christ, but also, in a certain way, the bread and wine. From thence, it does not follow that there are two sacrifices because these two things constitute the terms *a quo* and *ad quem* of the same sacrifice since the bread becomes the Body of Christ, by whose presence the species are sanctified." Suárez, *In tertiam partem*, disp. 75, no. 12, 653.

Cornelius à Lapide: Commenting on the passage of Saint Matthew (26:26), in which one reads that Our Lord blessed the bread before the Consecration, he writes, "Christ blessed, not the Father, as the heretics choose to say, but the bread and wine." Cornelius à Lapide, *St. Matthew's Gospel—chaps. 22 to 28*, vol. 3 in *The Great Commentary of Cornelius à Lapide*, trans. Thomas W. Mossman (London: John Hodges, 1887).

Diekamp: "In the Offertory of the Mass, the substances of the bread and wine are offered as a secondary host so that God may convert them into the primary host." Franciscus Diekamp and Adolphus M. Hoffmann, *Theologiae dogmaticae manuale* (Paris–Tournai–Rome: Desclée, edition of 1934), 4:224.

Camillus Callewaert (d. 1943): He defends the thesis that in the Offertory, there is not a mere preparation of the sacrifice but rather a true oblation, "a gift made to God with sacrificial intent." C. Callewaert, "De offerenda et oblatione in Missa," *Periodica de Re Morali, Canonica, Liturgica* 33 (1944), 70. He writes further, "As it appears, Luther was the first who rose against this traditional concept of the oblation. Intending to deny to the Mass the nature of true sacrifice, he reasoned against Catholics as follows: Nothing can be given to God, who already, of Himself, possesses everything. Therefore, one cannot make an oblation as a donation in the Mass. Therefore, in the Mass, there is no sacrifice." Callewaert, "De offerenda," 70.

The following express the same opinion: Joannes de Lugo, *Tractatus de eucharistia*, vol. 4 of *Disputationes scholasticae et morales* (Paris: Vivès, 1869), disp. 19, sect. 7, no. 99, 208–209; Jacques-Benigne Bossuet, *Explication de quelques difficultés sur les prières de la messe a un nouveau catholique*, in vol. 13 of *Oeuvres complètes de Bossuet* (Paris: Même Maison de Commerce, 1841), 45–46; Christian Pesch, *Praelectiones dogmaticae* (Fribourg: Herder, vol. 1, 1898; vol. 6, 1900; vol. 9, 1899), 6:382; Louis Billot, *De ecclesiae sacramentis* (Rome: Ex Typographia Pontificia in Instituto Pii IX, 1914), 1:599–600; Adrien Fortescue, *La messe* (Paris: Lethielleux, 1921), 391–92; Nicholas Gihr, *Le saint sacrifice de la messe* (Paris: Lethielleux, 1901), 196, 218–22, 233; M. Teixeira-Leite Penido, *O mistério dos sacramentos* (Petrópolis: Vozes, 1961), 288–89; Franciscus X. Abarzuza, O.F.M.Cap. *Manuale theologiae dogmaticae* (Madrid-Buenos Aires: Studium, 1956–1957), 4:280. See also: Council of Florence (Twelfth Ecumenical), *Decretrum pro Armeniis*. Denz.-Sch., 1320; José A. Jungmann, *El sacrificio de la misa* (Madrid: B.A.C., 1951), 51–54, 629–71, 741–44; Manuel Garrido Bonaño, O.S.B. and Augusto Pascual, *Curso de liturgia romana* (Madrid: B.A.C., 1961), 266–67; and also the liturgical texts and the numerous Church Fathers cited by the authors whom we indicate: Saint Irenaeus, Tertullian, Origen, Saints Cyprian, Hypolite, Augustine, Gregory the Great, and others.

(3) Through various prayers, the Roman Offertory highlights the propitiatory character of the sacrifice. We shall not explain this aspect of the Mass here, as we have examined it earlier.[183]

These three elements have disappeared in the new Offertory. In their stead are a simple "preparation of the offerings" or "presentation of the gifts," corresponding to a *concept of the Offertory fundamentally different from that of Saint Pius V*.

In addition, various expressions of other principles that distinguish Catholic doctrine from Protestantism were suppressed or attenuated. The allusion to the fall of our first parents was eliminated. The invocations to Our Lady, the angels and saints, have disappeared. The principle that God must accept the sacrifice for it to be agreeable to Him became unclear. The manifestations of sorrow for one's sins and humility were weakened, as was the affirmation of the hierarchical priesthood of the celebrant. There is no longer any explicit reference to the faithful departed.

All this becomes obvious through comparison, which we will do below, contrasting the Offertory of Saint Pius V and that of the new *Ordo missae*.

(1) The prayer "*Suscipe sancte Pater*," traditionally said by the celebrant on offering the bread, does not appear in the New Mass: "Accept, O holy Father, almighty and eternal God, this unspotted host, which I, Thy unworthy servant, offer unto Thee, my living and true God, for my innumerable sins, offenses, and negligences, and for all here present: as also for all faithful Christians, both living and dead, that it may avail both me and them for salvation unto life everlasting. Amen."

This prayer, full of unction in its terms and style, speaks of the propitiatory value of the sacrifice. Note that the priest offers the host for the people in a clear affirmation of his hierarchical function. He offers it for all the faithful living and dead, which contradicts the Protestant principle that the fruits of the Mass are inapplicable to those absent or the deceased. Luther, too, suppressed this prayer in his Mass.[184]

One point merits special attention here: The celebrant offers to God "this unspotted host." Now, the word "host," which can also indicate here the bread, more properly signifies "victim," and the adjective "unspotted" is not applied so much to the bread as to Jesus Christ, the only truly "unspotted host." Thus, at the same time that the priest in the old Roman Rite offers the bread to God with this prayer, he indicates, by anticipation, that the true sacrificial oblation will be that of Jesus in the sacrament, the "unspotted host."

All of this is abominable in the eyes of Protestants. As Lutheran pastor L. Reed affirms scornfully, "The central prayer of the offertory, *Suscipe sancte Pater*, is a perfect exposition of the Roman dictrine [*sic*] of the sacrifice of the Mass."[185] Luther saw in this and other Offertory prayers an "'abomination' which made

---

183. See chap. 3, sec. 2 (*The New Concept of the Offertory*) *supra*.
184. See chap. 5, sec. 3, item B (*The Lutheran Offertory*) *infra*.
185. Luther D. Reed, *The Lutheran Liturgy: A Study of the Common Liturgy of the Lutheran Church in America*, rev. ed. (Philadelphia: Fortress Press, 1947), 312. See this entire passage in chap. 5, sec. 3, item B (*The Lutheran Offertory*) *infra*.

'everything sound and smell of oblation.'"[186] The Protestants have a particular horror also of the anticipated offering of Our Lord, which this prayer realizes. In Reed's words, "They anticipated the consecration and the 'miracle of the Mass.'"[187]

(2) In addition, the prayer of the Roman Missal *Offerimus Tibi Domine*, with which the wine is offered, does not appear in the New Mass: "We offer unto Thee, O Lord, the chalice of salvation, beseeching Thy clemency, that it may ascend before Thy divine Majesty, as a sweet savor, for our salvation and for that of the whole world. Amen."

Like the prayer offering the bread, this one is also an anticipation since the "chalice of salvation" proper is that containing the Blood of Our Lord.

Here, too, one finds the notion of atonement for sins, expressed above all in the humble petition that the divine Majesty deign to accept the sacrifice. It is to be supposed, therefore, that the reasons which led to the suppression of this beautiful prayer are the same which inspired the elimination of the *Suscipe sancte Pater*.

(3) These two prayers, of the offering of the bread and wine, were replaced by the following:

> [*Offering of the bread*—] Blessed are you, Lord, God of all Creation. Through your goodness we have this bread to offer, which earth has given and human hands have made. It will become for us the bread of life....
>
> [*Offering of the wine*—] Blessed are you, Lord, God of all Creation. Through your goodness we have this wine to offer, fruit of the vine and work of human hands. It will become our spiritual drink.[188]

---

186. Reed, *The Lutheran Liturgy*, 312. We cite and comment on these affirmations of Luther in chap. 5, sec. 3, item B (*The Lutheran Offertory*) *infra*.

187. Reed, 312. We cite the whole text of L. Reed in chap. 5, sec. 3, item B (*The Lutheran Offertory*) *infra*. In part, the suppression of this prayer, as of various others, is according to the principle that "elements which, with the passage of time, came to be duplicated, or were added with but little advantage, are now to be discarded." Constitution *Sacrosanctum concilium* (on the Sacred Liturgy), no. 50; see also Paul VI, *Missale romanum*, par. 7.

As regards this prayer in particular, if not in any other way, it is obviously useful for affirming Catholic dogma against the Protestant heresy.

On the other hand, the systematic rejection of the duplications and anticipations seems contrary to the traditional mind of the Church. There is no room for a detailed exposition of the *raison d'être* of these duplications, repetitions, and anticipations in every order of being, especially in the doctrine and life of the Church. We should observe only that the metaphysics and theology of repetition, as well as anticipation, are those which explain the theory of the prefigures, the post-figures, and the anti-types, which form the essentially traditional foundation of the Church. They make the liturgical cycle intelligible, with its returning phases every year. They justify the litanies and so many other prayers in which one same idea—always old, always new—is said numerous times to nourish the piety of the faithful and express God's unchangeable eternity. In conclusion, we believe that only Protestant rationalism could condemn repetitions and anticipations as such.

188. *New ... Saint Joseph Sunday Missal: Prayerbook and Hymnal for 1972* (New York: Catholic Book Publishing, Co. 1972), 22–23.

Note that in these prayers, there is no reference to the true Victim, Jesus Christ; the offering of the gifts for us and our sins; the propitiatory character of the oblation; the hierarchical priesthood of the celebrant; and the principle that God must accept the sacrifice for it to be agreeable to Him. On the contrary, the expressions "It will become for us the bread of life" and "It will become our spiritual drink" insinuate that the true and essential end of the Mass is our spiritual nourishment. This thesis approaches one of the heresies condemned by Trent, as we have indicated.[189]

These new prayers *modify substantially, therefore, the very sense of the offering of the bread and wine.* The B.A.C. commentators[190] explain this profound change in the concept of the Offertory as follows:

> Not only is the text new, but its sense also. It is a prayer to bless, in a joyful exclamation in the presence of the symbol. It is an ascendant blessing directed to God that praises Him. Why do we praise God at this moment? For the creature bread. WE DO NOT ASK GOD'S BLESSING FOR THE BREAD. The bread we receive from God's generosity is the true descendant blessing because it brings us strength, life, and energy. The blessing which comes from God—grace, life, fecundity[191]—we pay back to Him, return to Him, in the sense and measure in which, through praise, we recognize that it proceeds from God. . . .
>
> Supported by and united to the innumerable biblical texts which call God "blessed" for the marvels that He does—and united to these texts— we bless Him in the moment of the presentation of the bread which will become, through the consecratory prayer, "bread of life." WE DO NOT OFFER BREAD TO GOD; rather, we bless Him through the bread. We offer God the Body and Blood of Christ—the eucharistized bread.[192]

The final affirmation that *we do not offer bread to God* merits emphasis. Undoubtedly, the sacrificial oblation which is the essence of the Mass is that which Jesus Christ makes of Himself, but we also offer ourselves to God, in union with Our Lord. Further, according to common doctrine, God is offered the bread as an expression of the oblation of the priest, the present and absent faithful, and, in sum, the entire Church. To deny that the bread is offered, therefore, is to deny the offering to God of ourselves, our good works and penances. It is also to deny that the other faithful, present and absent, and the whole Church, offer themselves to

---

189. See chap. 1, sec. 3 (*A Propitiatory Sacrifice*) *supra.*
190. We refer to the book *Nuevas normas de la misa*, mentioned at the beginning of chap. 1.
191. Note the naturalism of this concept: The "true descendant blessing" is the bread, which "brings us strength, life, and energy." In the following enumeration, "grace" appears beside "life" and "fecundity." It is not clear, therefore, that this means supernatural grace.

On the other hand, the phrase "We do not ask God's blessing for the bread" is founded on a radically Protestant conception of the Offertory, as we shall indicate further in chap. 5, sec. 3, item B (*The Lutheran Offertory*) *infra.*
192. Martín Patino, *Nuevas normas*, 39.

the Eternal Father in every Mass, in a sacrificial and propitiatory spirit. This point requires a little explanation, in addition to that given earlier.[193]

Even Protestants admit the propitiatory character of the sacrifice of the Cross. That is, they recognize that Jesus died to remit our sins. The error of Protestants here is on how the merits of Christ are applied to us. They say that only faith saves, that is, that our good works and sacrifices are unnecessary in union with the redemptive sacrifice of Christ.

According to Catholic doctrine, we must complement in ourselves as it were what was lacking in the sufferings of Our Lord (see Col. 1:24). By our good works and mortifications, done with the help of grace, we must apply the merits of Christ to ourselves, other men, and the faithful departed. We must, therefore, *offer ourselves* to God.

That offering of ourselves, our good works and penances, though, has meaning only if done in union with the redemptive sacrifice of the Cross, for only the death of Christ constitutes a worthy sacrifice for our sins.

On the other hand, God desired that the merits of the sacrifice of Calvary be applied to men through the Masses celebrated daily around the world until the end of time.[194] Being the unbloody renewal of the sacrifice of the Cross, the Mass is also propitiatory, in as much as Our Lord, truly present as Victim, offers Himself again to God the Father. Thus, the merits and satisfaction of the Passion are applied to all for whom the Mass is offered, according to Providence's designs.

This being the case, our good works and penances must be offered daily to God the Father in union with all the Masses being celebrated that day, especially those we arrange to have said for our intention or that we attend.

This union of the faithful with Christ—Who offers Himself to the Eternal Father in each Mass—is symbolized by the bread and wine offered on the altar, as we have already observed.[195] Consequently, this offering has the character of oblation and sacrifice. It is not only a "presentation of the gifts." It is an oblation made in a propitiatory spirit, while the true Victim, in the sacrifice of the Mass, is Our Lord, not the bread and wine. To deny that we truly offer God the bread and wine as a sensible and sacrificial expression of ourselves, our good works and penances, would lead to denying that the sacrifice of Christ needs to be, as it were, completed by us. This error is one step away from denying the propitiatory character of the Mass itself. For, if the sacrifice of the Cross needs no completion by us, then one does not see how to justify the daily renewal of the propitiatory sacrifice of Calvary.

True, the affirmation "we do not offer bread to God" appears only in the B.A.C. commentary, not in the text of the new *Ordo missae*. However, the B.A.C. commentators emphasize the tendency in the New Mass. It is implicit, but it is there.

---

193. See chap. 3, sec. 2 (*The New Concept of the Offertory*) supra.
194. For this reason, it is said that the sacrifice of the Cross is in the objective order of redemption, and that the Mass is in the subjective one, that is, that of the application to men of the merits obtained by Our Lord on the Cross. See Lercher, *Institutiones theologiae*, 4-2-1:307.
195. See chap. 3, sec. 2 (*The New Concept of the Offertory*) supra.

Indeed, as noted,[196] all the propitiatory expressions were eliminated from the new Offertory. Its title was changed to "preparation of the offerings."[197] Above all, the new prayers offering the bread and wine, which we are analyzing, insinuate that it is simply a presentation offering,[198] not a propitiatory one.

In addition, the 1969 *Institutio* and *Ordo* use of terms like *offer, oblations,* and so forth does not invalidate the quoted B.A.C. commentary. In the context, these terms have a sense that at least does not exclude the interpretation according to which "we do not offer bread to God."

On the other hand, we have noted[199] the equivocal meaning of the final expressions of the two new prayers in which the bread and wine are offered: "it will become for us the bread of life," and "it will become our spiritual drink." In their regard, the B.A.C. commentators write, "Note that the *Ordo missae* changed the sense of this rite, for the direct sense of offering was changed to a simple presentation of and placing upon the altar of the gifts which will become 'bread of life and drink of salvation.'"[200]

(4) In the traditional Offertory, before adding the water to the wine, the priest blesses it while saying the prayer *Deus qui humanae substantiae*. In the 1969 *Ordo*, this blessing disappeared, while, in the prayer, everything we show in parentheses was eliminated: "(O God, who, in creating human nature, didst wonderfully dignify it, and still more wonderfully restore it, grant that,) by the Mystery of this water and wine, we may be made[201] partakers of His divine nature, who vouchsafed to be made partaker of our human nature, (even Jesus Christ our Lord, Thy

---

196. See chap. 3, sec. 2 (*The New Concept of the Offertory*) *supra.*
197. Neither do the terms employed by the *Institutio* indicate a true sacrificial oblation but rather a "preparation of the offerings" or a "presentation of the gifts": *Praeparatio donorum* ("preparation of the gifts," see nos. 48, 49, 53), *dona afferuntur* ("the gifts are brought," see nos. 49, 50), *afferuntur panis et vinum* ("bread and wine are brought," see no. 48), *oblationes afferuntur . . . praesentantur . . . super altare deponuntur* ("the offerings are brought . . . are presented . . . are placed on the altar," see no. 49), *usquedum dona super altare deposita sunt* ("until the gifts have been placed on the altar," see no. 50), *dona in altari collocata* ("the gifts placed upon the altar," see no. 51), *depositione oblatorum facta* ("after the offerings have been deposited," see no. 53).
The word *Offertory* appears in various paragraphs of the 1969 *Institutio* (nos. 17, 50, 80c, 100, 133, 166, 167, 221, 235, 324). This is not enough, however, to give the traditional sense of offering to this part of the Mass. The proof is that Protestants do not reject the term *offertory.* See chap. 5, sec. 3, item B (*The Lutheran Offertory*) *infra.*
198. On this point, the translators of the *Ordo missae* to Portuguese were unfaithful to the letter of the original Latin, but not its spirit, for they translated *offerimus* as *apresentamos* ("we present"). **Publisher's Note:** See the observation made in footnote 29, on the chapter of the Portuguese original of this work, in which the author studies the Portuguese translation of the New Mass.
199. See chap. 3, sec. 2 (*The New Concept of the Offertory*), item (3), contrasting the Offertories in the traditional Latin and New Masses.
200. Martín Patino, *Nuevas normas,* 125–26. The translation of *potus spiritualis* as "*bebida/vinho de salvação*" ["drink/wine of salvation"] is one more infidelity of the Portuguese translation.
201. The elimination of the mentioned phrases demands that the verb *esse* of the traditional text be replaced here by *efficiamur.* The modification would be empty of doctrinal importance if it did not stem from suppressing the explicit petition: "grant us." As it appears in the new *Ordo,* the prayer is only optative and therefore less expressive than the text of petition in the traditional *Ordo.*

Son, who with Thee liveth and reigneth in the unity of the Holy Ghost, God: world without end. Amen).”

Besides eliminating the blessing of the water and mention of the Holy Trinity, note how reference to the Redemption, the essential purpose of the Incarnation, has also disappeared. That is one more modification that tends to weaken dogma, making the New Mass acceptable for non-Catholics.

(5) The following prayer stayed in the 1969 *Ordo*: “Accept us, O Lord, in the spirit of humility and contrition of heart, and grant that the sacrifice which we offer this day in Thy sight may be pleasing to Thee, O Lord God.”

The phrases “in the spirit of humility” and “contrition of heart,” taken from the prophet Daniel (3:39), are not enough to express the Catholic principles on the forgiveness of sins to distinguish us from Protestants.[202]

The term *sacrifice* appears here in a context where it is unclear that it is a propitiatory one.

(6) Another eliminated prayer: “Come, O almighty and eternal God, the Sanctifier, and bless this sacrifice, prepared for the glory of Thy holy Name.”

Note that the petition that God “bless this sacrifice” seems to hardly agree with the idea that “we do not ask God’s blessing for the bread”—an idea that, according to the B.A.C. commentators,[203] presided over the drafting of the new Offertory.

(7) All prayers in the *Ordo* of Saint Pius V accompanying the incensing of the offerings and altar were eliminated. Thus, the priest no longer blesses the incense. He no longer invokes Saint Michael the Archangel and all the elect. Nor does he offer God the incense.

(8) In the *Lavabo*, the verses from Psalm 25 were replaced with the following invocation from Psalm 50: “Lord, wash away my iniquity; cleanse me from my sin.”[204] On its own, this modification does not appear to have doctrinal consequences. Nevertheless, it is one more break with the liturgical tradition of many centuries.[205]

(9) The prayer to the Holy Trinity was eliminated: “Receive, O Holy Trinity, this offering which we make to Thee in remembrance of the Passion, Resurrection, and Ascension of our Lord Jesus Christ, and in honor of blessed Mary ever Virgin, of blessed John the Baptist, of the holy Apostles Peter and Paul, of these [the martyrs whose relics are in the altar] and of all the Saints: that it may avail to their

---

202. See chap. 5, sec. 3, item B (*The Lutheran Offertory*) *infra*.
203. See chap. 3, sec. 2 (*The New Concept of the Offertory*), item (3), contrasting the Offertories in the traditional Latin and New Masses.
204. *New . . . Saint Joseph*, 23.
205. In the Lutheran Supper, there are various references to sin. See chap. 5, sec. 3, item A (*The Lutheran “Confiteor”*) *infra*.

honor and our salvation: and may they vouchsafe to intercede for us in heaven, whose memory we keep on earth. Through the same Christ our Lord. Amen."

This prayer emphasizes that the sacrifice of the Mass is offered to the Most Holy Trinity. If, besides its elimination, we consider the already remarked reduction of the number of invocations to the Most Holy Trinity,[206] we can fear that the new *Ordo* leads to a weakening of faith in the principal Catholic dogma.

Note, further, the suppression of the prayer of intercession directed to Our Lady and the saints.

(10) The new Offertory retained the *Orate fratres* and its response:

> Priest: Brethren, pray that my sacrifice and yours may be acceptable to God, the almighty Father.
> People: May the Lord receive the sacrifice at your hands, to the praise and glory of His name, to our own benefit, and to that of all His holy Church.[207]

This prayer mentions sacrifice, but it in no way indicates that it is a propitiatory one.[208]

Here, in the distinction between *my* sacrifice and *yours*, an allusion to the priestly role of the celebrant is kept. Consequently, we say[209] that the new Offertory weakened but did not eliminate the affirmation of this doctrinal principle, suppressing the prayer *Suscipe sancte Pater*.[210]

A similar fact occurs with the principle that God must accept the sacrifice for it to become agreeable to Him; the petitions in this sense were eliminated in various prayers.[211] They remained, however, in the prayer *In spiritu humilitatis*[212] and the *Orate fratres*: "May be acceptable . . . ," "May the Lord receive. . . ."

3. The First Eucharistic Prayer or Roman Canon

The new Ordinary of the Mass has four "Eucharistic Prayers," which the priest selects from according to the rules in the 1969 *Institutio*, no. 322. The first Eucharistic Prayer, or Roman Canon, may always be used.

---

206. See chap. 5, sec. 3, item B (*The Lutheran Offertory*) *infra*.
207. **Translator's Note:** The author's comment applies to the Latin original, but I.C.E.L. rendered it differently in English: "Pray, brethren, that our sacrifice may be acceptable to God, the almighty Father." *New . . . Saint Joseph*, 23.
208. We recall that Protestants admit that there is a sacrifice in the Mass, but not one with a propitiatory character. See chap. 5, sec. 3 (*A Lutheran Work on the Liturgy*) *infra*.
209. See chap. 3, sec. 2 (*The New Concept of the Offertory*), item (3) *supra* on how the Roman Offertory highlights the propitiatory character of the sacrifice.
210. See the observation to the same effect in chap. 3, sec. 2 (*The New Concept of the Offertory*), item (1) *supra* on the Roman Offertory's prayer *Suscipe sancte Pater*.
211. See chap. 3, sec. 2 (*The New Concept of the Offertory*) *supra*, item (1) *Suscipe sancte Pater*, (2) *Offerimus tibi*, (7) *Per intercessionem*, and (9) *Suscipe Sancta Trinitas*.
212. See chap. 3, sec. 2 (*The New Concept of the Offertory*) *supra*, item (5) *In spiritu humilitatis*.

Considered superficially, the Roman Canon appears to have suffered only unimportant modifications. A more careful analysis, however, reveals that the alterations generally tend (at times subtly) to conform the text to a conception of the Eucharist as a simple agape, which is held by the community, under the presidency of the celebrant, to commemorate Our Lord's Passion and Resurrection.

As we shall see below, it has thus become a Canon that can no longer be called Roman.

In the Mass of Saint Pius V, there is a clear typographical separation between the narrative part of the Consecration and the words that effect the transubstantiation. To show unequivocally that the latter are said affirmatively, *in persona Christi*, not just narratively, the former ends with a period. Thus it becomes clear that the priest starts to speak in the name of Our Lord at that moment. In addition, the phrases in which the words of Consecration are found are printed in a larger type.

In the new *Ordo*, the text before the words of Consecration terminates with a colon, and although the larger type is kept in the phrases of the Consecration proper, new clauses were added so that a much larger number of words not essential to the transubstantiation appear in the larger type. As is obvious, this is one more measure that easily leads to the idea that the Consecration is nothing more than a historical narration of the institution of the Eucharist.[213]

So that the reader can distinguish these modifications of a typographical order introduced in the Consecration, we reproduce side by side the traditional and new texts:[214]

---

213. In chap. 1, sec. 4 (*The "Narrative of the Institution"*) *supra*, we indicate other manifestations of the same tendency in the New Mass.
214. The all caps and lowercase letters of the text in the St. Pius V missal are retained, but we skip the rubrics.

TEXT OF ST. PIUS V	TEXT OF THE NEW MASS
Who, the day before He suffered, took bread into His holy and venerable hands, and with eyes lifted up toward heaven, unto Thee, O God, His Almighty Father, giving thanks to Thee, did bless, break, and give unto His disciples, saying: Take and eat ye all of this.	The day before he suffered, he took bread in his sacred hands and looking up to heaven, to you, his almighty Father, he gave you thanks and praise. He broke the bread, gave it to his disciples, and said:
FOR THIS IS MY BODY.	TAKE THIS, ALL OF YOU, AND EAT IT: THIS IS MY BODY WHICH WILL BE GIVEN UP FOR YOU.
In like manner, after supper, taking also this excellent chalice into His holy and venerable hands: and giving thanks to Thee, He blessed, and gave to His disciples, saying: Take, and drink ye all of it.	When supper was ended, he took the cup. Again he gave you thanks and praise, gave the cup to his disciples, and said:
FOR THIS IS THE CHALICE OF MY BLOOD OF THE NEW AND ETERNAL TESTAMENT: THE MYSTERY OF FAITH; WHICH SHALL BE SHED FOR YOU, AND FOR MANY, FOR THE REMISSION OF SINS.	TAKE THIS, ALL OF YOU, AND DRINK FROM IT: THIS IS THE CUP OF MY BLOOD, THE BLOOD OF THE NEW AND EVERLASTING COVENANT. IT WILL BE SHED FOR YOU AND FOR ALL MEN SO THAT SINS MAY BE FORGIVEN. DO THIS IN MEMORY OF ME.[215]
As often as ye do these things, ye shall do them in remembrance of Me."	

---

215. *New . . . Saint Joseph*, 28.

As can be seen, the phrase following the Consecration of the wine was replaced. Note how the new text, "Do this in memory of me," is less removed from the idea that the Mass is a mere commemoration than the original: "As often as ye do these things, ye shall do them in remembrance of Me."

One ought to emphasize that the new text of the Consecration, resulting from the modifications which we have just pointed out, is not in itself unacceptable. In Oriental Catholic liturgies, for example, one encounters the punctuation adopted by the new *Ordo*, and one finds the phrase "which shall be delivered for you" annexed to the formula of the Consecration of the bread. What should be considered with reservation is that all these alterations have been made tending to move the Roman Canon closer to the new concept of the Mass expressed in the *Institutio*. In other words, the new texts of the Canon called Roman, although acceptable in themselves, are less clear than the ancient ones. Furthermore, that the core of the Mass has become less distant from Protestantism tends to create confusions that are inadmissible and extremely harmful to the Faith.

Also, in the so-called Roman Canon, twenty-four "Signs of the Cross" made by the celebrant were suppressed,[216] the reverential inclinations reduced from five to three, genuflections from six to two, and the two kisses of the altar were eliminated. These modifications tend to diminish the sacral nature of the Mass, with the consequent repercussions on faith in the Real Presence, the sacrificial character of the Mass, and God's transcendency.

* * *

Introducing the narration of the Supper, we find in the new *Ordo* the following rubric: "In the text that follows, the words of the Lord should be proclaimed clearly and distinctly, as their meaning demands."[217]

This prescription, which also holds for words of the Consecration proper, appears to be extremely grave:

(1) On the one hand, because it makes the Catholic Mass similar to the Suppers of Zwingli,[218] Luther,[219] and others like them;

(2) On the other, because this rubric not only determines that this central part of the Mass be said aloud but adds that the very nature of the words requires this. Now, this assertion has already been condemned by the Church. We indicated this when discussing a similar disposition in number 12 of the 1969 *Institutio*.[220]

---

216. Of the twenty-six "Signs of the Cross" prescribed by the traditional Roman Canon, only two remained: in the prayers *Te igitur* and *Supplices*. The sign of the Cross made during the *Sanctus* was also eliminated.

217. International Commission on English in the Liturgy, *The Sacramentary, Volume One—Sundays and Feasts* (Washington, D.C.: I.C.E.L., 1998), 272. The original Latin text is as follows: "In formulis quae sequuntur, verba Domini proferantur distincte et aperte, prouti natura eorundem verborum requirit."

218. See the text supported by footnote 382.

219. See the text supported by footnote 443.

220. See chap. 1, sec. 5 (*The President of the Assembly*), item C *supra*.

Let no one say that, in the rubric above, the conjunction *prouti* (as) is employed in a merely proportional sense, only indicating that the words which follow ought to be said aloud "in the measure that" it is required by each one's nature. In addition to violating the context and removing any reason for the rubric itself, such an interpretation is formally denied by number 12 of the 1969 *Institutio*.

The invocation of the greater part of the apostles and martyrs whose names appear in the traditional Mass was made optional.[221]

The reference to the mediation of Jesus Christ between us and God the Father in the Mass itself has also ceased to be obligatory in various prayers.[222] This modification contributes to moving the Mass closer to the liturgy of the Protestants. Indeed, according to these, the Mass is not a true propitiatory sacrifice. It is not a true renewal of the immolation of Our Lord on the Cross. Rather, it is simply a commemorative agape of the Last Supper. In such a heretical conception, the acceptance by God the Father of each new celebration of the Mass would be unnecessary. One could undoubtedly ask God that He accept this commemorative banquet, but such acceptation would not require the sacrificial mediation of Our Lord. There would thus be no reason for the particular insistence with which the Roman Missal affirms that the prayers of the priest rise to the Eternal Father "through Jesus Christ, Our Lord."

According to the new *Ordo*, the people must make an acclamation immediately after the Consecration, for which there are three texts. Two of these end by referring to Our Lord's second coming:

> "Christ has died, Christ is risen, Christ will come again."
> "When we eat this bread and drink this cup, we proclaim your death, Lord Jesus, until you come in glory."[223]

The expression "until he comes" is from Saint Paul (1 Cor. 11:26) and, therefore, cannot be censured. In the first Epistle to the Corinthians, the phrase indicates the expectation of Jesus's second coming. However, placed immediately after the Consecration, when Our Lord *has just come* substantially to the altar, this expression can lead one to think that *He is not present*, that *He has not come personally* under the Eucharistic species. Above all, when made in an epoch when Catholic circles show a shocking tendency to deny the Real Presence, such innovation has, as an inevitable consequence, the favoring of a diminishing of faith in transubstantiation.

---

221. In the prayers *Communicantes* and *Nobis quoque peccatoribus* of the *Ordo* of St. Pius V.
222. The invocations "through Christ, Our Lord. Amen" or "through the same Christ, Our Lord. Amen" have become optional at the end of the prayers *Communicantes*, *Hanc igitur* and *Supplices te rogamus*, and the memento of the dead.
223. *New . . . Saint Joseph*, 28–29.

4. The New Eucharistic Prayers

Compared to the traditional rite, one of the principal novelties in the 1969 *Ordo*[224] is the addition of three new Eucharistic Prayers to the so-called Roman Canon. For this reason, a true Canon has ceased to exist in the Mass, i.e., an exclusive rule according to which one must celebrate the sacrifice. Thus, the new Mass calls all of these prayers, including the Roman Canon, "Eucharistic Prayers."[225]

We shall indicate below some of the principal characteristics of the three new Eucharistic Prayers.

In the traditional Canon, the Consecration of the bread is preceded by the following words: "Who, the day before he suffered, took bread into His holy and venerable hands, and with eyes lifted up toward heaven, unto Thee, O God, His Almighty Father, giving thanks to Thee, did bless, break, and give unto His disciples, saying: Take and eat ye all of this."

In the new Roman Canon. this text was kept, with only the changes of punctuation and typographical order we have indicated.[226] This passage underwent profound and significant alterations in the three new Eucharistic Prayers.

Expressions emphasizing the sacred and holiest character of the act about to be carried out were eliminated. Thus, it only says that Our Lord took the bread without even mentioning His sacred hands. The phrase "with eyes lifted up toward heaven" was omitted. The loving reference to God the Father—"unto Thee, O God, His Almighty Father"—was suppressed in the second Eucharistic Prayer, replaced by a terse "to Thee" in the third, and exchanged for "to Thee, Holy Father" in the fourth.

In general, the words of the traditional Roman Canon immediately preceding the Consecration of the wine were retained, but some important modifications were introduced into the latter.

In addition to the mentioned punctuation and typographical changes and the suppression of the words "into His holy and venerable hands," the phrase "this excellent chalice" was simplified to "the chalice." This innovation is more important than it might seem. On the one hand, eliminating the adjective "excellent" (*praeclarus*) is one more desacralizing measure. On the other—an especially grave point—that the chalice is not qualified as "this" favors the theories according to which the priest does not act *in persona Christi*, that is, as Our Lord's representative. This point requires some explanation.

The 1969 *Institutio*, as we have seen, is not sufficiently explicit concerning the principle that the priest pronounces the words of the Consecration exclusively *in persona Christi*.[227] In the text we are examining, the traditional Mass uses one more

---

224. Even before the 1969 *Ordo*, Paul VI had introduced an identical modification in the Roman Missal, writing three new Eucharistic Prayers that could be substituted for the traditional Canon.
225. In the text supported by footnote 445, we show how Protestants preferred the nomenclature of "Eucharistic Prayer" to that of "Canon." Luther, who proclaimed so much the necessity of restoring the Mass of apostolic and evangelical times, also wrote new prayers for his Supper. See chap. 5, sec. 3, items A (*The Lutheran "Confiteor"*) and C (*The Lutheran Canon*) *infra*.
226. See chap. 3, sec. 2 (*The First Eucharistic Prayer or Roman Canon*) *supra*.
227. See chap. 1, sec. 5 (*The President of the Assembly*) *supra*.

symbolic recourse to indicate that the words of transubstantiation are pronounced in the name of Our Lord Himself. The chalice before the priest is referred to as if it were the same most sacred chalice in which Jesus converted wine into His Precious Blood for the first time. The elimination of this symbolism—so strong, rich, and vivid—is one more thing tending to debilitate the faith in the principle that Our Lord, the principal *sacerdos* in all Masses, is ministerially represented in them by the celebrating priest.

In the new Eucharistic Prayers, as in the new so-called Roman Canon, the number of Signs of the Cross made by the priest is minimal, as well as the number of reverential inclinations and genuflections. Also, the kisses of the altar were eliminated.

The rubrics also command that in the new Eucharistic Prayers, the words of Consecration be said aloud, "as their meaning demands."

In the new texts, the invocations to the apostles and martyrs by name disappeared completely. They were not made optional.

The references to Our Lord's mediation, almost all of which were made optional in the new Roman Canon,[228] are diminished further in the three new Eucharistic Prayers.

The fourth and last of these prayers "offers a summary of the whole history of salvation." "It is more appropriately used in a gathering of the faithful, who are gifted with a deeper understanding of Sacred Scripture." That is what is said by the 1969 *Institutio*, in number 322d. If we analyze its prayers carefully, however, we cannot avoid the impression that it is a text which will make possible future ecumenical celebrations with non-Catholics, especially Protestants. This being the case, one may fear that extremely progressive priests may believe that "the faithful, who are gifted with a deeper understanding of Sacred Scripture" that the *Institutio* refers to are the Protestants.

Let us analyze some passages of this fourth Eucharistic Prayer.

According to the rubrics, it does not have any memento for specific faithful departed. The reason for this strange instruction is given laconically by the *Institutio*, in number 322d: "Owing to its structure, a special formula for the dead is incapable of being inserted into this prayer."

It is difficult to comprehend why the "structure" of a Eucharistic Prayer cannot allow for the special mention of specific deceased persons. The concrete fact is that this rubric makes the text acceptable to the Protestants, who deny the applicability of the Mass to the dead.

Nor let it be said that the fourth Eucharistic Prayer has a general reference to the departed, which would be enough to distinguish it from the Protestant Supper. Luther's followers would not reject so vague a mention since they deny the applicability of the fruits of the Mass to the *faithful* departed but not that we may remember them in our prayers.[229]

---

228. We allude to the fact that in the Sacrifice of the Mass, Jesus Christ is the mediator between God the Father and ourselves. This mediation is indicated above all by the formula "through Christ, Our Lord," as commented in footnote 222 and its supported text.

229. See Reed, *The Lutheran Liturgy*, 314, 345.

Indeed, the reference to the dead in this fourth Eucharistic Prayer is sufficiently vague and emphasizes that we do not pray only for the faithful departed. Here are its terms: "Remember those who have died in the peace of Christ and all the dead whose faith is known to you alone."[230]

As one sees, it intercedes for those who, although not having died in the peace of Christ, were saved nevertheless because they had a faith that was only known to God. The formula causes perplexity, for though it can have an orthodox interpretation, it tends to salve the consciences of those who do not wish to belong to the Catholic Church. Maybe they have a "faith" that is unknown to men but is known to God.

The formula employed by this fourth Eucharistic Prayer to intercede for the living is no less "ecumenical": "Lord, remember those for whom we offer this sacrifice, especially *N.*, our Pope, *N.*, our bishop, and bishops and clergy everywhere. Remember those who take part in this offering, those here present and all your people, and all who seek you with a sincere heart."[231]

Once more, we have a formula that can be interpreted in an orthodox way but is ambiguous and dangerous. It insinuates that a vague and general *sincerity* in *seeking* God is sufficient for salvation.[232]

In conclusion: As a general rule, all that in the first Eucharistic Prayer, roughly imitating the traditional Roman Canon, sounds bad to Catholic ears, is found to be more accentuated in the three new Eucharistic Prayers.

In other words, the new so-called Roman Canon will probably be used only by certain traditionalist priests who do not like the Eucharistic Prayers that have now been composed. The progressive priests will probably use only the new Eucharistic Prayers, in such a way that these latter will end, in practice, by supplanting the so-called Roman Canon, making it fall into disuse.

Furthermore, introducing the new Eucharistic Prayers opens the way for further innovations. They constitute a blow against Tradition, which had, in the Canon of the Mass, an inflexible norm for the most sacred act of the sacrifice realized there.

5. The Communion Rite

In the rite for Holy Communion, the *Ordo* of Saint Pius V clearly distinguishes between the priest and the people.

Thus, for example, the priest prepares himself for Communion with his own prayers, which are said in the first person singular and distinct from those pre-

---

230. New ... Saint Joseph, 43.
231. New ... Saint Joseph, 42–43.
232. The existence of this insinuation is undeniable, for otherwise, one would not be able to explain why we do not pray for all men in general.

Furthermore, in no passage of this fourth Eucharistic Prayer is it emphasized that the Mass is offered in the first place for Catholics. Saint Thomas explains the dogmatic reason why "in the Canon of the Mass no prayer is made for them who are outside the pale of the Church." Saint Thomas Aquinas, *The Summa Theologica*, trans. Fathers of the English Dominican Province, www. documentacatholicaomnia.eu, III, q. 79, art. 7, ad 2.

ceding the Communion of the faithful. He receives Our Lord under two species, while the faithful communicate only under the species of bread. When the priest receives the Blood of Christ, the altar server says the *Confiteor*, after which the celebrant gives the absolution to the people, in an act that clearly expresses his priestly mission. The examples could be multiplied.

In the 1969 *Ordo*, various of these signs distinguishing the celebrant from the people were suppressed, and new prayers and rites were introduced, tending to conflate the priesthood of the priest with that of the faithful.

The cases in which the faithful were permitted to communicate under two species were greatly expanded.

The *Confiteor* and absolution preceding the Communion of the people were abolished.

The number of prayers in preparation for Communion said only by the priest, and in the first person singular, decreased substantially. Nine are in the traditional Roman Missal, and only four are in the new *Ordo*.[233] Of these four, in reality, only three are prayed by the celebrant in each Mass.[234] Even this number is considered excessive by the progressives, who would have liked to make the position of the priest as equal as possible to that of the faithful. Thus, for example, the B.A.C. commentators[235] write:

> As far as these private prayers of the celebrant are concerned, one should
> remember that they were a devotional product of the Middle Ages and
> that, in general, due above all to the epoch in which they appeared, they are
> decadent duplications. For this reason, during the gestation of the reform,
> there were strong pressures, coming from the better liturgiologists, above
> all, to bring about a total suppression of these obligatory private prayers:
> We believe this would have represented a liturgical advance. Indeed, if no
> private prayers are prescribed for the faithful, why does the celebrant have
> to be bound to fixed formulae of private prayers? Would he be considered
> so less capable than the faithful, for example, to prepare himself personally
> for communion that, therefore, one would like to oblige him to recite

---

233. These nine prayers are: *Domine Jesu Christe, qui dixisti*; *Domine Jesu Christe, Fili Dei vivi*; *Perceptio corporis*; *Panem coelestem*; *Domine, non sum dignus*; *Corpus Domini nostri*; *Quid retribuam*; *Sanguis Domini nostri*; and *Corpus tuum*.

Of these nine prayers, three were eliminated: *Panem coelestem*, *Quid retribuam*, and *Corpus tuum*; one came to be said in the first-person plural: *Domine Jesu Christe, qui dixisti*; and one became common to the priest and the people, who recite it simultaneously: *Domine, non sum dignus*.

There remain, therefore, only four prayers that are recited by the priest alone and in the first person singular: *Domine Jesu Christe, Fili Dei vivi*; *Perceptio corporis*; *Corpus Domini nostri*; and *Sanguis Domini nostri*. In reality, these four are reduced to three, as we shall indicate in the next footnote.

234. Indeed the new *Ordo* prescribes that, in each Mass, the priest must not recite the prayers *Domine Jesu Christe, Fili Dei vivi*, and *Perceptio corporis*, but only one of them, according to his own choice.

235. We refer to the work *Nuevas normas de la misa* mentioned at the beginning of chap. 1.

fixed formulas?[236] It is possible, and it is to be hoped for, that with the progress of liturgical culture, these prayers will tend to disappear. Indeed, and this is one of the best aspects of the *Institutio* and its reform, they have diminished notably.[237]

The Communion of the priest is no longer made with its own ritual and kept distinct from that of the faithful. Rather, he is only the first among those who communicate.[238] This change corroborates the impression the new *Ordo* gives that the priest is no more than the president of the assembly.

The new ritual of the sign of peace introduced among the acts preparing for Communion merits special attention. The priest says, "Let us offer each other the sign of peace,"[239] and those who are present greet one another with a handshake, a hug, or another greeting to be determined by the Episcopal Conferences "according to the character and customs of each people."[240]

It is not necessary to emphasize how such a practice, in the desacralized and sensual milieu of our days, can lend itself to abuses. From that perspective, there is no way to compare the "sign of peace" introduced by the new *Ordo* with analogous ceremonies in the Eastern liturgies and early Church. However, this is not the aspect of the innovation we wish to emphasize the most.

Above all, we wish to call the reader's attention to the fact that the salutation established by the *Ordo* of Paul VI does not start from the priest but from each Mass attendee who gives it to his neighbor. The B.A.C. commentators explain: "Note that, according to the new rubric, each one gives the sign of peace to those at his side, and receives it from them without waiting for it to come from the altar, as used to be done. Thus is restored a more ancient custom, and the duration of the sign of peace is diminished."[241]

In another passage, the same B.A.C. commentators recognize that this manner of proceeding has a more profound explanation than a simple archaism or love

---

236. As is evident, the question is not in any way the capacity of the priest to prepare himself personally for Communion. He can do that before Mass, and it is highly recommendable that he do so. Here, another question is under consideration: Everything the celebrant does during the Mass has a public and official note to a greater or lesser degree. In virtue of his priestly character and his condition as representative of Jesus Christ and the Church, even his private acts are incorporated into the sacrificial action as something radically distinct from the acts of devotion practiced by the people attending the Mass.

These truths cannot be unknown to the B.A.C. commentators and the would-be great liturgiologists they reference. We believe that the true reason moving the B.A.C. commentators to adopt the position indicated is at chap. 1, sec. 6 (*Jesus Christ, the Principal Priest [Sacerdos]*), where we pointed out how they conflate the hierarchical priesthood with that of the people.

237. Martín Patino, *Nuevas normas*, 89–90, note 13.

238. The only difference between the Communion of the priest and that of the people is in the words said before the reception of the Body and Blood of Christ. For his own Communion, the priest says, "May the body of Christ bring me to everlasting life" and "May the blood of Christ bring me to everlasting life." Before the Communion of each of the faithful, he says, "The body of Christ"; and when they communicate under two species, he also says, "The blood of Christ." *New . . . Saint Joseph*, 47.

239. *New . . . Saint Joseph*, 45. (*Offerte vobis pacem*).

240. 1969 *Institutio*, no. 56b, p. 27.

241. Martín Patino, *Nuevas normas*, 174.

of brevity. They write, "It is neither necessary nor fitting that the sign of peace come from the celebrant. Instead, each of the faithful must give it to others, each individual to whoever is at his left and right. The Christian peace is an effect of the Holy Spirit, who is in all the faithful."[242]

This affirmation is of no small gravity. Undoubtedly, the Holy Spirit dwells in every soul in the state of grace and moves it to the love of God and neighbor. However, it is necessary to keep in mind that we are at Mass here, in which we receive special grace, not because of the common action of the Holy Spirit in souls, but through the sacrifice of Christ, which is truly renewed on the altar by the ministry of the priest. In explaining that the salutation need not come from the priest because the Holy Spirit "is in all the faithful," the B.A.C. commentators insinuate again that the priesthood of the celebrant is not essentially different from that of the people.[243]

Moreover, the "peace" expressed in the new ritual is not presented as the result of the reconciliation between heaven and earth, effected by the redemptive sacrifice of Jesus Christ. Instead, it appears to come from the people, resulting from the strictly fraternal and human solidarity uniting those present.

As we have pointed out in a previous section, the part of the prayer *Perceptio corporis tui*, which contains an act of humility,[244] was suppressed. Moreover, the prayers *Quod ore sumpsimus*[245] and *Corpus tuum, Domine*, which express so well the notions of humility and sorrow for one's sins, and that, without grace, there is no perseverance in virtue, were also suppressed.[246] Also eliminated were various invocations to the Most Holy Trinity,[247] genuflections,[248] "Signs of the Cross,"[249] reverential kisses and inclinations,[250] and references to Our Lady and the saints in the prayer *Libera nos, quaesumus*.[251]

---

242. Martín Patino, 41–42.
243. See our observations in chap. 1, sec. 5 (*The President of the Assembly*) *supra*. Many are the other passages in which the B.A.C. commentators refer, in words that are at least suspect, to this presence of God among the faithful. Referring to singing, for example, they say, "One can affirm that the communal chant is a sign of true participation, for all the voices flow together in one sole and grand sonorous reality, which makes one feel the unity and perceive the presence of God." Martín Patino, 60. See also, in the same work, 31–32, 34, 82, 87, 91, 172–73.
244. See footnote 173.
245. This prayer was reintroduced in 1970; see the text supported by footnote 343.
246. See footnotes 174 and 175.
247. See footnote 178.
248. See the next section, 6 (*Other Modifications in the Rubrics*) *infra*.
249. See the observation in chap. 3, sec. 1 (*Suppressed and Altered Prayers*) *supra*, on reducing the external signs of worship.
250. See chap. 3, sec. 1 (*Suppressed and Altered Prayers*) *supra*.
251. Cf. the text supported by footnotes 380 and 413.

6. Other Modifications in the Rubrics

Beyond the changes we have pointed out, numerous alterations were introduced in the rubrics of the Mass. We present some of them below without attempting to make it an exhaustive study.[252]

The genuflections of both the priest and the people were almost all eliminated. Except in certain extraordinary cases, such as the presence of the Most Blessed Sacrament on the altar, only three genuflections of the priest (no. 233) and one of the people (no. 21) remain. Concerning the latter, which occurs at the Consecration, the *Institutio* stipulates, "Let the faithful kneel at the Consecration unless they are hindered by the lack of space, the great number of those attending, or other reasonable causes."[253]

Does the listing of such qualifying clauses—which common sense understands making mention of them superfluous—not come across as an invitation for the faithful not to kneel, even during the Consecration? That is how the B.A.C. commentators interpret them, saying that, from their viewpoint, having a large assembly is sufficient reason to suppress the genuflection.[254]

Following the same line, the booklet published by Vozes[255] for the use of the faithful in following the Mass, whose text was organized by the National Secretariat of the Liturgy of the National Conference of the Bishops of Brazil (C N.B.B.), purely and simply indicates that, at the Consecration, the faithful may either kneel or stand.[256]

Therefore, we see that in the Latin rite, the new rubrics almost eliminate the genuflection—the bodily position that is so fitting to symbolize adoration, humility, penance, and the spirit of supplication![257]

Numerous rules with which the traditional Mass surrounded the handling of the Eucharistic species were suppressed. All of these were originally ordered to express respect for our sacramental Lord, to prevent the loss of small consecrated particles, or to prevent these from being inadvertently subjected to less worthy treatment.

Thus, if a host now falls to the ground, one no longer proceeds to the purification ceremony of the spot.[258]

The fingers of the priest no longer must be purified in the chalice after Communion. Instead, it suffices that "when some fragment of the host has adhered

---

252. Obviously, the new rubrics we shall refer to in this item do not all merit the same reservation. It is also obvious that in their ensemble, they represent a very accentuated departure from the Tradition enshrined in the Mass of Saint Pius V.

253. 1969 *Institutio*, no. 21, p. 18.

254. See Martín Patino, *Nuevas normas*, 100.

255. **Publisher's Note:** Concerning the *Vozes* publishing house, see footnote 40.

256. See Secretariado Nacional de Liturgia da C.N.B.B., arr., *Ordinário da missa: De acôrdo com a edição típica do "Ordo missae,"* (Petrópolis: *Vozes*, 1969), 22.

257. On the genuflection in Sacred Scripture, see 3 Kings 19:18; 1 Esdras 9:5; Isa. 45:23; Dan. 6:11; Matt. 17:14; 27:29; Luke 5:8; Mark 1:40; 15:19; Rom. 11:4; 14:11; Phil. 2:10; Eph. 3:14.

258. See 1969 *Institutio*, no. 239, p. 54.

to his fingers . . . the priest removes it over the paten, or if necessary, he washes the fingers."[259]

The obligation that the priest hold the tips of his forefingers and thumbs together from the Consecration until the purification was suppressed. In the Roman *Ordo,* this rubric aimed to express the supreme reverence with which the sacred species must be handled.

The purification of the sacred vessels at the altar is no longer prescribed. It may be done after Mass and, "as much as possible," at the credence table.[260]

Except in the case of fixed altars, the use of the altar stone for the celebration of Mass is not obligatory.[261] Note how this disposition tends to facilitate Masses being celebrated in private homes, to which they wish to give the exterior appearances of simple meals.

The deacon may participate in the sacred functions without using the dalmatic, and the subdeacon, without the tunic, appearing, therefore, only with an alb.[262] Where there are many concelebrants, the impossibility of obtaining sufficient chasubles or other difficulties make them optional for the concelebrating priests. Only the principal celebrant is required to wear one.[263]

The *Institutio* determines that, considering the nature of the sign, not only the wine but also the bread "should look like food."[264] Consequently, it is appropriate that the bread "be made in such a way that the priest, in the Mass celebrated with the people, can divide the host into various portions and distribute them at least to some of the faithful."[265]

Thus, the B.A.C. commentators obey the dispositions of the *Institutio* when they provide a recipe and expand with much detail on how to cook up small loaves of coarse bread, each weighing 20 grams (.7 ounces) and being 12 millimeters (.47 inches) thick.[266]

The new rubrics tend to diminish the number of Requiem Masses. As ordered in number 316 of the *Institutio*, not to skip too many biblical readings indicated in the lectionary, the priest "will use Requiem Masses with restraint, since ANY MASS IS OFFERED AS MUCH FOR THE LIVING AS FOR THE DEAD, and in every eucharistic prayer there is a memento for the departed."[267]

Undoubtedly, the faithful should have Masses said, not only for the dead but also for the intentions of the Church Militant. This was always done. If there is any excess to correct in the matter of Requiem Masses, it is dangerous to do it in the name of the principle that "any Mass is offered for the living as well as for the dead." Not expressing the entire truth, such an assertion tends to dampen in the

---

259. 1969 *Institutio*, no. 237, p. 54.
260. 1969 *Institutio*, nos. 120, 238, pp. 38–39, 54.
261. See 1969 *Institutio*, no. 265, p. 62.
262. See 1969 *Institutio*, no. 81, p. 34.
263. See 1969 *Institutio*, no. 161, p. 45.
264. On the modifications introduced in this paragraph by the 1970 *Institutio*, see the text supported by footnotes 341 and 342.
265. 1969 *Institutio*, no. 283, p. 66.
266. See Martín Patino, *Nuevas normas*, 260–61.
267. 1969 *Institutio*, no. 316, pp. 71–72.

faithful the pious desire to have Masses said for certain deceased persons and the faithful departed in general (see 2 Mac. 12:41–46).

Number 337 reduced the number of Requiem Masses permitted, and number 340 abolished the *absolutio super tumulum* in the Masses in which the body is not physically present.

It is no longer necessary for the cross to be over the altar (nos. 79, 84, 236b, 270).

When there is Communion under two species, the faithful are obliged to receive it standing (nos. 244c, 244d, 245b, 245c, 246b, 247b, 249b). For Communion given only under the species of bread, the bodily posture of the faithful is not specified (nos. 56, 117).

Only one cloth is required to cover the altar instead of three as before (no. 79).

With permission from the episcopal conferences, except for the Gospel, the readings can be done by women (no. 66), and "the ministries exercised outside the sanctuary (*presbyterium*) can be confided to women."[268]

The Blessed Sacrament will normally be in some place other than on the altar on which Mass is celebrated (no. 276).

In principle, any artistic style is allowed in the construction of churches and manufacture of objects of worship (nos. 254, 287).[269] Great liberty is also granted regarding the form of the sacred vessels (no. 295).

Finally, we wish to call the reader's attention to the festive and busy character the New Mass takes on.

Many are those who exercise special functions during the Mass. In addition to the priest (or priests when there is a concelebration), the deacon, and subdeacon, there is a commentator, a reader (who can be a woman), a psalmist, the master of ceremonies, the ushers (in charge of receiving the faithful at the door of the church and leading them to their places), those who take up the collection, the thurifers, the candle-bearers, those in the entrance procession who carry the Missal, the cross, and possibly the bread, wine, and water.[270] There may be more than one deacon, subdeacon, commentator, reader, and psalmist. "The ministries exercised outside the sanctuary (*presbyterium*) can be confided to women," as mentioned.[271] There is also the cantor or choir director (nos. 64 and 78) and the *schola cantorum* (nos. 64 and 274).

Moreover, there will be two processions: the entrance procession, which will be carried out both in the common Masses (1969 *Institutio*, no. 82) and in the concelebrated ones (no. 162); and that of the Offertory (nos. 49–50), in which the people will bring to the altar the bread, wine, water, and possibly also other gifts for the sustenance of the poor and the Church.

---

268. 1969 *Institutio*, no. 70, p. 31.
269. The B.A.C. commentators even suggest that old churches "of excessive luxury" be transformed into museums and that sacred objects of "great beauty" be "retired from worship and placed in museums or adapted to other liturgical uses." Martín Patino, *Nuevas normas*, 63–64
270. See 1969 *Institutio*, nos. 65–73, pp. 30–32.
271. 1969 *Institutio*, no. 70, p. 31.

In addition, there will be acclamations and responses from the people (no. 15); the chants, which are given great importance (no. 19); the explanations and admonitions (nos. 11, 18). On various points, the celebrant is given great liberty in selecting prayers and rites.[272]

In number 66, the 1969 *Institutio* recommends that the reader be capable and prepared for that task "so that the faithful, on hearing the divine readings, may conceive a sweet and lively affection for Holy Scripture in their hearts."[273]

As can be seen, everything is oriented to give the Mass a festive tone of agape, pleasant commemoration—not that of the propitiatory sacrifice, where the Son of God immolates Himself for the sins and ingratitude of men.

Another significant expression of this carefree and agreeable banquet aspect they want the Mass to have is found in the B.A.C. commentary for number 280 of the 1969 *Institutio*. The "temple should have good visibility," we read, and the lights should be so positioned as to create "psychological rest" and "an atmosphere agreeable to the eyes." The seating arrangements should be such that the faithful can see the sanctuary well and one another, and "cleanliness ought to stand out in the temple more than anything else."[274]

The same B.A.C. commentators go on to write:

> Care should also be shown to odors, both to avoid the bad ones . . . and to perfume the area discreetly, before large gatherings, with one of those products so widely and cheaply available nowadays and commonly used in other meeting places such as theaters, cinemas, concert halls, and conference rooms, etc.
>
> Where possible, it would be of great pastoral efficacy to have a vestibule, hall, porch, or something similar, arranged with relative comfort, where people can meet one another on entering and leaving, exchange a few words, rest, wait for one another, buy a magazine, or even enjoy a refreshing drink in a small bar. These human signs admirably prepare and prolong the

---

272. Commenting on this point, Bishop Clemente Isnard, O.S.B., the Liturgy secretary at the Brazilian Bishops Conference (C.N.B.B.), writes, "The General Instruction which begins the new Roman Missal establishes new perspectives, very different from those which inspired the old body of rubrics. The guideline is flexibility, which frequently gives the celebrant selection opportunities. HE CEASES TO BE A MERE EXECUTOR OF RUBRICS TO ASSUME WITH SPONTANEITY THE PRESIDENCY OF THE LITURGICAL ASSEMBLY." "Presentation" of the new *Ordo missae* in *Presbiteral* (Petrópolis: *Vozes*, 1969), 5; and in *Liturgia da missa* (São Paulo: Edições Paulinas, 1969), 3.
273. 1969 *Institutio*, no. 66, pp. 30–31. Although it is most desirable that Scripture readings be done clearly and worthily, we cannot fail to emphasize that, in the context of the new *Ordo*, expressions like "conceive a sweet and lively affection for Holy Scripture in their hearts" take on a Protestant flavor. In chap. 5, sec. 1 (*A Slow and Cautious Reform*), we present the Lutheran concept on the effects of the biblical readings on the spirit of the faithful.
274. Martín Patino, *Nuevas normas*, 258.

liturgical one and give both pastor and people a good opportunity to meet one another.[275]

7. Conclusion

For the reasons presented, we do not see how to avoid the conclusion that, in conscience, it is impossible to accept the 1969 texts of the New Mass.

We leave, however, for the end of this study[276]—having analyzed the 1970 changes and the other theoretical and practical questions that we must consider—a more nuanced assessment of the attitude to be taken regarding the New Mass.

---

275. Martín Patino, 259. Among progressive writings, it is not easy to find texts which so clearly demand the transformation of churches into profane and desacralized environments. Indeed, the house of God is conceived of as a mere banquet hall in the above-cited passage. It is no wonder that, because of this, people prefer to frequent other banquet halls, which are more attractive, leaving the churches empty.
276. See Conclusion (*The New Mass and the Catholic Conscience*) *infra*.

CHAPTER FOUR

Changes to the 1969 *Ordo*

In May of 1970, the Latin edition of the new Roman Missal was published. In it, the *Institutio* and *Ordo* appear with numerous alterations, which we must analyze in the present chapter.

Paul VI had declared that the reform of the Roman Missal promulgated in 1969 was not improvised but was rather the result of profound studies.[277] Given this declaration and the importance of the matter itself, one can be sure that every proposition was carefully weighed, from both the theological and pastoral perspectives, given the predominantly pastoral preoccupations of this papacy.

Thus, it causes a certain surprise that numerous modifications have been made to such documents so soon after their promulgation. The Holy See must have considered it necessary or at least appropriate to make them, either from the theological or pastoral perspectives, or both.

These developments impose special circumspection on the studious person when analyzing the introduced changes, obliging him to use the greatest diligence and perspicacity in their individual examination. This is what we shall endeavor to do in this chapter, to the extent of our abilities.

1. The Principal Features of the Foreword in the 1970 *Institutio*

In an article about the reform of the 1969 *Ordo* published in the magazine *Notitiae* of the Sacred Congregation for Divine Worship, Fr. Annibale Bugnini, secretary of that Congregation, wrote, "The foreword is completely new and notably long. . . . It emphasizes three concepts: (a) the history of the Roman Missal, especially from the Council of Trent until the Second Vatican Council, to justify the changes introduced into the Missal according to the guidelines of the recent Ecumenical Council; (b) the theological and ritual fidelity of both Missals to the doctrine of the Church; (c) the presiding criteria for the reform."[278]

Undoubtedly, this foreword is quite concerned with enunciating certain Catholic doctrinal teachings that were absent from the 1969 *Institutio* or incorrectly expounded there:

---

277. See Paul VI, *Missale romanum*, 4ᵗʰ par.
278. Annibale Bugnini, "De editione missalis romani instaurati," *Notitiae* 54 (May 1970), 161.

—it insists on the principle of the ministerial priesthood of the celebrant;
—it refers to the Real Presence of Our Lord in the Eucharist
  and transubstantiation;
—it contains numerous citations from the Council of Trent;
—it affirms the sacrificial character of the Mass several times;
—it declares that, in the Mass, there is a sacramental renewal of the
  sacrifice of the Cross;
—one article states explicitly that the Mass is a propitiatory sacrifice;
—it repeatedly professes the purpose of maintaining itself faithful to
  Tradition, and so forth.

A hurried reading of these passages in the foreword could lead one to believe that it corrects all the imprecisions, insufficiencies, and doctrinal deviations being pointed out in the New Mass. Unfortunately, however, an attentive consideration of these same passages, as well as the other items of the foreword and even the 1970 *Institutio*, does not justify thinking that the introduced changes result in a substantial alteration in our earlier observations about the New Mass.

2. The Priesthood of the People

Indeed, in the traditional-flavored passages themselves, in which the foreword affirms previously omitted or dubiously expressed points, we find formulations that are entirely insufficient or even deserving of grave reservations. Let us see some examples.

We read in item 4:

> 4. The nature of the ministerial priesthood of the celebrant who offers the sacrifice in the person of Christ, and who presides over the holy people, is clearly manifested not only by the way in which the rite is conducted, but also by the prominent position and unique functions allotted to the priest. These are explained more fully in the Preface of the Chrism-Mass on Maundy Thursday, the day on which the institution of the priesthood is commemorated. This Preface mentions how the priestly powers are conferred by the imposition of hands, and it describes the various duties of the priestly ministry whereby the power of Christ, High Priest of the New Testament, is continued.[279]

---

279. Howell, *General Instruction*, foreword item 4, pp. 8–9. **Translator's Note:** For quotations from the 1970 *Institutio*, the English translation prepared by Fr. Clifford Howell, S.J., is used wherever possible.

On the one hand, it is true that, in the text being analyzed, it is affirmed that the celebrant acts in the person of Christ (*in persona Christi*) and that his power is a continuation of Our Lord's priestly power.[280]

On the other, however, the text establishes a dangerous parallel between *the offering of the sacrifice* and *the presiding over the holy people* because this second function, while truly priestly, is, nevertheless, secondary, accidental, and simply a consequence of the first. Even when there is no assembly of "the holy people," the celebrant fully exercises his priestly function in the Mass. The emphasis thus given to the presidential role of the priest in the Mass favors in the faithful the impression that they and the priest equally celebrate the sacrifice.[281]

Furthermore, that passage does not exclude the heterodox interpretation that the B.A.C. commentators,[282] for example, give to the principle that the priesthood of the celebrant is *ministerial*. According to these authors, the priest is essentially a minister, that is, a representative and servant of Our Lord—a truth which is affirmed here—*as well as of the people*. He would thus have no greater dignity than that of the laity.[283]

Given the *Institutio* context—the criticisms rightly made of this point and the erroneous interpretations it engendered—it would be suitable, indispensable even, for the corrected 1970 *Institutio* to have eliminated this very dangerous error, which completely subverts the doctrine of the Catholic priesthood. It would be necessary to affirm not only the *ministerial* character of the priesthood but also its *hierarchical* nature, which places it essentially above any representation of Christ existing in the lay faithful or proceeding from them.

Item 5 of the foreword takes on an even greater gravity since it confirms the apprehensions induced by item 4. It states:

> 5. But the very nature of the ministerial priesthood sheds light upon another kind of priesthood of great dignity, namely, the royal priesthood of the faithful whose spiritual sacrifice is accomplished through the ministry of the priest in union with the sacrifice of Christ, the One Mediator. For THE CELEBRATION OF THE EUCHARIST IS AN ACT OF THE

---

280. In chap. 1, sec. 5 (*The President of the Assembly*) *supra*, we show that in the context of the 1969 *Institutio*, expressions such as *in persona Christi* are insufficient to indicate how the priest represents Our Lord in the Mass.

281. See, in this regard, chap. 1, sec. 5 (*The President of the Assembly*) *supra*, as well as our commentary about item 5 of the foreword, *infra*.

282. We are referring to the B.A.C. commentators, the authors of *Nuevas normas de la misa*, the work mentioned at the beginning of Chapter 1.

283. See chap. 1, sec. 6 (*Jesus Christ, the Principal Priest [Sacerdos]*) *supra*.

WHOLE CHURCH.[284] Everyone at Mass is to do all of, but only, those parts which pertain to his office according to his status within the people of God.[285] A consequence of this principle is that certain features of the celebration are now receiving greater attention than was formerly accorded to them during some of the preceding centuries. The celebrating people are in fact the people of God, purchased by the Blood of Christ, convened by their Lord, nourished by his word, A PEOPLE CALLED ON TO LAY BEFORE GOD THE ENTREATIES OF ALL MANKIND. They are a people who give thanks to God for the mystery of salvation in Christ by OFFERING HIS SACRIFICE; a people who grow together in unity by being united with his Body and Blood, a people, holy by origin, who continually grow in holiness by active, conscious, and fruitful participation in the eucharistic mystery.[286]

When we consider the terms of this item 5 carefully, we see that they reaffirm, and clearly, the conception of the priesthood of the people, which we have pointed out previously as unacceptable.[287]

Indeed, what are these "features of the celebration [which] are now receiving greater attention than was formerly accorded to them during some of the preceding centuries"? One is that the holy people are "called on to lay before God the entreaties of all mankind." Another is that they "give thanks to God for the mystery of salvation in Christ by *offering* his sacrifice"!

As is readily seen, we return to the same imprecisions and ambiguities of the 1969 *Institutio* and their B.A.C. commentary. For, although one can say, in a broad and analogical sense, that the simple faithful "lay before God the entreaties" of others and "offer [Christ's] sacrifice," in their proper understanding, these expressions indicate *only* the specifically priestly mission of the celebrant, on which the foreword seemingly insists.[288]

---

284. In its proper sense, the "celebration of the Eucharist" is exclusively an action of Christ and the priest who, in the Mass, represents Him. Pius XII condemned the proposition according to which "they look on the Eucharistic sacrifice as a 'concelebration,' in the literal meaning of that term, and consider it more fitting that priests should 'concelebrate' with the people present." Pius XII, *Mediator Dei*, no. 83.

The faithful can and ought to unite themselves to the celebrant in offering the Victim Who is immolated, and in this sense, the Mass is really an action of the whole Church. The offering made by the faithful, however, *is* essentially distinct from that of Our Lord. One cannot say, in any sense, that because of this offering, the simple faithful become authentic "celebrants" of the Mass.

There is no doubt that, in an analogous sense, the term "celebration" may have broader acceptations, but it is not legitimate to juggle such acceptations to insinuate that the faithful have a "celebration" function proper. For this reason, the phrase under analysis—"the celebration of *the Eucharist is an action of the whole Church*"—is shown to be ambiguous within the context of item 5 of the foreword.

285. This is exactly the concept expressed by the B.A.C. commentators in the quotation supported by footnote 107.

286. Howell, *General Instruction*, item 5, p. 9.

287. See footnote 284, as well as chap. 1, secs. 5 *(The President of the Assembly)* and 6 *(Jesus Christ, the Principal Priest [Sacerdos])* supra.

288. The foreword insists on this point in item 4. We comment at chap. 4, sec. 2 *(The Priesthood of the People)* supra.

This passage establishes a strange distinction between the "people of God" and "all mankind," for it says that the former, by the priestly action it exercises in the Mass, raises to God the prayers "of all mankind." Taking the expression in its natural sense, it indicates that the "people of God" exercise a function of mediation between the whole human race—including non-Catholics, non-Christians, atheists, etc.—and God. However, such mediation belongs properly to the priesthood.

Furthermore, since the immediately following phrase attributes to this same "people of God" the role of "offering [Christ's] sacrifice," it appears that, through the Mass, the prayers of *all men*—non-Catholics, non-Christians, polytheists, atheists, and so forth—are indiscriminately presented to God and made pleasing to Him. Such a conception of the Mass is all the stranger since it dovetails with a certain heterodox ecumenism spreading in large sectors of the Catholic public.

These dangerous ambiguities in item 5 of the foreword aggravate our fears regarding item 4. The silence in the latter about the *hierarchical character* of the ministerial priesthood of the celebrant and the absence of a clear understanding of the *representation of Christ by the priest* favor and prepare an erroneous notion of the priesthood of the faithful.

3. Return to the Norms of the Church Fathers

Items 6 to 9 of the foreword seek to demonstrate that the new *Ordo missae* is not opposed to traditional Catholic principles, particularly those mentioned at Trent, but that it confirms them.

The foreword tries to defend this thesis by alleging that the Second Vatican Council ordered "that certain rites were 'to be restored to the vigor which they had in the days of the holy Fathers.'"[289] This expression is found *ipsis litteris* in the apostolic constitution *Quo primum*, with which Saint Pius V promulgated the Tridentine Missal.

This point of extrinsic resemblance seemed sufficient to the foreword authors to prove that the New Missal follows the same tradition as that of Saint Pius V. Given the depth of their conviction, they did not bother demonstrating in the following lines how the New Mass implements Tridentine teachings. They limited themselves to declaring that as far as restoring "the norms of the holy Fathers" was concerned, "the new Missal is a considerable improvement on the old one."[290] Accordingly, the affirmations made in the previous items of the foreword about transubstantiation and the sacrificial and propitiatory character of the Mass remain, as it were, suspended in the air. There is no explanation for how these truths are not contradicted by the New Mass passages being shown to be contrary

---

289. Howell, *General Instruction*, item 6, p. 9.
290. Howell, items 9, 6, pp. 11, 10.

to the doctrines of Trent.[291] They rely on an extrinsic element, i.e., the purpose of restoring the rites according to the norms of the holy Fathers.

How does the foreword purport to prove that the Mass of Paul VI, like that of Saint Pius V, obeyed this purpose?

Obviously, the differences between the two Masses are so great that the foreword authors' main difficulty was explaining how the *same rule* could lead to *such different results.* In other words: How could the same purpose of restoring the rites according to the norms of the Church Fathers lead to such different ways of celebrating the Mass?

As a first response to this question, the foreword authors write, "In those troubled days, St. Pius V was unwilling to make any changes in the rites except minor ones; he was intent on preserving more recent tradition because at that time attacks were being made on the doctrine that the Mass is a sacrifice, that its ministers are priests, and that Christ is really and abidingly present under the eucharistic species."[292]

In the following items, the foreword affirms that since the ancient liturgies are much better known today than in the sixteenth century, it is now possible to reform the Mass in a much more profound manner.[293] All of this means "that the new Missal [of Paul VI] is a considerable improvement on the old one [of Saint Pius V]."[294]

4. Do These Errors No Longer Exist Today?

The suggestion that it is not necessary to retain the traditional rite because the dogmas concerning the sacrificial character of the Mass, the ministerial priesthood, and the Real Presence are not endangered today as they were in the times of Saint Pius V is quite perplexing.[295]

We cannot understand how what is public and notorious can be denied in this way. Large and influential sectors of Catholic opinion today, in the most varied

---

291. As mentioned in Chapter 2, to defend a text from the accusation of heterodoxy, it is not enough to prove that it contains the truth. It is, above all, necessary to demonstrate that it does not contain the errors it is accused of having, for doctrinal deviations are frequently presented in juxtaposition with, and at times even amalgamated with, truths that are contrary to them.

As is evident, the foreword cannot express itself in polemical terms, but it is equally clear that it is possible to confute objections raised against a document using a non-polemical style.

292. Howell, *General Instruction*, item 7, p. 10.

293. See Howell, items 7–9, pp. 10–11.

294. Howell, item 6, p. 10.

295. Further on, the foreword alleges that one can now celebrate in the vernacular because "no Catholic would now deny the legitimacy and efficacy of a liturgical rite celebrated in Latin." Howell, *General Instruction*, item 12, p. 12. It also says that "in our own days no one disputes the doctrinal principles which legitimize the reception of Communion under the species of bread only." Howell, item 14, p. 13.

The foreword authors seem not to consider, in any way, the harmful influences that the new *Ordo* can have on non-Catholics, for it is incontestable that the errors pointed out exist, at least among them. In the times of ecumenism that we live in, it is indispensable to present the doctrine of the Church clearly, both to her children and those who are not, for only in this way will it be possible to avoid dangerous misunderstandings, which in the concrete order necessarily lead to deforming the principles of the Faith.

countries, accept and spread the gravest errors about the principal tenets of Eucharistic doctrine, particularly the truths that the foreword affirms go unchallenged.

To avoid referring to the relevant documents of Pius XII—which condemned numerous practices adopted by the new *Ordo*—we shall mention only some more recent facts.[296]

In the encyclical *Mysterium fidei*, Paul VI declares that the errors regarding private Masses, transubstantiation, Eucharistic symbolism, and so forth are, for him, causes of "serious pastoral concern and anxiety."[297] The same document insists that "the distinction between the universal priesthood and the hierarchical priesthood is something essential and not just a matter of degree."[298] Would Paul VI have denounced heresies in this encyclical that no one today professes?

The *Dutch Catechism* and those like it in other countries fall into the same errors.[299]

How can one deny that the highly regarded Father Schillebeeckx, for example, proposes the notions of "transfinalization" and "transignification" in terms that are irreconcilable with Church doctrine[300] and which have already been condemned by Paul VI?[301]

How can one deny that in the very *Consilium ad Exsequendam Constitutionem de Sacra Liturgia*,[302] now replaced by the Sacred Congregation for Divine Worship, there was someone who subscribed to the errors mentioned above? Indeed, according to what we have shown at length and with documentation, the work *Nuevas normas de la misa*, whose main author was a *Consilium* expert, professes the same doctrinal deviations—sometimes clearly, sometimes in a veiled way.[303]

We have noted our surprise that the documents introducing the New Mass mention only the favorable aspects of the liturgical movement of the time of Pius XII, while the very grave errors infecting large sectors of that movement[304] and which led the pope to write the encyclical *Mediator Dei* are passed over in complete silence. The foreword authors now affirm that such errors do not exist. A scientific and objective analysis of these pronouncements obliges one to hypothesize that the foreword authors have embarked on a known and dangerous

---

296. See Pius XII, *Mediator Dei*; Instruction of the Holy Office (July 30, 1952); "Allocution, Royalty of Our Lady" (Nov. 1, 1954); "Allocution, Congress on Pastoral Liturgy" (Sept. 22, 1956).
297. Paul VI, encyclical *Mysterium fidei* (Sept. 3, 1965), no. 9.
298. Paul VI, *Mysterium fidei*, no. 31
299. See, for example, in the Brazilian edition of the *Dutch Catechism*—Hoger Katechetisch Institunt, *O novo catecismo* (São Paulo: Herder, 1969)—the passages on the Real Presence (397–99) and the priesthood of the faithful (403–404). See also the commentaries in this regard by Fr. Candido Pozo, S.J., in *El credo del pueblo de Dios* (Madrid: B.A.C., 1968), 177ff.; and Cunha Alvarenga, "Pedras e serpentes para as almas que pedem pão," *Catolicismo*, no. 231 (Mar. 1970).
300. See Schillebeeckx, "Transignification," 175–89.
301. See Paul VI, *Mysterium fidei*, no. 11.
302. About this organ of the Holy See, see our brief explanation in footnote 22.
303. On the importance and influence of the book *Nuevas normas de la misa*, see what we write at the beginning of Chapter 1.
304. See our commentary on the apostolic constitution *Missale romanum* at the beginning of Part One.

dialectical process. They admit in the abstract that certain doctrines are heretical. They deny, however, that anyone professes them in the real world. From those premises, they proceed to actions which, in the order of ideological propaganda and in real life, end up favoring or even promoting error.[305]

To these considerations, we must add another. The non-existence of such doctrinal deviations is alleged in the foreword[306] as a reason for introducing into the Mass innovations that Saint Pius V rejected because, since such deviations existed then, the introduction of those innovations would have gravely harmed the Faith. Therefore, given that similar errors exist today—and they obviously do—the very arguments presented by the foreword authors testify against them.

5. Adaptation to Present-Day Conditions

As we have observed,[307] the foreword insists that the new *Ordo* follows the Council of Trent because, like the latter, it seeks to restore the rites according to the ancient norms of the Church Fathers.

The argument is insufficient. The return to the norms established by the Church Fathers is a simple material criterion. It will become specified formally by the orientation according to which the patristic texts are interpreted, the passages to be introduced into the liturgy are selected, and so forth.

Thus, Pius XII condemns the efforts of some who, to readopt "ancient rites and ceremonies,"[308] would "revive the exaggerated and senseless antiquarianism to which the illegal Council of Pistoia gave rise. . . . [and] reinstate a series of errors which were responsible for the calling of that meeting as well as for those resulting from it."[309]

Along the same line, Dom Guéranger pointed out that demand for the "rights of *antiquity*" was one of the tactics employed by "all the sectarians" to destroy the real liturgical traditions and thus introduce their new forms of worship—which in reality will not correspond to the ancient traditions.[310]

On the other hand, it is known that an expression legitimately used by a Church Father can, through changed circumstances, become one that favors heresy in a later age. This happens, for example, with Saint Augustine's expression "faith saves," which the Protestants abused, interpreting it in a sense that is irreconcilable with good doctrine.[311]

---

305. On how this dialectical process was realized in the times of Jansenism, see chap. 2, sec. 2 (*Second Answer: The Contradictory Character of All Heresies*), item E. See Mayer, "Problemas do apostolado moderno," 25–26; Carreyre, "Jansénisme," in *D.T.C.*, 8–1e.:488–89.
306. See Howell, *General Instruction*, item 7, p. 10. See our commentaries on this matter at chap. 4, sec. 3 (*Return to the Norms of the Church Fathers*) *supra* and sec. 5 (*Adaptation to Present-Day Conditions*).
307. See chap. 4, sec. 3 (*Return to the Norms of the Church Fathers*).
308. Pius XII, *Mediator Dei*, no. 61.
309. Pius XII, no. 64.
310. Guéranger, *Institutions liturgiques*, 1:417–18.
311. See our essay "Não só a heresia pode ser condenada pela autoridade eclesiástica," *Catolicismo*, no. 203 (Nov. 1967).

As we have pointed out, the 1969 reform established worship tending to desacralization, to confusion between the hierarchical priesthood and that of the people, the putting on equal footing of the "liturgy of the word" and the "eucharistic liturgy," to a break, in the final analysis, with the most venerable traditional rites and customs.

What does this reform have in common with that of Saint Pius V? Unhappily, only the *material and extrinsic* element which consists in the formulation, both by Saint Pius V and Paul VI, of the purpose of restoring some rites according to the norms of the Church Fathers.

Sensing the need to explain better how this restoration was made so differently in one case and the other,[312] the foreword authors dedicated their six final items to the matter.[313]

"When the Fathers of the Second Vatican Council," we read in item 10, "repeated the dogmatic pronouncements of the Council of Trent, they were speaking in a profoundly different epoch of the world's history. For this reason, they were in a position to put forward in the pastoral sphere proposals and directives which, FOUR CENTURIES AGO, COULD HARDLY HAVE BEEN IMAGINED."[314]

As is readily seen, the expression used is so strong that it shows how the foreword authors radically understood the distance separating the documents of Trent from those triggering the recent liturgical reforms.

In the following items, they try to explain that since the sixteenth-century errors regarding Eucharistic worship no longer exist today, they can, therefore, introduce:

—the vernacular (items 11 and 12);
—Communion under two species for the simple faithful (item 14);
—new texts of the Mass and prayers (item 15);
—formulations adapted to modern theological language (item 15),
    and so forth.

Since it is not our purpose to analyze the foreword exhaustively here, we will only make some observations about these final paragraphs, which show clearly how they repeat grave deviations which already existed in the 1969 *Institutio*.

6. "The Eucharistic Sacrifice Is Above All an Action of Christ"

The dominant concern in these final paragraphs is to show that, since the danger of confusion between the hierarchical priesthood and that of the faithful no longer existed, it was possible to permit greater participation of the people in the liturgical ceremonies.

---

312. At chap. 4, sec. 3 (*Return to the Norms of the Church Fathers*, we have already indicated a first explanation which the foreword tries to give to this fact.
313. See Howell, *General Instruction*, items 10–15, pp. 11–14.
314. Howell, item 10, p. 11.

To justify this way of proceeding, the foreword affirms that "the circumstances prevailing in those days forced the Council [of Trent] to a conclusion . . . that there was an imperative need to emphasize once again a traditional doctrine of the Church. This was the doctrine that the eucharistic sacrifice is in the first place an action of Christ himself, and that its intrinsic efficacy is independent of the manner in which the faithful take part in it."[315]

It is incomplete and dangerous to formulate the relations between Our Lord's priesthood and that of the faithful in this way. This is a delicate matter. The question does not consist only, nor above all, in knowing whether the sacrifice is *affected* in some manner by the participation of the faithful. Rather, it consists in ascertaining if the faithful are *concelebrating* the Mass with the priest *when they participate*; in other words, if, like the priest, the faithful are official *representatives* of Our Lord for carrying out the liturgical functions.

It is in this aspect of the question that the changes introduced into the 1970 *Institutio* fail lamentably once more.

In the context of the paragraph we are now analyzing, the word "*imprimis*" (above all, principally, in the first place) declares that *in its essential element*, the sacrifice is the *action of Christ*. However, it does not explicitly exclude that it is *also the action of the faithful*. Furthermore, within the perspective of the entire foreword, such non-excluded action of the faithful is considered even an element of great importance in celebrating the Mass.[316] Now, the sacrificial immolation, properly speaking, is *exclusively* Our Lord's action, represented by the celebrant, who participates as an instrument. It is not, *in any way*, however, an action of the faithful. They can and must unite themselves to it in spirit, offering the Victim and themselves in union with the Victim, but in no way do they perform *the sacrificial action itself*.[317]

The text under analysis is unclear in this regard. It also leaves the way open once more for an erroneous concept of the priesthood of the faithful. Consequently, in the context of the New Mass, the reasons alleged immediately afterward to justify that the new *Ordo*—unlike that of Saint Pius V—introduced the vernacular and Communion under both species are invalid because such practical measures favor an erroneous and modernistic notion of the priesthood of the faithful.

7. The Language of Modern Theology

In item 15, the foreword has the following paragraph:

---

315. Howell, item 11, p. 11. "Ad talem quidem postulationem, Concilium, rationem ducens adiunctorum illa aetate obtinentium, sui officii esse arbitrabatur doctrinam Ecclesiae tralaticiam denuo inculcare, secundum quam Sacrificium eucharisticum imprimis Christi ipsius est actio, cuius proinde efficacitas propria eo modo non afficitur, quo fideles eiusdem fiunt participes." Foreword to the 1970 *Institutio*, item 11.

316. See Howell, *General Instruction*, items 4–5, pp. 8–9. We commented at chap. 4, sec. 2 (*The Priesthood of the People*) *supra*.

317. See Antonio de Castro Mayer, "Carta pastoral sobre o santo sacrificio da missa," (Sept. 12, 1969), in *Por um cristianismo autêntico*, 329–53 (São Paulo: Editora Vera Cruz, 1971).

To change a phrase or two here and there in the venerable treasury of prayers inherited from the past so as to relate them to present-day circumstances[318] is in no way to undervalue them. Such changes have been made so that the mode of expression may be in harmony with that of modern theology and with the facts of contemporary Church discipline. That is why some phrases concerning the estimation and use of earthly things or the external forms of penance formerly in vogue in the Church have been altered.[319]

This passage is symptomatic. The "language of modern theology" is no longer that of Patristic theology, nor is it that of Scholastic theology, nor that of Trent. Will the "evaluation" or the "use" of "earthly things" have to be expressed in another manner for semantic and grammatical reasons, or because the new prayers provide an "opening" for the desacralization of Catholic life? In abolishing "the external forms of penance formerly in vogue in the Church," will the reformers not be preparing the way for an anthropocentric religion without crosses and Protestant-flavored?

Furthermore, these norms of a linguistic nature adopted by the foreword of the *Institutio* try to explain and justify the profoundly desacralizing orientation which, in general, presided over the translations of the new *Ordo* into the living languages of the West.[320]

---

318. "*Ob eandem porro aestimationem novi status mundi, qui nunc est.*" Centre National de Pastorale Liturgique (France) gives the following translation to this phrase, conceived in the style of the so-called prophetic groups: "De même, parce qu'on *prenait conscience* de la situation nouvelle du monde contemporain." [Likewise, because we *became aware* of the new situation of the contemporary world.] *La Documentation Catholique* (June 21, 1970), 568.
319. Howell, *General Instruction*, item 15, p. 14.
320. We refer to translations which the Sacred Congregation for Divine Worship has approved. Issue no. 54 (May 1970) of the magazine *Notitiae*, which gives information about the modifications then introduced into the New Mass, contains a long study of the translations of the Roman Missal (194–213). The article is written by Dom Antoine Dumas, O.S.B., a member of both the commission in charge of reviewing the Latin text of the new Roman Missal and that which prepares French translations (*Notitiae*, 197). After saying that those who revised the original Latin sought "a fundamental adaptation of the texts to the contemporary mentality" (196) and after eulogizing the liturgical language of the Protestants (197), Dom Antoine presents principles and examples that very clearly demonstrate the desacralizing orientation which is being followed in these matters by the respective commissions of the Sacred Congregation for Divine Worship. We indicate here some characteristic cases: "*hostia*" never has the sense of "victim" (198); "*forma*" and "*substantia*" must not be translated in a manner to "overcharge the prayers with irrelevant philosophical technicalities" (206); "*quaesumus*" must never be interpreted as having a sense of supplication (209); "*continentia*," "*moderatio*," "*temperari*," "*castigatio*," and "*ieiunium*" "are to be translated by expressions which are quite general and adapted to the contemporary mentality" (208–9). Antoine Dumas, O.S.B., "Pour mieux comprendre les textes liturgiques du missel romain," *Notitiae*, no. 54 (May 1970), 194–213.
    It would be very difficult to conceive of a better way of realizing the modernist ideal of adapting the Church to the mentality of the world. The faithful had this same temptation at the time of Saint Paul: "Be not conformed to this world" (Rom. 12:2); "Keep that which is committed to thy trust, avoiding the profane novelties of words" (1 Tim. 6:20); "There shall be a time, when [men] will not endure sound doctrine; but according to their own desires, they will heap to themselves teachers, having itching ears; and will indeed turn away their hearing from the truth, but will be turned unto fables" (2 Tim. 4:3–4).

8. The 1970 Revision of the *Institutio*

In presenting the alterations introduced in 1970 to the *Institutio*, the magazine *Notitiae*[321] states:

> Once the 1969 Ordinary of the Mass, *Institutio generalis missalis romani* was published, various criticisms, both rubrical and doctrinal, were raised in its regard. Some points were not presented entirely clearly, above all on account of the difficulty of having all the material before one's eyes, which was expounded in various places. However, certain strong censures were made based on a preconception opposed to any novelty; therefore, considering them did not seem necessary since they lack any foundation. Indeed, the *Institutio* had been submitted to the examination of the *Consilium* Fathers and the experts, before and after publication, and no reason was found to alter the disposition of the material, nor was any doctrinal error discovered. It is a pastoral and rubrical document that orders the celebration of the Mass according to the doctrine of the Second Vatican Council, the encyclical of Paul VI *Mysterium fidei* . . . and the Instruction *Eucharisticum mysterium*. . . .
>
> However, to avoid any difficulties and to clarify certain expressions, it was resolved that, together with the publication of the typical edition of the new Roman Missal, the text of the *Institutio* would be completed or rewritten here and there (see the "Declaration of Sacred Congregation for Divine Worship of Nov. 18, 1969," *Notitiae* 5, 1969, 417–18). However, nothing entirely new was done. Thus, the enumeration of the *Institutio* continued as it was in the first writing.
>
> The amendments are really few and, at times, slight or only stylistic.[322]

If we wished to examine these lines thoroughly, we would have numerous and important observations to make. We would demonstrate how the allegation that important criticisms of the 1969 *Institutio* have originated from the simple "difficulty of having all the material before one's eyes" is unfounded. We would prove that, in the real order, the so-called "preconception opposed to any novelty" is nothing more than the love of Catholic doctrine. We would observe that the fact that the *Consilium* Fathers and the experts have not found doctrinal errors in the document testifies heavily against them. We would emphasize how it is inconceivable for one still to insist on the merely "pastoral and rubrical" character of the 1969 *Institutio* when it obviously contains numerous passages of an incontestably doctrinal nature.[323] We would also make even more corrections to the text.

Since our objective, however, is only to show that important points in the 1970 *Institutio* continue to clash with Catholic doctrine despite the "at times,

---

321. The article "Variationes in 'Institutionem generalem missalis romani' inductae," *Notitiae* 54 (May 1970), 177–90.
322. "Variationes in 'Institutionem,'" 177.
323. See our observations in this regard in footnote 51.

slight" modifications it has undergone, we shall consider more attentively only one aspect of the quotation translated above: the authors' concern with stating that the amendments were not intended to correct doctrinal errors or deficiencies, but only to make clearer what the document already contained.

If this is so, one can fear, even before analyzing the aforementioned corrections, that they have sometimes been incomplete and contradictory in that they have not exempted the 1970 *Institutio* overall from the suspicion hanging over it. *A priori,* one may fear that the revision of the document represents a mere tactical retreat. This withdrawal creates certain difficulties in the concrete order for those pointing out the errors of the *Institutio.* In reality, though, it consolidates those same errors, sometimes reaffirming many of them clearly, and at others in a disguised and subtle language.

Let us go on then with the analysis of the 1970 changes to the *Institutio generalis missalis romani.*

9. Number 7 of the 1970 *Institutio*

The much-attacked number 7 of the *Institutio*[324] now has the following text:

> In the Mass or Lord's Supper the people of God are called together into one place where the priest presides over them and acts in the person of Christ [*personam Christi gerente*]. They assemble to celebrate the Memorial of the Lord, which is the sacrifice of the Eucharist. Hence the promise of Christ: "Wherever two or three are gathered together in my name, there am I in the midst of them" (Matt. 18:20) applies in a special way to this gathering of the local church. For in the celebration of the Mass whereby the sacrifice of the Cross is perpetuated, Christ is really present in the very community which has gathered in his name, in the person of his minister, [in his words,] and also substantially and continuously under the eucharistic species.[325]

The corrections to which this new text of number 7 is susceptible are almost as serious as the old one.

The appearance of a definition of the Mass has been removed, it is said that the priest acts in the person of Christ, a reference to the sacrifice has been added (albeit Eucharistic, they do not say propitiatory), and it is declared that Our Lord

---

324. On the original wording of this paragraph, and the corrections it needed, see our observations in chap. 1, sec. 2 (*Number 7 of the 1969* Institutio) *supra.*

325. Howell, *General Instruction*, no. 7, p. 16. "In Missa seu Cena dominica populus Dei in unum convocatur, sacerdote praeside personamque Christi gerente, ad memoriale Domini seu sacrificium eucharisticum celebrandum. Quare de huiusmodi sanctae Ecclesiae coadunatione locale eminenter valet promissio Christi: 'Ubi sunt duo vel tres congregate in nomine meo, ibi sum in medio eorum' (Matt. 18:20). In Missae enim celebratione, in qua sacrificium Cruces perpetuatur, Christus realiter praesens adest in ipso coetu in suo nomine congregato, in persona ministri, in verbo suo, et quidem substantialiter et continenter sub speciebus eucharisticis."

is substantially and permanently present under the Eucharistic species. Nevertheless, ambiguities and deviations subsist that are by no means small.

The gravest of its faults is the affirmation that it is the *people* who *celebrate* the memorial of the Lord or Eucharistic Sacrifice.[326] Note, indeed, that the word *celebrandum* has as agent *populus Dei*. After all that we have said about the gravity of this concept,[327] we deem it superfluous to spend further time on this point. This notion returns again and again in the new text of the *Institutio*.[328] That observation suffices. This recurring error alone shows how far the document strays from Church teaching.[329]

Even in the new text of number 7, the strange imprecisions about the various manners of Our Lord's "presence" in the Mass continue. True, it declares that the presence under the Eucharistic species is "substantial and permanent." The expression is perfectly exact, but the word "*enim*" (for) establishes a connection that is not very clear and is very dangerous between that substantial presence and the principle enunciated earlier: "Where two or three are gathered together in my name, there am I in the midst of them." What relation would there be between these two "presences"? Would the "communal" character of the "community which has gathered" in Christ's name contribute to His becoming present under the Eucharistic species or for this second presence to be realized more fully, or do the "people of God" gathered together at least exercise some active function to make Our Lord's substantial presence in the Eucharist effective? The text permits dangerous ambiguities to settle around this point, especially because of what was affirmed above, that the "people of God" *celebrate* the sacrifice.

Neither do the authors establish the necessary distinctions between the several modes of the non-substantial presence of Christ, that is, in the gathered community, in the person of the minister, and in the word of Scripture. That the assembly is named before the minister is noteworthy. It could indicate that Our Lord's presence in the people is, if not superior to, at least more fundamental for the Eucharistic celebration than His presence in the person of the minister. Furthermore, as we have observed,[330] the simple use of the expression "*personam Christi gerens*" is insufficient, in the context of the *Institutio*, to eliminate the ambiguities the document creates regarding this matter.

Even in its new formulation, this number 7 sounds so strange as to require several additional corrections:

---

326. See what we said in this regard in footnote 284.
327. See chap. 1, secs. 5 (*The President of the Assembly*) and 6 (*Jesus Christ, the Principal Priest [Sacerdos]*) *supra*.
328. The same deviation, indeed, was already pointed out at chap. 4, secs. 2 (*The Priesthood of the People*), 4 (*Do These Errors No Longer Exist Today?*), and 6 ("*The Eucharistic Sacrifice Is Above All an Action of Christ*") *supra*, and we shall refer to it again, especially in the Conclusion (*The New Mass and the Catholic Conscience*) *infra*.
329. We recall that we do not present these observations in a spirit of contestation or revolt against the powers and the authority which the hierarchy has, according to the laws and doctrine of the Church. What we desire is to verify in what measure these laws and doctrine, in their purest and most authentic expressions, oblige us to accept or reject the New Mass.
330. See chap. 1, sec. 5 (*The President of the Assembly*) *supra*.

—In the Mass, Our Lord *becomes* present under the Eucharistic species, but one cannot say without further ado that in the Mass He *is* substantially and permanently present under the Eucharistic species.

—The clause "*sacerdote praeside personamque Christi gerente*" appears to subordinate the priest's function as representative of Christ to his function as president of the assembly. In reality, what happens is the reverse.

—In the context, that the expression "real presence" is not reserved for the presence resulting from the transubstantiation tends to weaken the faith in the "*Real* Presence," by antonomasia, introducing into Catholic circles a terminology agreeable to certain Protestants.

—Nor is it said *how* the sacrifice of the Cross is perpetuated in the Mass, for the classic term "is renewed" is not used.

The commentary in the magazine *Notitiae* regarding number 7 in its new formulation only aggravates the ambiguities of the text. Here is one example: "The structure of the eucharistic celebrations is drawn from the communal Mass, or the Mass with the people, in which THE 'ACTION OF CHRIST AND THE CHURCH' takes place IN FULL MEASURE, that is, the action of the people of God hierarchically organized, although ONE SHOULD RECOGNIZE THE ENTIRE EFFICACY AND DIGNITY of the private Mass or the Mass without the people."[331]

It is not easy to comprehend why "one should recognize the entire efficacy and dignity" of the private Mass when in it, the "action of Christ and the Church" does not take place "in full measure." Either this phrase has no meaning, or it insinuates that in the "communal" Mass, the faithful present really *concelebrate* with the priest, the "action of Christ and the Church" attaining thus its "full measure."

10. The Other Numbers That Have Been Changed

The beginning of number 48 now has the following text: "Christ our Lord instituted the paschal sacrifice and meal at the Last Supper. In this the sacrifice of the Cross is continually made present in the Church whenever. . ."[332]

As can be seen, the expression "memorial of His death and resurrection" has been replaced by "paschal sacrifice and meal," still referencing the sacrifice of the Cross. However, the ambiguity surrounding the term *presence,* which we pointed out, has remained.[333] On the other hand, unfortunately, it is not said that the sacrifice is propitiatory: This precision only appears in number 2 of the foreword. Accordingly, the modification introduced in number 48 did not go far enough to substantially alter the *Institutio*'s evaluation.

---

331. "Variationes in 'Institutionem,'" *Notitiae* 54, 178. (Internal citation omitted.)
332. Howell, *General Instruction*, no. 48, p. 26. The 1969 text of this number of the *Institutio* is in chap. 1, sec. 1 (*The 1969* Institutio *and the Dogma of Transubstantiation*) *supra.*
333. See chap. 1, sec. 1 (*The 1969* Institutio *and the Dogma of Transubstantiation*) *supra.*

Number 55d was given the following formulation: "*The Institution Narrative AND CONSECRATION*: Through the words and actions of Christ THERE IS ACCOMPLISHED THE VERY SACRIFICE WHICH HE HIMSELF INSTITUTED AT THE LAST SUPPER when, under the species of bread and wine, he GAVE his Body and Blood TO HIS APOSTLES to eat and drink, and commanded them in turn to perform this same sacred mystery."[334]

Undoubtedly, the changes introduced in this paragraph are an important correction in the *Institutio*. It was inadmissible that in this central passage of the document, the title used only the words "Narrative of the Institution" and did not even speak of sacrifice. It was also to be hoped for that the insinuation that, at the Last Supper, Christ gave his Body and Blood only to the apostles, without offering them for all men, would be eliminated. The ambiguity about the notion of *presence* disappeared.

The insistence on considering the Mass a memorial of Our Lord's Death *and Resurrection* was also suppressed. As noted,[335] that insistence was such as to favor an erroneous concept about the Holy Eucharist. There is no doubt that the Resurrection has a special relationship with the Mass, for the theologians consider it to be a manifestation of the acceptance of the sacrifice of Calvary by God the Father, but the excessive insistence that the Eucharist *also recalls the Resurrection* contributes to dissimulating the sacrificial and propitiatory character of the Mass.

Despite these modifications, the text of number 55d ought to be more complete. Given the importance of this passage, it should contain a reference to the sacrifice of the Cross and the propitiatory character of the Mass.

In any event, the amendments made here were also insufficient to make the *Institutio* acceptable in its ensemble, all the more so because, as we shall see further on,[336] passages in which the document insinuates the same errors now expurgated from number 55d were not corrected.

In number 60, where it read, "The priest celebrant also presides over the assembly which has met, acting in place of Christ, . . ." it now reads, "IN VIRTUE OF HIS ORDINATION the priest is THE MEMBER OF THE COMMUNITY OF THE FAITHFUL WHO POSSESSES THE POWER TO OFFER SACRIFICE IN THE PERSON OF CHRIST. It is his function, therefore, to preside over the community."[337]

Undoubtedly, this correction introduces the notion of the instrumental priesthood of the celebrant, but its favorable effect is inadequate to undo what is censurable in the various passages whereby, as we have shown, the *Institutio* affirms explicitly that the people *also* celebrate.

In the same number 60, an additional change was made: Where it said that the priest "participates with his brethren in the bread of eternal life," it now says that

---

334. Howell, *General Instruction*, no. 55d, p. 29. See the former text in chap. 1, sec. 1 (*The 1969 Institutio and the Dogma of Transubstantiation*) *supra*.
335. See chap. 1, sec. 8 (*Memorial of the Resurrection and Ascension*) *supra*.
336. See Conclusion (*The New Mass and the Catholic Conscience*) *infra*.
337. Howell, *General Instruction*, no. 60, p. 33.

"he DISTRIBUTES to his brethren the Bread of eternal life, and himself receives it with them."[338]

As one sees, the new text alludes to the priestly function of the priest, but it does not, in any way, undo the ambiguities pointed out earlier.[339]

Lesser modifications, which do not require commentary, were made in various other parts.

In the final paragraph of number 59, where it read, "If however the bishop does not celebrate the Eucharist, but delegates someone else to do it," it now says, "However, if the bishop is not personally celebrating the Eucharist but DELEGATES another to do so."

In number 56, it is now said that only "the faithful in good dispositions should" receive Holy Communion. The previous formulation opened the way for an interpretation of a Protestant nature, according to which all the faithful must always communicate.[340]

Number 56a introduced a change, probably to eliminate the dangerous ambiguity of the original text, according to which the Body of Christ appeared to be entirely identified with the "daily bread" which we ask for in the "Our Father"

In numbers 80c and 117, using the paten for the Communion of the faithful was reintroduced.

Number 109 was modified to admit the optional use of bells at the Consecration.

Number 125, in its new text, made the kiss of the altar at the end of the Mass optional in certain circumstances. This is one more desacralizing measure. Numbers 141, 152, and 208 were altered in the same manner.

Number 276 clarifies that, outside the Mass, the faithful should not only pray before the Blessed Sacrament but also adore It.

Number 283 has a new clause in which it says that "bread used for the Eucharist, even though unleavened and of the traditional shape. . ."[341] One does not see the point of this change, all the more so since the commentary of *Notitiae* admits that such hosts may be, in their "size, thickness, and color," different from the traditional one.[342] Anyway, the introduction of this clause allows one to perceive that the authors of the New Mass sensed how far they had departed from the traditional *Ordo*.

Various numbers introduce modifications of a merely disciplinary, rubrical, stylistic, or typographical order: 30; 32; 76; 95; 99; 120; 121; 143; 153, item 1; 157; 158; 158a; 158c; 158d; 234a; 235; 242, item 4; 242, item 7; 242, item 8b;

---

338. Howell, no. 60, p. 33.
339. See especially chap. 4, secs. 2 (*The Priesthood of the People*) and 9 (*Number 7 of the 1970 Institutio*). The custom, every day more generalized, of lay men and even women (at times during the very celebration of the Mass) distributing Holy Communion shows very well how these simple modifications to number 60 are insufficient to undo everything opposed to Church Tradition in the structure of the new *Ordo*.
340. Howell, *General Instruction*, ncs. 59, 56, pp. 33, 29.
341. Howell, no. 283, p. 70.
342. "Variationes in 'Institutionem,'" *Notitiae*, no. 54, 186.

242, item 14, 290; 299; 300; 308a; 308b; 315; 316; 319; 322e; 329a; 330; 332; 333; 334; 336; and 337.

These modifications are of no (or only very slight) doctrinal importance. We only highlight the broadening of the situations when Communion under both species by the faithful and concelebration are permitted.

11. Modifications in the Fixed Parts of the Mass

Various changes were also introduced in the *Ordo* proper, that is, in the fixed parts of the Mass.

Many new prefaces were added, which caused a considerable increase in volume and required an important modification in the enumeration of the paragraphs.

It was also determined that, on purifying the sacred vessels, the celebrant must say in a low voice the prayer *Quod ore sumpsimus*, which had been previously eliminated.[343]

We shall not comment on other alterations introduced in the *Ordo* because they do not affect our earlier criticisms of the 1969 *Institutio*. Here are some examples of these alterations:

—before the Gospel, the words: "Reading of the Holy Gospel according to N." are said;

—it became permissible in any Mass to sing the parts of the Eucharistic Prayer which can be sung in the concelebrated Masses;

—the *Communicantes* and the *Hanc igitur* of Easter must be prayed until the Second Sunday after Easter and not only until Saturday "in albis";

—it is required that the priest pronounce the *Pax Domini* always facing the people.

12. Conclusion

In conclusion, the texts of the New Mass of 1970, like those of 1969, cannot be accepted in conscience.

As we have said,[344] we shall leave for the end of this study[345] a more detailed critique or evaluation of the conclusions to be drawn from the considerations we are making.

---

343. See footnotes 174 and 245.
344. See chap. 3, sec. 7 (*Conclusion*) *supra*.
345. See Conclusion (*The New Mass and the Catholic Conscience*) *infra*.

CHAPTER FIVE

The New Ordinary of the Mass and the Protestant Supper

Various theologians have called the Catholic public's attention to the Protestant, especially Lutheran, inspiration of the new *Ordo missae*. A study of the matter shows that they are not mistaken. We will illustrate this in the following pages, basing our work on Catholic and Protestant documents dealing with the Reformation and its liturgical innovations.

Unfortunately, as the analysis of these documents demonstrates, the Lutheran Supper and the New Mass share more than superficial features. It is not a question of seeming or occasional resemblance. Rather, the similarity between the two is rooted in their very premises.

1. A Slow and Cautious Reform

In the article "Luther" in the *Dictionnaire de théologie catholique*, J. Paquier describes the new worship introduced by Luther as follows: "Logically, the new religion should perhaps have only one cult: the interior cult of faith. To stimulate this interior worship, it would be possible to add a sacrament: the Word.[346] But the Catholic past of Luther and his good sense prevented him from drawing the logical consequences of his ideas.[347] The new worship will be a prudent and timid reduction and transformation of Catholic worship, which retained much of the past."[348]

See, then, how insufficient it is to allege, in defense of the new *Ordo*, that it preserves much of the traditional Missal.

Paquier continues:

---

346. We already pointed out the singular importance attributed to the "Liturgy of the Word" by the *Institutio*. See chap. 1, sec. 7 (*A Tendency to Make the "Liturgy of the Word" Equal to the "Eucharistic Liturgy"*).

347. Note that it is peculiar to heretics to go little by little, only revealing their real designs when the resistance of the faithful is overcome. This point will be expounded in greater detail further on, above all in the text supported by footnotes 374, 376, and 380 *infra*.

348. Paquier, "Luther," *D.T.C.*, 9–1e :1304–5.

The center of Catholic worship is Jesus Christ. The great prayer of the Church, the most important act of her worship, is the Mass, at the same time a sacrifice and the realization of a sacrament. As sacrifice, it is, above all, a tribute of man to God. As a realization of a sacrament, it is principally a source of sanctification for men. This sacrament is the *sacrament* of the Eucharist, or simply the *Sacrament*, as they said in the days of Luther.

Regarding this doctrine, Luther always preserved the belief in the real presence of Jesus Christ in the Eucharist. It distinguished him clearly from Zwingli,[349] Bucer, and Calvin, in a word from those who, perhaps with a certain irony, were called *sacramentarians*.[350]

Note, therefore, how right Pius VI[351] was in condemning the Synod of Pistoia for not speaking of *transubstantiation* while admitting the Real Presence. Once again, it becomes clear how grave the omission by the 1969 *Institutio* was in using only the word "presence" and not even mentioning the *Real Presence* to indicate how Jesus is present in the Eucharist.[352]

Paquier states:

Evidently, though, he submitted this dogma to profound modifications. First of all, this sacrament, like the others, will not produce grace; it only stimulates within us the confidence that our sins were forgiven.[353] On the other hand, the bread and wine remained after the Consecration, together with Christ's Body and Blood. There was no change of substance, no transubstantiation, but rather an "*impanatio*" ("inbreadification").[354] In other words, both as man and God, Jesus was present everywhere. Therefore, what difficulty would there be in admitting his presence in the Eucharist?[355] Besides that, when is Jesus Christ present in the bread and wine? Luther generally tells us that He is present only at the moment of the Consecration and Communion. But on this point, as in others, his contradictions are abundant.[356] One will easily comprehend that, after his death, this belief in the Real Presence was compromised among his followers.

---

349. On Zwingli's liturgical reform, see text supported by footnote 382.
350. Paquier, "Luther," 9–1e.:1305.
351. See the last five paragraphs of chap. 1, sec. 1 (*The 1969* Institutio *and the Dogma of Transubstantiation*) *supra*.
352. See chap. 1, sec. 1 (*The 1969* Institutio *and the Dogma of Transubstantiation*) *supra*.
353. By weakening the sacrificial and propitiatory character of Eucharist worship, the New Mass establishes one more connecting tie with the Lutheran Supper.
354. Therefore, the affirmation of the presence of the "Body of Christ" in the Eucharist is also insufficient to distinguish Catholics from Protestants. The use of the term *transubstantiation* is indispensable. See our observations in this regard in chap. 1, sec. 1 (*The 1969* Institutio *and the Dogma of Transubstantiation*) *supra*.
355. As can be seen, Luther, for his part, took advantage of the inherent ambiguities of the concept of *presence*. Regarding how the 1969 *Institutio* makes use of this concept, see chap. 1, sec. 1 (*The 1969* Institutio *and the Dogma of Transubstantiation*) *supra*.
356. Contradictions are also abundant in progressive writings. See chap. 2, sec. 2 (*Second Answer: The Contradictory Character of All Heresies*) *supra*.

Finally, and above all, Luther rebelled against the idea of sacrifice.[357] The idea of the Mass put him in a true fury. The Mass and the papacy[358] were what received the most offense from him.[359]

Immediately afterward, the article in the *Dictionnaire de théologie catholique* describes Luther's violent attacks against receiving stipends for Masses. According to him, the effect of stipends was the maintenance of innumerable priests in idleness and the abusive promotion of foundations. Consequently, he called the Mass "the work of the devil"[360] and "the greatest and most horrible of papal abominations, the tail of the dragon of the Apocalypse."[361] As Paquier observes, the abuse of Mass stipends was nothing more than a "circumstantial reason" for Luther's attacks against the Mass.[362] In reality, the logic of his doctrine would lead to the total abolition of the Mass.

Paquier explains this in greater detail:

> Against the Mass, however, Luther had an infinitely more important argument: The Mass opposed his understanding of religion. In ancient times, the center of religion was God. More than anything else, worship was, therefore, an homage offered to God, and, in this tribute, the sacrifice was the act par excellence. For Luther, the center of religion was now no longer God but man. Religion's purpose is to enlighten man. Even more, it is to console him. Thus, what is the point of an immolation offered to God to recognize His sovereign dominion over His creature?[363] Undoubtedly, Luther still admitted the sacrifice of the Cross but made this sacrifice an ancient stage of religion and placed it in opposition to our religious life today. On the one hand, in the ancient stage were Christ and his merits; on the other, in the present, would be ourselves, who would have nothing more to merit but would have only to attract the merits of Jesus Christ upon us through our confidence in Him (Weimar, 8:442, 28 f. (1521); etc.[364]

---

357. The new *Ordo* weakens the notion that the Mass constitutes a sacrifice. See chap. 1 sec. 2 (*Number 7 of the 1969* Institutio) *supra*.
358. The traditional notion of the Mass and the papal primacy are perhaps the Catholic truths most attacked by neomodernists today.
359. Paquier, "Luther," *D.T.C.*, 9–1e.:1305.
360. Paquier, 9–1e.:1305. He cites Weimar, 8:499, 13 (1521).
361. Paquier, 9–1e.:1305. He cites Weimar, 50:200, 8; 204, 15 (1537).
362. Paquier, 9–1e.:1305.
363. For that reason, Luther desired the abolition of the Offertory. See chap. 5, sec. 3, item B (*The Lutheran Offertory*) *infra*. In the new *Ordo*, the Offertory practically disappeared. See chap. 3, sec. 2 (*The New Concept of the Offertory*) *supra*.
364. Paquier, "Luther," *D.T.C.*, 9–1e.:1305–6. The notion that we have nothing to merit is not without affinity to the slight emphasis the new *Ordo* gives to the propitiatory character of the Mass.

Here one could ask if any tendency to lead the faithful away from frequent Communion or to diminish devotion to the Holy Mass is observable among the indoctrinators of progressivism.

At first glance, this question deserves a negative answer, as they continuously cast themselves as ardent paladins of the liturgy in general and the Eucharistic liturgy in particular. They extol the excellence of the Mass so often that they would seem to outdo traditional Catholics significantly.

However, we cannot forget that when one exalts something in terms not entirely in accordance with sound doctrine, one generally ends up denigrating, sometimes even denying, the very thing which was so highly praised in the beginning. That is what history teaches. Rationalism led to the suicide of reason itself. Jansenist false Eucharistic fervor ended up separating souls from the Blessed Sacrament. Liberalism led to totalitarianism. The earthly paradise promised by Communists proves to be a real-world hell from which entire populations try to flee.

Will the same rule hold for the unsound liturgical movement, already denounced by Pius XII?

Unfortunately, there are reasons to fear that such is the case. We shall point out some of them:

(1) The already mentioned B.A.C. commentary says that the priest must never celebrate a private Mass—now called a "Mass without the people"—for mere personal devotion.[365]

(2) Explaining the paragraph of the 1969 *Institutio* that declares that the Mass has a "communal" character, the B.A.C. commentators write:

> In our pastoral care, we ought to draw forth all the consequences of these words of the *Institutio*. For example, not multiplying Masses when there is no true communion necessity, especially during weekdays. Consequently, could one not sustain that on Sundays, all the faithful will be content with one Mass in the morning and another in the evening, at the most convenient times for the majority? In this case, if there are more priests than the number of Masses, why should they not concelebrate, grouping people together in this way as much as possible?[366]

Why not multiply the Masses, we ask, given that Catholic doctrine permits and even recommends this, to facilitate Mass attendance by the faithful as much as possible—all the more so since the Mass's true "common" character does not cease to exist in a private celebration?[367]

---

365. Martín Patino, *Nuevas normas*, 214, commentary on number 209 of the 1969 *Institutio*.
366. Martín Patino, 91, commentary on number 14 of the 1969 *Institutio*.
367. See Council of Trent, Denz.-Sch., 1747; Lercher, *Institutiones theologiae*, 4–2–1:276n14.

(3) On the other hand, the notion that Communion outside of the Mass clashes with the recent liturgical reforms is increasingly spreading among priests and faithful.

Paquier's exposition continues:

> The Mass now is not a sacrifice. Luther will eliminate all that brings this characteristic to mind.[368] Other reasons will contribute to the modifications he will introduce. Luther and Melanchthon were professors. Teaching will replace the sacrifice, and the chair will replace the altar. The professor does not like pompous apparatus. Thus, the new worship will be simple.[369] All Christians are priests. Therefore, all communicate under both species.[370] In the Eucharist, Jesus Christ is not constantly present, but He is present only in the moment of the function and the Supper. Therefore, outside the scheduled service time, one should not go to church to pray.[371] And, crowning all the rest, the vernacular—formerly used in the early Church—will be introduced in the worship and replace Latin, the official language of the Church of the West. In this way, Luther approached the

---

368. On the tendency of the new *Ordo* to consign the sacrificial character of the Mass to the shadows, see chap. 1, sec. 2 (*Number 7 of the 1969* Institutio) *supra.*

369. Emphasizing the weaknesses of professors, which would have given rise to certain errors of Luther and Melanchthon, Paquier seems not to note that egalitarianism, and, therefore, pride and sensuality, is at the heart of the state of soul, which gave rise to Protestantism. On the central role of egalitarian metaphysics in the explosion of the Protestant Revolution, see Plinio Corrêa de Oliveira, *Revolution and Counter-Revolution*, 3rd ed. (York, Penn.: The American Society for the Defense of Tradition, Family, and Property, 1993), 46–51.

370. It is with profound uneasiness that anti-progressive Catholics have noted the multiplication of Mass situations in which Communion under both species is authorized.

371. About the tendency of the heterodox liturgical movement to condemn all private devotions, Pius XII wrote:

> 173. When dealing with genuine and solid piety, We stated that there could be no real opposition between the sacred liturgy and other religious practices, provided they be kept within legitimate bounds and performed for a legitimate purpose. In fact, there are certain exercises of piety which the Church recommends very much to clergy and religious.
>
> 174. It is Our wish also that the faithful, as well, should take part in these practices. . . .
>
> 176. In keeping with your pastoral solicitude, Venerable Brethren, do not cease to recommend and encourage these exercises of piety. . . . Above all, do not allow—as some do, who are deceived under the pretext of restoring the liturgy or who idly claim that only liturgical rites are of any real value and dignity—that the churches be closed during the hours not appointed for public functions, as has already happened in some places: where the adoration of the august sacrament and visits to our Lord in the tabernacles are neglected; where confession of devotion is discouraged; and devotion to the Virgin Mother of God, a sign of "predestination" according to the opinion of holy men, is so neglected, especially among the young, as to fade away and gradually vanish. Such conduct most harmful to Christian piety is like poisonous fruit, growing on the infected branches of a healthy tree, which must be cut off so that the life-giving sap of the tree may bring forth only the best fruit. (Pius XII, *Mediator Dei*, nos. 173–74, 176)

See also Pius XII, "Allocution, Congress of the Pastoral Liturgy" (Sept. 22, 1956).

people and interested them in the cause of the Reformation.[372] Finally, the sermon will be in the most important place; prayer will be in the second; and confession and the supper only in the third place.[373]

However, the changes will be made timidly. And that is what a certain good sense in Luther and the falsity of his attitudes require. It is necessary to reassure the people or, to use his expression, "to temporize with the conscience of the weak" [Weimar, 12:48, 20 (1523)]. In the churches, people will encounter more or less the same rites as before. The very name of "Mass," derived from the idol "Maozim," described by Daniel ["Tischreden," 4:5037 (1540)], that horrid name will be preserved. Thus, long years after becoming Lutherans, there will be Christian communities who ignore that they have separated from Rome and the Catholic Church.[374]

Luther's temporizing measures had incredible success in circles that would have reacted energetically had they only seen from the beginning where they were being misled.

In our own days, this history lesson creates for many souls the grave obligation of alerting their brothers in the Faith against the process that envelops us.

As readily seen, profound and grave reforms can develop "timidly" and very gradually. One wonders then, with apprehension, to what point the liturgy can evolve, starting from the *Institutio* and the new *Ordo*. All the more so, when such evolution will be multiform and *ipso facto*, very free, in light of the faculties granted to bishops and episcopal conferences to introduce in their territories, with the authorization of the Holy See, innovations not provided for in the liturgical books. To this should be added the now very broad attributes the same episcopal conferences enjoy in implementing *Institutio* norms.[375]

One can fear that, as they exercise such faculties conditioned by the peculiarities of each region and moved by the internal logic of things, the process of liturgical modernization will be delayed to ensure its unique effectiveness in moving toward radicalizations and exaggerations. In Holland, for example, innovations may be numerous and extreme, while in Brazil, they will develop more flexibly and gradually. In all countries, eventual resistance will be mollified through conciliatory measures while, simultaneously, advancing the process as fast as possible.

Eventual recourse to such "temporiz[ations] with the conscience of the weak" would be even more dangerous since many traditionalist Catholics do not appear

---

372. Here, too, it does not seem that Paquier has grasped the true importance of an aspect of the Protestant Reformation. Would Luther have introduced the vernacular in the Liturgy to please the people? Or was it, above all, to eliminate the sacral character of worship, to confuse the celebrant with the people-priest, and to destroy a venerable tradition of the Church?

373. Another affinity. The new *Ordo* emphasized more the "Liturgy of the Word" and the homily while abbreviating the *Confiteor* and the Canon and eliminating the absolutions given by the priest to the faithful.

374. Paquier, "Luther," *D.T.C.*, 9–1e.:1306.

375. See the final paragraph of Chapter 5.

to have their eyes open to the danger of such slow marches of the Revolution.[376]
Paquier states:

> It was with these doctrinal and practical preoccupations that Luther
> reformed the Mass. Toward the end of 1523, he wrote, still in Latin, his
> *Brief Exposition of the Mass and Communion*. At the beginning of 1526,
> in German, *The German Mass and the Ordinary of the Service of God.* . . .
> The first mass in German was celebrated in Wittenberg on October 29,
> 1525.[377] In contemporary Lutheranism, this mass is preserved integrally.[378]

As readers will note, the Lutheran revolutionary process stalled somewhat, and
it became impossible for it to reach the ultimate consequences of Luther's ideas.
Indisputably, other sects and schools will later assume the responsibility of carrying on the march of the Revolution,[379] but we must emphasize here the stagnation
which detained Lutheranism in its journey. It was provoked above all by reactions
of a certain traditionalist origin that arose in Lutheran circles, especially due to the
energetic and salutary measures adopted by the Council of Trent.

This is one more history lesson, showing us how vigorous and uncompro-
mising Catholic reactions have great possibilities of success. It also demonstrates
the caution the pseudo-Reformers had to use to avoid the stagnation of the revolutionary processes they had unleashed. According to Paquier, "In general, the
Lutheran mass or supper was only celebrated on Sundays. Daily worship was
maintained, however, replacing the mass with a reading from the Bible followed
by a sermon, prayers, and the singing of psalms. Little by little, the feasts of the
Saints disappeared. In any case, there should only be an honorific reverence for the

---

376. See Corrêa de Oliveira, *Revolution and Counter-Revolution*, 24–25, 29–34, 96–100.
377. Note the extreme slowness of the liturgical reform carried out by Luther. The publication of
his Ninety-Five Theses on indulgences dates from 1517, and his condemnation by Leo X, from
1520. However, it was only in 1525 that he celebrated his first mass in German.
378. Paquier, "Luther," *D.T.C.*, 9–1e.:1306.
379. See Corrêa de Oliveira, *Revolution and Counter-Revolution*, 15–16, 24–25, 29–35.

Virgin and the other saints, which avoids seeing them as intercessors before God. It was also in this sense that their statues would be retained."[380]

After describing the modifications introduced by Luther into the liturgy of the other sacraments, Paquier makes an observation that also suggests curious parallels with contemporary events: "Those are the principal features of the nascent Lutheran worship. Many details remained vague, varying from year to year and city to neighboring city."[381]

To complete this section, we transcribe below a brief exposition by historian Jean Rilliet regarding Zwingli's liturgical reform:

> On Maundy Thursday, April 13, 1525, and on the following Good Friday and Easter Day, under the amazed arches of the Great Minster, divine service took place according to an absolutely new rite. The German language completely excluded the Latin of the liturgy. Choral music was absent. Only the voices of Zwingli and his two assistant priests could be heard at the entrance of the choir, reciting antiphonally texts taken from psalms or the creed. At certain moments the crowd which thronged the Cathedral church supported them by its responses: "God be praised, Amen," or again, kneeling, would recite with them the *Our Father*. The Lord's Supper supplanted the mass. . . .
>
> The elements of the holy meal were placed on an ordinary table. Zwingli officiated facing the congregation, instead of taking as in the Roman rite the eastward position. Assistant ministers then distributed the bread to the congregation who remained in their seats, each taking a piece and placing it in his mouth. The cup, carried round in the same way, then passed from one communicant to another. Zwingli insisted that the wine should be poured into wooden chalices, so as openly to reject any suggestion of pomp.

---

380. Paquier, "Luther," 9–1e.:1306. Note, in this last paragraph, how Luther only permitted images to be kept to not contradict profound desires of the people.

The 1969 *Institutio* has only one paragraph dedicated to the veneration of images, number 278. Please note that one does not encounter there a single word of encouragement for this veneration so praised by the Church, but only a permission, and that is fully focused on avoiding possible dangers from devotion to images:

> 278. In the sacred edifices, the images of Our Lord, the Blessed Virgin Mary and the Saints, according to the ancient tradition of the Church, are legitimately proposed for the veneration of the faithful. However, take care, on the one hand, that the number be not excessive and, on the other, that their disposition is made in due order, to not distract the attention of the faithful from the celebration itself (see Conc. Vat. II, Const. On the Sacred Liturgy S. C., no. 125). Let there not be more than one image of a given saint. In a general way, in the ornamentation and arrangement of the Church, try to favor the piety of the whole community. (1969 *Institutio*, no. 278, p. 65)

Does the phrase "let there not be more than one image of a given saint" also apply to Our Lady? Does the *Institutio* include her among the "saints," contrary to Church custom? The text is not clear. But the B.A.C. commentary interprets it in this anti-Marian sense: "neither is it appropriate to multiply images of the Virgin." Martín Patino, *Nuevas normas*, 257.

381. Paquier, "Luther," *D.T.C.*, 9–1e.:1307.

These sensational innovations met with little opposition. The facility with which the Church freed itself from an age-long tradition is amazing. For several years, those who upheld the ancient faith were authorized to go to church on Sundays in Aargau or Schwyz territory, at Dietikon, Baden, or Einsiedeln. There they found again sacerdotal vestments, incense, the Kyrie Eleison, the "Gloria," the confession, all of which had disappeared from the churches of Zurich.

When relations between the Confederate states grew strained, shortly after the adoption of the reformation in Berne in 1528, toleration came to an end.[382]

2. Luther's Temporizations

In the same *Dictionnaire de théologie catholique*, J. Rivière presents some other suggestive data about the liturgical innovations of the early Protestants:

> Grave disputes arose from the beginning among the Reformers about the meaning and value of the Eucharist. But all, Lutherans and Sacramentarians, agreed in denying the Mass the sacrificial character which Christianity had always recognized in it. . . .[383]
>
> . . . It was reserved for the German Reformation to simultaneously unleash the war against the Catholic Church and organize the communities conquered for the new Gospel. If the first task authorized the most complete doctrinal radicalism, the second demanded certain temporizations with inherited customs. The theoretical and practical position of Lutheran Churches regarding the Mass was affected by this double inspiration.[384]
>
> . . . All of his principles and passions as a reformer united in Luther to make him reject the traditional doctrine on the Mass. . . . Thus, this point is one of those against which he had to harden himself especially. His reason was that he felt that he did not merely stand up against a secondary point but the cornerstone of the Catholic stronghold.[385] "Having overthrown the Mass," he wrote in his work *Against King Henry of England* (1522), "I

---

382. Jean Rilliet, *Zwingli: Third Man of the Reformation*, trans. Harold Knight (Philadelphia The Westminster Press, 1964), 92–93.
383. Once again, one notes the dangers involved in any weakening of the sacrificial aspect of the Mass.
384. Is it not obvious that neomodernists find themselves in an analogous situation? How, then, can one judge their works only based on their seemingly traditional passages while ignoring the blatantly heterodox ones? Or, as some would have it, how can one deny the obvious meaning of their heterodox passages based on orthodox ones?
385. Luther had more than enough reasons to think this way. For, as Pius XII wrote, "The mystery of the most Holy Eucharist . . . is the culmination and center, as it were, of the Christian religion." Pius XII, *Mediator Dei*, no. 66.

believe we will have triumphed totally over the pope." . . . The importance of the situation easily explains the violence of the assault.[386]

A little later, J. Rivière emphasizes that one principle admitted by Luther before his break with the Catholic Church showed his future orientation:

> Luther did not allow the eucharistic communion to be separated from the words of God. . . .[387] ["For one should receive the Sacrament and the Gospel at the same time."] From that, he concluded, . . . ["Therefore it is not licit to celebrate the Mass without the Gospel: a private reading in a private Mass and a public "reading in a public Mass."] . . . But this still does not show that he already raised doubts about the reality of the sacrifice of the Mass.[388] . . .
>
> It is not necessary to insist on the fact that Luther at times gives the Mass the name of "sacrifice of praise." . . . For that very true aspect does not prevent the Mass from also being presented under other aspects, and the Reformer recognizes, in the same places, that the Mass acts "ex opere operato." However, he urges that one add personal sacrifice to it.[389]
>
> In a sermon in German about the Blessed Sacrament, printed in 1520 . . ., Luther still kept silent about the question of the sacrificial value of the Mass. . . .[390] But he was not going to wait long to express his opposition to this article of the Catholic faith.
>
> His conviction was already formed in the celebrated sermon about good works in 1520, . . . where he outlined it in a few words, announcing a greater development to come later. This was the object of a special sermon "about the New Testament, that is, about the Holy Mass,"[391] distributed in the same year. . . . The author sustains that to conceive the Mass as a sacrifice is "the worst of abuses," . . . that it is only a testament, i.e., a favor

---

386. J. Rivière, "La messe," in *D.T.C.*, 10–1e.:1085. The importance of the situation in which we find ourselves today, similar in so many ways to that of the Church in the first steps of Lutheran radicalization, explains our firmness in analyzing the new Ordinary of the Mass.

387. On the exaggerated emphasis on the "Liturgy of the Word" and on the neomodernist tendency to disallow Communion outside of the Mass, one may see, respectively, chap. 1, sec. 7 (*A Tendency to Make the "Liturgy of the Word" Equal to the "Eucharistic Liturgy"*), and Pius XII, *Mediator Dei*.

388. These steps in the process of Luther's apostasy seem extremely revealing regarding the generally slow and progressive march of schisms and heresies. This history lesson ought to be remembered by anyone wishing to accept the new *Ordo* because it retains numerous rubrics of the traditional Mass.

389. It is not strange, therefore, that neomodernist documents admit true doctrines side by side with heterodox ones, in frank contradiction, and at times in the same paragraph. Lutheranism, and in the main all heresy, is constrained to act this way for tactical and metaphysical reasons. See Chapter 2.

390. In the development of heresies, silencing a dogma usually precedes its explicit denial.

391. Note this identification between the Mass and the New Testament, as well as the explanation that follows. Here are the reasons alleged by Luther against the Offertory—which practically disappeared from the new *Ordo*.

received from God, not an offering made to God.[392] There is only sacrifice in the prayers of thanksgiving, which we direct to God in recognition of the blessings we receive from Him. Luther was referring to the early times when the faithful brought to the church gifts "in natura," which the priest blessed and over which he pronounced a eucharistic prayer. He sees a survival of this custom in the rite of the offertory. Except for this, nothing in the Mass indicates that it is a sacrifice.[393]

In the paragraphs which follow, J. Rivière expounds on the theory of Luther, which we have just analyzed,[394] about the non-sacrificial character of the Mass. Concluding this topic, he writes that, according to Luther, "Christ did not carry out a ritual act, but a meal; everything that was later added on to the simplicity of this first supper is no more than a ceremonial without value."[395]

Further on, J. Rivière observes that Luther "did not prohibit priests from celebrating, as long as they interpreted the formulae of the Missal in the sense of his theology of sacrifice, and that they did not have any other goal except to give communion to the faithful and pray for them."[396]

We shall close this item with a brief enumeration of other facts from the beginnings of Protestantism related by J. Rivière:

(1) In a letter addressed to Melanchthon on August 1, 1521, Luther proposed to never again celebrate a private Mass on his own initiative.[397]

(2) The Augustinians of the Wittenberg monastery, following in Luther's footsteps, introduced very serious modifications into the liturgy. They began to distribute Communion under both species, even prohibited Communion under just one, and abolished private Masses.[398]

---

392. We have already observed—see chap. 3, sec. 2 (*The New Concept of the Offertory*), item (3), contrasting the Offertories in the traditional Latin and New Masses—that, according to the B.A.C. commentators, in the Offertory of the new *Ordo*, one does not ask God that He accept our offerings. Rather, one praises God for the good things He has given us, which we now present to Him. It is difficult to sustain that this interpretation of the new Offertory is unfounded.

393. Rivière, "La messe," *D.T.C.*, 10–1e.:1086. **Translator's Note:** Rivière shows Luther's quotations in Latin. An English translation is provided [in square brackets] for the reader's convenience.

394. See footnote 364 and the text it supports.

395. Rivière, *D.T.C.*, 10–1e.:1086. It is not without foundation that numerous theologians today have seen as suspect the insistence of the new *Ordo* in affirming that the Mass is a supper—above all, given that such insistence has been accompanied by a marked de-emphasis on the sacrificial character of the Mass.

396. Rivière, 10–1e.:1087. Therefore, for a while, Luther found himself forced to tolerate the use of the traditional Mass, although he obliged his followers to interpret it in line with his heresies. It is impossible not to see a suggestive similarity between this Lutheran temporization and that adopted by today's neomodernists, who still see themselves forced to use, against their will, certain traditional expressions of the new *Ordo*, though interpreting them in the sense of their heterodox doctrines.

397. See Rivière, 10–1e.:1087.

398. See Rivière, 10–1e.:1087–88.

(3) Melanchthon, together with declaring himself in favor of Communion under both species, said that a private Mass "is nothing more than a mere sham, a pure act of theatre" (*"nisi merum ludibrium, mera scena"*).[399] He denied the sacrificial character of the Mass. He insisted on the principle of the universal priesthood, conflating the priesthood of the priest with that of the people.

(4) Luther also, in a work published in January 1522, "takes pains to show that Scripture does not know any priesthood, besides Christ's, in which all Christians participate equally."[400]

(5) About the doctrine on the Mass in the celebrated *Confession of Augsburg*, the first and principal symbol of faith for the Lutheran churches, Rivière writes:

> The Mass is the object of a long, although not very explicit exposition, in the *Confession of Augsburg*. . . .
>
> On no other point, perhaps, is the writing of this celebrated document so clever and tempered. The Mass does not figure in the first part, consecrated to the "principal articles of faith," but only in the second, among "the articles enumerating the abuses which have been eliminated." It comes after the questions of the communion of the faithful from the chalice and the marriage of priests. Evidently, this was calculated to have it understood that they were merely dealing with disciplinary matters.
>
> "The accusation against our Churches, that they have abolished the Mass, is false. For the Mass is preserved among us and is celebrated with great reverence." A comforting declaration! The scruple is carried to the point of proclaiming an almost complete liturgical conformism: "Almost all the customary ceremonies are preserved." The only difference is that songs in the vernacular were added to the Latin hymns, and nothing could be more natural and more beneficial than that. The people are then invited to communion, being prepared for it through pious instructions on the value of the sacrament. This worship is evidently carried out with the end of glorifying God and promoting the good of souls. Therefore, this slightly ironic conclusion: "For this reason, we do not see that Masses are celebrated with greater piety among our adversaries than among ourselves."[401]

---

399. Rivière, 10–1e.:1088. On placing the lay Catholic on the same footing as the priest in the reforms introduced by the new *Ordo*, see chap. 1, sec. 5 (*The President of the Assembly*) *supra*.
400. Rivière, 10–1e.:1088. The B.A.C. commentators defend a similar idea. See chap. 1, sec. 6 (*Jesus Christ, the Principal Priest [Sacerdos]*).
401. Rivière, 10–1e.:1089–90.

3. A Lutheran Work on the Liturgy

To complement the observations made so far about Luther's liturgical reforms, we shall now analyze certain elements furnished by Luther D. Reed's work *The Lutheran Liturgy*. The author, an American Lutheran pastor, published numerous books on the topic. He taught liturgy in the Lutheran Theological Seminary of Philadelphia for thirty-four years. He is one of the principal figures of a movement that has been trying to give some uniformity to the Lutheran liturgy in the United States for the last fifty years.

Since we have discussed the great doctrinal principles of the Lutheran liturgical reform, we shall only present some of Reed's observations in this regard. We shall pay special attention to his considerations of the liturgical order since they will furnish material to contrast the new *Ordo* and the Lutheran Supper.

We start with the repudiation of the notion of the Mass as a propitiatory sacrifice:

> The idea of *sacrifice* cannot be dissociated from the Sacrament, for the memorial which our Lord commanded his disciples to make centers in the thought of his body given and his blood shed for the salvation of men. All Christians recognize Christ's sacrifice on the cross as the only and all-sufficient sacrifice for sin. Where they differ is in their views concerning subjective aspects of sacrifice, and the manner and extent to which believers share in the sacrifice of Christ.
>
> We cannot compromise with pagan or Roman (rather than earlier Gallican) conceptions of the offering of material things and of our own human action as a propitiatory sacrifice. We do, however, recognize the eucharistic sacrifice of praise and thanksgiving. There are other ideas of sacrifice too, which, though valid, fell under suspicion in the violence of Reformation debate and the necessity of opposing the massive medieval belief in propitiatory sacrifice.[402]

We follow this with some general characteristics of Luther's liturgical reform:

> Luther's constructive efforts also definitely promoted vernacular services and active congregational participation in worship. He gave the sermon great importance, restored the chalice to all communicants, and greatly increased frequency of communion.[403]
>
> The Lutherans, in Germany and Scandinavia particularly, found in worship a new and significant possession in which all might share and rejoice. L. Fendt says: "Nowhere does the pulse [Blutwelle] of the Reformation beat so warmly as in its worship. Worship is the body in which Luther's spirit entered into the life of the people." When we understand

---

402. Reed, *The Lutheran Liturgy*, 256. On the negation of the propitiatory character of the Mass, see also pp. 55, 59, 107, and 339 in the same book.
403. Reed, 80.

worship as including within its framework not only the liturgy but extensive readings from Scripture, effective preaching, and a great development of congregational song and artistic choral music, we know that this is not an overstatement.[404]

We now consider the communal character of Lutheran worship:

> The medieval church destroyed the earlier unity and the sense of corporate worship by emphasizing the priestly class and by relieving the laity of active participation. The Reformation corrected this and reemphasized the priesthood of believers and the congregational character of worship. Masses without communicants were forbidden and actual communion by the people was promoted. The use of the vernacular, together with the development of hymnody and of popular preaching, were significant factors. THE WORLD-WIDE LITURGICAL MOVEMENT IN THE ROMAN CHURCH TODAY IS A BELATED EFFORT TO DEVELOP INTELLIGENT ACTIVE LAY PARTICIPATION IN THE MASS SO THAT THE PEOPLE MAY THINK OF THEMSELVES AS "CO-CELEBRANTS" WITH THE PRIEST.[405]

Now, for what Reed has to say on the Lutheran *Confiteor*, Offertory, and Canon: "The most radical reform of the liturgy made by Luther and his followers was the omission of the Offertory and Canon. Up to this point the outline of the medieval Mass was followed closely, and, except for the *Confiteor*, comparatively few changes were made in the text."[406]

Let us examine then with special attention the *Confiteor*, Offertory, and Canon of the Lutheran Supper.

A. The Lutheran "Confiteor"

In comparing the *Confiteor* of the new *Ordo missae* with that of the Lutherans, we should remember that the pseudo-Reformers had great difficulty writing a *Confiteor* that expressed their doctrines suitably. "Providing an evangelical form of confession was a slow and uneven procedure."[407]

The main reason for that difficulty was that all the known texts were of medieval composition. This being the case, the Reformers "could not use existing forms because of their doctrinal impurity."[408]

However, common characteristics between the *Confiteor* of the new *Ordo* and that of the Lutherans call our attention.

---

404. Reed, 107 (internal citations omitted).
405. Reed, 234. In the following paragraphs, Reed emphasizes the communal character of the worship according to Luther.
406. Reed, 334.
407. Reed, 258.
408. Reed, 257.

Luther Reed writes, "Recognizing the principle of the priesthood of all believers, the Confession was made a congregational instead of a priestly act."[409]

Accordingly, certain parts of the Lutheran *Confiteor* are said only by the minister. Others are dialogued between the minister and the people. Others, finally, are said jointly by the minister and the people.[410]

Similarly, in the new *Ordo missae,* the *Confiteor* has some parts said only by the priest, others that are dialogued with the people, and a *Confiteor* proper which is recited by the priest and the people jointly.

Justifying this way of proceeding, the Liturgical Commission's *Institutio* included the "penitential act" among the "parts which are very useful to manifest and favor the active participation of the faithful, and which are assigned to all the assembly" (no. 16). It is also placed among the rites "whose end is to bring it about that the gathered faithful constitute one community and dispose themselves to hear as they ought the word of God and to celebrate the Eucharist worthily" (no. 24). It emphasizes that "the penitential act" "is done by the whole community, through a general confession" (no. 29).[411]

In incisive terms, the B.A.C. commentators emphasize the communal character of the new "penitential rite":

> The purpose of the entrance ritual liturgy is to reveal the presence of God in the assembly, create a community of faith, and prepare it to hear the divine word and offer the sacrifice.
>
> In the context of the entrance, the penitential rite receives special emphasis and can be considered a novelty of the new *Ordo*, which prepares and disposes us for the celebration of the sacred mysteries.[412]

In Luther Reed's work, we read, "It [the Confession] was addressed [by the Reformers] to God alone, and all references to intercessions by the Virgin and the saints were omitted."[413]

The "penitential rite" of the new *Ordo* consists of three formulae, among which the priest will select the one he judges most opportune. The second and third do not contain any reference to Our Lady or the saints. The first, which is a bad copy of the traditional *Confiteor*, eliminates in the introductory part, that is, in the confession of sins, the reference "to Blessed Mary ever Virgin, to Blessed Michael the Archangel, to Blessed John the Baptist, to the Holy Apostles Peter and Paul, and to all the saints." In the final part, it keeps a laconic petition of intercession, "I ask blessed Mary, ever virgin, all the angels and saints. . . ."[414]

As is known, according to Protestant doctrine, the sins of men are not pardoned properly speaking through the merits of Christ and the practice of

---

409. Reed, 257. On the communal character of the initial rites in both the Lutheran Mass and the new *Ordo*, compare *Institutio*, nos. 7 and 24, and Reed, 252.
410. See Reed, 255–56.
411. 1969 *Institutio*, nos. 16, 24, 29, pp. 17, 19, 20.
412. Martín Patino, *Nuevas normas*, 34.
413. Reed, *The Lutheran Liturgy*, 257.
414. *New . . . Saint Joseph*, 14.

good works, but are only, as it were, covered over, in him who believes, by Our Lord's merits.

Although the Lutheran liturgy contains such expressions as "remission of sins," "penance," and "pardon,"[415] such terms must be interpreted according to Protestant doctrines. There are unmistakable signs this is the interpretation they accept: At the end of the Confession, the minister does not give the absolution but makes a so-called "Declaration of Grace."[416] In the liturgical text, there is no clear reference to the conversion of the sinner, but "believing in the name of Christ" is sufficient to make one a son of God.[417]

Also, the new *Ordo missae* keeps terms seemingly sufficient to express the Catholic doctrine on the remission of sins. It speaks of *penance, confession of sins, pardon, contrite hearts,* and so forth.

However, several innovations make one fear that these terms will be given meanings differing from the traditional ones, leading to a lessening of faith in certain dogmas touching on the forgiveness of sins.

Thus, the B.A.C. commentators attribute to the 1969 *Institutio*, in this regard, an intention frankly irreconcilable with Catholic doctrine. They say, "The following introductory admonition is proposed for the three formulae of the penitential act: 'Brethren, before celebrating the sacred mysteries, let us recognize our sins,' which is followed by a brief silence.[418] Prescribing this brief introductory admonition avoids the danger of anyone at this moment making a short homily to stir up sentiments of conversion."[419]

Note that, while the priest and the commentator may give numerous explanations and make various admonitions during the New Mass,[420] it is seen as a "danger" that the priest attempt to stir up "sentiments of conversion" before the *Confiteor.*

On the other hand, the new *Ordo* eliminated two prayers of the traditional Missal that clearly recall the Catholic principles on the forgiveness of sins:

(1) "May the almighty and merciful Lord grant us pardon, absolution, and remission of our sins. Amen."

(2) "Take away from us, we beseech Thee, O Lord, our iniquities, that we may be worthy to enter with pure minds into the holy of holies. Through Christ our Lord. Amen."

B. The Lutheran Offertory

In the early Church, the faithful carried their gifts to the altar at the moment of the Offertory. They symbolized in this way the giving of themselves to God while

415. See Reed, 255–56.
416. Reed, 259.
417. See Reed, 255–56.
418. Another small resemblance between the Lutheran liturgy and the new *Ordo missae* is that in both, the *Confiteor* is accompanied by brief silence for meditation on one's sins. Among the Lutherans, this silence comes after the Confession; in the new *Ordo*, it is before.
419. Martín Patino, *Nuevas normas*, 36.
420. See 1969 *Institutio*, nos. 11, 68a, pp. 16, 31.

simultaneously providing for the support of priests, the needs of the poor, and so forth.

Over time, this ceremony was enriched with magnificent prayers that expressed the sacrificial sense of the Mass and its propitiatory purpose, and in which we pray to God for the living and the dead. When the Offertory procession fell into disuse, these prayers remained, although they were evidently contrary to Luther's concepts on the purpose of the Mass.

Expounding on the Protestant attitude toward the Offertory, Reed writes:

> The offertory procession was continued in many localities until late in the Middle Ages. When it finally ceased its place was taken by a series of ceremonies and prayers of entirely different character. These developed as a sacerdotal function instead of an action of the people. They anticipated the consecration and the "miracle of the Mass"[421] and invoked the divine blessing in view of the eucharistic sacrifice to be offered.
>
> By the fourteenth century this so-called "little canon" included, besides the prayers, the mingling of the water with the wine, the offering of the host and of the chalice, the incensing of the altar and the elements, and the washing of hands. The Offertory prayers were of mixed origin, chiefly Gallican. They were admittedly of poorer quality than the prayers of the Canon which followed. The central prayer of the Offertory, *Suscipe sancte Pater*, is a perfect exposition of the Roman dictrine [*sic*] of the sacrifice of the Mass. . . .[422]
>
> All the Reformers rejected the Roman Offertory and its idea of a sin offering by the priest instead of a thank offering by the people. Luther, with his conviction of the Sacrament as a gift of God to man and not an offering of man to God,[423] called the Roman Offertory an "abomination" which made "everything sound and smell of oblation." "Repudiating all things which reek of sacrifice and of the Offertory, together with the entire

---

421. See footnote 187 for the sense in which there is in the Offertory a legitimate and praiseworthy anticipation of the true offering of Our Lord to God the Father, which will be made after the Consecration.

422. Reed is quite right on this point. If Luther and his followers rejected the Catholic Offertory so categorically, ultimately, it was not for historical reasons. Rather, it was due to the unmistakably priestly and propitiatory character of its main prayers. Proof of this is that Luther and his followers did not hesitate to introduce new prayers and ceremonies when there was a question of making their equally new concepts on the Mass evident. That is what happened, for example, with the prayers of the *Confiteor*, composed by the sixteenth-century pseudo-Reformers—see chap. 5, sec. 3, item A (*The Lutheran "Confiteor"*)—as well as with the novelties adopted in the "prayers of the faithful," so that they "stressed Lutheran ideas." Reed, *The Lutheran Liturgy,* 318. The same thing also occurred with Luther's repudiation of the sacrificial character of the Mass while recognizing its patristic origins.

423. As pointed out—chap. 3, sec. 2 (*The New Concept of the Offertory*), item (3), contrasting the Offertories in the traditional Latin and New Masses—in the new *Ordo*, according to the B.A.C. commentators, we no longer ask for God's blessing over the bread and wine, but praise Him for the bread and wine which He has given to us, and which we now present to Him. The Reed text cited here clearly shows the Lutheran character of this concept of the Offertory, which could appear orthodox to an incautious reader.

Canon [wrote Luther], let us retain those things which are pure and holy, and thus order our Mass" (*Formula Missae*, 1523).[424]

The new Offertory retains certain expressions which, at first sight, would seem to clash with Luther's doctrines on the forgiveness of sins and the Mass in general: *sacrifice, contrite heart, offering* of the bread and wine, and *wash me* of my iniquity.

However, a careful analysis of the texts reveals that those expressions are found in almost identical terms in the psalm verses and other Offertory texts of the Lutheran Mass:

> The sacrifices of God are a broken spirit: a broken and contrite heart, O God, thou wilt not despise. . . .
> Then shalt thou be pleased with the sacrifices of righteousness: with burnt-offering and whole burnt-offering. . . .
> I will offer to thee the sacrifice of thanksgiving. . . .
> Create in me a clean heart, O God [and so forth.][425]

The Lutherans reduced the Offertory to the presentation of the gifts of the people and the preparation of the bread and wine to be distributed in the communion.[426]

In the new *Ordo*, the Offertory also appears to be oriented in this direction. The Offertory procession, restored in many Lutheran communities,[427] emphasizes the part of the offering of the gifts by the people. The new name of the Offertory, "Preparation of the gifts,"[428] tries to introduce among Catholics the idea that, in this part of the Mass, the action of the priest consists essentially in "preparing" the bread and wine for its administration to the people, at the same time that certain prayers are recited or sung as a mere accompaniment.[429]

*   *   *

The "Prayer of the Church," also known as "Universal Prayer," "General Prayer," and "Prayer of the Faithful," is part of the Lutheran Offertory.

This part of the Mass, which had ceased to be used, was reintroduced before the Offertory by the Second Vatican Council[430] and is now presented by the *Institutio* as a prayer in which the people "exercise their priestly function" (no.

---

424. Reed, 312.
425. Reed, 310–11.
426. See Reed, 308ff.
427. See Reed, 309, 312.
428. 1969 *Institutio*, no. 49, p. 25.
429. Reed references Lutheran rubrics, stating:

> If there is to be a communion, the minister now prepares for the administration. . . .
> When there is a Communion, the Minister, after Silent Prayer, and during the singing of the Offertory, shall uncover the Vessels and reverently prepare for the Administration of the Holy Sacrament. (Reed, *The Lutheran Liturgy*, 310)

430. See *Sacrosanctum concilium*, no. 53.

45). The B.A.C. commentators also attribute great importance to this prayer, saying that "it is a priestly intercession of the people of God," "pertaining to the very structure of the celebration," "as one among several fixed, invariable, and mandatory elements."[431]

On the Prayer of the Faithful, Reed writes:

> It is one of the outstanding elements in the liturgy and probably the one above all others which illustrates the congregation's active exercise of its functions as a priesthood of believers. We instinctively feel that the principal service of the Lord's Day or festival could not be complete without some such lofty, pure, and acceptable form of prayer.[432]
>
> The Reformation restored this general church prayer to the Lutheran and the Anglican liturgies after it had degenerated in medieval times into a series of commemorations of the departed, invocation of the saints, etc., scattered through the Offertory and Canon.[433]

Both for Lutherans and the new *Ordo*, the Prayer of the Faithful asks God for religious and civil authorities, men of every condition, and the salvation of the world.[434] The Lutherans say it without interruption or with the following response of the people after each invocation: "We beseech thee to hear us, good Lord."[435] Following the post-conciliar reforms and the new *Ordo*, the people answer each invocation made by the priest with: "Lord, hear our prayer."

Referring to the Offertory and the Prayer of the Faithful in the Protestant liturgies, Reed writes, "Reformation developments thus restored to the Communion Service [that is, to the Mass] two important features of early Christian worship— the people's offering of gifts and the people's offering of praise and intercession."[436]

These elements are also found in the new *Ordo missae*.

C. The Lutheran Canon

Luther Reed writes:

> The lengthy prayers of the Roman Canon definitely interpret the Eucharist as a propitiatory sacrifice. They also include commemorations of the living and the dead, venerations of the Virgin, the apostles and the saints, prayers for the departed, etc. These all lead to an embellished form of the Words of Institution, of which recitation by the priest is supposed to secure the miraculous change of the elements into the very body and blood of Christ....

---

431. Martín Patino, *Nuevas normas*, 119.
432. Reed, *The Lutheran Liturgy*, 315.
433. Reed, 316.
434. See 1969 *Institutio*, nos. 45–46, pp. 23–24; Reed, *The Lutheran Liturgy*, 312ff.
435. Reed, 313.
436. Reed, 309.

Because the prayers of the Roman Canon, with their ceremonies
... were such truthful expositions of corrupt medieval doctrine, all the
Reformers denounced them. Many attempts were made to revise them in
an evangelical sense.[437]

In the Eucharistic Prayers of the new *Ordo,* the references to the Mass as a
propitiatory sacrifice[438] were weakened; the invocations to Our Lady, the apostles and saints were reduced;[439] the prayers for the departed were diminished;[440]
numerous acts of veneration and respect which the Protestants would classify as
"anti-evangelical embellishments": inclinations, blessings, genuflections, kisses,
etc.,[441] were suppressed.

After mentioning some less important reforms of the Canon made by Protestants, Reed writes:

Zwingli replaced the Canon by four prayers which led to the Verba.[442]
Calvin at Geneva developed an elaborate and heavily didactic Preface and
omitted practically everything of the ancient Canon. Archbishop Cranmer
in the English *Book of Common Prayer* (1549) reached out constructively
in an extended prayer of consecration which recast much of the Canon in
an evangelical sense and combined with it certain features from the Eastern
and other Western liturgies.

Luther was the most vehement of all the Reformers in denunciation of
the Canon. He characterized it as the "mangled and abominable Canon
gathered from every source of filth and corruption," and declared that it
changed the very nature of the Sacrament into "cursed idolatry and sac-
rilege." He said that by the silent repetition of the Verba "the devil has in
a masterly manner stolen from us the chief thing in the Mass and put it
to silence." Taking advantage of the fact that the Canon was said secretly,
he suggested that all that sounded of sacrifice could be omitted without
offense to the people inasmuch as they did not hear it. His *Formula Missae*
[text of the Mass in Latin] cut out everything in the Canon except the
Verba, which the minister was ordered to chant aloud. The Lord's Prayer
and the Pax followed immediately. In his German Mass he placed a para-
phrase of the Lord's Prayer first and followed this by the Verba.

This was Luther's most radical liturgical reform [of the Canon]. . . .
With a single bold stroke he completely changed the character of the

---

437. Reed, 339–40.
438. See chap. 1, sec. 3 (*A Propitiatory Sacrifice*).
439. See the text supported by footnote 221, the paragraph before the text supported by footnote
228, the new *Confiteor,* and so forth.
440. See the multi-paragraph commentaries on the faithful departed toward the end of chap. 3,
sec. 4 (*The New Eucharistic Prayers*).
441. See footnote 216, the text it supports, and paragraph.
442. The Protestants frequently call the formulae of the consecration "*Verba*" ("Words").

liturgy at this point. The Holy Communion became again a sacrament, or gift from God, instead of a sacrifice offered to God.[443]

In the new *Ordo*, the Canon came to be called the "Eucharistic Prayer," which is characterized as "a prayer of thanksgiving and sanctification."[444] The expression was common in early times. The term *Canon* is kept only for the first Eucharistic Prayer: the Roman Canon.

Reed writes, "EUCHARISTIC PRAYER: in the Lutheran use, the Prayer of Thanksgiving in the Holy Communion."[445] In what follows, he shows that he is dealing with a part corresponding to the Canon. Reed also reserves the term "Canon" for the Roman Canon, although he admits that historically it has a broader sense.[446]

An age-old controversy between Catholics and Protestants has to do with the moment of Consecration. Denying the transubstantiation, the latter have no motive to admit that Our Lord becomes present in the exact moment in which the words of Consecration are pronounced.

Charles M. Jacobs, a Lutheran author who is much respected in his sect, writes:

> The Real Presence of Christ with the bread and wine of the Eucharist presents no difficulties to faith. If we believe that Jesus died and rose again and is our living Lord and Savior, why should we not believe that He can be really present, where and as He will? If we believe that the Christ who now lives is the same Jesus who endured the suffering of the Cross, why should we doubt that His humanity, as well as His deity, is present in and with the Sacrament? If we believe that, in the Resurrection, Christ's human body was transformed, and became, in St. Paul's phrase, "a spiritual body," why should we stumble at the thought of a "bodily presence"? . . .
>
> We who believe in this Presence are sure that it is "real." It is not contingent upon the faith of those who receive or those who administer the Sacrament, but is for all alike, for believers and unbelievers, for the godly and the ungodly. It depends in no way upon our perception of it. But to those who are conscious of it, it becomes an additional assurance of the promise, which the Sacrament confers, "of forgiveness of sins, life and salvation." It belongs to the "sign" by which our faith is strengthened and increased.[447]

As readily seen, there is no place for transubstantiation in this mind frame, nor for determining a precise moment when Our Lord becomes present on the altar.

---

443. Reed, *The Lutheran Liturgy*, 340–41.
444. 1969 *Institutio*, no. 54, pp. 25–26.
445. Reed, *The Lutheran Liturgy*, 764. (All caps in the original.) See also Reed, 751.
446. See Reed, 761, 334ff.
447. Charles M. Jacobs, "The Ministry and the Sacraments," in *The Ministry and the Sacraments: Report of the Theological Commission Appointed by the Continuation Committee of the Faith and Order Movement*, ed. Roderic Dunkerley (London: Student Christian Movement Press 1937), 143–44; see Reed, *The Lutheran Liturgy*, 232.

Consequently, and as we have observed,[448] the Protestants deny what they call pejoratively the "miracle of the Mass" believed by Catholics. For identical reasons, Reed writes, "The Roman church shifted the emphasis from the offering and the thanksgiving to the consecration, and limited this latter to a precise moment."[449]

In consideration of these Protestant concepts, item 2, of no. 48 of the 1969 *Institutio,* and its respective B.A.C. commentary, take on a special gravity. It reads, "In the eucharistic prayer, thanks are given to God for the whole work of salvation, and the offerings become the Body and Blood of Christ."[450]

On this point, the B.A.C. commentators observe, "In item 2, it is said that in the eucharistic prayer the human bread is converted into the bread of Christ, and in this way the Church can unite herself to Jesus Christ, thus having the oblation, the true offering, the true sacrifice of the Church. It is the vertical and ascendant sense of the Christian life. Note the deliberate indetermination of the moment of conversion of the eucharistic species, to avoid entering into scholastic disquisitions about the precise instant in which the conversion is realized."[451]

Note, however, that while not entering into those scholastic disquisitions, they institute an *Ordo missae* that is acceptable to Lutherans and, above all, cast a veil of doubt over the dogma of transubstantiation.

Regarding the text of the consecration, Reed writes, "Luther in his Latin Service (1523), omitted several medieval embellishments and added the scriptural phrase, 'which is given for you' (also in the Mozarabic), after the words 'This is my Body.' The English *Book of Common Prayer* followed the Lutheran form."[452]

The 1969 Ordinary of the Mass also added the words "which will be given for you" ("*quod pro vobis tradetur*"—1 Cor. 11:24) to the consecratory formula "For this is My Body" ("*Hoc est enim corpus meum*").[453]

The *Institutio* establishes that the words of the Consecration be pronounced aloud (nos. 10, 12).

In his Latin and German masses, Luther also determined that these words should be said aloud.[454] This procedure, common among Protestants, still holds in present-day Lutheran liturgies.[455]

---

448. See footnotes 421 and 422 and the text they support.
449. Reed, *The Lutheran Liturgy*, 335.
450. 1969 *Institutio*, no. 48, item 2, p. 24. See this text quoted in chap. 1, sec. 1 (*The 1969* Institutio *and the Dogma of Transubstantiation*).
451. Martín Patino, *Nuevas normas*, 123–24.
452. Reed, *The Lutheran Liturgy*, 360.
453. There have been theologians according to whom the clause "which will be given for you" would be essential for the Consecration of the bread (see Pesch, *Praelectiones dogmaticae*, 6:772). This thesis is no longer defended today. It is to be feared, however, that on this point, once again, the 1969 *Institutio* furnishes an occasion to resuscitate old doubts about the essential form of the Consecration and the exact moment in which the transubstantiation occurs.
454. See Reed, *The Lutheran Liturgy*, 72, 78.
455. See Reed, 360; *Liturgia Luterana* (Porto Alegre: Casa Publicadora Concordia), 19, a publication authorized by the "Evangelical Lutheran Church of Brazil."

D. Other Aspects of the Lutheran Supper

Having made these observations regarding the *Confiteor*, Offertory, and Canon, it is fitting that we make additional comments about the Lutheran supper.

As we have seen,[456] the new *Ordo* greatly reduced the number of the Signs of the Cross made by the priest during the Mass.

In Reed's work, we read, "The church at the time of the Reformation reacted against the excessive and superstitious use of the sign of the cross which had characterized the late Middle Ages."[457]

In the traditional Catholic liturgy, the *Kyrie eleison* consists of nine invocations: three times *Kyrie eleison*, three times *Christe eleison*, and then again three times *Kyrie eleison*.

The new *Ordo* reduced these to six. As we have mentioned, each supplication is said once by the priest and repeated by the people.[458]

Among the Lutherans also, the *Kyrie* is said in six invocations.[459]

As seen,[460] in the 1969 *Institutio* from the Liturgical Commission, the Consecration was simply indicated by the words "Narration of the Institution." The Lutherans also use this expression. Thus, in enumerating the various parts of the Eucharistic Prayer, Reed says that one of these is the "narrative of Institution of the Sacrament."[461]

In another passage, he observes, "Luther rejected the entire Canon and retained only the scriptural narrative of the institution and the Lord's Prayer."[462]

Let no one say that for Lutherans, it is a question of a mere historical narration, while in the context of the *Institutio,* it is made clear that the bread and wine become the Body and Blood of Our Lord by these words. For the Lutherans also admit this, as long as one does not mean transubstantiation:

> The use of the Verba at this point is more than the recital of a historic event or the citation of authority to engage in this holy proceeding. It is a solemn, corporate act of prayer, an exalted liturgical celebration, in which the worshiping congregation apprehends and holds aloft the divine promises, claims the divine warrant and invokes the divine blessing. It becomes a vivid and exalted rite as the minister not only repeats our Lord's own words, but in a measure imitates his actions. In the scriptural narrative the actions are given importance equal to that of the words.[463]

Reed follows this passage with a quotation on the topic from *The Lutheran Cyclopedia*: "*The Words of Institution* are addressed to God. They are the warrant

---

456. See footnote 216 and the text it supports.
457. Reed, *The Lutheran Liturgy*, 254.
458. See footnote 180 and the text it supports.
459. See Reed, 271, 767.
460. See chap. 1, sec. 4 (*The "Narrative of the Institution"*).
461. Reed, 764.
462. Reed, 335. The expression "narrative of the institution" also appears on pages 337 and 357.
463. Reed, 360.

of the act in which we are engaged, and of the faith nourished by the sacrament, and they ask and receive from the Risen Lord the grace by which the Bread and Wine become to those who receive them his Body and his Blood."[464]

Further on, Luther Reed writes: "The consecration is completed by the administration, apart from which there is no sacrament."[465]

At every step, Reed admits that the Body and Blood of Our Lord are present in the communion.[466] It is in explaining the concept of transubstantiation that he really distinguishes himself from Catholics on this point: "TRANSUBSTANTIATION: the doctrine of the Roman Catholic Church which defines the method of the change in the elements at the consecration in the Mass: the substance of the bread and wine is changed into the substance of the body and blood of Christ—and thereafter only the "accidents" remain; the doctrine is specially [sic] repugnant to Protestant Christians."[467]

As one sees, the references of the 1969 Institutio to the Body and Blood of Christ[468] are absolutely insufficient to exclude any Protestant interpretation of how Our Lord is present in the Eucharist.[469]

Concerning the doctrine of the Real Presence, Reed writes: "By the Real Presence is understood the presence of the whole Christ in the Sacrament—the human as well as the divine Christ. The Lutheran denies as strongly as does the Calvinist the teaching of transubstantiation, but he believes as strongly as does the Roman Catholic in the Real Presence itself."[470]

Once more, then, the gravity of the complete omission from the 1969 text of the Institutio, not only of the term transubstantiation but even of the expression Real Presence, becomes clear.[471]

*   *   *

In the early Church, the formulae "the Body of Christ" and "the Blood of Christ" were used to distribute Communion. The people responded: "Amen." Later, other expressions were introduced.

---

464. E.T. Horn, "Liturgy," in The Lutheran Cyclopedia, ed. Henry Eyster Jacobs and John A.W. Haas (New York: Charles Scribner's Sons, 1911), 282; see Reed, The Lutheran Liturgy, 360.
465. Reed, 360.
466. See, for example, Reed, 132, 230ff., 360, 375ff. The same thing is admitted in various Lutheran Eucharistic Prayers cited by Reed: the "Pfalz-Neuberg Church Order, 1543" (753); "King John's Liturgy, Sweden, 1576" (753–54); "The First Prayer Book of King Edward VI, 1549" (754–55); "Agenda of the Lutheran Church in Bavaria, 1879" also adopted by the "Liturgy of the Joint Synod of Ohio" in 1884 (755–56); "Book of Worship of the Lutheran Churches in India, Guntur, 1936," (756–57); "Book of the Common Order of the Church of Scotland, 1940" (757–58); "The Order for Holy Communion of the Protestant Episcopal Church" of 1928 (725ff.).
467. Reed, 772. (All caps in the original.)
468. See chap. 1, sec. 1 (The 1969 Institutio and the Dogma of Transubstantiation).
469. For what the 1970 Institutio says regarding this particular, see chap. 4, sec. 9 (Number 7 of the 1970 Institutio).
470. Reed, The Lutheran Liturgy, 231.
471. See chap. 1, sec. 1 (The 1969 Institutio and the Dogma of Transubstantiation). On the manner in which these terms appear in the 1970 text, see chap. 4, sec. 1 (The Principal Features of the Foreword in the 1970 Institutio) and chap. 4, sec. 9 (Number 7 of the 1970 Institutio).

In his 1523 Mass in Latin, Luther retained the traditional formula—"May the Body of Our Lord Jesus Christ preserve your soul unto eternal life. Amen." "He gave no formula in his German Mass (1526)."[472] In this matter, there were variations among his followers. Various present-day Lutheran liturgies use the formulae introduced in the last few years among Catholics, which the new *Ordo* retains: "the Body of Christ" and "the Blood of Christ."[473]

* * *

There is among Protestants a general tendency to put the bread and chalice into the communicants' own hands. This practice, immediately adopted by Zwingli, became generalized later among the Anglicans and is permitted to Lutherans.[474]

The new *Ordo* does not authorize this practice. Nevertheless, it is becoming more and more prevalent in Catholic circles.

* * *

For a long time, Lutherans have been striving to obtain a certain uniformity in their liturgy. To justify that, they based themselves on the principle that, constituting one single Church, they should have one book of prayers, which is the same in each country: "one Church, one book."[475] But, together with one text adopted for all, they would also like that there be "ample room for differences in practice" within each "congregation."[476]

Without prejudice to the great liberty the *Institutio* grants bishops, priests, and even the simple faithful,[477] this basic uniformity of the liturgy in each country, subject to local variations, makes one think of the broad powers episcopal conferences currently enjoy in liturgical matters in the Catholic Church.[478]

---

472. Reed, 375.
473. Reed cites the "Common Liturgy" of American Lutherans, Swedish Lutherans, and the Augustana Church among Lutheran liturgies that adopt these formulae. Also included is "given for thee," an expression added by Luther, with precedents in certain oriental liturgies. See Reed, 375–76.
474. See Reed, 376. On Zwingli, see the text supported by footnote 382.
475. Reed, vii, 182, and others.
476. Reed, xi.
477. In the systematic index of the B.A.C. commentary, see the entries "*Conferencia episcopal*" and "*fieles.*"
478. See the text supported by footnote 375.

Chapter Six

The Infallibility of the Church in Liturgical Laws

The following objection can be made to our considerations about the New Mass: Since the principle that the Church is always infallible in its universal laws is commonly accepted among theologians, it is unlawful to even doubt the doctrinal purity of the 1969 *Ordo*. This question, which has been discussed frequently of late, either in connection with the New Mass or other subjects, leads us to examine the following problems in this Chapter 6:

—From the dogmatic and moral viewpoint, are the universal laws of the Church always guaranteed by infallibility?

—Would expressing doctrinal reservations about a universal ecclesiastical law not imply a denial of the infallible authority of the person who promulgated the law?

—Applying this to the case at hand: Can a true pope impose on the whole Church an *Ordo missae* susceptible to reservations in its dogmatic aspect?

—If, on the other hand, an ecclesiastical law only involves infallibility when it fulfills *certain conditions*, then has the 1969 *Ordo* fulfilled these conditions?

1. A Theologically Certain Thesis

To properly present the traditional thesis of infallibility in ecclesiastical laws, we must first insert it in its due place within the ensemble of theses on infallibility in the Church as studied in dogmatic theology.

Theologians customarily distinguish between direct and indirect objects of the infallible Magisterium.

They first demonstrate that the Church cannot err when she solemnly defines revealed truths, that is, truths of faith or morals that are formally contained in the deposit of Revelation, whether explicitly or implicitly. They constitute the direct and primary object of infallibility.

Then, the treatises go on to study infallibility as far as its indirect and secondary object is concerned. By this, they mean the truths which, although not formally revealed, are nevertheless so intimately connected with Revelation that they are necessary for the deposit of faith to be integrally preserved, duly explained, and effectively defined.[479]

Among the truths constituting the indirect object of infallibility are included:

(1) the philosophical presuppositions, or preambles of faith;

(2) theological conclusions, that is, truths deduced from two premises, of which only one is revealed;

(3) dogmatic facts, that is, those which have not been revealed but are necessarily connected with the exposition and preservation of the deposit of faith. For example, the legitimacy of an ecumenical council, the orthodoxy or heterodoxy of a particular book, the heroism of the virtues and eternal salvation of the saints who are presented for the veneration of the faithful;

(4) disciplinary decrees, among which theologians include liturgical laws;

(5) approval of the rules of religious orders.

To defend the traditional doctrine on the indirect object of infallibility, handbooks usually present a general thesis at the outset, wherein they demonstrate that the Magisterium enjoys infallibility regarding all truths which, although unrevealed, are nevertheless necessary to preserve the deposit of faith. This is proved both by documents of Tradition and by the argument that the Church would lack the indispensable means to accomplish her mission if she could not teach those truths infallibly. This general thesis is usually qualified as being, at least, *theologically certain*.[480]

Next, the treatises normally contain a special thesis for each category of truths constituting the indirect object of infallibility. This procedure is fully justifiable. In addition to the generic reasons applied to all categories, there are very different specific reasons justifying infallibility for each group. For example, special arguments may be adduced about the preambles of faith that are inapplicable to the

---

479. In this respect, one can see, for example, Iragui and Abarzuza, *Manuale theologiae dogmaticae*, 1:444ff.

480. Among those who consider it *theologically certain* are, for example, Hervé, *Manuale theologiae dogmaticae*, 1:500, and Auguste-Alexis Goupil, *L'Église: Insititution, constitution, pouvoir* (Laval–Mayenne: Goupil, 1946), 109. Other authors attribute to this thesis higher theological notes. Cardinal Billot considers it "a truth most certain in itself." Louis Billot, *De credibilitate ecclesiae, et de intima ejus constitutione*, vol. 1 of *Tractatus de ecclesia Christi* (Rome: Gregoriana, 1921), 1:394. Billot continues, citing Cardinal Franzelin: "It is so certain theologically that its negation would be a very grave error, or even, according to the opinion of the majority, heresy." [J.B. Franzelin, *Tractatus de divina traditione et scriptura* (Rome–Turin: Marietti, 1870), th. 12, sch. 1, 112]. Billot, *Tractatus de ecclesia*, 1:395. Salaverri judges it to be "at least theologically certain" and "proximate to the Faith in virtue of the [First] Council of the Vatican." Salaverri, *De ecclesia Christi* (no. 713), 1:742. Iragui classifies it as "at least theologically certain, or rather, proximate to the Faith." Iragui and Abarzuza, *Manuale theologiae dogmaticae*, 1:446.

disciplinary decrees or the approval of religious orders. Furthermore, infallibility in defining theological conclusions may be demonstrated with arguments that, for instance, would not be valid for the canonization of saints.

Concerning the *theological note* attributable to each of these specific theses, there is some diversity among the theological writers. However, they are unanimous in holding that there is no doubt about the abovementioned theses. Here are some examples:

(a) The thesis concerning *theological conclusions* is considered "theologically certain" by Hervé[481] and Van Noort,[482] and "at least certain" by Tanquerey.[483] Pesch qualifies it as follows: "at least a theological conclusion, which is not only recognized by the theologians as certain but which has also been approved and confirmed, although not defined, by the doctrine and practice of the ecclesiastical authority."[484]

(b) The thesis about *dogmatic facts* is declared "theologically certain" by Hervé,[485] Van Noort,[486] and Diekamp;[487] and "certain" by Tanquerey.[488]

(c) The thesis on the *canonization of the saints*, taken by many theologians as a separate study, is qualified as "common and certain doctrine" by Hervé;[489] as "common opinion today" by Van Noort;[490] and as a "common and true opinion" by Tanquerey.[491] Pesch writes on it, saying: "The judgments of the theologians concerning the certainty of this doctrine differ considerably because according to some of them it is "pious," and according to others it is of faith (see Benedict XIV, *De servorum Dei*, 1:45). More commonly they think that it is theologically certain, and we ought to abide by this judgment."[492]

Benedict XIV makes the following pronouncement on this matter:

> We would qualify the person who dared to affirm that the sovereign pontiff had erred in this canonization or the other and that any saint whatsoever canonized by him should not be honored by dulia worship, if not as a heretic, then as temerarious; as a scandal to all the Church; offensive to the saints; a favorer of the heretics who deny the authority of the Church to

481. Hervé, *Manuale theologiae dogmaticae*, 1:502.
482. G. Van Noort, *Christ's Church*, vol. 2 of *Dogmatic Theology*, trans. rev. John J. Castelot and William R. Murphy (Westminster, Md.: The Newman Press, 1959), 111.
483. Tanquerey, *Synopsis theologiae dogmaticae*, 1:920.
484. Christian Pesch, *Compendium theologiae dogmaticae* (Freiburg: B. Herder, 1921), 1:247.
485. Hervé, *Manuale theologiae dogmaticae*, 1:506.
486. Van Noort, *Christ's Church*, 112.
487. Diekamp and Hoffman, *Theologiae dogmaticae manuale*, 1:76.
488. Tanquerey, *Synopsis theologiae dogmaticae*, 1:622. On the distinction between a proposition that is "certain" and one that is "theologically certain," see Sisto Cartechini, *Dall'opinione al domma* (Rome: Editoriale Civiltà Cattolica, 1953), 8.
489. Hervé, *Manuale theologiae dogmaticae*, 1:507.
490. Van Noort, *Christ's Church*, 117.
491. Tanquerey, *Synopsis theologiae dogmaticae*, 1:624.
492. Christian Pesch, *Compendium theologiae dogmaticae* (Freiburg: B. Herder, 1921), 1:256.

canonize saints; as having a savor of heresy, for he would open the way for the infidels to mock the faithful; as a defender of erroneous propositions, and as being subject to the gravest penalties.[493]

(d) The thesis about *disciplinary decrees*, which include liturgical ones, is declared "theologically certain" by Hervé,[494] Van Noort,[495] Tanquerey,[496] and Pesch.[497]

(e) The thesis about the decrees approving rules of *religious orders* is considered "theologically certain" by Hervé,[498] Van Noort,[499] Tanquerey,[500] and d'Herbigny.[501]

*   *   *

As is obvious, we do not intend to study the problem of infallibility in all of the abovementioned aspects, but will only deal with the liturgical element. Since, as stated, dogmatic theology usually groups liturgical dispositions among disciplinary decrees when dealing with infallibility, it is not appropriate for us to study them separately right away. Thus, in the following items,[502] we shall consider the liturgical[503] and disciplinary laws simultaneously and strictly. Then, in the topic expounding what we judge to be the solution to the problem we are dealing with,[504] we shall restrict our attention exclusively to the liturgy. Furthermore, we believe the conclusions reached regarding the liturgy will be equally valid, in their basic lines, for disciplinary decrees in the strict sense.

We shall refer to the approval of religious orders, canonizations, and beatifications only to the extent indispensable to present our theme.

2. The Church Is Infallible in Matters of Discipline and Liturgy

We shall adduce some documents to show that the thesis on the infallibility of the Church in disciplinary laws has solid support in Tradition.

To facilitate the understanding of the texts, it is appropriate to make some general observations first:

---

493. Benedict XIV, *De servorum Dei beatificatione, et sanctorum canonizatione*, in vol. 1 of *Opera omnia* (Venice: Remondini, 1767), book 1, chap. 45, no. 28.
494. Hervé, *Manuale theologiae dogmaticae*, 1:508.
495. Van Noort, *Christ's Church*, 114.
496. Tanquerey, *Synopsis theologiae dogmaticae*, 1:625.
497. Pesch, *Compendium theologiae*, 1:254.
498. Hervé, *Manuale theologiae dogmaticae*, 1:509.
499. Van Noort, *Christ's Church*, 116.
500. Tanquerey, *Synopsis theologiae dogmaticae*, 1:625.
501. Michel d'Herbigny, *Theologica de ecclesia* (Paris: Beauchesne, 1921), 2:303.
502. Up to the end of chap. 6, sec. 4 (*Hesitations and Restrictive Expressions in Testimonies of Tradition*).
503. In this matter, when the expressions *liturgical laws*, *liturgy*, or similar ones are used, they indicate determinations of the Church concerning all that is prescribed for public worship: texts of prayers, rubrics, ceremonies, acts, gestures, objects, and so forth.
504. See chap. 6, sec. 5 (*Conditions Under Which Liturgical Laws Involve Infallibility*), *infra*.

(1) The thesis on the infallibility of the Church in disciplinary decrees applies only to decrees promulgated for the universal Church because all recognize there may be an error in an individual case. Here, the universal Church is equivalent to the Latin rite, which, besides representing the largest part of the Catholic world, is proper to the Roman See, Head of All the Churches. For the same reason, in the specifically liturgical field, the universal liturgy is equivalent to the Roman one.

(2) All authors affirm that infallibility extends only to matters of faith and morals. Thus, in the Breviary lessons, the facts reported in the biographies of the saints are not guaranteed by infallibility. What is guaranteed is the moral doctrine contained in those facts.

(3) The thesis deals with infallibility only regarding the doctrine explicitly or implicitly contained in everything that the law prescribes—acts, words, attitudes, and so forth; or, in the strictly liturgical field: prayers, ceremonies, rubrics, gestures, objects, and the like. The thesis, however, does not deal with whether the law is opportune or fitting, for it is known that there may be errors in universal ecclesiastic laws as far as these prudential aspects are concerned.

(4) The thesis does not affirm, by any means, that the law must be the most perfect possible, nor that it ought to contain implicitly all the doctrine about the point in question. Rather, it deals only with the non-existence in what the law prescribes of any implicit or explicit error in matters of faith and morals

Having made these preliminary observations, we can now proceed with the study of some documents of Tradition, which at least seem to affirm or presume the thesis that the Church is always infallible in its universal laws, both strictly disciplinary and liturgical.

(a) **Saint Augustine** wrote, "But the Church of God that is situated amid much straw and many weeds tolerates many things, and yet she does not approve, does not pass over in silence, and does not do those things that are opposed to the faith or a morally good life."[505]

In another work, the bishop of Hippo expressed himself as follows: "'So what then?' somebody says. 'Does an infant too need a liberator? Certainly it does. . . . The proof is its mother the Church receiving the baby to be washed clean. . . . Who would dare to take the stand against such a mother?"[506]

(b) The **Sixteenth Council of Carthage**, held in 418, teaches that even the just need God's forgiveness, and to demonstrate this principle, it uses a liturgical

---

505. St. Augustine, "Letter 55," in *Letters 1–99*, vol. 1 in *The Works of Saint Augustine: A Translation for the 21st Century*, ed. John E. Rotelle, O.S.A., trans. Roland Teske, S.J. (Hyde Park, N.Y.: New City Press, 2001), 234.
506. St. Augustine, "Sermon 293," no. 10, in *Sermons 273-305A*, vol. 8 in *The Works of Saint Augustine: A Translation for the 21st Century*, trans. Edmund Hill, O.P., ed. John E. Rotelle, O.S.A. (Hyde Park, N.Y.: New City Press, 1994), 155.

argument. The Council observes that the just also must say, "Forgive us our trespasses," and that in this prayer, they ask for grace, not only for others but also for themselves. Now, this being the official meaning of the prayer of the Church, it is inadmissible that the just should pray in this manner out of simple humility, but lying to God. The Council argues, "For who would tolerate one praying and lying, not to men, but to the Lord himself, who says with his lips that he wishes to be forgiven, and in his heart holds that he does not have debts to be forgiven?"[507]

(c) The *Indiculus*—Annexed to a letter of Pope Saint Celestine I (d. 432), there used to appear the famous "Indiculus on the Grace of God," in which semi-Pelagian errors are refuted and condemned. Nowadays, we know that this document was not written by Saint Celestine I.[508] Its authority, however, continues to be enormous because various subsequent popes explicitly or implicitly approved it.

Showing that the Pelagians had against them the unanimous Tradition of the Church, the *Indiculus* says, "Besides these hallowed ordinances of the most blessed and Apostolic See . . . let us be mindful also of the sacraments of priestly public prayer, which, handed down by the Apostles, are uniformly celebrated in the whole world and in every Catholic Church, in order that the law of supplication may support the law of believing."[509]

The final part of this text was later transformed into a theological adage: "*Lex orandi lex credendi*" ("The law of prayer is the law of faith"). With variations in its formulation but substantially identical meanings, this axiom was also used in recent years by Pius IX, Pius XI, Pius XII and Paul VI.

Further along in the text, referring to the ceremonies of baptism, for example, the exorcisms and breathings by the priest upon the person being baptized, expressing the expulsion of the devil, the "Indiculus" declares that such practices are not an idle spectacle for us; therefore, what they express is true.[510]

(d) **Saint Thomas** taught, "The custom of the Church has very great authority and ought to be jealously observed in all things."[511]

The Angelic Doctor frequently uses liturgical arguments to demonstrate his theses. We give one example. To prove that the transubstantiation of the bread happens before that of the wine, he recalls that the Host is presented for the adoration of the faithful immediately after its consecration. "Otherwise, the priest would sin immediately after the words of the consecration by showing an unconsecrated host to the people to be adored, unless the body of Christ were already there; because he would be inducing the people to idolatry."[512]

---

507. Sixteenth Council of Carthage, can. 8, Denz.-Sch., 230; Denz.-Umb., 108. On this document, see Fr. Manuel Pinto, S.J., *O valor teológico da liturgia* (Braga: Livraria Cruz, 1952), 191.
508. The *Indiculus* is attributed today to Prosper of Aquitaine; see Denz.-Sch., 238.
509. *Indiculus*, cap. 8, Denz.-Sch., 246, Denz.-Umb., 139.
510. See *Indiculus*, cap. 9, Denz.-Sch., 247, Denz.-Umb., 140
511. *Summa Theologica*, II–II, 10, 12, c.
512. St. Thomas Aquinas, *Commentary on the First Epistle to the Corinthians*, trans. Fr. Fabian Larcher, O.P., isidore.co/aquinas/SS1Cor.htm#116, 11:25, no. 673.

(e) The **Council of Trent** often used liturgical arguments to justify its decisions. Thus it is that in canon 4 about the sacrament of Holy Orders, we read, "If anyone says that by sacred ordination, the Holy Spirit is not imparted, and that therefore THE BISHOPS SAY IN VAIN: 'RECEIVE YE THE HOLY SPIRIT' . . . let him be anathema."[513]

In the decree on the veneration of the relics and images of the saints, the Council approved the traditional practices as being "in accordance with THE USAGE OF THE CATHOLIC AND APOSTOLIC CHURCH, received from primeval times of the Christian religion, and with the consensus of opinion of the holy Fathers and the decrees of sacred Councils."[514]

Still regarding the relics and images of the saints, the Council of Trent condemned "those who affirm that veneration and honor are not due to the relics of the saints, or that these and other memorials are HONORED BY THE FAITHFUL WITHOUT PROFIT, and that the places dedicated to the memory of the saints for the purpose of obtaining their help are visited IN VAIN."[515]

(f) **Sixtus V** declared, "The sacred rites and ceremonies . . . contain great teachings for the Christian people and a profession of true faith."[516]

(g) **Saint Robert Bellarmine**, in his opinion, read in the Sacred Congregation of the Holy Office, in the presence of the pope, about the possible definition of the dogma of the Immaculate Conception, stated: "If a formal definition is not made now, then it should at least be prescribed for all the secular and regular ecclesiastics that they should recite the Office of the Immaculate Conception, as the Church does: for thus, without any definition, we would obtain what is desired."[517]

(h) **Pius VI**, in the bull *Auctorem fidei*, which condemned the Jansenist Synod of Pistoia, used numerous arguments based on the legislation and practice of the Church. Here we reproduce some of them:

> As if the Church, which is ruled by the Spirit of God, could have established discipline which is not only useless and burdensome for Christian liberty to endure, but which is even dangerous and harmful and leading to superstition and materialism.[518]

---

513. Denz.-Sch., 1774, Denz.-Umb., 964.
514. Denz.-Sch., 1821, Denz.-Umb., 984.
515. Denz.-Sch., 1822, Denz.-Umb., 985.
516. Sixtus V, apostolic constitution *Immensa aeterni Dei* (Jan. 22, 1587), in vol. 2 of *Bullarium romanum*, Cherubinorum edition (Rome: Ex Typographia Rev. Camerae Apostolicae, 1638), 2:465.
517. Quoted in Philippus Oppenheim, O.P., *Principia theologiae liturgicae*, vol. 7 of *Institutiones systematico-historicae in sacram liturgiam* (Turin: Marietti, 1947), 107, and Pinto, *O valor teológico*, 297.
518. Denz.-Sch., 2678, Denz.-Umb., 1578.

> As if the present order of the liturgy, received and approved by the
> Church, had emanated in some part from forgetfulness of the principles
> by which it should be regulated.[519]

Pius VI also condemned the proposition of the Council of Pistoia, according to which "the institution of new feasts derived its origin from neglect in the observance of the older feasts, and from false notions of the nature and end of these solemnities."[520]

(i) **Dublanchy** expressed himself as follows in the *Dictionnaire de théologie catholique*:

> The infallibility of the Church ought to be extended to all dogmatic
> or moral teaching which, in the practical order, is included in what is
> IMPOSED, APPROVED, OR AUTHORIZED by *the general discipline
> of the Church.* . . .
>   This is the rigorous consequence of the teaching of the New Testament. For the infallibility which Jesus Christ guaranteed to his Church
> . . . APPLICABLE TO ALL TEACHING really and effectively given
> by the ecclesiastical magisterium, ought also to be applied to all teaching
> necessarily included in the laws, practices, or customs ESTABLISHED,
> APPROVED, OR AUTHORIZED by the universal Church since this
> practical or indirect teaching is, above all, since it is an authority which is
> in itself infallible, as real and efficacious as the direct doctrinal teaching.[521]

This passage of Dublanchy appears to merit special attention because, as we shall see, many theologians want to restrict infallibility to disciplinary decisions which *impose* the practice of an act. Now, if the Church has, in her universal legislation, absolute infallibility, without any distinctions, we do not see how this infallibility can be restricted to her preceptive pronouncements—for *to approve* or *to authorize positively* certain actions can be as important, for morality, as to impose others. The true solution does not lie in distinguishing the preceptive decrees from those which are not, but rather, as we shall show further on, in establishing the *conditions* in which the Church is infallible in its decrees in general.[522]

(j) **Haegy**, in his *Manuel de liturgie et cérémonial*, wrote, "The acts of the liturgy have dogmatic value; they are the expression of the worship of God in the Church. Now, the exterior manifestation of worship has an intimate relation with faith. To be rational, worship cannot fail to be in accordance with faith."[523]

---

519. Denz.-Sch., 2633, Denz.-Umb., 1533.
520. Denz.-Sch., 2673, Denz.-Umb., 1573.
521. Dublanchy, "Église," in *D.T.C.*, 4:2197.
522. These conditions are presented in chap. 6, sec. 5 (*Conditions Under Which Liturgical Laws Involve Infallibility*), *infra*.
523. Joseph Haegy, *Manuel de liturgie et cérémonial selon le rite romain*, rev. 11th ed. (Paris: Librairie Victor Lecoffre, 1922), 1:2.

(k) **Pius XI** declared, in the apostolic constitution *Divini cultus*, that, through the liturgy, "we proclaim our faith."[524] Further, in the papal bull *Inter multiplices*, the same pontiff taught, "The missals . . . have always been considered of great importance as monuments of Christian piety and remote antiquity, in which the Church affirms her living faith."[525]

(l) **Wernz and Vidal**: "The Roman Pontiffs are infallible in making *universal* laws about the ecclesiastical discipline, in such a way that they might never establish anything against faith and morals, even though they do not reach the supreme degree of prudence."[526]

(m) **Pius XII**, referring to the sacred liturgy, wrote, "The integrity of faith and morals ought to be the special criterion of this sacred science, which must conform exactly to what the Church out of the abundance of her wisdom teaches and prescribes."[527]

3. A Thesis to Be Considered in Its Nuances

As we have seen, the thesis that the disciplinary and liturgical decrees promulgated for the universal Church are always guaranteed by infallibility seems to have the full support of Tradition.

However, before we go on to ask if there are testimonies to the contrary within Tradition, it seems that one can and should doubt that the thesis of infallibility in the disciplinary and liturgical decrees has the amplitude that certain theologians judge they can attribute to it.

Indeed, the studies carried out during the last hundred years have made it clear that even in their direct and expressly doctrinal pronouncements for the universal Church, the pope and the council are not necessarily infallible. This affirmation is based on the fact that the pope and the council can use their magisterial authority to a greater or lesser degree as they consider opportune in each specific case.

Now, one could ask, if even in its universal scope, the Magisterium does not always apply its infallibility to specific doctrinal pronouncements, why should it do so in pronouncements that only indirectly and implicitly involve doctrine? If, when they teach *ex professo* on matters of faith and morals, the pope and the council do not always wish to define infallibly, it is difficult to sustain that they always want to do so when teaching in a merely indirect and implicit manner.

Moreover, the study of the history of the liturgy—including the Roman one—raises serious doubts about the necessarily infallible character of Church

---

524. Pius XI, apostolic constitution *Divini cultus* (Dec. 20, 1928).
525. Pius XI, bull *Inter multiplices* (Dec. 6, 1924), in *Missale bracarense* (Rome: Typis Polyglottis Vaticanis, 1924).
526. Franciscus Xavier Wernz and Petrus Vidal, *Ius canonicum* (Rome: Gregoriana, vol. 1, 1938; vol. 2, 1923; vol. 7, 1937), 2:410; see also 1:278.
527. Pius XII, *Mediator Dei*, no. 9.

decisions regarding her official worship. For example, it is not easy to explain, given the natural meaning of the words, certain texts referring to the Assumption, the Sacrament of Holy Orders, prayers for the dead, and the "consecration of wine by contact."[528]

It does, however, seem legitimate to ask if a phenomenon similar to what happened with the explicitly doctrinal teachings may not have also occurred with the implicitly doctrinal ones. Regarding the explicitly doctrinal teachings, one frequently finds in ancient authors, and even recent ones, the unqualified affirmation, generally made only in passing, that these *always* involve infallibility, as long as they are directed to the universal Church. However, we also find in Church practice and authors of all centuries testimonies to the contrary, that is, documents that introduce important nuances and limitations into the thesis. Based on these last documents, it was possible to show, without breaking with Tradition, that, in fact, the direct doctrinal teachings of the universal Magisterium only involve infallibility to the degree that there is the intention of using it.

Could not something similar have happened with the thesis of the infallibility of the Church in matters of discipline, liturgy, and the like? To answer this question, it is necessary to check Catholic Tradition, for it is never lawful for a son of the Church to reason contrary to Tradition in matters revealed or necessarily connected with Revelation.

Now, once we have examined Tradition, a certain ambiguity and imprecision are noted around the thesis of infallibility in the implicitly doctrinal teachings. Even authors who affirm it absolutely in one passage place an unexpected restriction, an equivocal term, or a sign of hesitation in others.

This is what we desire to prove next.

4. Hesitations and Restrictive Expressions in Testimonies of Tradition

To guide the reader in the examination of the texts we are going to present, we would like to point out, from the start, that the principal hesitations and restrictive expressions concerning infallibility in ecclesiastical laws can be reduced to three points:

(1) Certain authors seem to restrict infallibility in the subject we are studying to laws that "impose," "prescribe," or "make obligatory" a certain act.[529] When reading these theologians, we would say that infallibility is not involved

---

528. These points—some of which are highly delicate—are discussed further on: the Assumption (text supported by footnotes 570, 638, and 652); Holy Orders (text supported by footnotes 579–82); prayers for the dead (text supported by footnotes 577–78); and "consecration by contact" (text supported by footnotes 583–84).
529. That is what we shall see further on in the texts of Cano, Pesch, Hurter, Lercher, Hervé, Cartechini, and Iragui.

in laws that only recommend, insinuate, or positively permit the practice of a certain act.[530]

(2) In other texts, infallibility in the ecclesiastical laws seems to be restricted to what constitutes "serious matter," "mortal sin," or that could bring "grave detriment" to the universal Church.[531] This being the case, one is inclined to ask if universal laws regarding light matters are excluded from the scope of infallibility.

(3) Other theologians declare that infallibility is only involved in universal laws in which the pope pronounces "solemnly," "in a definitive manner," or "with his supreme authority," or when the legal disposition becomes "settled and stable."[532] Such expressions seem to signify that infallibility is only involved in a law when, in one way or another, for intrinsic or extrinsic reasons, the pope or the Church express their intention of teaching infallibly the doctrinal truth which the given legal disposition implies.

*   *   *

As we shall see,[533] these hesitations and restrictive expressions are explained by the fact that only in recent times have the *conditions* under which the Church or the pope are infallible in disciplinary decrees been formulated satisfactorily.

This being established, let us now examine the texts. They are all post-sixteenth century since Melchior Cano[534] was the first theologian to enunciate the thesis of infallibility in ecclesiastical laws explicitly and *ex professo*.

(a) **Melchior Cano** wrote, "In making laws for the whole people IN GRAVE MATTERS and those which INFLUENCE NOTABLY in forming Christian customs, the Church can ORDAIN nothing contrary to the Gospel or natural law.[535]

(b) **Suárez**, pointing out one of the reasons that papal infallibility is involved in the approval of the rules of religious orders, observed, "The pontiff cannot err, in matters of morals, WITH GRAVE DAMAGE to the universal Church; now, the error referred to, would be of this type."[536]

In the same order of ideas, he wrote a little further on, "By the very fact of a religious order having been approved, it is declared that to profess this state of

---

530. See our observations about this matter in the paragraph supported by footnote 522, commenting on the passage from Dublanchy.

531. See the citations from Cano, Suárez, Cartechini, and Iragui.

532. See the texts of Dom Guéranger, Bouix, Pius IX, Pesch, Lercher, Hervé, and Goupil to this effect.

533. See chap. 6, sec. 5 (*Conditions Under Which Liturgical Laws Involve Infallibility*).

534. "Cano (d. 1560) is the first to express this principle, implicitly admitted by medieval theologians and Church Fathers." Dublanchy, "Église," in *D.T.C.*, 4:2185.

535. Melchior Cano, O.P., *De locis theologicis*, in *Opera* (Venice: Bassani, 1776), book 5, chap. 5, concl. 2, 124.

536. Suárez, *De religione*, in vol. 15 of *Opera omnia* (Paris: Vivès, 1859), lib. 2, cap. 17, no. 18, 212.

life is to embrace the evangelical counsels. Therefore, the contrary error would be VERY PERNICIOUS IN THE CHURCH. Therefore, even here, there is no lack of assistance from the Holy Spirit, so such error is not introduced into the Church."[537]

(c) The Spanish Jesuit, **Fr. Gabriel Vasquez** (d. 1604), resolving a difficulty about the possibility of error in the Roman liturgy, expressed the following opinion: "Furthermore, somebody may answer that, concerning the essence and substance of the sacraments, the Church always approves, by words and acts, a doctrine which is certain and not subject to doubts; but, in that which deals with other things, which are accidental, she sometimes does something following in practice an opinion which is not entirely certain, but probable, in as much as it has not been positively declared a dogma of the Faith."[538]

(d) Fr. **Francisco Antonio Zaccaria**, an eighteenth-century Jesuit (d. 1795),[539] may be considered "the first writer of a treatise, although partial, on the theological value of the Liturgy."[540] In his work *De usu librorum liturgicorum in rebus theologicis*, after defending the theological authority of the books mentioned above, he established principles such as the following:

> **Canon III.** That which appears in the Liturgy should be taken in its true and proper sense, UNLESS THERE IS SOMETHING CONTRARY TO THIS.[541]

> **Canon VII.** If a text in the liturgical books seems obscure or to contain a DOCTRINE WHICH IS NOT CAREFULLY EXPRESSED, then it must be explained in the light of other passages in the same book.[542]

(e) Studying the various senses that Tradition may have, **Dom Guéranger** wrote, "The second state of *Tradition* is that in which it is *professed* by the Church,

---

537. Suárez, *De religione*, no. 21, 213.
538. Gabriel Vasquez, S.J., *Disputationibus de eucharistia, & missae sacrificio*, vol. 3 in *Commentariorum ac disputationum in tertiam partem sancti Thomae* (London: Pillehote, 1620), disp. 227, cap. 3, no. 22, 451.
539. Francisco Antonio Zaccaria, S.J., *De usu librorum liturgicorum in rebus theologicis* in *Theologiae cursus completus* (Paris: J.P. Migne, 1860), 5:207–310. Fr. Zaccaria was a great defender of the papacy against the attacks of the Jansenists. About him, we read in the *D.T.C.*: "Saint Alphonsus Liguori cites him with the greatest eulogies. At Saint Alphonsus's request, Zaccaria composed an *Introductory Dissertation on the Origins, Places, and Importance of Casuistic Theology*, which the holy Doctor inserted into his *Teologia moralis*." J.P. Grausem, "Zaccaria, François-Antoine," *D.T.C.*, 15–2e.:3644.
540. Pinto, *O valor teológico*, 300. Before Zaccaria, many popes, Church Fathers, Doctors, and theologians frequently used liturgical arguments to demonstrate theological theses, but they never systematically studied the exact measure in which infallibility is involved in the liturgical dispositions. As it is easy to perceive, this gap noted among the ancients is, in great part, at the root of the confusion that today still hangs over this important theme.
541. Zaccaria, *De usu librorum*, 5:286.
542. Zaccaria, 5:298.

in the formulae which she uses, as the Church; in the usages and customs which she FOLLOWS AND IMPOSES WITH AUTHORITY, either as an EXPRESSION OF HER BELIEF or as a RULE OF MORALS. In this second state, *Tradition* is guaranteed by the authority of God, who could not permit that the Church *indirectly* teach error."[543]

(f) The French canonist **Marie Dominique Bouix** (d. 1870) ardently defended the thesis that the liturgy cannot err when it *clearly* enunciates a doctrine. Even here, one notes some limitation of the principle of infallibility in liturgical matters, in that the field remains open for *unclear* expressions that insinuate error, favor heresy, and so forth.

Bouix, however, was radical in his assertions. Trying to refute Vasquez, who accepted infallibility in what is essential to the sacraments but doubted it concerning accidental matters,[544] he argued:

> I confess that with such a doctrine, if it were true, the dogmatic value of the liturgy would be destroyed; . . . for, accepting this distinction referred to, I could not conclude from the liturgy the truth of any dogma, unless it were previously made clear to me that the dogma deals with something *essential.* This, however, could not be made clear to me through the liturgy itself, BUT ONLY FROM SOME OTHER PLACE. Therefore, using only the liturgy, one could not conclude the truth of any doctrine which refers either to the *essential* or to the *accidental.*[545]

Bouix considers this consequence to be contrary to the teachings of Saint Augustine and Tradition in general. However, a little further on, he was obliged to recognize that reasons taken "from some other place" can be necessary to evaluate the dogmatic sense of the liturgical text. In reality, when explaining how the Immaculate Conception could have been celebrated throughout the whole Church for several centuries—since before the time of Suárez (d. 1617)—without involving infallibility, Bouix indicated the special meaning which he attributes to the term *clear*:

> To refute the doctrine we uphold on the dogmatic value of the liturgy with the referred-to fact, it would have been necessary for the liturgy at the time of Suárez to have *clearly* expressed the dogma of the Immaculate Conception. Now, the liturgy of that time did not yet express this dogma *clearly.* The Holy See had indeed approved an office and feast celebrating the abovementioned privilege of the Mother of God, but at the same time declared that it did not approve, by that concession, the opinion favoring that privilege, except as being the most likely: "The very pontiff who

---

543. Prosper Guéranger, O.S.B., *Nouvelle défense des institutions liturgiques—II partie: Deuxième lettre à monseigneur l'évêque d'Orléans* (Le Mans: Fleuriot, 1846), 2ⁿᵈ part, 7.
544. We cite this passage from Vasquez in the text supported by footnote 538.
545. Marie Dominique Bouix, *Tractatus de jure liturgico* (Paris: Ruffet, 1873), 47.

approved that feast—says Suárez—declared that he only approved that opinion as being pious and more probable." And although the words of the office then granted roughly indicated Our Lady's preservation from all stain of original sin, THE SAID DECLARATION HINDERED THEM FROM EXPRESSING THAT DOGMA *CLEARLY*. THAT PUBLIC DECLARATION SO RESTRICTED THEIR SENSE that those words were not allowed in the liturgy except with the disclaimer that that opinion was pious and most probable, but not entirely certain.[546]

Therefore, Bouix found himself obliged to admit that in the study of the theological value of the liturgy, one cannot ignore elements that do not appear in the liturgical books.

This being the case, it is necessary to see, in all its nuances and theological rigor, each of the terms of the following proposition enunciated by Bouix: "When the Church MANIFESTS, EXPRESSES, AND PROFESSES what she BELIEVES in, she cannot ERR, neither in great nor in small things."[547]

(g) **Pius IX**, in the papal bull *Ineffabilis Deus*, in which he defined the Immaculate Conception, wrote, "But since the things which belong to external veneration are clearly, by an intimate connection, coupled with the object of the same, and that those cannot continue settled and stable, if the object be fluctuating and floating in the region of doubt, our predecessors the Roman pontiffs, wishing with all care to enlarge and extend the public devotion in honor of the Conception, devoted themselves accordingly with all possible pains to declare its object, and to inculcate the precise doctrine."[548]

Note, therefore, that even that which belongs to worship—and by the context, it is clear that Pius IX is dealing with universal worship—cannot become settled and stable, that is, it is not infallibly proposed, as long as its object is dogmatically doubtful and ambiguous.[549]

(h) **Pesch**, dealing with infallibility in disciplinary decrees, says that the Church cannot "ORDAIN for all the faithful, THROUGH HER SUPREME AUTHORITY, something contrary to faith and morals."[550]

---

546. Bouix, *Tractatus de jure*, 51–52.
547. Bouix, 48.
548. In Latin: "Quoniam vero quae ad cultum pertinent, intimo plane vinculo cum ejusdem objecto conserta sunt, neque rata et fixa manere possunt, si illud anceps sit et in ambiguo versetur, idcirco Decessores Nostri Romani Pontifices omni cura Conceptionis cultum amplificantes, illius etiam objectum ac doctrinam declarare et inculcare, impensissime studuerunt." Pius IX, bull *Ineffabilis Deus* (Dec. 8, 1854), in *The Bull 'Ineffabilis' in Four Languages; on The Immaculate Conception of the Most Blessed Virgin Mary*, ed. and trans. Ulick J. Bourke, 4–83 (Dublin: John Mullany, 1868), 18–21.
549. We cite the commentary Fr. Manuel Pinto, S.J. made on this passage from Pius IX in the text supported by footnote 634.
550. Pesch, *Praelectiones dogmaticae*, (no. 542), 1:328.

(i) **Hurter:** "The Church cannot approve a general and OBLIGATORY discipline for all, which is contrary to faith or morals, or which redounds in grave damage to religion."[551]

(j) **Lercher**, as soon as he expounds the general thesis[552] about the secondary object of infallibility, writes, "The PEREMPTORY judgment of the Church in matters that are connected with the Faith in this way (and the DEFINITIVE condemnation of the opposite error) is infallible."[553]

A little further on, while dealing specifically with disciplinary decrees, Lercher adds, "We refer to the decrees whereby a certain norm of life is PRESCRIBED, for the *universal* Church, BY HER SUPREME POWER, through a law which is in itself stable."[554]

Immediately after, we read that the Church would not attain her end "If she could, BY HER OWN SUPREME POWER, OBLIGE all the faithful to a norm of life which was not in agreement with the true faith and good morals."[555]

(k) **Hervé** observes that the Church "would *cease* to be *holy*" and, therefore, "would cease to be the true Church of Christ" if "she COMMANDED all the faithful, USING HER SUPREME AUTHORITY, something contrary to faith and morals."[556]

(l) In his well-known course of theology in French, **Goupil** teaches, "It is certain that the Church cannot fall into error when she SOLEMNLY approves a devotion, a feast, and a doctrine implicit in this feast."[557]

Commenting next on the axiom "the rule of prayer is the rule of faith," he writes:

> This does not mean that everything in the liturgy is infallible truth. One could say, in general, that this axiom APPLIES MORE TO DOCTRINE than facts. The historical fact will often be rather the occasion than the direct object of worship. The formulae indicate as much: "It is said that," "It is reported that," etc. It is equally necessary to distinguish between the feasts of the universal Church and those which are only local, as also AMONG THE SEVERAL PARTS OF THE LITURGY. Thus, in the Mass, the Canon is certainly free from error;[558] the text of the Masses has more authority than that of the Breviary; the historical information of the

551. Hugo Hurter, *Theologiae dogmaticae compendium*, (Innsbruck, Austria: Wagneriana, 1883), no. 385, 1:271.
552. See chap. 6, sec. 1 (*A Theologically Certain Thesis*).
553. Lercher, *Institutiones theologiae*, no. 504, 1:300.
554. Lercher, no. 510, 1:304.
555. Lercher, no. 510 (a), 1:304.
556. Hervé, *Manuale theologiae dogmaticae*, 1:508.
557. Goupil, *L'Église*, 112.
558. The author refers to the traditional Roman Canon, which the Council of Trent defined as free from all error.

Breviary and the Martyrology is less certain. It is as necessary to distinguish theologically what is taught infallibly or not as it would be incorrect, on the other hand, to think that where the Church has not brought her infallibility into play, one is free to doubt her teachings or even reject them; this would not be heresy, but rather rashness and disrespect. Therefore, although DISTINGUISHING THE VARIOUS DEGREES OF CERTAINTY, one will accept filially the pious customs and traditions that the Church approves, and one will have, at the same time, the disposition to correct any errors which may be found there.[559]

(m) Justifying the principle of infallibility in disciplinary decrees, **Cartechini** writes, "If the Church were to include MORTAL SIN in her laws, SHE WOULD oblige men to lose eternal life."[560]

To restrict the argument only to mortal sins causes some perplexity, the more so because the author goes on to establish an absolute principle: "In the *Code of Canon Law*, there can be nothing which is opposed IN ANY WAY whatsoever to the laws of faith and the holiness of the Gospel."[561]

A few lines further on, however, we find another restrictive expression: "In the *Code*, in as much as the Church TEACHES some practical and speculative truths as being contained in the deposit of Revelation, and in as much as she explains and proposes them IN AN OBLIGATORY WAY, it cannot be denied that some dogmas are clearly expressed."[562]

(n) Arguing in favor of infallibility in disciplinary laws, **Iragui** observed, "If the Church should IMPOSE a false doctrine in her decrees which are universally OBLIGATORY, then the true faith and customs would be GRAVELY damaged, people would be led away from salvation, and her very condition as the true Church would be endangered."[563]

(o) **Liturgical Feasts**—In finishing the item dealing with the hesitations and limitations we find in the traditional doctrine on infallibility in ecclesiastical laws, it is necessary to present some considerations about the liturgical veneration of Our Lady, the saints, and the blessed.

As all admit, the simple inclusion of a name in the Roman Martyrology, without a formal declaration by the pope that the person is a saint, does not involve infallibility. In ancient times, many names were thus included in the Martyrology and are still there today. Now, the Roman Martyrology is a liturgical book and one of morally universal use.

---

559. Goupil, *L'Église*, 112.
560. Cartechini, *Dall'opinione*, 48.
561. Cartechini, 48.
562. Cartechini, 48.
563. Iragui and Abarzuza, *Manuale theologiae dogmaticae*, 1:453.

This being the case, one may ask, "How do we know that infallibility is not involved in simply including a name in the Martyrology?" The matter is certainly connected with Revelation because it refers to the canonization of saints.

The solution is that theologians explicitly affirm that infallibility is not involved since the Church has no intention of declaring saints those whose names are only included in the Martyrology.[564] Therefore, the following *conclusion* imposes itself: Here is one more restriction, in traditional theology, of infallibility in liturgical matters.

Another important limitation is found in the doctrine related to beatifications. As is generally recognized,[565] these do not involve infallibility. For this same reason, the veneration of a beatified person is not, in principle, extended to the whole Church. However, at least in the abstract, it is admitted that a beatified person may receive universal veneration without this meaning that the infallibility of the Church guarantees his sanctity. This is what Benedict XIV, for example, affirms when he cites and agrees with Dominique de la Sainte-Trinité (d. 1687), who stated:

> The Church may celebrate a feast in two ways: First, with her absolutely positive judgment or universal assent about the sanctity of the person whose feast is celebrated. Second, by mere concession or permission, without such judgment or assent. When the feast is celebrated in the first manner, as is the case in canonization, one can deduce someone's sanctity with perfect assurance. . . . However, that does not occur if the feast is celebrated only in the second manner, which simply means that celebration is not censurable. . . . This happens in beatification, in which there is no definitive judgment by the Church but only her permission, NOT ALWAYS [EXTENDED TO] THE UNIVERSAL CHURCH. . . . EVEN IF THE UNIVERSAL CHURCH CELEBRATES the feast of a beatified person, AND THERE IS A SPECIFIC DECLARATION NOT TO CONDEMN THE OPPOSITE OPINION—AS HAPPENS IN THE CELEBRATION OF THE FEAST OF THE IMMACULATE CONCEPTION—one cannot deduce with absolute certainty from a solemnity accompanied by such declaration, the sanctity of the person whose feast is being celebrated.[566]

This doctrine will be better understood if one keeps in mind the following: Infallibility in the canonization of a saint does not stem from his liturgical worship having been imposed on the universal Church—an imposition which is not always made—but from the pope's intention when declaring solemnly and

---

564. See Benedict XIV, *De servorum Dei*, book 1, chap. 43, no. 14, 147; Pesch, *Praelectiones dogmaticae*, 1:332; Hervé, *Manuale theologiae dogmaticae*, 1:507.
565. See G. Van Noort, *Tractatus de ecclesia Christi* (Bussum, Netherlands: Brand, 1954), 107 Goupil, *L'Église*, 112; d'Herbigny, *Theologica de ecclesia*, 2:109.
566. Dominicus a Sanctissima Trinitate, *Tractatus de summo pontifice romano*, in vol. 10 of *Biblioth. Pontif.*, 496, quoted by Benedict XIV, *De servorum Dei*, 143.

definitively that the saint is in eternal glory and constitutes a model of virtue for all the faithful. This is Benedict XIV's explanation: "The ultimate difference between beatification and canonization must by no means be based either on the permission for his veneration or on its limitation to particular persons and places—which in beatification is different than in canonization—but rather on the ultimate and definitive pronouncement on the sanctity, that pronouncement which ordains by canonization the veneration due in the universal Church to some saints, while it absolutely does not ordain it in beatification."[567]

In the same order of ideas, Pesch observes that the universal obligation to venerate a saint is not necessarily concerned with his liturgical cult, but signifies that "all the faithful are obliged to consider him, as undoubtedly a saint, that is, worthy, as such, of public veneration."[568]

In the above-cited text of Dominique de la Sainte-Trinité, there is a most enlightening reference to the Feast of the Immaculate Conception, and we must say a word about it. In 1708, Clement XI extended this solemnity to the whole Church. Would this act involve the infallibility of the Church regarding that sublime prerogative of Our Lady? No. As Benedict XIV observed, after indicating various constitutions in which the popes praised the Immaculate Conception, this was because

> up to the present time, there has appeared no definition of the Church about the Immaculate Conception of the Virgin, and the Roman pontiffs themselves, in the abovementioned constitutions, declared that by the concessions which were made they by no means desired to decide the question. Theophilus Raynaud himself, and, with him, Natal (Alexandre) . . . deduce that the cult, the feast, and everything else which has been approved in honor of the Virgin as having been preserved from Original Sin in her Conception, absolutely do not result in that preservation (from Original Sin) being held as certain, as a matter of Faith.[569]

Based on the absence, in those times, of a dogmatic definition of the Assumption, Benedict XIV shows that neither might one deduce from the liturgical feast that the elevation of Our Lady, body and soul to heaven, is a truth of faith. Further, he emphasizes that that was the common opinion of the theologians.[570]

Along the same line, the following commentary made by X. Le Bachelet in connection with the papal bull extending the Feast of the Immaculate Conception to the whole Church is also significant: "Therefore, the supreme pontiff extended, in an imperative manner, the feast of the Immaculate Conception to the entire Church. Thence arises the importance of his act; for, according to the commonly accepted principles, the extension of a feast to the whole Church . . . involved the

---

567. Benedict XIV, book 1, chap. 39, no. 14, 124.
568. Pesch, *Praelectiones dogmaticae*, (no. 547), 1:331.
569. Benedict XIV, *De servorum Dei*, book 1, chap. 42, no. 14, 143.
570. See Benedict XIV, book 1, chap. 42, no. 15, 143.

certainty of its object: not a certainty of divine faith but A CERTAINTY OF THE MORAL ORDER."[571]

* * *

Given the documents of Tradition we have just presented, it becomes clear that it is not possible, without further considerations, to affirm that the disciplinary and liturgical decrees promulgated for the universal Church are always guaranteed by infallibility. Rather, it is necessary to study the *conditions* that would give them such a guarantee if fulfilled. Only thus will one be able to come to a conclusion having the due distinctions, which would fully correspond to the teaching of the Church about this important matter.

In the following item, we shall try to investigate the conditions of infallibility in ecclesiastical laws, relying on the more in-depth studies that have been made recently.

5. Conditions Under Which Liturgical Laws Involve Infallibility

During the last decades, aiming above all at combating Modernism and neomodernism, numerous traditional theologians have been paying special attention to the problem of the infallibility of the sovereign pontiff and the Church. Besides this, the doctrinal authority of the liturgy has been the object of profound studies having the goal of giving new precision to the traditional principles in this matter. Thus, certain truths, which the ancient authors accepted only in an implicit and obscure manner, are being explained and justified more and more. As we shall see in the following pages, these recent studies show that both liturgical and directly doctrinal texts only involve infallibility when they fulfill well-defined and precise conditions.

As indicated, taking this topic as a starting point, we shall base our argument exclusively upon liturgical grounds[572] so as not to find ourselves obliged to extend our considerations farther than necessary.

A. Msgr. Camillus Callewaert

In his treatise *De sacra liturgia universim*, the illustrious Belgian liturgiologist Camillus Callewaert (d. 1943) writes:

> The argument taken from the liturgy *proves with full certainty* the truth of a doctrine of the faith, IF BY THIS MEANS—as is demanded of any argument within the dogmatic tradition—IT IS SEEN THAT THE CHURCH MORALLY AS A WHOLE, at some time ACCEPTED OR PROFESSED such a doctrine as belonging WITH CERTAINTY to

---

571. X. Le Bachelet, "Immaculée Conception," in *D.T.C.*, 7–1e.:1186.
572. See the last two paragraphs of chap. 6, sec. 1 (*A Theologically Certain Thesis*).

the DEPOSIT OF FAITH. For it is impossible that the whole Church err in this matter.

Such a condition can be fulfilled—and this is not rare—more easily in the liturgical documents than in the writing of the Holy Fathers.... Finally, BY THE MANNER AND FREQUENCY OF THE TESTIMONY, BY THE NATURE OF THE RITE in which it is expressed, and BY THE IMPORTANCE OF THE DOCTRINE ITSELF, it may be made manifest, in a way leaving no room for doubt, that the Church professes such a doctrine as belonging to the deposit of faith. And thus, by how the Church commands us to pray, it can SOMETIMES be deduced with full certainty what ought to be believed.[573]

B. Fr. Philippus Oppenheim, O.S.B.

In his highly esteemed liturgy manual, Fr. Philippus Oppenheim, O.S.B., dedicates a special volume (vol. 7) to the "principles of liturgical theology."

We are giving special attention to this work because, as Fr. Manuel Pinto, S.J. rightly observes,[574] it constitutes a compilation of what the most ancient authors wrote about the subject.

While defending with the greatest zeal the thesis that "the Liturgy of the Church expresses the faith and doctrine of the Church,"[575] Oppenheim shows that infallibility is not always involved in liturgical texts, even in those of the Roman rite. He states:

> In the Church, the persuasion that there is an intimate relationship between liturgy and faith, and even that the law which orders public worship establishes the law of faith, is most ancient and firm. This affirmation is well-known to many. Few, however, really know the genuine and original meaning of this axiom, on what grounds it is based, and if, as far as divine worship is concerned, it can be accepted really and as fully lawful, in a general manner and without any exception or limit, or whether, on the other hand, it ought to be restricted to certain cases and conditions.[576]

To establish the exact outlines of the doctrine of infallibility in liturgical material, the author cites and analyzes several texts of the Roman liturgy which contain or insinuate errors. Here are some examples:

(1) in the Offertory of the Mass for the dead and the liturgy for the day of death (the prayer *Deus cui proprium est*), prayers are found that express eschatolog-

---

573. C. Callewaert, *De sacra liturgia universim*, vol. 1 of *Liturgicae institutiones* (Bruges: Beyaert, 1944), 44.
574. See Pinto, *O valor teológico*, 7. We analyze this book in chap. 6, sec. 5 (*Conditions Under Which Liturgical Laws Involve Infallibility*), item C *infra*.
575. Oppenheim, *Principia theologiae*, 8.
576. Oppenheim, 77.

ical dogmas in a less perfect manner,[577] seeming to insinuate that the Church prays that the damned should be taken out of hell, or that those who died in a state of mortal sin should not be cast into hell.[578]

(2) In the Roman Pontifical, there was a rubric instructing the bishop administrating the sacrament of Holy Orders to present to each ordinand "successively a chalice, containing wine and water, and a paten upon it, with a host."[579] In light of the principle of the infallibility of the Church in liturgical matters, a naive consideration of this rubric could lead one to think that in it, the following dogma is indirectly defined: The priestly character is imparted in the bestowal of the instruments on the ordinand. However, even at the time when Oppenheim wrote his book, it was generally recognized that the matter of the sacrament of Holy Orders is the imposition of the hands, not the bestowal of the instruments. At that time, the Holy See itself, through a Roman Congregation,[580] had already made a pronouncement to this effect. Later, Pius XII defined this truth,[581] and the Sacred Congregation of Rites had the abovementioned rubric removed from the Roman Pontifical.[582]

---

577. Oppenheim, 117.
578. On the interpretations traditionally given to these prayers, see Pesch, *Praelectiones dogmaticae*, 9:300–301.
579. Lynch, *The Rite of Ordination*, 65. [**Translator's note:** The Roman Pontifical also says that in presenting the chalice and paten, the ordinant states, "Receive power to offer sacrifice to God and to celebrate Mass, as well for the living as for the dead, in the name of the Lord." The ordinand responds, "Amen."]
580. See Oppenheim, *Principia theologiae*, 121.
581. See Pius XII, apostolic constitution *Sacramentum ordinis* (Nov. 30, 1947—on the sacrament of Holy Orders), no. 4.
582. See A.A.S., 1950, 449. Oppenheim's explanation (*Principia theologiae*, 121) of why the aforementioned rubric appears in the Roman Pontifical does not seem satisfactory. According to him, even supposing that the instruments' bestowal was not the matter of Holy Orders, the Church would not have erred "in respect to something which touches the faith interiorly" since, as the rite included the imposition of hands, the sacrament did not become invalid. Indeed, in this hypothesis, the sacrament undoubtedly did not become invalid because the bishop not only bestowed the instruments but made the imposition of hands. But would such a rubric not establish a "false" principle in a question of dogmatic theology, namely, what the matter of a sacrament is, as Oppenheim seems to concede a little earlier?
   As we shall see further on—chap. 6, sec. 5 (*Conditions Under Which Liturgical Laws Involve Infallibility*), item C *infra*—the true explanation for the fact is provided by authors after Oppenheim, such as Fr. Manuel Pinto, S.J. They show that a liturgical law only involves infallibility when, considered in its context and circumstances, it becomes obvious that it contains an irreformable definition, that is, that the Church wished to use this means to teach a doctrine infallibly. We shall study this matter further on—see chap. 6, sec. 5 (*Conditions Under Which Liturgical Laws Involve Infallibility*), items C (from footnote 620 on) and D (from footnote 647 on) *infra*. Regarding the matter of Holy Orders, the Church always considered this an open question until Pius XII. Church-approved theologians disputed freely in this respect, dividing themselves into various schools. This clearly shows that the Holy See did not intend to make an irreformable definition when it introduced the abovementioned rubric into the Roman Pontifical.
   Moreover, it is appropriate to note that the difficulty this rubric created cannot be resolved on the grounds that, as some argue, the bestowal of the instruments was the matter of Holy Orders before the apostolic constitution *Sacramentum ordinis*. While Pius XII did not condemn this thesis, and it may be defended, few today consider it probable. This notwithstanding, in no way did it constitute a *dogma of faith*, as anyone refusing to consider the thesis of infallibility in liturgical laws with its proper nuances would have to admit.

(3) On the well-known subject of "consecration by contact," Oppenheim writes:

> According to a rubric in thirteenth-century Roman pontificals, uncon-
> secrated wine is transubstantiated into the Blood of Christ on contact
> with the consecrated Host. A dogmatically *certain* conclusion may not
> be deduced from this rubric for the same reason mentioned above (in
> the matter of Holy Orders). The case in question is about the rite of com-
> munion for the sick, according to which the consecrated Host is dipped
> into the wine and then given to the sick person. Now, whoever receives
> Communion under this rite, really and truly receives Christ, although
> only under the species of Bread, and does not lose any grace necessary for
> salvation.[583] The case would be different if it affected the true reception of
> the Sacrament.[584]

Oppenheim is quite right in observing that infallibility is fully involved in liturgical dispositions affecting the very validity of the sacraments. Thus, it is known that Extreme Unction is validly administered if given with a single anointing on the forehead, for the *Code of Canon Law* permits that the priest proceed in this manner if necessary.[585] It is known that the physical and simulta-neous presence on the altar of the two consecrated species is not required for the validity of the sacrifice of the Mass, for under extraordinary circumstances, this presence is not required.[586] Yet further examples of the same principle are given by Oppenheim.[587]

Among the author's conclusions in his study of this topic, we highlight those concerning the distinctions to be kept in mind when accepting the thesis of the infallibility of the Church in the approval of liturgical texts.

Among the necessary conditions for a liturgical text to be used as a *certain* argument in favor of a dogmatic thesis, Oppenheim lists the following: that the text enunciate a particular truth in a *univocal manner*.[588] The reason for this con-dition seems evident, for nothing can be deduced *with certainty* from a vague or

---

583. In a footnote, Oppenheim indicates the Tridentine definition of the full value of Commu-nion under one species: Section 21, chap. 3.

584. Oppenheim, *Principia theologiae*, 121–22. Here, too, Oppenheim's argumentation appears incomplete. He explains appropriately that the Church did not deprive a sick person of the graces she promised to give, but he fails to explain how the Church could permit that the faithful be induced to material idolatry by adoring unconsecrated wine. A different and complementary explanation becomes necessary, i.e., although presented in a liturgical text, the principle of "conse-cration by contact" was not taught as a truth of faith.

There is no room for a more detailed analysis of this question. On the historical aspect of the "consecration by contact," see Michel Andrieu, *Immixtio et consecratio: La consécration par contact dans les documents liturgiques de moyen âge* (Paris: Picard, 1924).

585. See 1917 CIC, can. 947, p. 330. See Oppenheim, *Principia theologiae*, 119–20.

586. See *De defectibus in celebratione missae occurrentibus*, 4:4–5; Oppenheim, *Principia theolo-giae*, 119.

587. See Oppenheim, *Principia theologiae*, 119–22.

588. See Oppenheim, 116.

ambiguous phrase. However, this condition becomes richer and more precise as Oppenheim adds: "This *univocality* may result from either a declaration of the Church, according to which a given text must be explained in a certain way, or because of the common explanation from theologians."[589]

As one sees, internal criteria such as grammatical and semantic analyses of the text and context are insufficient to prove this univocality. One must also appeal to external criteria such as an explicit declaration of the Magisterium on the significance of the liturgical text in question or a morally unanimous interpretation of theologians. We are thus getting close to the principle that the mere fact of appearing in all liturgies, or only in the Roman Liturgy, does not guarantee a text with the infallibility of the Church. That prerogative can only be attributed to it based on declarations of the Magisterium, the teaching of theologians, and the like. While Oppenheim undoubtedly did not fully enunciate this principle, his writings about this important question attained a considerably advanced stage.

Besides univocality, Oppenheim lists two more conditions under which a liturgical text may be used as a *certain* argument to defend a thesis in dogmatic theology: (a) the text should have an internal and necessary relationship with faith,[590] and (b) it should have been accepted by all Catholic liturgies or by the Roman Liturgy.[591] When these three conditions are fulfilled simultaneously, the liturgical text expresses a truth that is *certain* but not necessarily—and let this be clear—a dogma or teaching guaranteed by the infallibility of the Church.[592]

Indeed, in theology, *certain* is an adjective applied not only to what is proposed under the guarantee of infallibility but to any teaching against which there are no serious doubts. Thus, as Oppenheim explains, there may be several degrees of certainty, from that which is opposed to simple temerity to that which, based on a solemn declaration of the Magisterium, is opposed to heresy.

How does one determine the degree of certainty in a truth implicitly taught in a liturgical text? According to Oppenheim, such a determination should be based upon *external* and *internal* reasons.[593]

The *external* reasons are, for example, declarations made by the Church concerning the theological value of a text (as when the Council of Trent defined infallibly that there is no error in the Roman Canon) and the frequency with which a text appears throughout the liturgical cycle.

The *internal* reasons refer to the greater or lesser degree of relationship between the text and the Faith. For example, that which is connected with the validity of the sacraments enjoys, for this reason, great theological value

---

589. Oppenheim, 116.
590. See Oppenheim, 114–15. The author alludes here to the fact that the miracles of the saints, private revelations, and so forth are not guaranteed by infallibility, even when accepted by the universal or Roman liturgy. See our general observations at the beginning of chap. 6, sec. 2 (*The Church Is Infallible in Matters of Discipline and Liturgy*) supra.
591. See Oppenheim, 115–16. See our general observations at the beginning of chap. 6, sec. 2 (*The Church Is Infallible in Matters of Discipline and Liturgy*) supra.
592. See Oppenheim, 116–17.
593. See Oppenheim, 117.

Furthermore, the author observes that, in liturgical content, "when the Church manifests, expresses, and professes what it believes, it can err neither in great nor small matters."[594]

Note that the terms "manifests, expresses, and professes" do not indicate any teaching whatsoever, but only that which has special clarity and solemnity.[595] Note also that the expression "what it believes" does not apply to every truth that the Church teaches, but only to those proposed as being of faith, that is, which the Church imposes on her children as truths that must be *believed*.

On the other hand, the continuity with which the Church teaches a given doctrine plays a very important role in establishing the infallibility of a teaching of the ordinary and universal Magisterium. Oppenheim formulates an analogous thesis about the liturgy, as seen from his statements below. We show in all caps his words referring to continuity in teaching: "The true Church of Christ cannot err, nor profess error in a known, public, and CONTINUOUS manner, nor propagate it."[596]

The truth of numerous dogmas "may be legitimately and rigorously deduced from the mere fact of their being expressed, in a clear and PERMANENT manner, in the Roman liturgy."[597]

Summing up, Oppenheim does not accept indiscriminately the principle of the infallibility of the Church in approving liturgical texts, but says that, in the liturgy, "*by the manner and frequency of the testimony, by the character of the rite* in which it is expressed, and *the importance of the doctrine itself*, without a doubt it may be manifest that the Church professes such a doctrine AS BELONGING TO THE DEPOSIT OF FAITH. This being the case, then, SOMETIMES, from how the Church commands us to pray, one may deduce, with full certainty, what should be believed."[598]

C. Fr. Manuel Pinto, S.J.

In 1952, Fr. Manuel Pinto, S.J. published the book *O valor teológico da liturgia* (The Theological Value of the Liturgy),[599] which reproduces his doctoral thesis prepared in Granada and Rome, and defended in the Faculty of Theology of Granada in 1951.[600]

The work is of great interest for the subject we are discussing since it aims at studying this problem: "Given that the Liturgy is a *theological source*, what are the conditions of its value?"[601] Furthermore, the author observes that, although

---

594. Oppenheim, 129.
595. See Oppenheim, 129.
596. Oppenheim, 82.
597. Oppenheim, 84.
598. Oppenheim, 114.
599. See Pinto, *O valor teológico*.
600. See Pinto, vii–viii.
601. Pinto, 3. In determining the objective of his work, the author also presents this suggestive formulation: "To ascertain how the *liturgy* is a *theological place* for the theologian, and with what value or *theological note* one can qualify what it contains." Pinto, 9. (Our emphasis.)

Zaccaria, Bouix, Guéranger, Oppenheim,[602] and others had already taken up the question of the theological value of the liturgy, no systematic work had been written until then with the double objective of checking the sources to verify what is known about the matter and mapping out what remains unknown.[603] Fr. Pinto writes:

> We thus recognize Oppenheim has written the most necessary and complete compilation on the present scientific state of the question, beyond which we shall try to extend our investigative work. We cannot presume that our work will be the ultimate expression of the problem showing its whole context, scientific investigation, method employed, and the complex theory that might stem from its conclusions. It is only an essay on this subject, and we can say, within these lines, that it is the first one to be published.[604]

The value of Father Pinto's study is heightened by its being carried out under the direction of theologians of renown[605] and its good acceptance in specialized circles.[606]

As may be seen from Father Pinto's just quoted text, his thesis is not presented as an exhaustive and final monograph on the theme. In another passage, he explains the limitations of his work better: "We wish to try to determine the theological value of the liturgy. We do not want to try and study various particular liturgies to extract their theological content. That work would be endless. We only seek to indicate to and determine for the theologian the conditions under which he can evaluate the testimony of the liturgy. The field is very broad. We only wish to clear the ground."[607]

---

602. See text supported by footnotes 540 and 574.
603. See Pinto, 5, 7.
604. Pinto, 307.
605. Fr. Pinto writes that the thesis was suggested to him by Fr. Joseph A. de Aldama, S.J. (see Pinto, vii); that he received orientation from Fr. Miguel Nicolau, S.J., who discarded the idea of publishing a work of his own on the theme, and placed at Fr. Pinto's disposal the elements he had gathered (see Pinto, vii–ix). He also says that he had the help of Fr. J. Filograssi, S.J. (see Pinto, ix).
606. See, for example: Agostinho Veloso, S.J., *Brotéria* 56 (1953), 240; *La Civiltà Cattolica*, Oct. 3, 1953, 581; *Revista Eclesiástica Brasileira* 13 (1953), 812–13; J.M. Granero, in *Razón y Fe* 149 (1954), 284; L. Renwart, *Nouvelle Revue Théologique* 87 (1955), 421; Cyprian Vagaggini, *Theological Dimensions of the Liturgy: A General Treatise on the Theology of the Liturgy*, trans. Leonard J. Doyle and W.A. Jurgens (Collegeville, Minn.: The Liturgical Press, 1976), 511; Garrido and Pascual, *Curso de liturgia*, 64, 70.
  From the fact that we give great attention to Fr. Pinto's works, one must not deduce that we agree with him wholesale. There are some serious points where we would not subscribe to his assertions. Such is the case, for example, with his evaluation of the bull *Auctorem fidei*, by which Pius VI condemned the Jansenist Synod of Pistoia. We believe that Fr. Pinto diminishes the importance of the bull in saying that "the propositions (of Pistoia) of a liturgical character are rejected generally in the measure *they are contrary to the customs* accepted in the Church, or introduced by ecclesiastical authority" (Pinto, *O valor teológico*, 232). However, our points of divergence with Fr. Pinto are collateral to the central thesis he develops, to which we would subscribe entirely.
607. Pinto, 7.

To attain this objective, Father Pinto initially studies the notion of the liturgy and the theological process.[608] Then, taking up his specific theme, he tries to determine the theological value of the liturgy[609] with arguments drawn from Scripture,[610] the testimony of the universal Church,[611] the Councils,[612] pontifical documents,[613] Church Fathers,[614] theologians,[615] and reason.[616] After each item, the author draws partial conclusions. These are recapitulated and completed in the final section, in which he systematically expounds on the result of his work.[617]

We have sketched the general lines of Father Pinto's work to give the reader a panoramic view of the study. We shall not follow it step by step but only point out some considerations and conclusions that seem to shed light on the problem under study.

In the beginning, Father Pinto observes that, given the decisions of the Magisterium, the teachings of the Church Fathers and theologians, and constructions of theological reason, it is

> a settled and clear point that there is generally a relationship between dogma and liturgy.
>
> But there are, at the same time, difficulties in determining this relationship.[618]

The author then points out that the infallibility of the Church is not involved in the historical facts undergirding certain liturgical feasts, such as the Presentation of Our Lady in the Temple and the Translation of the Holy House of Loreto. He adds:

> There are objections of another order, possibly more important than those. One, for example, is that in various ancient missals, one finds a special Mass to alleviate the pains of hell.
>
> On the one hand, the abovementioned and acknowledged generic relationship and, on the other, these and many other doubt-triggering objections *make one desire a clear and ample determination of the relationship between the liturgy and dogma.*[619]

---

608. See Pinto, Part I, 11–78.
609. See Pinto, Part II, 79–333.
610. See Pinto, 83–91.
611. See Pinto, 93–160.
612. See Pinto, 161–97.
613. See Pinto, 199–244.
614. See Pinto, 245–76.
615. See Pinto, 277–310.
616. See Pinto, 311–33.
617. See Pinto, 335–51.
618. Pinto, 4.
619. Pinto, 4.

For a proper application of the principle of the *Indiculus*,[620] "*lex orandi lex credendi*," Father Pinto lists the following rules:

> The law of faith, which is based on the law of prayer, will have value:
>
> (a) **according to the competence** or origin of the person from whom the law proceeds: Christ or the Church. If it proceeds from a *divine source*, what is expressed by the Liturgy will always be true because God is infallible in everything. If its origin is *ecclesiastical*, the universal liturgy will have objective value in matters of faith and morals or things connected with them, for the universal Magisterium of the Church has competence over these things. IN THESE CASES, ONE MUST INTERPRET THE TEXT ACCORDING TO THE SENSE INTENDED BY THE CHURCH IN THE LAW OR LITURGICAL INSTITUTION....
>
> (b) **according to the sense** intended by the Church, and only within these limits, will the sensible *object, act, formula*, or liturgical *feast* have value as a law of faith.
>
> (c) **The theological qualification** that one must give to such an affirmation of the liturgy will depend on the *nature* of what is affirmed, the *manner* in which it is expressed, and the *intention* of the Church in affirming it.[621]

We call the reader's attention to the observation made in item (c), which we have just cited. Father Pinto enunciates what we could call the *golden rule* for the theological qualification of the doctrines contained in the liturgy. These doctrines would have more or less authority according to whether the Church *intended* to engage her authority to a greater or a lesser degree. An examination can ascertain such intention of the liturgical text within the context of all its surrounding circumstances.

Some of the examples given by Father Pinto clarify this principle further:

(1) The doctrine of the efficacy of prayer is a dogma that can be demonstrated with exclusively liturgical arguments. The numerous prayers imposed by the Church in all liturgical ceremonies and over the centuries could not be in vain. It is evident, therefore, that the Church obliges one to believe in this truth when prescribing the liturgical prayers.[622]

(2) It is a dogma, also demonstrable with exclusively liturgical arguments, that the grace of Christ expels the devil. Indeed, "the exorcisms and breathings of the priest upon the catechumens are done to signify the expulsion of the devil by Christ's grace."[623] In retaining these rites in her ceremonies from the earliest times

---

620. On the *Indiculus*, see footnote 508.
621. Pinto, *O valor teológico*, 120–21.
622. See Pinto, 103ff.
623. Pinto, 120.

and giving them a precise significance, the Church is obliging us to believe in the truth they express.

(3) The Presentation of Our Lady in the Temple is not a dogma, for, although there is a liturgical feast with this title, it is manifest that the Church does not intend to present this historical fact as a truth of faith.[624]

In the conclusion of each topic of his study, Father Pinto again insists on the nuances that form part of the infallibility thesis in liturgical matters. Here are some significant texts:

Terminating the study of "Liturgy in Heresies, Schisms, and Controversies," the author writes, "It is easy to see that not all the liturgical disciplinary laws have a dogmatic or even doctrinal intention or presupposition. We only have to admit this intention or presupposition when it is clear by the very *nature* of the law. For example, the one that commands us to adore the Consecrated Host before the consecration of the [wine in the] chalice.[625] Or then, by the *circumstances*. Thus, by specific declarations, one knows the conventional significance of the drop of water put into the chalice."[626]

"The doctrinal value of [the liturgy's] elements, and, therefore, the *theological notes* with which one must qualify them," we read further in the same chapter, "depend upon the circumstances."[627]

Regarding certain definitions of the Council of Trent, the author observes:

> Thus, the value of a liturgical institution or law of prayer depends on the *competency* of its originating source.
>
> If the institution is *divine*, God's authority guarantees its truth in all its elements, for example, the original text of Scripture.
>
> If the institution is *ecclesiastical*, i.e., *definitively approved* by the Church, whether explicitly by decree or implicitly by longstanding use, then the institution rests on a dogmatic foundation. It has, for this reason, secure doctrinal consequences in *matters of faith and morals* since this field alone is under the Church's direct authoritative doctrinal competency. This is the case with the Vulgate, the Canon of the Mass, and the complete text of the professions of faith.
>
> If it is not definitively approved, it does not have the same authoritative value, as is the case now, with the new translation of the Psalms.[628]

Regarding the argument founded on an omission, Father Pinto writes:

---

624. See Pinto, 120.
625. The author alludes to the fact that the genuflection made before the Consecration of the wine proves that the transubstantiation of the bread is realized before and independently of that of the wine (see Pinto, 146, 281).
626. Pinto, 158.
627. Pinto, 160.
628. Pinto, 183.

There are elements in the liturgy that are not necessary but *merely fitting*, for example, the Feast of Corpus Christi. From its existence, one can argue the truth it presupposes; from its omission, however, one could not argue the denial of the doctrine it expresses.

But when the liturgy *necessarily* had to make a pronouncement and did not, one may argue from the omission. For example, from the fact that in the formulae of the Mass (to whose essence the oblation pertains), it is never said that the former is offered to the saints, one concludes that it is not offered to the saints but only in their honor, as is clear from the liturgical text.[629]

Continuing his comments regarding the Council of Trent, Father Pinto states, "From the time when the Orientals were Catholics, the prolonged use of the Greek Liturgy in the Church is a strong guarantee of doctrinal purity. This is one basis for the authority of the Septuagint."[630]

Commenting on the passage we cited,[631] in which Pius IX declares that a liturgical disposition whose object is doubtful and ambiguous cannot be *settled and stable*, Father Pinto observes:

> In worship, it is very important to know how to distinguish what can be called *settled and stable* or, properly speaking, the *"law of* prayer." In books of the Roman liturgy, there were passages, now suppressed, which would be at variance with today's more explicit dogma.[632] Such passages could not have been called *settled and stable* with the stability of the *"law of prayer."* They corresponded to opinions not condemned by the Church at that time,[633] whereas, when it exists, stability indicates the permanent mind of the infallible Church. But what is the *criterion* to discern what is stable in the Liturgy? One cannot always know this through the Liturgy alone, but also extrinsically thanks to an explicit or implicit declaration of the Church.[634]

Regarding the liturgical argument as used by the supreme pontiffs, Father Pinto says that an encyclical is more decisive doctrinally than the liturgy.[635] That declaration is important because it is known that the encyclicals, as such, do not

---

629. Pinto, 186.
630. Pinto, 187.
631. See text supported by footnote 548.
632. In a footnote, the author cites the cases of "consecration by contact" (see our reference to this in the text supported by footnote 584), the matter of the sacrament of Holy Orders (referred to in the text supported by footnotes 579 to 582), and also the following: "From the Roman Breviary was suppressed a lesson unduly attributed to St. Jerome in which the bodily Assumption of Mary was questioned." Pinto, 236n87.
633. Although not condemned by the Church—we would add—these opinions were objectively erroneous. The examples adduced are very enlightening, for they show that, in principle, the possibility of having errors in the liturgical texts that are not *settled and stable* is not excluded.
634. Pinto, *O valor teológico*, 236–37.
635. See Pinto, 242.

constitute dogmatic definitions. Therefore, there is even less reason to attribute such a prerogative to liturgical texts that are not *settled and stable*.

Based on two documents of Saint Pius V, the author observes, "One cannot lightly assume that *particular liturgies* which have maintained themselves in communion with Rome for *two hundred years* contain errors of faith and morals."[636]

Among the conclusions of the chapter referring to Saint Augustine, we read:

> In matters of faith and morals, the *qualification* of propositions included in liturgical prayers and rites of the universal Church depends, then, on how the Church considers them in the latter. If she considers them as a matter of faith, that is, clearly and evidently as a truth professed and lived by her, then they will be propositions of faith. If she considers them as accepted Catholic doctrine, then they will be Catholic doctrine. If she considers them as certain, they will be certain doctrine. If she considers them as probable, they will be probable doctrine. Absolution at a distance and absolution of an unconscious agonizing person, practiced in the Church as being of probable efficacy, are an argument for the probability of this efficacy.[637]

The following considerations of Father Pinto regarding the position of Saint Peter Canisius on this matter are enlightening:

> The *Letter to Paula*—falsely attributed to Saint Jerome and for this reason removed from the lessons of the office of the Assumption—which questions the bodily Assumption, was replaced by the homilies of Saints Athanasius and John Damascene, which affirm the doctrine of the bodily Assumption. On being retired from the liturgy, says Saint Peter Canisius, it lost much of its authority. This fact and the commentary of the holy Doctor indicate that the authority of Breviary lessons is, in the mind of the Church, that of those to whom they are officially attributed, although the Church corroborates them with her approbation, for she commands their reading. But she does not give them decisive doctrinal force by this act as long as the contrary is not made clear by the circumstances.
>
> Despite the certainty that the Feast already gave to the doctrine of the bodily Assumption at the time of Saint Peter Canisius, the Church had not made a pronouncement, and the same saint explained, distinguishing *three classes of truths* of the faith: *explicit dogmas*, which one must believe under pain of heresy; *truths accepted by the faithful* and sanctioned by the practice of the Church which it is rash to deny, and *certain truths expressed by the public worship*, whose authority continues to increase as the teachers of the Church go on corroborating them with more interest and as they go on penetrating the convictions of the faithful.

---

636. Pinto, 244; see also 229–30.
637. Pinto, 263.

At the time of Saint Peter Canisius, the doctrine of the Assumption of Mary was in this latter category, as he says immediately afterward.[638]

One more observation regarding Father Pinto's work: Earlier,[639] we said we considered that there was a marked analogy between how the Church exercises her Magisterium regarding what constitutes the direct object of infallibility and how she exercises it concerning the indirect object of infallibility—Liturgy, Canon Law, approval of religious orders, beatification and canonization of saints, and so forth.

Father Pinto admits this analogy[640] and makes a very suggestive comparison between the functions of the Magisterium regarding the Liturgy and Sacred Scripture. In both cases, it belongs to the Church to pronounce on the true sense of the texts. In both cases, the declarations of the Magisterium can involve varying degrees of authority, and, in both cases, infallibility can only be involved in what concerns truths that touch on faith and morals directly or indirectly.[641]

These considerations of Father Pinto help one to understand that the principles presiding over the action of the Magisterium in the most varied fields are substantially the same.

D. Fr. C. Vagaggini, O.S.B.

Fr. Cyprian Vagaggini, O.S.B. stands out among contemporary authors who have studied the question of infallibility in the liturgy. A figure of great renown in the Congregation for Divine Worship, and professor at the College of Saint Anselm, in Rome, he has been one of the fiercest champions of the new *Ordo missae*.

If we cite a notorious progressive like Father Vagaggini, it is for two reasons. On the one hand, because, in this particular case, he presents various arguments that seem to be absolutely conclusive. ("But prove all things; hold fast that which is good," 1 Thess. 5:21). On the other, those who defend the new *Ordo*, alleging the desire to conform their own thinking to present-day Roman theological circles, cannot be indifferent to his influence in the Congregation for Divine Worship.

The first edition of his work *Il senso teologico della liturgia*[642] was published in 1957. In a long chapter titled "Liturgy and Faith," he studies the theme now before us.

While Father Vagaggini disagrees with Father Pinto on various matters, they are collateral to the specific thesis we have been defending—that not all texts of the Roman or universal liturgy are guaranteed by the infallibility of the Church. Father Vagaggini is clear and incisive on this particular point, as we shall see below.

---

638. Pinto, 296–97.
639. See the last two paragraphs of chap. 6, sec. 1 (*A Theologically Certain Thesis*) and chap. 6, sec. 3 (*A Thesis to Be Considered in Its Nuances*).
640. See, for example, Pinto, *O valor teológico*, 332, 350.
641. See Pinto, 325–33.
642. Citations of this work are from its fourth Italian edition of 1965.

He begins the chapter to which we refer with two questions: "What are the precise relations between liturgy and faith, and between liturgy and theology? In particular, to what point does the liturgy oblige the faith of the believer, and what use can and should be made of the liturgy in theology?"[643]

Having thus established the object of the chapter, he expounds on certain basic concepts for a solution to the question. He observes that in the last centuries, a more precise knowledge has been obtained "of the fact that what the magisterium proposes to the faithful it proposes with very different degrees of authority and of authenticity."[644]

After a detailed study of the liturgy as *didascalia* (means of instruction) in the Church,[645] the author takes up the theme which now interests us in a paragraph under this subtitle: "Some General Rules to Determine the Extent to Which the Church Imposes Anything in the Liturgy as Being a Matter of Faith."[646]

This section begins with the following paragraph:

> Since the liturgy, as a means of teaching, is a means of teaching of the ordinary magisterium and, since, as a whole, it is less precise conceptually than the other means, in many cases it poses special difficulties to a theologian exploring it to find out to what extent, in a given case, he can resort to the liturgy to know the teaching of the magisterium conceptually.
>
> This difficulty is felt especially when one seeks to determine precisely, on a certain point, what is properly *de fide* in the liturgy and what is not, and what degree of adherence one must give to each element.[647]

To resolve the question, the author proposes four rules, two of which are of direct interest to the matter under discussion. The second rule reads: "What the magisterium proposes in the liturgy for the adherence of the faithful, which the faithful accept, is proposed with varying degrees of dogmatic authority, according to the matter in question; likewise, provided they are well informed of the magisterium's intention, the faithful respond with an adherence that varies in degree and quality."[648]

Explaining this rule, Father Vagaggini writes:

> This is simply a rule of general theological methodology: not everything the magisterium proposes is proposed with the same degree of authoritative force or intention of engaging its responsibility or doctrinal authority and the faith of believers in the same manner.
>
> The magisterium proposes some points to be believed with divine and Catholic faith under the pain of shipwreck in the faith; it engages all its

---

643. Vagaggini, *Theological Dimensions*, 509.
644. Vagaggini, 511.
645. See Vagaggini, 512–18.
646. Vagaggini, 518.
647. Vagaggini, 518.
648. Vagaggini, 522.

infallible authority in those points. It proposes other points to a lesser authoritative degree. In turn, this may vary from the degree which theologians call proximate to faith . . . to opinion simply admitted as such; to a mere hypothesis, more or less generally admitted, which the magisterium does not intend to contradict for the moment, nor to assume any special responsibility for even when presupposing it. There can be an indefinite number of degrees and nuances between these stances.

Nor are the faithful supposed to give the same degree and kind of adherence to whatever the teaching authority proposes. The general rule is simply that the believer give to every single proposition of the magisterium that degree and kind of adherence it requires of him, neither more nor less. . . .

This general rule also holds for doctrine the magisterium proposes through the liturgy in its various elements and to very different degrees. Those degrees are all the more diverse and hard to distinguish because, as has been explained, the liturgy's teaching function is only indirect, with very rare didactically explicit and precise expressions.[649]

The fourth rule reads: "In practice, only by means of exhaustive theological study of each individual problem can one determine the degree of authority of any point of the liturgy, historical or present-day."[650]

Commenting on this proposition, Father Vagaggini writes:

This fourth rule is by far the most important. If one admits the preceding observations, the crucial point for a theologian or believer concerned to gauge the doctrinal value of an element in historical or current liturgies, is to know how to determine, in individual cases, the degree of authority the magisterium gave that element at a given epoch and gives it today.

Can the study of the liturgy alone lead to this result? Sometimes it is possible to have indications even from the liturgy alone. The importance given to an element, whether it is found in one or several liturgies, or quite clearly in all, can suggest that the teaching authority is engaged more or less notably in it. The universality of the feast of the Assumption and its high degree of solemnity may suggest a notable engagement of the ordinary and universal magisterium in proposing this point of doctrine.

But even supposing—which is not always the case—that the very meaning of an element can be determined sufficiently from the liturgy alone, for the most part it will be exceedingly difficult, if not downright

649. Vagaggini, 522–23.
650. Vagaggini, 526.

impossible,[651] to determine from the liturgy alone, with sufficient precision, the degree of authority the magisterium engages in proposing
that element.

The very antiquity and universality of an element is not an absolutely apodictic proof that the magisterium proposes it in the liturgy as
a matter of divine and Catholic faith. One must not forget that, to argue
apodictically from the ordinary and universal magisterium alone that the
Church proposes a doctrine as being of divine and Catholic faith, it is not
enough to show there is moral unanimity among the bishops united with
the Roman pontiff in proposing that doctrine; one must also prove they
propose it with moral unanimity precisely as a matter of faith.[652]

After examining, from this perspective, the historical examples of the Immaculate Conception and the Assumption and writing about other aspects of the
theory on which he expounds, the author says:

> On the other hand, it follows that to satisfy his legitimate questions, a
> theologian focused on this aspect of things must have recourse to an
> exhaustive theological study of the issue with which he is concerned. Only
> this general theological study of the issue, employing the usual criteria of
> theology, can provide as certain an answer as possible about the degree of
> authority and the sense in which the ordinary magisterium imposes a given
> liturgical element for the adherence of the faithful, and hence, to what
> degree and kind of adherence the faithful are held.[653]

---

651. Concerning this point, Fr. Vagaggini exaggerates the difficulty of demonstrating a dogma
based only on the liturgy. Undoubtedly, a theologian ought to study all aspects of a question to
argue about it, but this principle also holds for liturgical, scriptural, patristic, and other arguments.
It is not the problem in focus here. What matters is to maintain that, having thoroughly studied
a dogmatic question, a theologian can frequently draw from the liturgy absolutely decisive arguments that would suffice to demonstrate the doctrine taught by the Church. Fr. Vagaggini passes
over this second aspect of the problem in silence and insists that it is "difficult, if not downright
impossible," to determine the value of a particular teaching of the Magisterium with precision
using just the liturgy. Therefore, he does not seem to adequately express the truth about this matter and weakens the doctrine on the theological value of the liturgy.
In other words, although he admits the general and indisputable principle that the faithful
have in the liturgy an expression of their faith (see Vagaggini, 509–18), moving on to the concrete
case, Fr. Vagaggini excessively restricts this didactic value of the Sacred Liturgy. At any rate, there
is no way to deny that in numerous cases, it is impossible to determine the degree of authority of
liturgical texts only using arguments drawn from the liturgy itself. This conclusion is sufficient
for us for the moment, for we are only seeking to demonstrate that not all liturgical dispositions
involve the infallibility of the Church.
Furthermore, we wish to call the attention of those who are defending the new *Ordo* based on
the unqualified concept of the infallibility of the liturgy to the fact that Fr. Vagaggini himself, a
figure of great prestige in the Congregation for Divine Worship, would not subscribe to this way
of thinking.
652. Vagaggini, 525–26.
653. Vagaggini, 527–28.

6. The New Missal and the Infallibility of the Church

Before examining the specific case of the new *Ordo*, we shall summarize the principles explained up to this point and fix with clarity the state of the question:

(1) we saw that, in general, the neo-scholastic manuals consider as theologically certain the thesis that the universal laws of the Church, among which are included the liturgical laws, involve infallibility;[654]

(2) we showed, next, that this thesis has—or appears to have—solid support in Tradition;[655]

(3) we emphasized that, despite the adduced testimonies of Tradition, grave doctrinal and historical reasons exist for us to doubt that the universal liturgical laws *always and necessarily* engage the infallibility of the Church;[656]

(4) we observed that this doubt has support in Tradition, for we find in numerous documents hesitations and restrictive expressions regarding the thesis of infallibility in disciplinary and liturgical matters;[657]

(5) we found, finally, that in the theology of the last few decades, it is becoming ever clearer that the universal liturgical dispositions involve the authority of the Church in varying degrees, according to the measure in which the Holy See or the sacred Hierarchy have engaged their own authority in each specific case;[658]

(6) therefore, to resolve the question formulated in the introduction of this Chapter 6, it only remains for us to ask in what measure the documents referring to the New Mass reveal that Paul VI had desired to engage his authority in that matter. This is what we shall see next.

*   *   *

On the one hand, it is true that in various pronouncements, Paul VI declared the New Mass, in principle, obligatory.[659] It is necessary, however, not to forget that the obligation of a law is not, by itself, an absolutely clear sign that infallibility

---

654. See chap. 6, sec. 1 (*A Theologically Certain Thesis*).
655. See chap. 6, sec. 2 (*The Church Is Infallible in Matters of Discipline and Liturgy*).
656. See chap. 6, sec. 3 (*A Thesis to Be Considered in Its Nuances*).
657. See chap. 6, sec. 4 (*Hesitations and Restrictive Expressions in Testimonies of Tradition*).
658. See chap. 6, sec. 5 (*Conditions Under Which Liturgical Laws Involve Infallibility*).
659. We say obligatory "in principle" because, as we shall see later, the Missal of Saint Pius V continues in force, side by side with that of Paul VI.
　　We should emphasize that we refer here to the strictly canonical aspects of the documents relative to the new *Ordo*. We abstract, therefore, from the dogmatic aspect of the question, as well as from its eventual canonical implications.

is involved in it. In the past, there have been liturgical dispositions, later revoked, which, although obligatory, were not guaranteed by infallibility.[660]

On the other hand, the Congregation for Divine Worship[661] and the Holy Father[662] determined that the Missal of Saint Pius V would still be in use until November 1971.[663]

Now, the fact that the Missal of Saint Pius V continues canonically in use is an indication—evidently not decisive[664]—that Paul VI did not intend to engage his infallibility in the new texts of the Missal.

However, concerning this question, there is a truly decisive document. It is the general audience of November 19, 1969, in which Paul VI, referring to the new *Ordo*, says, "the rite and the respective rubrics ARE NOT by themselves A DOGMATIC DEFINITION; they are SUSCEPTIBLE OF THEOLOGICAL QUALIFICATION OF VARYING VALUE, according to the liturgical context to which they refer; they are gestures and terms which are related to a religious action, lively and living, of an ineffable mystery of the divine presence, which is not always realized in the same manner, an action which only theological criticism can analyze and express in doctrinal formulae which are logically satisfactory."[665]

Therefore, if Paul VI himself declared explicitly that the rites and rubrics of the New Mass "are susceptible of a theological qualification of varying value," it

---

660. See, for example, chap. 6, sec. 5 (*Conditions Under Which Liturgical Laws Involve Infallibility*), item B.
661. See Instruction (Oct. 20, 1969).
662. See Paul VI, General audience (Nov. 26, 1969).
663. As the Diocesan Chancery of Campos, Brazil, made clear in a communiqué of September 1, 1970, "Every priest can always celebrate in Latin," and "the Sacred Congregation for Divine Worship grants to every priest who celebrates in Latin, the faculty of retaining the *Ordo missae* of Saint Pius V." H.C. Fischer, "Missa em latim," *Catolicismo*, no. 237, (Sept. 1970), p. 8. Moreover, various canonists have declared that independent of the postponing of the question until November 1971, the *Ordo* of Saint Pius V was not formally prohibited. In defense of this thesis, they allege, on the one hand, the not very clear terms with which the apostolic constitution *Missale romanum* makes the new *Ordo* obligatory; and, on the other, the fact the age-old and immemorial customs in opposition to the new *Ordo*, have not been expressly revoked according to the terms of canon 30. See Un groupe de canonistes, "Consultation, témoignage et voeu sur le nouvel *Ordo missae*," *La Pensée Catholique* 122 (1969), 44–47; "La nouvelle ordonnance de la messe: Vers une messe oecumenique," *Courrier de Rome* (Paris), no. 49 (June 25, 1969), 7; "La Messe polyvalente de Paul VI: L'instruction Bugnini, une pause tactique," *Courrier de Rome* (Paris), no. 56 (Nov. 10, 1969), 4–5; Abbé Georges de Nantes, "L'interdit jeté sur la sainte messe romaine," *La Contre-Réforme Catholique au XXe Siècle* (Saint-Parres-les-Vaudes, France), no. 33 (June 1970), 7–8; Philippe Beauchamp, "La nouvelle messe est-elle obligatoire?" *Cices—Bulletin du Cercle d'Information Civique et Sociale* (Paris), no. 104 (May 31, 1970), 1–2. **Publisher's Note:** On this point, in accordance with what is said in the Publisher's Note at the beginning of this book, the author believed until his September 2018 death that there was nothing to be modified in his affirmations about the right of *every* priest to continue *celebrating* Mass in Latin and according to the *Ordo* of St. Pius V. Regarding the dispositions of the Holy See on this matter at the time of the promulgation of the *novus Ordo missae*, see Abbé des Graviers, "La messe tridentine est-elle morte?" *Courrier de Rome* (Jan. 1974).
664. It is a question of an *indication* since—see chap. 6, sec. 4 (*Hesitations and Restrictive Expressions in Testimonies of Tradition*)—various theologians declare that an ecclesiastical law only involves infallibility when it *obliges* one strictly to practice a certain act. However, such an indication is not *decisive* because other theologians think differently—see chap. 6, sec. 2 (*The Church Is Infallible in Matters of Discipline and Liturgy*).
665. Paul VI, General audience (Nov. 19, 1969).

does not seem possible to sustain that the texts of the New Mass, as such, involve the infallibility of the Church. In this specific case, this conclusion would impose itself even if doubts remained, in the theoretical plane, about the existence of universal ecclesiastical laws that do not involve the infallibility of the Church.

PART TWO

Can a Pope Be ... a Heretic?

THE THEOLOGICAL HYPOTHESIS OF A HERETICAL POPE

Presentazione
BY ROBERTO DE MATTEI

Prof. Roberto de Mattei wrote this foreword in 2016 for an Italian printing of this Part Two. It is republished here with his permission.

The existence of a crisis in the Church is now evident to many, but its antecedents have been identified since the 1960s and 1970s, and even before that, by authors endowed with the *sensus fidei* (sense of the faithful) and intellectual acuity.

In 1970, a young Brazilian scholar, Arnaldo Vidigal Xavier da Silveira, published a study titled *Considerações sobre o Ordo missae de Paulo VI*, which was divided into two parts. One was dedicated to a critical analysis of the *Novus Ordo missae* of Paul VI (1969), and the other dealt with the theological hypothesis of a heretical pope, also written to answer possible objections to the first part. The writing was encouraged and approved by Most Rev. Antonio de Castro Mayer (1904–1991), bishop of Campos, and by Prof. Plinio Corrêa de Oliveira (1908–1995), in whose school Xavier da Silveira was formed. In 1962, during the first session of the Second Vatican Council, Xavier da Silveira went to Rome, accompanying Bishop Mayer, Archbishop Sigaud, ordinary of Diamantina, state of Minas Gerais, and Prof. Corrêa de Oliveira, to help them establish a "Small Committee" of anti-progressive bishops and theologians. It would become the nucleus of the *Coetus Internationalis Patrum.*[666]

Xavier da Silveira's study appeared in a mimeographed edition in Portuguese, later in Spanish and English, and a French edition was published by Chiré, a publishing house known for spreading good books. While this French edition was in preparation, on September 24, 1973, Vicente Cardinal Scherer (1903–1996), then archbishop of Porto Alegre and president of the National Conference of Bishops of Brazil, delivered to Bishop Mayer an order from Paul VI forbidding the dissemination of the book. The preparation continued, however, and the work appeared in 1975 with the title, *La nouvelle messe de Paul VI: Qu'en penser?*[667]

At the time of the dissemination campaign, Bishop Mayer urged the author and Prof. Corrêa de Oliveira to heed Paul VI's request. Out of respect for the

---

666. See Roberto de Mattei, *The Second Vatican Council: An Unwritten Story*, trans. Patrick T. Brannan, S.J., Michael J. Miller, and Kenneth D. Whitehead, ed. Michael J. Miller (Fitzwilliam, N.H.: Loreto Publications, 2012), 202–210.

667. See Arnaldo Vidigal Xavier da Silveira, *La nouvelle messe de Paul VI: Qu'en penser?* (Chiré-en-Montreuil, France: Diffusion de la Pensée Française, 1975).

authority of the bishop of Campos, with whom they had closely collaborated, Prof. Corrêa de Oliveira and the author agreed to limit the circulation of the book. Even though only a few copies reached the European public, the work circulated among specialists, imposing itself by the intellectual rigor with which the author tackled unprecedented problems.

Forty years have passed, but while the literature on the new liturgy has grown to some extent, with rare exceptions, the issue of the heretical pope began to arouse the attention of theologians and pastors only after Benedict XVI's resignation and the election of Pope Francis.[668] Articles by the American Jesuit Fr. James V. Schall in *The Catholic Thing*,[669] Robert J. Siscoe in *The Remnant*,[670] Jacob W. Wood in *Crisis Magazine*,[671] as well as the publication by Fr. Jean-Michel Gleize of the French translation of the *Tractatus de comparatione auctoritatis papae et concilii* (1511) by Cardinal Cajetan,[672] have opened a lively and fruitful debate. Reading the study by Xavier da Silveira, which is now presented in this updated edition, will certainly offer a precious contribution to guide a discussion that, as is easily predictable, will become ever more intense.

According to Louis Cardinal Billot (1846–1931), one of the few twentieth-century authors addressing the topic, the Church does not rule out the possibility of a pope falling into heresy, although the French theologian finds it unlikely that it would ever happen.[673] As a historian, not a theologian, I find it useful to offer a historical synopsis helping to define the solid points within which the theological hypothesis examined by Xavier da Silveira lies.

A nemine est judicandus, nisi a fide devius . . .

In its July 18, 1870 session, the First Vatican Council sanctioned the principle that the pope may not be judged,[674] as summarized in the formula, *prima sedes a nemine judicatur* (No one will judge the First See [i.e., Rome]).[675]

No authority on Earth is superior to the pope, the Vicar of Christ. In a letter to Michael, Emperor of the Orient, Pope Saint Nicholas I (858–867) summarizes the doctrine of the Roman primacy,[676] of which one of the first axioms is *prima*

---

668. Among these are studies of a sedevacantist line known as "Theses of Cassiciacum," by Fr. Michel Guérard de Lauriers (1898–1988). See "Le siège apostolique est-il vacant? (*Lex orandi, Lex credendi*) in Cahiers de Cassiciacum," no. 1, May 1979.
669. James V. Schall, "On Heretical Popes," *The Catholic Thing*, Nov. 11, 2014.
670. See Robert J. Siscoe, "Can the Church Depose an Heretical Pope?" *The Remnant*, Nov. 18, 2014.
671. See Jacob W. Wood, "Can a Pope Be a Heretic?" *Crisis Magazine*, Mar. 4, 2015.
672. See Thomas de Vio Cajetan, O.P., *Le pape el le concile—Tractatus de comparatione auctoritatis papae et concilii cum apologia ejusdem*, trans. ann. Fr. Jean-Michel Gleize, S.S.P.X. (Condé-et-Poireau: *Courrier de Rome*, 2014).
673. See Billot, *Tractatus de ecclesia*, q. 14, tes. 29.
674. See Denz.-H., 3063.
675. Canon 1556 of the 1917 CIC, gives a lapidary definition of the principle *Prima sedes a nemine iudicatur*. Canon 1404 of the 1983 Code of Canon Law also reiterates *Prima sedes a nemine iudicatur*.
676. See Denz.-H., 638–642.

sedes non iudicabitur a quoquam [the first see will not be judged by anyone].[677] However, this rule admits an exception, as Gratian points out in his famous *Decretum* (1140), namely, the sin of heresy.[678]

Summarizing an assertion attributed to Saint Boniface, bishop of Mainz, and quoting from Saint Ivo of Chartres,[679] Gratian states that the pope, "*a nemine est iudicandus, nisi deprehendatur a fide devius.*"[680] This judgment, according to an authoritative Church historian, Msgr. Victor Martin, undoubtedly reflects a tradition that was already solid in the eighth century.[681] This principle is reaffirmed by the *Summae decretorum* of Rufinus (ca. 1157–1159), bishop of Assisi and later archbishop of Sorrento, and by Huguccio of Pisa (ca. 1180–1190),[682] bishop of Ferrara, who is considered to be the most famous *Magister Decretorum* of his century. Along this line, in one of his sermons, Pope Innocent III affirms that "The faith is necessary for me to such an extent that, while having God as my only judge in all other sins, I could be judged by the Church for a single sin that I might commit against the faith."[683] Comparing his union with the Church to a marriage in which the bridegroom "does not seek to divorce, neither resigns nor could be deposed," he observes, "however, the Roman Church could repudiate the Roman pontiff because of fornication: I am not saying carnal, but spiritual fornication, that is, an error in faith, for those who do not believe are already judged (John 3)."[684]

As attested by great canonical treatises, the possibility of judging the pope if he becomes guilty of heresy was "an undisputed maxim throughout the Middle Ages."[685] Fr. Salvatore Vacca, who traced the history of the axiom *prima sedes a nemine judicatur,* recalls that "the thesis on the possibility of a heretical pope was taken into consideration . . . throughout the Middle Ages until the time of the Western Schism (1379–1417)."[686]

---

677. See St. Nicholas I, "Epistula ad Michaelem imperatorem," *P.L.*, 119:940 (926–962). This text is inserted in the *Decretum* of Gratian. dist. 21, chap. 7, *Nunc autem.*

678. On the heresy clause, see also James M. Moynihan, *Papal Immunity and Liability* (Rome: Gregorian University Press, 1961), 25–42.

679. See Ivo of Chartres, *Decretum*, pars V, chap. 23, *P.L.*, 161:330.

680. Gratian, *Decretum*, pars 1, dist. 40, c. 6, *P.L.*, 187:215: "Huius (i.e., papae) culpas istic redarguere presumit mortalium nullus, quia cunctos ipse iudicaturus a nemine est iudicandus, nisi deprehendatur a fide devius." (Let no mortal presume to contradict the faults of this one (i.e., the pope), for he that should judge all is judged by no one unless he is caught erring from the Faith.)

681. See Victor Martin, "Comment s'est formée la doctrine de la supériorité du concile sur le pape," *Revue des Sciences Religieuses*, no. 2 (1937), 124–25.

682. Huguccio Pisanus, *Summa decretorum*, pars 1, dist. 40, chap. 6, "Tunc enim demum papa potest condemnari de heresi si pertinax fuerit aliter non ar [truncated in paper original] qui dixit apostolus (C. 24, q. 3, c. 29) . . . prima [sedes] id est romana non iudicabitur nisi de heresi ut dixl. si papa." (Therefore, only then can a pope be condemned of heresy, if he should be persistent [truncation in paper original] which apostle said (C. 24, q. 3, c. 29) ... the first [see], that is, the Roman [one], will not be judged except concerning heresy as said in [canon] 40, 'Si papa.')

683. "In tantum enim fides mihi necessaria est, ut cum de caeteris peccatis solum Deum judicem habeam, propter solum peccatum quod in fide committitur possem ab Ecclesia judicari." Innocent III, "Sermo II in consacratione pontificis maximi," *P.L.*, 217:656.

684. Innocent III, "Sermo II," *P.L.*, 217:664–65.

685. Martin, "*Comment s'est formée*," 127.

686. Salvatore Vacca, O.F.M.,Cap. *Prima sedes a nemine iudicatur : Genesi e sviluppo storico dell'assioma fino al Decreto di Graziano* (Rome: Editrice Pontificia Università Gregoriana, 1993), 254.

The Gallican and conciliar theories of the fourteenth and fifteenth centuries took the hypothesis of a heretical pope as a pretext to deny the principle *prima sedes a nemini judicatur*. Gallicanism is an error that, before being established as a system in the modern era by Honoré de Tournely (1658–1729) and Archbishop Henri-Louis Maret (1805–1884), dated back to the legists of Philip the Fair.[687] The chief exponent of Conciliarism was William of Ockham,[688] whose *Dialogus* on the heretical pope was taken up by some authors of the Great Schism era until the Council of Florence restored the doctrine of the Roman primacy.[689] However, even the best anti-conciliarist authors, such as Juan de Torquemada (1388–1468),[690] admit the possibility of a heretical pope. An isolated opinion is that of Dutch theologian Alberto Pighi (1490–1542), who believes that it is impossible for the pope to be heretical, for otherwise, the gates of hell would have prevailed against the Church. Pighi's opinion was opposed by Melchior Cano (1509–1560),[691] who upholds as certain, though exceptional, the possibility of a heretical pope since one or two examples can be seen in history.[692]

Cano speaks particularly of Pope Honorius's case, recalling Pope Adrian II's words at the Fourth Council of Constantinople. That pope was anathematized, Adrian II explained, because "Honorius . . . was accused of heresy, the only crime which makes legitimate the resistance of inferiors to superiors, as well as the rejection of their pernicious doctrines."[693]

At the July session of the First Vatican Council, the general rapporteur, Bishop Vinzenz Gasser (1809–1879), dismissed the accusation to the Deputation, made by some Council Fathers, that they followed Alberto Pighi's view that the pope could never fall into heresy. He explained that the Vatican's doctrine is neither that

---

687. See V. Martin, *Les origines du gallicanisme* (Paris: Bloud & Gay, 1939), 130–33; Brian Tierney, *Foundations of the Conciliar Theory* (Leiden: Brill, 1998), 144–46. Philip the Fair allied himself with two cardinals of the Colonna family, Giacomo (1250–1318) and Stefano (1265–1349), who in 1297 denounced the election of Boniface VIII as invalid, denying the legitimacy of the papal abdication. See Valerio Gigliotti, *La tiara deposta: La rinuncia al papato nella storia del diritto e della chiesa* (Florence: Leo S. Olschki, 2013), 196–212.

688. William of Ockham, *Dialogo sul papa eretico*, ed. Alessandro Salerno (Milan: Bompiani, 2015). First translation in vernacular of the first part of *Dialogus* (ca. 1332–1334).

689. See Denz-H., 1307.

690. See Juan de Torquemada, *Summa de ecclesia*, book 2, chap. 112. On the author, see Pacifico Massi, *Magistero infallibile del papa nella teologia di Giovanni da Torquemada* (Turin: Marietti, 1957).

691. See Melchior Cano, *De locis theologicis*, trans. Juan Belda Plans (Madrid: B.A.C., 2006), book 6, 407–10. Cano defines Pighi's position as "new" (see p. 408). Among others, Cano was followed by Fr. Domingo de Soto, a sixteenth-century Dominican: "Quamvis in quantum papa errare non possit: hoc est statuere errorem nequeat tamquam articula fidei, quia spiritus sanctus id non permittet, tamen ut singularis persona errare in fide potest, sicut alia peccata committere, quia non est impeccabilis." (The extent of a pope's unerringness: He cannot decree an error regarding articles of Faith since the Holy Ghost will not permit it. Nevertheless, as a particular person, he can err regarding the Faith, as he can commit other sins since he is not impeccable.) Domingo de Soto, *In quartum sententiarum*, dist. 22, q. 2, a. 2 (Venice: H. Zenarius 1584), 1:1088.

692. See Cano, *De locis* (Spanish), 409.

693. Council of Constantinople IV, Actio 7, in Joannes Dominicus Mansi, *Sacrorum conciliorum nova et amplissima collectio* (Venice: Antonium Zatta, 1771), 16:126.

of Alberto Pighi nor the extremist opinion of any school, "but that of Bellarmine, who admits this possibility in his *Controversies*."[694]

Therefore, the real problem is not the hypothesis of a heretical pope, which is admitted by the vast majority of theologians.[695] The point on which there is still no consensus is regarding the conditions and time when a heretical pope loses his office. Indeed, once the possibility of heresy is admitted, who can judge the heretical pope if no one is superior to him?

Haereticus deponendus aut depositus?—Ought a heretic to be deposed, or is he already deposed?

The authors who develop this theme more profoundly are Cardinal Cajetan, in the *Tractatus de comparatione auctoritatis papae et concilii*,[696] and Saint Robert Bellarmine, who, in *On the Roman Pontiff*,[697] also presents a broad classification of different theological opinions.

For Cardinal Cajetan, "*Papa haereticus deponendus est:* A heretical pope must be deposed."[698] It is up to a legal corpus, possibly a General Council, to depose him in the case of heresy.[699] The heretical pope maintains his position for as long as the Church has not issued a legal ruling. Fr. Francisco Suárez (1548–1617), while

---

694. Mansi, *Sacrorum conciliorum nova et amplissima collectio* (Arnheim-Leipzig: Société Nouvelle d'Édition de la Collection Mansi, 1927), 52:1218. "Deputatio iniuste traducitur ac si voluisset extreman opinionem, scilicet illam Alberti Pighii, ad dignitatem dogmatis evehere [sic]. . . . Doctrinam quae habetur in schemate non esse illam Alberti Pighii, sed extremam cuiusdam scholae, sed illam unam eandemque quam Bellarminus in loco a reverendissimo oratore citato docet." (The decision is unjustly insinuated as if it intended to raise the extreme opinion [namely, that of Albert Pighi] to the dignity of a dogma. . . . The doctrine followed in the schema is not that of Albert Pighi, or the extreme of a certain [other] school, but is rather that taught by Bellarmine in the place quoted by the most reverend speaker.)

695. See, for example, the Salmanticenses, who defined this opinion as "longe probabilior et communior inter theologos." (More widely accepted and common among theologians.) In *De fide*, Tractatus 17 of *Cursus theologicus* (Paris: V. Palmé, 1879), 40:253.

696. See Cajetan, *De romani pontificis institutione et auctoritate*, c. 13; In *Sum. Theol*. II-IIae. c. 39. See also Vittorio Mondello, *La dottrina del Gaetano sul Romano Pontefice* (Messina: Arti Grafiche di Sicilia, 1965).

697. See St. Robert Bellarmine, *On the Roman Pontiff*, vol. 2 of *De controversiis*, trans. Ryan Grant, 2nd ed. (Post Falls, Id.: Mediatrix Press, 2017), book 2, chap. 30, 338–44. Reprinted with permission.

698. Translator's Note: "Papa, si a fide deviat, deponendus est." Thomas De Vio Cajetan, *De comparatione auctoritatis papae et concilii: Cum apologia eiusdem tractatus*, ed. Vincentius M Iacobus Pollet (Rome: Institutum Angelicum, 1936), chap. 20, 125.

699. See Cajetan, *De auctoritate papae et concilii*, chaps. 20–21.

doubting that the pope may fall into heresy, states, "Si fiat, juridice est declarandus." (Should it happen, it must be declared juridically.)[700]

Cardinal Cajetan and his followers, such as Suárez and John of St. Thomas (1589–1644),[701] are certainly not conciliarists, but attaching the deposition of a heretical pope to a legal statement by a Council is likely to contradict the principle that the pope may not be judged, thus falling into semi-Conciliarism. Xavier da Silveira sees the thesis of Saint Robert Bellarmine as more appropriate, according to which *Papa haereticus depositus est*: the heretical pope is deposed *ipso facto* when his heresy becomes public and notorious. This statement cannot have the character of a verdict, for no one is superior to the pope. Another eminent Jesuit, Cornelius à Lapide (1567–1637), issued a similar opinion in the seventeenth century: It is not a question of deposing the pope but of finding that the pope has fallen from his office because of heresy.[702]

If Xavier da Silveira leans to Saint Robert Bellarmine's position, it is also because he belongs to the ultramontane and infallibilist school, and is opposed to any, even mitigated, forms of Conciliarism. He also believes that a heretical pope loses his office when his heresy becomes manifest and known by the *sanior pars* [healthier or sounder part] of the Catholic faithful, including at least some cardinals, bishops, priests, religious, and lay people.

To avoid misunderstandings, it must be noted that Xavier da Silveira has never been a sedevacantist and has polemicized with various exponents of Sedevacantism. Given the Church's necessary visibility, Xavier da Silveira asks whether a pope's defection might result in a prolonged vacancy of the see. He believes that although there is a root incompatibility between heresy and papal jurisdiction, the pope does not lose his mandate until his heresy becomes manifest. Since the Church is a visible and perfect society, the loss of Faith by her visible Head must be a public fact, clearly knowable by common believers. Jesus Christ Himself maintains the person of the heretical pontiff in his jurisdiction on a precarious basis until the Church realizes that he stands deposed.

---

700. Francisco Suárez, *Tractatus de legibus*, in vol. 5 of *Opera omnia* (Paris: Vivès, 1856) book 5, no. 10, 5:361. "Unum ergo superest Ecclesiae remedium, scilicet, ut in concilio generali juridice declaretur haereticus; nam eo ipso cadit a dignitate, non tam potestate humana quam divina. Sicut enim quando eligitur, non accipit potestatem ab electoribus, sed a Christo: ita in eo speciali casu a Christo ipso deponitur post juridicam declarationem." (One Church remedy, therefore, remains, namely, that in a general council, he [the pope] be juridically declared a heretic since he falls from the office of his own accord, not so much as regards human, but [rather] divine power. When elected, he does not receive his power from the electors but from Christ. So also, in this particular case, he is deposed by Christ after a juridical declaration.) Suárez, *De legibus*, 5:361. See also Francisco Suárez, *De fide theologica*, in vol. 12 of *Opera omnia* (Paris: Vivès, 1858), disp. 10, sect. 6, no. 11, 318–20.
701. See Iohannes a Sancto Thomas, *De auctoritate summi pontificis* (Quebec: Université de Laval, 1947).
702. "The pope receives his power not from the Church but directly from Christ. Wherefore, under no circumstances can he be deposed by the Church, but can only be declared to have fallen from his pontificate, if, for the sake of example, he should chance (which God forbid) to fall into public heresy, and should therefore, *ipso facto*, cease to be pope, yea, to be a Christian believer." Cornelius à Lapide, *St. Matthew's Gospel, chaps. 10 to 21*, vol. 2 in *The Great Commentary*, trans. Thomas W. Mossman, 3rd ed. (London, John Hodges, 1887), 305.

The position that Xavier da Silveira develops in the wake of Saint Robert Bellarmine is very close to that of a prominent Veronese theologian, Fr. Pietro Ballerini (1698–1769),[703] who, with the collaboration of his brother Gerolamo (1702–1781), authored writings that excel in orthodoxy and erudition.

Ballerini believes that if the pope advocated an error manifestly contrary to the faith, he should be warned and corrected. If he persisted in error, he would thereby declare himself a heretic, separate himself from the body of the Church, and lose his pontificate without the need for any statement or judgment by others.[704]

Ballerini does not see the work of a Council as necessary in the case of heresy; on the contrary, he deems it unfit for the purpose. "It (a Council) is unnecessary because, simply as a declaration which does not imply jurisdiction, an admonition is useless. Convening a Council is a long and difficult process, and, amid serious danger, the need for remedy requires the shortest possible time. Therefore, instead of a correction and public declaration, he prefers that the cardinals, the clergy, or the Roman Synod take care of it."[705] The judgment of the Church is nothing but a finding of fact.

The greatness of Xavier da Silveira's study is not only that it provides us with a comprehensive and exhaustive view of the various theological positions on this issue, but it also proposes a reasonable and balanced solution. His position seems to be in continuity with that of the medieval decretists, who explain that by falling into an error against the Faith, the pope ceases to be the Head of the Church. According to the teaching of Huguccio, the pope would lose his office without the need for a Council, even if convoking a Council might be useful to publicize the sentence. Indeed, the pope does not lose the papacy if his heresy is secret and

---

703. Pietro Ballerini, *De vi ac ratione primatus summorum pontificum et de ipsorum infallibilitate in definiendis controversiis fidei. Liber singularis in quo utrumque deducitur et constituitur ex principiis concessis ab iis ipsis adversariis, contra quos disputatio futura est*, (Verona: M. Moroni, 1766); *De potestate ecclesiastica summorum pontificum et conciliorum generalium liber. Una cum vindiciis auctoritatis pontificia contra opus Iustinii Febronii. Accedit appendix de infallibilitate eorundem pontificum in definitionibus fidei*, (Verona: M. Moroni, 1768).

In his first work, Ballerini addresses the problem regarding papal primacy and infallibility; in the second, that of the relationship between the pontiff and the Council. In both cases, one finds a vigorous and well-documented refutation of Gallican ecclesiology on a dogmatic and historic-exegetic plane. On Ballerini, see the entry by Osvaldo Capitani, in *Dizionario biografico degli italiani*, Istituto della Enciclopedia Italiana, (1963), 5:575–87; Tarcisio Facchini, "Il papato principio di unità e Pietro Ballerini di Verona," *Il Messaggero di S. Antonio* (Padua) 1950.

704. "Qui nimirum semel et bis correctus non resipiscit, sed pertinax est in sententia dogmati manifesto aut definito contraria; hac sua publica pertinacia, cum ab haeresi proprie dicta, quae pertinaciam requirit, excusari nulla ratione potest; tum vero semetipsum palam declarat haereticum, hoc est a fide catholica et ab Ecclesia voluntate propria recessisse, ita ut ad eum praecidendum a corpore Ecclesiae nulla cujusquam declaratio aut sententia necessaria sit." (Certainly, he who is corrected once and twice and does not return to reason but is obstinate in an opinion contrary to defined dogma, then by this his public obstinacy—when he can no longer be excused from heresy, which requires pertinacity—he openly declares himself a heretic, that is, to have departed from the Catholic Faith and the Church, by his own will, so that no declaration or sentence of anyone is needed to separate him from the Church.) Pietro Ballerini, *De potestate ecclesiastica summorum pontificum et conciliorum generalium* (Rome: Typis S. Congr. De Propaganda Fide, 1850), 105.

705. Facchini, "Il papato principio di unità," 128.

only suspected.[706] According to Huguccio, he can be deposed when he publicly manifests a heresy and refuses to abandon it after being admonished.

It would be logical to imagine that even if there is no need for a legal declaration, the recognition of heresy cannot be made by mere religious or lay people but by a qualified group of bishops and cardinals. In this regard, the fourth and fifth opinions enumerated by Saint Robert Bellarmine might find a meeting point.

These pages by Xavier da Silveira help readers to orient themselves in the confusing situation the Church finds herself in today. The author considers his thesis not only intrinsically probable but theologically certain for the objective reasons he adduces. This does not detract from the fact that other opinions are extrinsically likely since important authors uphold them.

In principle, all opinions are theologically free until Church authority directly or indirectly determines with certainty their degree of truth through the consensus of "tried" theologians. Today, however, the discussion has ceased to be academic, and, for Church pastors attempting to solve it, it can become a problem of conscience from which there is no escape. For their part, baptized Catholics "according to the knowledge, competence, and prestige which they possess have the right and even at times the duty to manifest to the sacred pastors their opinion on matters which pertain to the good of the Church and to make their opinion known to the rest of the Christian faithful, without prejudice to the integrity of faith and morals, with reverence toward their pastors, and attentive to common advantage and the dignity of persons."[707]

Therefore, it is hoped that this important study by Arnaldo Xavier da Silveira will give rise to serious theological debate and that the confrontation of opinions maintains an elevated and dispassionate tone, as the delicate question deserves, reaching a common position as soon as possible.

Roberto de Mattei
May 2016

---

706. See Huguccio's comments on *nisi, deprehendatur vevius*: "De crimine haeresis potest papa accusari si haeresim publice predicat et non vult desistere quamvis tale crimen non sit notorium, sed de alio crimine non potest accusari nisi sit notorium. Ergo de occulto crimine non potest accusari." (The pope can be accused of the crime of heresy if it is publicly declared and he does not want to recant, even if it is not notorious—though concerning another crime, he cannot be accused unless it is notorious. Therefore, he cannot be accused of a hidden crime.) Tierney, *Foundations of the Conciliar*, 227–28.
707. *Code of Canon Law*, 212, §3.

Introduction to Part Two

In various troubled periods in Church history, the theological question of a pope who falls into heresy attracted great interest.[708] During those anguishing years, theologians, moralists, and canonists devoted themselves to examining this delicate problem without arriving at a uniform and common opinion.

When those difficult moments had passed, the debates about the possibility of a heretical pope ceased to attract scholarly attention. Generally, authors dedicate only a few lines to the issue, as if this were a purely academic problem that would never again be of urgent interest.

The uncontested possession of the Roman See by a long series of popes in the last centuries has consigned the question of a heretical pope to oblivion. Above all, theologians dedicating themselves to this topic's study are rare from the seventeenth century to the present day.[709]

Beginning with the pontificate of John XXIII, however, an attentive observer could note that the delicate matter was once more beginning, little by little, to garner interest in specialized circles.[710] This notwithstanding, to our knowledge, a systematic and up-to-date study of the matter has not been published recently despite the relative frequency with which the question is reappearing.

Consequently, in our opinion, the debates on the subject are greatly impaired so that, generally, our contemporaries have studied the hypothesis of a heretical pope with partial or even false notions of the *status quaestionis* (the state of investigation). This, at least, is what we have been observing with growing concern. For this reason, several of them have fallen into evident errors and simplifications,

---

708. Such was the case, for example, in the eighth century, on account of the ambiguous attitudes of Pope Honorius I in the face of Monothelitism; in the twelfth century, when Paschal II weakened in the Investiture Controversy; and in the fifteenth and sixteenth centuries on account of the scandals of Alexander VI.

709. Rightly then, does Dublanchy, in the *Dictionnaire de théologie catholique*, after analyzing the opinions of the classic theologians on the possibility of a heretical pope, write, "We terminate our studies at the end of the seventeenth century, because from then on, the theological controversy is not very interesting, in as much as the positions remained the same and in most cases, the question merits, on the part of the theologians, only a brief mention." Dublanchy, "Infaillibilité du pape," in *D.T.C.*, 7–2e.:1716.

710. Various factors have given rise to the current situation. First, the convocation of the Second Vatican Council, a fact making all theological questions about the relationship between pope and Council most timely. Second, the profound symptoms of crisis in the Church, which already at that time worried many souls. Third, the efforts of certain progressives in proclaiming the possibility of a heretical pope, aiming to weaken pontifical authority.

rendering it more difficult to offer a lucid and coherent analysis of the grave the-oretical and practical problems involved.

There are some who, knowing only the position of one author and those who follow him, analyze contemporary events solely from that scholar's perspective. They do not consider that other theologians of great authority subscribe to different theories.

It is not enough to say, for instance, as Cajetan or Suárez teach, that the cardinals and bishops should declare the pope deposed were he to become a heretic. Indeed, some heavyweight theologians hold that a true pope can never fall into heresy. Others, who also enjoy great authority, admit the hypothesis of one falling into heresy but claim that the pope's deposition happens *ipso facto*, with no declaration being needed. There are many holding other positions, as we shall see later.

On this issue, several opinions enjoy at least extrinsic probability.[711] Accordingly, what right has anyone these days to attach himself to one of them, imposing it without further debate? There is no doubt that extrinsic probability yields to intrinsic evidence, but where are the well-founded and exhaustive studies that would permit a reevaluation, in new terms, of the basic data on this momentous matter?[712]

Therefore, we deem it extremely urgent to present an overview of the various opinions of the great theologians from the past on the theme of a heretical pope. This is only an initial but indispensable step, enabling one to move on from the stagnation these studies have lain in since the seventeenth century, as noted above by Dublanchy.[713]

---

711. "A proposition or opinion is called probable when it has in its favor reasons or motives of such weight that a prudent person can assent to it, not in a firm manner (as in the case of certainty), but with a fear of error." H. Noldin, S.J., A. Schmitt, S.J., and G. Heinzel, S.J., *Summa theologiae moralis* (Innsbruck: Rauch, 1962), 1:215, no. 225. The intrinsic or internal probability "is founded upon reasons drawn from the very nature of the thing"; the extrinsic or external is "based directly upon the authority of the learned." Noldin, Schmitt, and Heinzel, 1:215, no. 226. "The external probability per se supposes the internal, that is, it supposes that the learned have been led by internal reasons to embrace the truth." Noldin, Schmitt, and Heinzel, 1:215, no. 226. "Given that the external probability is based essentially upon the internal, it is not licit to appeal to the external probability when one knows that the opinion is false and does not have any internal probability of being correct, even when authors of great name defend the opinion. External probability without internal probability can only be invoked when one is dealing with an obscure matter wrapped in difficulties and still insufficiently clarified by the authors." Noldin, Schmitt, and Heinzel, 1:225, no. 238.

712. One must keep in mind the grave risks in embracing absolutely one of the opinions admitted among the theologians, to the exclusion of all others, without having objectively decisive reasons for this. Those who came before us did not succeed in establishing such reasons. Let us suppose that, confronted with a hypothetically heretical pope, someone would judge him to be *ipso facto* deposed, as St. Robert Bellarmine teaches, and draws the practical consequences stemming from that. Indeed, this person would risk falling into schism, which would be the result, should the opinion of Cajetan or Suárez, for example, prove true. They claim that a declaration of heresy for such a pope is required to be effectively deprived of his office.

Conversely, suppose that someone took for certain, without further investigation, the opinion of Suárez. In sound logic, this person would have to accept as dogma a solemn definition made by a heretical pope before the declaration of his sin of heresy was pronounced. Now, such an acceptance would be rash for, according to the opinions of distinguished doctors, such a pope could already have ceased to be legitimate and therefore could define as dogma something false.

713. See footnote 709.

Thus, we have two purposes in mind in the second part of this work. On the one hand, to show the various opinions on this matter in detail. On the other, to convey certain conclusions that reflection and the analysis of the sources have brought us, intending to make a small contribution to the debate so that theologians might reach a common opinion.[714]

We restrict our considerations to the fields of dogmatic theology, morals, and canon law, setting aside the historical problems. Without a doubt, given what is known today on the question of a heretical pope, a reevaluation of the pontificates of Liberius, Honorius I, Paschal II, Alexander VI, and so forth would be most opportune.[715] In the present work, however, there is no room for such deep research.[716]

To clarify the question of a heretical pope, it is also necessary to consider certain problems connected to it, which we take up in the final chapters: the hypotheses of a schismatic pope and a dubious pope (Chapter 14), the possibility of errors and heresies[717] in pontifical and conciliar documents (Chapters 15 and 16), and the right of public resistance to eventual iniquitous decisions of ecclesiastical authority (Chapter 18).

---

714. As is evident, for an opinion to be classified as "common," it is not necessary to have the approval of theologians of a notoriously doubtful orientation.

715. Refuting the objections that can be made against the doctrine of infallibility, St. Robert Bellarmine studies the cases of forty popes. This number represents about 17 percent of the sovereign pontiffs who had reigned until that time (*On the Roman Pontiff*, book 4, chaps. 8–14).

716. In dogmatic material, it is obvious that we will pay more attention to what Tradition says than to the arguments of reason. Such being the case, when we allude to historical facts, it will not be to analyze them as such, but only to seek the aid of Church history for the clarification of Tradition in the matter.

717. In Chapters 7 to 13, dedicated to analyzing the various theological opinions on the question of a heretical pope, we will consider only the possibility of heresy in the pope as a *private person*, for that is the only hypothesis that the authors treat explicitly and *ex professo*. In Chapter 16, however, we will show that sacred theology does not exclude the possibility of heresy in the pope as a *public person*, that is, in official pontifical documents. As is evident, such a possibility is limited to the documents which do not involve infallibility.

CHAPTER SEVEN

The Five Opinions Regarding the Hypothesis of a Heretical Pope Enumerated by Saint Robert Bellarmine

Analyzing the various theological opinions regarding the hypothesis of a heretical pope, we will adopt the classification presented by Saint Robert Bellarmine. It is entirely valid, even today, in as much as the studies about the matter have made practically no progress in the last centuries. For this reason, many recent authors follow in the footsteps of the great doctor of the Counter-Reformation.[7-8] When, however, it appears that Saint Robert's classification does not precisely distinguish all the nuances characterizing certain schools, we will suggest subdivisions within his classification.

He lists five opinions worthy of study:[719]

1—The pope cannot be a heretic;

2—Falling into heresy, even merely internal heresy, the pope loses the papacy *ipso facto*;

3—Even though he falls into heresy, the pope does not lose his office;

4—The heretical pope is not deposed *ipso facto*. Rather, the Church must declare him deposed;

5—The heretical pope is deposed *ipso facto* when his heresy becomes manifest.

---

718. See, for example, Wernz and Vidal, *Ius canonicum*, 2:433ff.; Guidus Cocchi, *Commentarium in codicem iuris canonici* (Turin: Marietti, 1940), 3:25–26; Eduardus Regatillo, *Institutiones iuris canonici* (Santander: Sal Terrae, 1961), 1:299. Others adopt the classification of Saint Robert Bellarmine but make small alterations. See Marie Dominique Bouix, *Tractatus de papa* (Paris: Lecoffre, 1869), 2:654ff.; Stephanus Sipos, *Enchiridion iuris canonici* (Rome: Herder, 1954), 156, item d.

719. See St. Robert Bellarmine, *On the Roman Pontiff*, book 2, chap. 30. We will not consider St. Robert Bellarmine's observations about this matter in other writings.

In establishing this classification, Saint Robert Bellarmine only sought to order the matter in a manner convenient for showing the reasons and objections that can be alleged regarding each opinion. He did not intend to make a complete and systematic presentation of the principal positions taken over the centuries regarding the theological hypothesis of a heretical pope. He does not refer, for example, to Conciliarism, which had enormous importance in the past, and which, though condemned by the Church,[720] is resurfacing in numerous progressive writings. The great Jesuit saint did not clearly set out his logical criteria for ordering the matter. All this creates a certain difficulty in understanding his classification, and, at the same time, it may give rise to misunderstandings.

To avoid these drawbacks, without abandoning Saint Robert's classification, we present below a Synoptic Outline of the several opinions. Organizing the material according to logical criteria, we seek to give a global vision of the matter and insert the five opinions, which we will analyze later, into the systematic whole wherein they must be considered.

---

720. See Denz.-Sch., systematic index, item G 4 d b.

Synoptic Outline of the Opinions About the Theological Hypothesis of a Heretical Pope

Preliminary Notes

(1) As noted, we refer here only to the classification presented by Saint Robert Bellarmine in *On the Roman Pontiff*, book 2, chap. 30.

(2) The authors whose names are marked with an asterisk deem it more probable that a pope could not fall into heresy but do not consider this position certain. For this reason, they analyze the possibility that a pope could become a heretic and take a position concerning his eventual loss of the papacy. Therefore, these authors appear twice in the "Principal Defenders" column of the various opinions. They are listed among those who follow the thesis that the pope will never fall into heresy (first opinion in Saint Robert's classification) and those who make statements on the loss of the papacy by a heretical pope (fifth opinion in Saint Robert's classification).

(3) Given the criteria adopted for categorizing the "various opinions," it becomes clear that positions B, B.II, and B.II.3 are generic opinions, which are made more specific by those that immediately follow. Accordingly, we do not indicate their "principal defenders" as they obviously are listed in the following opinions.

THE VARIOUS OPINIONS	SAINT ROBERT'S CLASSIFICATION	PRINCIPAL DEFENDERS	OBSERVATIONS	INDEX
A: The pope cannot fall into heresy	FIRST OPINION	Bellarmine,* Suárez,* Matthaeucci, Bouix,* Billot*	Subdivided, the opinion might be considered: (i) a truth of faith; (ii) by far the most probable; (iii) only more probable than the others. See p. 175.	Chap. 8; Billot, see pp. 173-75; Suárez, see pp. 175-76; Bellarmine, see p. 175; Salaverri, see pp. 184-85; Refutation, see pp. 176-83; we do not follow this opinion, see chap. 13.
B: One cannot exclude the hypothesis of a heretical pope	Indirectly referred to by Bellarmine	See the following items (3)	For Bellarmine, the first opinion is not certain	Explanation by references, see chap. 9.
B.I: He never loses his office for heresy	THIRD OPINION	Bouix*	Of the 136 authors examined, only Bouix adopts this opinion	Chap. 10; we do not follow it, see chap. 13.
B.II: The heretical pope loses the papacy	Expounded by Bellarmine together with the fourth opinion	See the following items (3)		Bellarmine, see pp. 202-5; objections by Bouix, see pp. 191-94; WE FOLLOW THIS OPINION, see chap. 13.

B.II.1: He loses papacy when he falls into internal heresy	SECOND OPINION	Torquemada	Opinion abandoned by the theologians	Chap. 9; Suárez, see pp. 197-201; refutation by Bellarmine, see pp. 202-5; we do not follow it, see chap. 13.
B.II.2: He loses papacy when his heresy becomes manifest	FIFTH OPINION	Bellarmine,* Billot,* Cano	Becomes "manifest" when heresy is: (i) merely exteriorized; (ii) has come to the knowledge of others; (iii) "notorious and publicly divulged (Wernz and Vidal)	Chap. 12; WE FOLLOW THIS OPINION, version (iii), see chap. 13.
B.II.3: He loses papacy when Church declares his heresy	Expounded on by Bellarmine together with the fourth opinion	See the following items (3)	Declaration by a Council, cardinals, groups of bishops, etc.	Exposition and refutation by Bellarmine, see pp. 202-5; we do not follow it, see chap. 13.
B.II.3a: This declaration would be a deposition proper	Bellarmine does not list this heretical opinion	Conciliarists: Gerson, Pierre d'Ailly, etc.	This opinion is appearing in numerous progressive writings in the form of neo-Conciliarism	Opinion condemned by the Church, see p. 197; neo-Conciliarism, see p. 197.
B.II.3b: This declaration would be a mere act declaring the loss of the papacy	FOURTH OPINION	Cajetan, Suárez*	As to who ought to make this declaration, see the passage of Suárez that we cite at pp. 197-201.	Chap. 11; Suárez, see pp. 197-201; refutation by Bellarmine, see pp. 202-5; we do not follow it, see chap. 13.

CHAPTER EIGHT

The First Opinion: God Will Never Permit That the Pope Fall Into Heresy

Based on rational arguments, Scripture, and Tradition, the defenders of this first opinion believe that Our Lord will never permit a successor of Saint Peter to lose his faith.[721]

The first defender of this opinion seems to have been Albert Pighi, a sixteenth-century Dutch theologian, in his work *Hierarchiae ecclesiasticae assertio*.[722]

Since then, numerous authors have subscribed to this position. For the authority they enjoy and attention devoted to the matter, the most significant among them are Suárez,[723] Saint Robert Bellarmine,[724] Cardinal Billot,[725] and the nineteenth-century French canonist Bouix.[726]

Let us see how Cardinal Billot defends his position:

> Given the hypothesis that the pope should have become *notoriously* heretical, one must concede, without hesitation, that he would lose *ipso facto* his pontifical power since, *by his own will, he has put himself outside the body of the Church, becoming an unbeliever....*
>
> I said, *given the hypothesis.* But it appears much more probable that this is a mere hypothesis, never reducible to act, considering what Saint Luke

---

721. Obviously, we are not discussing the possibility of the pope being in material heresy. No one denies that mistakenly or inadvertently, the supreme pontiff can fall into material heresy as a private person. Regarding the equal possibility concerning official but not infallible documents, see Chapter 16.

722. See Albert Pighi, *Hierarchiae ecclesiasticae assertio* (Cologne: 1538), book 4, chap. 8, 131 ff., quoted by Dublanchy, "Infaillibilité du pape," in *D.T.C.*, 7–2e.:1715.

723. See text supported by footnotes 733 and 767 *infra*.

724. See text supported by footnotes 765 and 768 *infra*.

725. We cite his arguments in this section. See *infra*.

726. See Chapter 10. To avoid misunderstandings, we wish to insist on a point already emphasized in the second note to the Synoptic Outline at the end of Chapter 7. Almost all the defenders of this first opinion consider it not certain. For this reason, they also analyze the hypothesis of the pope falling into heresy, giving their opinions on his possible deposition in this eventuality. One should not wonder then that several followers of this first opinion are also listed among the followers of other opinions. This is the case for St. Robert Bellarmine, Suárez, Cardinal Billot, and Bouix. See in this regard chap. 8, sec. 4 (*A Merely Probable Opinion*).

says (22:32): "I have prayed for you, that your faith not fail, and you, once being converted, confirm your brethren." That this ought to be understood of Saint Peter and all his successors is what the voice of Tradition attests to, as we shall demonstrate *ex professo* later on when dealing with the infallible magisterium of the Roman pontiff. For the time being, we shall consider this as absolutely certain.[727] Now, even though these words of the Gospel refer principally to the pontiff, as a public person who teaches *ex cathedra*, one ought to affirm that they extend, by a certain necessity, also to him as a private person regarding his preservation from heresy.[728] To the pontiff, in effect, was given the ordinary function of confirming the rest in faith. For this reason, Christ—who for His dignity is heard in everything—asks for him the gift of an indefectible faith. But in favor of whom, I ask, is this petition made? Of an abstract and metaphysical person, or, rather of a real and living person, upon whom it is incumbent to confirm the rest? Or perhaps he will be called indefectible in the faith, who cannot err in establishing what the others must believe, but personally can become shipwrecked in the faith?

And—please note—even though the Roman pontiff, falling into notorious heresy, would lose *ipso facto* the papacy, he would logically fall into heresy before losing his office. Accordingly, the defectibility in the faith would co-exist with the duty of confirming his brethren, which the promise of Christ would seem to exclude absolutely. Moreover, if one considers the Providence of God, it cannot happen that a pontiff fall into hidden or merely internal heresy, for this would cause much worse concomitant evils. Now, the order established by God absolutely requires that, as a private person, the supreme pontiff cannot be a heretic, not even by losing the faith in the internal forum alone. "For," writes Saint Robert Bellarmine (*On the Roman Pontiff*, book 4, chap. 6), "the pope not only should not, but cannot preach heresy, but rather should always preach the truth. He will certainly do that since the Lord commanded him to confirm his brethren. . . . How, I ask, will a heretical pope confirm the brethren in faith and always preach the true faith? Certainly God can wrench the confession of the true faith out of the heart of a heretic just as he placed the words in the mouth of Balaam's ass. Still, this will be a great violence, and not in keeping with

---

727. Cardinal Billot does not qualify it as "absolutely certain" that the pope cannot become a heretic, but rather that the Scripture passage alluded to refers to Saint Peter and his successors. No Catholic author would deny this, whatever may be the exact meaning of the promise made here by Our Lord.

728. In general, the authors do not admit that the quoted passage of the Gospel must be applied necessarily to the person of the pope in his non-*ex cathedra* pronouncements. This is what we show in chap. 8, sec. 2 (*Arguments Contrary to This Opinion*), citing Palmieri, Van Laak, Straub, and Dublanchy.

the providence of God that sweetly disposes all things."[729] Finally, if the hypothesis of a pope who turned notoriously heretical became a reality, the Church would be thrown into such and so many afflictions that *a priori* one can perceive that God would never permit it.[730]

1. Nuances Within This First Opinion

There are certain nuances among the positions adopted by the defenders of this first opinion that we must highlight.

Some believe that this opinion is a truth of the faith. Such was, for example, the thinking of Augustine Matthaeucci, a Franciscan theologian who died in 1722.[731]

Other authors, among them the above-cited Cardinal Billot, do not think this opinion constitutes a truth of faith. However, they consider it the most probable by far, tending to lessen the probability of opposing opinions.

Others, finally, defend this position in an even less rigid way. Such is the case of Suárez and Saint Robert Bellarmine. They do not consider the passage of Saint Luke (22:32) decisive. At the same time, they acknowledge that certain documents of Tradition that admit the hypothesis of a heretical pope have a greater value than that attributed to them, for example, by Cardinal Billot.

We can see, for example, that even the tone of Suárez's argument differs from that in the cited passage of Cardinal Billot:

> Though many[732] may hold, with verisimilitude [that the pope can fall into heresy], to me, however, in a few words, it appears more pious and probable to affirm that the pope, as a private person, can err by ignorance but not contumaciously. Because although God could prevent a heretical pope from damaging the Church, nevertheless, the smoother manner of Providence's acting would be that having promised that the pope would never err in defining, God would consequently provide that he would never

---

729. For the reasons stated further on—especially in chap. 8, sec. 2 (*Arguments Contrary to This Opinion*) and Chapter 13—it does not seem that the argument adduced here by St. Robert Bellarmine or Cardinal Billot demonstrates that the thesis they sustain is the most probable. Nevertheless, this argument has an undeniable residue of truth: Providence could not permit a pope's adhesion to heresy to be frequent and, as it were, habitual. On the contrary, such a thing could only be admitted as exceptional, characterizing one of the most dramatic and profound trials to which the Church Militant might be subjected.

Taking the very example of Balaam's donkey given by St. Robert Bellarmine and other followers of this first opinion, we would say that Providence would not have to permit that donkeys normally and frequently speak, but rather that one donkey, Balaam's, spoke.

730. Billot, *Tractatus de ecclesia*, 1:609–10. This last argument presented by Cardinal Billot does not appear conclusive. Could Our Lord, Who permitted the malice of men to injure His very Person to the point of having Him die on the Cross, not permit that the ingratitude and malice of men subject the Holy Church to a new *Via Crucis*? That this could come about without breaking the promise of divine assistance is obvious and was even prefigured in the fact that, during the Passion, not a single bone of the Sacred Body of Our Redeemer was broken.

731. See Ferraris, "Papa," *Prompta bibliotheca* (Paris: Migne, 1865), 5:1843, no. 65; 5:1845. This passage of Ferraris is reproduced by Bouix, *Tractatus de papa*, 2:658. The affirmation cited from Matthaeucci is from his work *Controversiae fidei de ecclesia* VII, chap. 1, no. 7.

732. Suárez refers to St. Robert Bellarmine here, *On the Roman Pontiff*, book 4, chap. 7.

become a heretic. Furthermore, one ought to hold that that which until now has never happened in the Church, by order and Providence of God, cannot happen.[733]

2. Arguments Contrary to This Opinion

Against this first opinion can be alleged, on the one hand, that the cited passage of Saint Luke (22:32) is, in general, *only* applied to pontifical teachings involving infallibility. On the other, there are numerous testimonies from Tradition favoring the possibility of heresy in the person of the pope.

A. Sacred Scripture

As to the exact sense of Saint Luke's text, numerous theologians sustain that for the fulfillment of the promise of Our Lord, it is enough that there exist no errors in the infallible documents. Thus, they conclude that there is insufficient reason to hold that the confirmation of the brethren also postulates the pope's indefectibility in the faith as a private person. Let us see how Palmieri, for example,[734] expounds on this argument:

> It is not necessary that the indefectible faith be, in reality, distinct from the confirmation of the brethren, but it is enough that it be distinguished by reason. For if the authentic and solemn preaching of faith is infallible, he can confirm the brethren; for this reason, the infallible faith and that which confirms are one and unique; being infallible, it also enjoys the power to confirm his brethren. The indefectibility of the pontiff in the Faith was asked so that he might confirm his brothers. Therefore, from Christ's words, one can only infer the indefectibility necessary and sufficient to attain that end. Such is the infallibility of authentic preaching.[735]

B. Tradition

We present here some documents from Tradition that admit the possibility of the pope falling into heresy.

---

733. Suárez, *De fide*, disp. 10, sect. 6. no. 11, 319. Neither does it seem that this last argument alleged by Suárez is decisive. Our Lord prophesied terrible happenings at the end of the world (see, for instance, Matt. 24:1–41; Mark 13:1–31; Luke 21:5–33), which in numerous aspects will have had no historical precedent.

734. The following theologians declare in the same sense: H. Van Laak, *Institutionum theologiae fundamentalis repetitorium* (Rome: Gregorian, 1921), 1:508–9; Antonius Straub, *De ecclesia Christi* (Innsbruck: Rauch-Pustet, 1912), 2:1068, 479–80; Dublanchy, "Infaillibilité du pape," in *D.T.C.*, 7–2e.:1717.

735. Dominicus Palmieri, *Tractatus de romano pontifice* (Rome: Ex Typographia Polyglotta, 1877), 631–32.

a. Documents Referring to Pope Honorius

Historical proofs authorizing one to affirm that Pope Honorius I was a heretic do not exist. It is certain, nevertheless, that his letters to the Patriarch Sergius favored the Monothelite heresy (according to which in Our Lord there is only one will). Since this refers to a pope favoring heresy, not papal heresy per se, the case of Pope Honorius does not refer directly to our topic.

However, we need to observe that this case, more perhaps than other analogous ones recorded in history, provided an occasion for popes, Councils, saints, bishops, and theologians to manifest their conviction that the hypothesis of the pope falling into heresy was not theologically absurd. Thus, we present documents that directly admit the possibility of a heretical pontiff and others which do so only indirectly. In the second group are, for example, the documents showing the pope's orthodoxy to have been positively suspected. As is evident, such a suspicion would be vain and absurd for one who believed in the impossibility of a pope's defection from the faith. The accusations of favoring heresy are also included in this second group when, by the terms in which they are formulated or by other circumstances, it becomes probable that, in reality, it had been at least positively suspected that the pope was a heretic.

*   *   *

The Third Council of Constantinople (and Sixth Ecumenical one) declared that it had analyzed Patriarch Sergius's dogmatic epistles and a letter written to him by Honorius I. It continues, "Having discovered that these [letters] are entirely alien to the apostolic teachings and to the decisions of the holy councils and to all the eminent holy Fathers but instead follow the false teachings of the heretics, these we entirely reject and loathe as soul-destroying."[736]

After anathematizing the principal Monothelite heresiarchs,[737] the Council condemns Honorius: "Along with these we have seen fit to banish from the holy Church of God and to anathematize also Honorius, the former pope of the elder Rome, because we have discovered in the letters written by him to Sergius that he followed in everything the opinion of that one and confirmed his impious dogma."[738]

*   *   *

Condemning Honorius as a favorer of heresy, Pope Saint Leo II (611–683) wrote, "We, in like manner, anathematize the inventors of the new error: Theodore, bishop of Pharan, Cyrus of Alexandria, Sergius, Pyrrhus . . . and also

---

736. Denz.-Hün., 550.
737. See Denz.-Hün., 551.
738. Denz.-Hün., 552. The terms of this condemnation authorize one to conclude that the Council had anathematized Honorius as a heretic, but this is not the sense generally attributed to the document. Moreover, in other writings, St. Leo II, who approved the Third Council of Constantinople, condemned Honorius only as a favorer of heresy. (We will present these pronouncements of St. Leo II to complete the documentation on this point.) We cite these passages from the Sixth Ecumenical Council and St. Leo II in terms of the observations made in the text supported by footnote 736, at the beginning of item 2 a.

Honorius, who did not purify this apostolic Church by the doctrine of the apostolic tradition, but rather, *attempted to subvert the immaculate faith by profane treason.*"[739]

In a letter to the bishops of Spain, the same Saint Leo II declared that Honorius was condemned because "he did not immediately extinguish the flame of the heretical teaching, as would befit the apostolic authority, but supported it by his negligence."[740]

In a letter to Erwig, King of Spain, Saint Leo II repeated that, together with the mentioned heresiarchs, "Honorius of Rome, who allowed the immaculate rule of apostolic tradition that he had received from his predecessors to be stained," was also condemned.[741]

Regarding the case of Pope Honorius I, R. Bäumer writes:

> Afterward, that condemnation [of Honorius, by the Sixth Ecumenical Council] was renewed by the Synods "in Trullo" of 692 (Mansi, 11:938), by the Seventh General Council (Mansi, 13:377) and by the Eighth (Mansi 16:181). Leo II, who accepted the decision of the Sixth General Council, extenuated the fault of Honorius. . . . The account of the condemnation of Honorius even entered into the *Liber diurnus*. Every newly-elected pope had to condemn the authors of the new heresy, "together with Honorius, who favored their errors." The very *Liber pontificalis* and the Roman Breviary mentioned the condemnation in the second nocturn of the feast of Pope Saint Leo II.[742]

*　*　*

Therefore, the affirmation of V. Mondello, according to which a tradition already solid in the eighth century said that "a Council can judge a heretical pope,"[743] had a historical foundation.

*　*　*

Among the documents related to the case of Pope Honorius I, perhaps none has such importance for our theme as the passage cited below, extracted from an allocution of Pope Adrian II to the Eighth Ecumenical Council. As we shall see, regardless of the judgment made in the case of Honorius I, here we have a pontifical declaration admitting the eventuality of a pope falling into heresy.[744]

---

739. Denz.-Hün., 563.
740. Denz.-Hün., p. 195.
741. Denz.-Hün., p. 195.
742. R. Bäumer, "Honorius I," in *Lexikon für theologie und kirche* (Freiburg: Verlag Herder, 1960), 5:475.
743. Mondello, *La dottrina del Gaetano*, 25; see also 164. The author reproduces, in these topics, the affirmation made by V. Martin in his work, *Les origines du gallicanisme*, chap. 1, 2:12–13. As is evident, the term "judged" does not necessarily indicate, in this Mondello passage, that a Council could pass true "judgment" on a pope. Rather, in context, the term signifies, according to the traditional authors, that a Council can pronounce judgment on someone who was pope and ceased to be because he fell into heresy. We explain this problem in more detail in Chapter 13.
744. St. Robert Bellarmine's commentary is in the text supported by footnote 765.

Adrian II's words were uttered in the second half of the ninth century, more than two centuries after the death of Honorius I. "We read that the Roman pontiff has always judged the chiefs of all the Churches [i.e., the patriarchs and bishops], but we do not read that anyone has ever judged him. It is true that, after his death, Honorius was anathematized by the Orientals. Still, one must remember that he was accused of heresy, the only crime which makes the resistance of inferiors to superiors legitimate, as well as the rejection of their pernicious doctrines."[745]

b. Paschal II (1099–1118)

During the pontificate of Paschal II, the Investiture Controversy shook Christendom again. Emperor Henry V, holding the pope prisoner, extorted from him concessions and promises irreconcilable with Catholic doctrine. Recovering his liberty, Paschal II hesitated for a long time to retract the acts he had made under duress. Despite being admonished repeatedly by saints, cardinals, and bishops, he always postponed his retraction and the hoped-for excommunication of the emperor. A murmur against the pope began to arise throughout the Church, classifying him as suspect of heresy and adjuring him to turn back under pain of losing the papacy.

We cite some facts and documents of the struggle that saints, cardinals, and bishops organized against Paschal II. One will see that the theology of the times admitted the hypothesis of a heretical pope and judged that, on account of such a sin, he would lose the papacy.[746]

* * *

In Italy, Saint Bruno, bishop of Segni and abbot of Monte Cassino, was at the head of the movement opposed to Paschal II. We do not possess any document in which he has declared that he judged the pope to be suspect of heresy. Nevertheless, this is the accusation that his letters and acts unequivocally insinuated.

To Paschal II, he wrote:

> I esteem you as my father and lord. . . . I must love you; nevertheless I must love even more Him who created you and me. . . . I do not praise the pact [signed by the pope], so horrible, violent, done so treasonably, and contrary to all piety and religion. . . . We have the Canons; we have the constitutions of the Fathers, from the times of the Apostles up to you. . . . The Apostles condemned and expelled from the communion of the faithful all those who obtained charges in the Church through secular power. . . . This determination of the Apostles . . . is holy, Catholic, and whoever would contradict it is not Catholic. For they alone are Catholics who do

---

745. Adrian II, "alloc. 3, lecta in conc. VIII," in Mansi, *Sacrorum conciliorum*, 16:126. See also Charles-Joseph Hefele and Dom H. Leclercq, *Histoire des conciles* (Paris: Letouzey et Ané, 1911–1912), 5–1e.:471–72.
746. In this case, as in that of Pope Honorius I, it is not our objective to take a stand regarding a historical question. We only wish to show that theologians of authority admitted the possibility of heresy in the person of the supreme pontiff.

not oppose the faith and the doctrine of the Catholic Church, and, on the contrary, they are heretics who obstinately oppose the faith and doctrine of the Catholic Church.[747]

In another letter, Saint Bruno stresses that he only considered heretics those denying the Catholic principles in the Investiture Controversy, not those who, in the concrete order and pressed by circumstances, act contrary to true doctrine.[748] However, the reservation is not sufficient to exempt Paschal II from the suspicion of heresy since, even when the coercion had ceased, he refused to correct the evil done.

The pope knew quite well that Saint Bruno did not shrink from the hypothesis of declaring him deposed, for he resolved to depose the saint first from the influential position of abbot of Monte Cassino based on this allegation: "If I do not remove him from the rule of the monastery, he with his arguments will take away from me the government of the Church."[749]

When the pope finally retracted, before the Synod convened in Rome to examine the question, Saint Bruno of Segni exclaimed, "God be praised! For behold, it is the pope himself who condemned this pretended privilege [of investiture by the temporal power], which is heretical."[750]

With this phrase, for the first time, Saint Bruno let it be known publicly how much he suspected the orthodoxy of Paschal II. His enemies protested energetically at this. The most salient among them was the abbot of Cluny, Jean de Gaete, "who did not wish to permit that the pope be accused of heresy," as we read in Hefele and Leclercq.[751]

*　*　*

Saint Bruno of Segni was not the only saint of the time who admitted the possibility of heresy in Paschal II. In 1112, Archbishop Guido of Vienne, the future Pope Callistus II, convoked a provincial Synod in Vienne, which was attended, among other bishops, by Saints Hugh of Grenoble and Godfrey of Amiens. With the approval of these two saints, the Synod revoked the decrees extorted from the pope by the emperor and addressed the pope as follows: "If, as we absolutely do not expect, you choose another way and refuse to confirm the decisions of our authority, may God help us, for thus you will be separating us from obedience to you."[752]

747. St. Bruno of Segni, "Letter to Paschal II" (1111), *P.L.*, 163:463. See also Baronius, *Annales*, ad ann, 1111, no. 30, 228; Hefele and Leclercq, *Histoire des conciles*, 5–1e.:530.
748. See St. Bruno of Segni, "Letter to the Bishops and Cardinals," *P.L.*, 165:1139. See also St. Bruno, "Letter to the Bishop of Oporto," *P.L.*, 165:1139, quoted also by Baronius, *Annales*, ad ann. 1111, no. 31, 228.
749. Caesaris Baronius, *Annales Ecclesiastici*, ad ann. 1111, no. 32, 228. See also: Hefele and Leclercq, *Histoire des conciles*, 5–1e.:530: René-François Rohrbacher, *Histoire universelle de l'Église catholique* (Paris: Gaume Frères, 1844), 15:130.
750. Hefele and Leclercq, *Histoire des conciles*, 5–1e.:555.
751. Hefele and Leclercq, *Histoire des conciles*, 5–1e.:555.
752. Bouix, *Tractatus de papa*, 2:650. See also: Hefele and Leclercq, *Histoire des conciles*, 5–1e.:536; Rohrbacher, *Histoire universelle*, 15:61.

These words contain a threat of rupture with Paschal II that can only be explained by the fact that, in the spirit of the bishops who met in Vienne, three notions came together: First, they were convinced that it constituted heresy to deny the doctrine of the Church on investitures; second, they suspected that the pope had embraced that heresy; and, third, they considered that a pope in the eventuality of being heretical, would lose his office, and should not, therefore, be obeyed anymore.[753] This interpretation is confirmed by the letters Saint Ivo of Chartres wrote at the time, which we allude to below. They eliminate any doubt.

After narrating the events of the Synod of Vienne, Hefele and Leclercq write, "The result was that, on October 20th of that same year, the pope confirmed, in a brief letter and in vague terms, the decisions taken in Vienne, and praised the zeal of Guido. Fear of a schism led the pope to take this attitude."[754]

*   *   *

Against this provincial Synod of Vienne, one could argue that another saint, Ivo, bishop of Chartres, refused to participate in it, alleging that no one could judge the pope.[755]

We do not intend here to study the history of the Synod of Vienne. We cite it only to show that, in those times, two saints and a future pope took an attitude toward Paschal II based on the principles that there could be a heretical pope and that, in such an eventuality, he would lose the papacy. Therefore, we shall analyze the position of Saint Ivo of Chartres only from this perspective.

He, too, was opposed to the concessions made by Paschal II to the emperor. He said that the pope ought to be warned and exhorted by the bishops so that he might repair the evil done. However, he dissented from the Synod of Vienne because he did not consider that the pope's attitude in the Investiture Controversy involved heresy.[756] He affirmed, as a consequence, that Paschal II could not be

---

753. Geoffroi, abbot-cardinal of Vendôme, gave the same opinions. See Rohrbacher, *Histoire universelle*, 15:63–64.

754. Hefele and Leclercq, *Histoire des conciles*, 5–1e.:536–37.

755. See Bouix, *Tractatus de papa*, 2:650–51; Rohrbacher, *Histoire universelle*, 15:61–63. Saint Ivo of Chartres, who took that decision together with some other bishops, explains his attitude in a letter addressed to the archbishop of Lyon. See *P.L.*, 162:238ff.

756. As it seems, this dispute, which even divided the saints who opposed Paschal II, originated in confusion that remained about the concept of a heretic. Some said that since the pope had not affirmed the heresy, he was not a heretic. Others maintained that having acted in a manner contrary to a defined dogma, he was a heretic. Later, theology clarified better the principle that it is possible to fall into heresy not only by denying a dogma explicitly but also through acts that unequivocally reveal a heretical spirit—see our essay "Acts, Gestures, Attitudes, and Omissions Can Reveal a Heretic," in *Catolicismo*, no. 204 (Dec. 1967). See Chapter 17.

Therefore, Saint Ivo was correct in sustaining that, through *merely* acting contrary to dogma, Paschal II had not made himself a heretic, but, by his writings, one does not see that he had considered the other aspect of the question, namely, that acting in a continuous way contrary to dogma can suffice to reveal a heretic.

In their turn, the bishops who met in Vienne were correct when they said that it is possible to fall into heresy not only by words but also by acts; but it is not certain that they had taken into account that such acts only reveal a heretic when, considered in all their circumstances, they unequivocally reveal a heretical spirit. Simple pusillanimity, for example, even though prolonged, does not constitute heresy. As historians generally admit, that must have been the case with Paschal II.

submitted to the judgment of men, no matter how grave his weaknesses might have been. Nevertheless, Saint Ivo recognized explicitly in his letter that, in the hypothesis of being a heretic, the Roman pontiff would lose his office. This constitutes an important testimony to the possibility of the pope's defection from the faith. Here are his words: "We do not wish to deprive the principal keys of the Church [that is, the pope] of their power, whoever be the person placed in the See of Peter unless he manifestly departs from the evangelical truth."[757]

Therefore, the attitude taken by Saint Ivo of Chartres is not opposed, from the point of view that concerns us now, to that of Saints Godfrey of Amiens and Hugh of Grenoble. On the contrary, it corroborates it.[758]

c. From Gratian to Our Days

The following canon appears in the *Decretum* of Gratian, attributed to Saint Boniface the Martyr: "Let no mortal presume to accuse the pope of fault, for, it being incumbent upon him to judge all, he should be judged by no one, unless he departs from the faith."[759]

In the *Dictionnaire de théologie catholique*, Dublanchy cites evidence for the influence of this canon in establishing medieval thought concerning the question of a heretical pope:

> One finds in the *Decretum* of Gratian this assertion attributed to Saint Boniface, archbishop of Mainz, and already cited as his by Cardinal Deusdedit (d. 1087), and Saint Ivo of Chartres, *Decretum*, V, 23.
>
> After Gratian, this same doctrine is found even among the most convinced partisans of the papal privileges. Innocent III refers to it in one of his sermons. . . . In general, the great scholastic theologians did not pay attention to this hypothesis. However, the canonists of the twelfth and thirteenth centuries knew and commented on the text of Gratian. All admitted without difficulty that the pope could fall into heresy, as any other grave fault. Their sole concern was to investigate why and in what conditions he could, in that case, be judged by the Church.[760]

---

757. St. Ivo, "Epistola 236," in *P.L.*, 162:240.

758. The *Decretum* attributed to Saint Ivo of Chartres also references the possibility of a heretical pope, as we show. We do not give it special emphasis because its authority is questioned today. It is nevertheless undeniable that this *Decretum* receives no small recognition as an expression of medieval thinking.

759. Pars I, dist. 40, chap. 6, canon "Si papa." The *Decretum* of Gratian was composed in the first half of the twelfth century, probably around 1140.

760. Dublanchy, "Infaillibilité du pape," in *D.T.C.*, 7–2e.:1714–15. Another of Gratian's canons is also interpreted, by authors like Cajetan (*De comparatione*, 170) and Suárez (*De fide*, disp. 10, chap. 6, n. 15, 320), in the sense that once his heresy was declared, a heretical pope was deprived of his charge. This had to do with the chapter *Oves* (C. 13, c. 2. q. 7), attributed to Pope Saint Eusebius (this canon would be from Pseudo Isidore, according to what Bernardi concludes, "Gratian. Canon. Geniun.," pars 2, tom. 2, cap. 29, 138, quoted by Georges Phillips, *Du droit ecclésiastique* [Paris: Lecoffre, 1885], 1:179–80).

A portion of a sermon of Pope Innocent III: "The faith is necessary for me to such an extent that, having God as my only judge in all other sins, I could, however, be judged by the Church for the sins which I might commit in matters of faith."[761]

One understands then how correct Mondello was to write: "Many in the Middle Ages admitted that a Council could judge[762] a heretical pope. We can go so far as to say that it was a most common doctrine in that time, even among the very defenders of the pope."[763]

* * *

To show that Tradition furnishes weighty reasons against the first opinion enumerated by Saint Robert Bellarmine—according to which a pope could not turn heretic—we believe that it is unnecessary here to extend our investigation to later centuries. Indeed, in the following chapters, we will adduce many documents of the last six centuries, making it superfluous to present them here.

3. The Answer From the Defenders of This Opinion

What reasoning is used by the partisans of the first opinion to oppose such testimonies from Tradition and so many others that could be alleged?

Some of these authors, like Saint Robert Bellarmine and Suárez, recognize that such documents weaken the thesis of the impossibility of a heretical pope.

Others, however, like Cardinal Billot, try to contest the value of these documents.[764] He sustains that the allocution of Adrian II proves nothing, in as much as Pope Honorius I, in reality, had not been a heretic. He contests the authenticity of the canon *Si papa* of Gratian. He sees in the words of Innocent III only oratorical hyperbole.

Cardinal Billot did not deny, however, nor could he, that the Church has always left open the question of the possibility of heresy in the person of the pope. This fact alone constitutes a weighty argument in the evaluation of Tradition. It is what Saint Robert highlights in the following passage, where he refutes, three centuries beforehand, his future brother cardinal and fellow member of the glorious Ignatian militia: "Here the fact must be remarked upon that, although it is probable that Honorius was not a heretic, and that Pope Adrian II was deceived by corrupted copies of the Sixth Council [the Third Council of Constantinople] which falsely reckoned Honorius was a heretic, we still cannot deny that Adrian, with the Roman Council and the whole Eighth Synod [the Fourth

---

761. Innocent III, "Sermo II," *P.L.*, 217:656. See also Innocent III, "Sermo IV in consecratione pontificis," *P.L.*, 217:670. Though such pronouncements evidently are not definitions of faith, they nevertheless have great authority, as coming from a pope who was an intransigent and fearless defender of papal prerogatives.

762. For the non-conciliarist understanding of the term "judged" in this context, see footnote 743.

763. Mondello, *La dottrina del Gaetano*, 25.

764. See Billot, *Tractatus de ecclesia*, 1:610–12. See also: Bouix, *Tractatus de papa*, 2:658–59; Phillips, *Du droit ecclésiastique*, 1:179–80.

Council of Constantinople], sensed that in the case of heresy, a Roman Pontiff can be judged."[765]

4. A Merely Probable Opinion

As observed in brief notes,[766] generally, the partisans of this first opinion do not refuse to study what procedure is to be adopted in case the pope falls into heresy. They act this way because they do not consider their position absolutely certain, recognizing that the other opinions enjoy at least extrinsic probability. This explains the seemingly strange fact that followers of this first opinion are often also identified as partisans of others.

Here is how Suárez expresses his thinking on this point:

> It seems consistent with the sweet Providence of God never to permit him to err in the faith, to whom it is never permitted that he teach error. Therefore, it is said that these two promises are included in the words "I have prayed for thee, Peter, that thy faith not fail." Since, however, this opinion is not generally accepted, and the General Councils have sometimes admitted the hypothesis in discussion [of heresy in the pope], supposing it to be thus at least possible, one must say that, should he become a heretic, the pope would not fall *ipso facto* from his dignity, through the loss of faith.[767]

Saint Robert Bellarmine writes, "There are five opinions on this matter. The first is of Albert Pighius, who contends that the pope cannot be a heretic, and hence would not be deposed in any case. Such an opinion is probable, and can easily be defended, as we will show in its proper place. Still, because it is not certain, and *the common opinion is to the contrary*, it will be worthwhile to see what the response should be if the pope could be a heretic."[768]

*   *   *

On the same matter, the following passage, from an eminent contemporary theologian, the Spanish Jesuit Fr. Joachim Salaverri, is also enlightening:

> *As a private person, can the pope fall into heresy?* Theologians dispute this question. To us, "it seems more pious and probable" to admit that God will take care, by His Providence, "that never will a pope be a heretic." Because this opinion, sustained by Saint Robert Bellarmine and Suárez, was also praised in the First Vatican Council by Bishop Federico Maria Zinelli (of Treviso), Speaker of the Faith, in the following terms: "Confident in supernatural Providence, we judge it to be quite probable that this will

---

765. St. Robert Bellarmine, *On the Roman Pontiff*, book 2, chap. 30, 339.
766. See preliminary note 2 of the Synoptic Outline, and footnote 726.
767. Suárez, *De legibus*, book 4, chap. 7, no. 10, 361. See Suárez defend his opinion in chap. 11, sec. 1 (*Defense of This Opinion by Suárez*).
768. St. Robert Bellarmine, *On the Roman Pontiff*, book 2, chap. 30, 338. (Our emphasis.)

never happen. But God does not fail in the necessary things; therefore, if He permits so great an evil, the means to remedy such a situation will not be lacking" (Conc. Vatic., Mansi 52, 1109).[769]

---

769. Salaverri, *De ecclesia Christi* (no. 657), 1:718.

CHAPTER NINE

Second Opinion: Falling Into Heresy, Even Merely Internally, the Pope Loses the Papacy *Ipso Facto*

Because of the arguments already mentioned,[770] the followers of this second opinion do not deny that the pope might become a heretic. Admitting that there is a complete incompatibility between heresy and ecclesiastical jurisdiction—above all pontifical jurisdiction—they maintain that the heretical pope loses the papacy *ipso facto*, even before the external manifestation of his heresy.

1. Arguments in Favor of This Opinion

Various arguments support this opinion, which Suárez explains and refutes.[771] After showing, based on passages of Scripture, that the Faith is the foundation of the Church, Suárez writes:

> Therefore, if the faith is the foundation of the Church, it is also the foundation of the papacy and the hierarchical order of the Church. This is confirmed by the fact that it is the reason presented to explain why Christ asked Saint Peter for a profession of faith before promising him the papacy (Matt. 16). A second confirmation: Frequently, the Fathers say that he who does not have faith cannot hold jurisdiction in the Church, for example, Saint Cyprian (referred to in the chapter "Novatianus," 7, q. 1; chap. "Didicimus," 24, g. 1), Saint Ambrose (chap. *Verbum*, de Poenitentia, q. 1), Pope Saint Gelasius (chap. "Achatius," 1) and Alexander II (chap. "Audivimus," 24, q. 1), Saint Augustine (*epist. 48 ad Vincent.*; lib. *De Pastoribus*), Saint Thomas (II–II, q. 39). A third confirmation, by way of a very simple argu-

---

770. In this matter, as is evident, the arguments in favor of one opinion constitute, in general, objections to the others, and vice-versa. Accordingly, in the chapter dedicated to each opinion, we present only the reasons pro and con that offer something new.

In the present case, it is not necessary to indicate the foundations of the thesis that the pope can become a heretic, for they are enunciated in the objections raised against the previous opinion.

771. In the last centuries, no author we have heard of defended this opinion. Among the ancients, its principal defender was Cardinal Thomas de Torquemada (uncle of the inquisitor of the same name).

ment: a heretic is not a member of the Church and in consequence, neither is he the head. Further: the heretic should not even be saluted. Rather he should be absolutely avoided, as Saint Paul teaches (Tit. 3) and Saint John (2 John). Much less, therefore, ought he to be obeyed. Finally: The heretical pontiff denies Christ and the true Church. Consequently, he denies himself and his office. Consequently, for this same reason, he is deprived of that office.[772]

2. Reasons Against This Second Opinion

The arguments opposed to this second opinion are mainly grounded on the visible character of the Church, because of which it is impossible to declare the loss of jurisdiction for reasons unknowable and unverifiable by the faithful. Here is how Suárez develops his argument in this regard:

> The loss of faith for merely internal heresy does not cause the loss of the power of jurisdiction. . . . This is proved in the first place by the fact that the [ecclesiastical] government would become very uncertain if the power depended on interior thoughts and sins. Another proof: given that the Church is visible, her governing power must also be visible, dependent, therefore, on external actions and not on mere mental cogitations. This is an *a priori* reason, for, in such a case, the Church does not take away the power through her human law since it does not judge what is internal, as we shall see further on. Neither is the power taken away through mere divine law, for this either is natural, that is to say, co-natural to the supernatural gifts themselves or established by a positive determination. The first part of the dilemma cannot be accepted, for it is impossible to demonstrate a necessary connection between faith and the power of jurisdiction by the very nature of things. Further, because the power of orders is even more supernatural but it is not lost. This constitutes a truth of faith, as is shown more amply in the treatise on the sacraments in general and as Saint Thomas teaches (II–II, q. 39, a. 3). Therefore, while the faith is the foundation of sanctification and of the gifts that pertain to it, it is not, however, the foundation of the other powers and graces, which are conceded for the benefit of other men. The second part of the dilemma is eliminated with the simple observation that neither by Tradition nor Scripture is it possible to demonstrate the existence of this positive divine law. Finally, it is consistent with reason that just as ecclesiastical jurisdiction is only conferred through some human act—whether it be only designative, that is elective of the person, as in the case of the supreme pontiff, or be it the conferring of power, as in the other cases—neither should it be taken away except

---

772. Suárez, *De fide*, disp. 10, sect. 6, no. 2, 316.

through some external action, for in both situations due proportion must be observed, considering the condition and nature of man.[773]

3. An Abandoned Opinion Today

As seen, this second opinion—of the loss of the papacy through merely internal heresy—is rooted in the thesis, today abandoned by the majority of theologians, that even a heresy that is not manifested externally causes the loss of membership in the Church.[774] Among these two positions, there does not exist, however, a necessary connection. Thus, while admitting that merely internal heresy excludes from the Church,[775] Cardinal Journet is nevertheless inclined to believe that the heretical pope is not *ipso facto* removed.[776] Suárez also considered that the internal heretic ceased to be a member of the Church.[777] However, he thought it would require a declaratory act for the heretical pope to fall from the Chair of Peter.[778]

In more general terms, it is opportune to observe that, while an intimate connection exists between exclusion from the Church and the loss of the papacy, many theologians do not hold that the former determines *ipso facto* the latter.[779]

It is understood, then, that the opinion whereby merely internal heresy determines the loss of the papacy has been completely abandoned by theologians.

---

773. Suárez, *De legibus*, book 4, chap. 7, no. 7, 360.
774. The various positions of theologians regarding the moment when a heretic ceases to be a member of the Church can be seen in Salaverri, *De ecclesia Christi*, 1:881–82.
775. See Charles Journet, *L'Église du Verbe Incarné*, 2nd ed. rev. (Bruges: Desclée de Brouver, 1962), 2:575n3; 821n3; 1064 (where he cites a section of the bull *Ineffabilis Deus* of Pius IX).
776. See Journet, *L'Église*, 2:821n3.
777. See Salaverri, *De ecclesia Christi*, 1:881.
778. See the text of Suárez in chap. 11, sec. 1 (*Defense of This Opinion by Suárez*).
779. On this point, see the considerations of Suárez—chap. 11, sec. 1 (*Defense of This Opinion by Suárez*)—and Saint Robert Bellarmine—chap. 11, sec. 2 (*Refutation of This Opinion by Saint Robert Bellarmine*).

CHAPTER TEN

Third Opinion: Even If He Falls Into Notorious Heresy, the Pope Never Loses the Papacy

This third opinion—which Saint Robert Bellarmine classifies as "exceedingly improbable"[780]—is defended by a single theologian among the 136 ancient and modern theologians whose position on this matter we could verify. We are speaking of the French canonist Bouix, and he argues as follows:[781]

> 2. There is insufficient reason to think that Christ had determined that a heretical pope could be deposed. The reason allegeable in favor of that deposition would be the enormous evil that would befall the Church if such a pope were not deposed. Now this reason does not hold: for, on the one hand, a heretical pope does not constitute an evil so great that it necessarily leads the Church to ruin and destruction;[782] and, on the other, the deposition would be a remedy much worse than the evil itself.[783]

---

780. St. Robert Bellarmine, *On the Roman Pontiff*, book 2, chap. 30, 338.

781. As seen in the following pages, Bouix judges it more probable that the pope could not fall into heresy. Given such a hypothesis, however, he maintains that the sovereign pontiff would retain his office. Note also that Bouix affirms explicitly that faced with a heretical pope, the faithful should not remain motionless but should resist his iniquitous decisions. (On the right of resistance, even public resistance, to the decisions of ecclesiastical authority, see Chapter 18).

782. Bouix argues here by way of hyperbole. No author has said that the Church would necessarily be brought "to ruin and destruction" if the heretical pope retained the papacy. That which constitutes the common opinion—which Bouix seems to underestimate or even deny—is that the permanence of such a pope in his office would cause great evils for the Church and the salvation of souls, for heresy "spreads like cancer" (2 Tim. 2:17—see also the commentary of Suárez on this passage—cited by us at chap. 11, sec. 1 (*Defense of This Opinion by Suárez*), points 5–7—and, once installed in the See of Peter, it would constitute "a peril for the faith so imminent and among all the gravest." Ballerini, *De potestate ecclesiastica*, 104; we quote this text in chap. 12, sec. 2 (*Defense of This Opinion by Father Pietro Ballerini*).

783. The principal reason allegeable against the permanence of the heretical pope in the papacy is not the evil which would arise thereby for the Church but the incompatibility between heresy and ecclesiastical jurisdiction, as we show in chap. 13, sec. 2 (*Incompatibility in Root*). In this regard, see also the explanations given by Saint Robert Bellarmine—chap. 12, sec. 1 (*Defense of This Opinion by Saint Robert Bellarmine*) and Ballerini—chap. 12, sec. 2 (*Defense of This Opinion by Father Pietro Ballerini*). As for the affirmation that the loss of the papacy by the heretical pope would bring about greater evils than his holding on to the office, see footnote 802.

In the first place, therefore, we have said that the papal heresy we discuss here does not constitute an evil so grave that it necessarily obliges one to think that Christ would desire the deposition of such a pontiff. It is a question, in effect, of exclusively *private*[784] heresy, that is, professed by the pontiff not as Pastor of the Church and in his papal decrees and acts, but only as a private doctor and solely in his private speeches and writings. Now, as long as the pope teaches the true faith whenever he defines or makes pronouncements as pontiff, the faithful will be sufficiently safe, even though it be known, at the same time, that the pope himself adheres privately to some heresy. All would easily understand that an opinion defended by the pope as a private doctor would be deprived of authority and that he should only be obeyed when he defined or imposed truths of faith officially and with pontifical authority. If anyone, despite this, insists that the private heresy of the pope could be harmful to such a point that Christ would not be able to leave His Church without a remedy against so great an evil,[785] we respond that we also hold this opinion as being the most probable. Still, as a remedy, we point to the special Providence of Christ so that the pope does not fall into heresy, not even as a private doctor. We absolutely deny, however, that Christ could have established the deposition of the pope as a remedy.

For—this is our *second* assertion—such a remedy would be worse than the evil itself. Indeed, one either supposes that this deposition would be carried out by Christ Himself as soon as the pope were declared a heretic by a General Council, according to the doctrine of Suárez, or one supposes that it would be realized through the authority of the General Council itself. Now, in both cases, the evil would be aggravated and not remedied. For the doctrine according to which Christ himself would depose the heretical pope, as soon as the General Council declared him a heretic, is no more than an opinion, rejected by many, and with which it is licit, for anyone whatsoever, to disagree. Suárez himself judges this opinion less probable, in as much as he reputes it to be more *probable* that there cannot be a heretical pope, not even privately. Such being the case, even after a General Council declared that a particular pope was a heretic, it would absolutely not become certain that the pope would be deposed. In such a

---

784. In this passage, Bouix does not consider all the possible hypotheses. He says it is a matter of exclusively private heresy, as long as the pope does not err when he defines and imposes truths of faith. In these, however, the possibility of errors and even heresies is not excluded, as we show in Chapters 15 and 16. Therefore, the argument presented here by Bouix is not conclusive since it is based on an inadequate division.

785. Note that Bouix tries to refute the text of Suárez, which we present in chap. 11, sec. 1 (*Defense of This Opinion by Suárez*), points 6–7.

doubt, one must rather continue to respect his authority.[786] If another pope were elected, not only would he be of uncertain legitimacy, but he would even have to be branded as an intruder. Therefore, the remedy of a deposition made by Christ in the moment of a Conciliar declaration not only would not remedy the evil but would create a graver one, that is, a most intricate schism. Consequently, one should not think that Christ established such a remedy. But neither should one think that He established as a remedy deposition by the authority of a Council itself. For, the deposition of a pope by a Council, besides being impossible,[787] as will be said further on, would be followed by a worse evil if it were possible. In fact, the concession to a Council, by Christ, of such authority over a heretical pope is no more than a simple opinion most commonly rejected by Catholic doctors and even intrinsically inadmissible, as is easily demonstrated. Then, after such deposition, it would not be certain that the heretical pope would have been deprived of the pontifical primacy. Many would brand as an intruder whoever was elected in his place, and he would be licitly rejected. This measure, therefore, would not bring a remedy but rather a schism, confusion, and dissension.[788]

2. It would be most harmful to the Church if the pope were deposed *ipso facto* for being a heretic because this would be done when he was a notorious and public heretic, for hidden external heresy, or even internal heresy. If it were for public and notorious heresy, doubts would arise concerning the degree of notoriety or infamy necessary for the pontiff to be considered deprived of the papacy.[789] Thence would arise schisms, and everything would become uncertain, the more so if, despite the alleged notoriety, the pope were to retain his office by force or any other means and continued to perform many papal acts. If the deposition were made on the grounds of external but hidden heresy, there would arise even greater evils. For all the acts of such a pontiff, secretly heretical, would be null and invalid, but this would only be known to a few persons. Such difficulty

---

786. Bouix is correct when he affirms that, when there is doubt, one should continue to respect the authority of the pope in all things that are not opposed to the principles of the Faith for the loss of jurisdiction is only effected when it is demonstrated (*melior est conditio possidentis*).

We believe, however, that the doubt to which Bouix alludes can be resolved today by the joint action of the theologians, for there are ways for them to reach a *common opinion* in this matter—see last three paragraphs of Introduction to Part Two and chap. 13, sec. 6 (*Conclusion*).

787. On this point, Bouix is undoubtedly correct, for a Council could only depose a pope *by its own authority* if it were superior to him, and it is a dogma of the faith that a Council is not, in any circumstance, above the pope.

788. Bouix, *Tractatus de papa*, 2:670–71.

789. It does not seem that Bouix is correct here. Many rights and obligations are based on concrete facts whose complexity can furnish a margin for discussion. Nevertheless, for all that, one ought not to deny, in principle, the existence of such rights and obligations.

The point we made—see last five paragraphs of Introduction to Part Two—about the necessity of a more profound study of the whole question of a heretical pope holds in connection with the disagreement which could arise among theologians over the case analyzed here by Bouix.

would be even greater, as is obvious if the pope were deposed *ipso facto* on account of internal heresy. . . .[790]

3. Faith is not necessary for a man to be capable of ecclesiastical jurisdiction nor to exercise true acts that require such jurisdiction. Because, as taught in the treatises on penance and censures, a heretical priest can absolve in case of extreme need. However, absolution requires and supposes jurisdiction. Moreover, the power of orders, which in its way is superior, can remain without faith, that is, with heresy. Therefore, ecclesiastical jurisdiction can do so, too. . . .

5. To the texts in which some Fathers teach that he who has not faith cannot have jurisdiction in the Church, we answer: this ought to be understood in the sense that without faith, ecclesiastical jurisdiction cannot be exercised appropriately, and in the sense that a heretic deserves to be deprived of jurisdiction: some of these texts must be interpreted as determinations of Canon Law relative to the bishops, in particular, determinations which declare them to be deposed *ipso facto*. . . .

6. To the argument that *not being a member of the Church, the heretical pope is not the head of the Church either*, . . . [o]ne can answer: I concede that the heretical pope is not a member and head of the Church insofar as the supernatural life which commences by faith and is completed by charity, by which all the members of the Church are united in one body supernaturally alive. I deny, however, that he might not be a member and head of the Church regarding the governing power proper to his office. Indeed, it is not absurd to suggest that Christ wishes that the pope (the same might be said of a bishop concerning his diocese), while he might not be part of this body supernaturally alive due to heresy, should nevertheless still retain the power of governing the Church, exactly as if he had not lost the supernatural life mentioned above.[791] Regarding the power of orders, there is no doubt that Christ did not wish that either heretical priests or bishops be deprived of this power, although because of heresy, they have already ceased to be a member of the Church in the sense indicated. Now, the permanence of jurisdiction in a bishop would not be more absurd than in a heretical pope, whether the heresy is only internal or external.[792]

---

790. The argument of Bouix against the loss of the papacy by a pope who is only secretly a heretic, or only internally a heretic, seems decisive. It is founded upon the visible character of the Church.

Note that the hypothesis of merely internal heresy corresponds to the second opinion enumerated by Saint Robert Bellarmine—see position B.II.1 in the synoptic outline at the end of Chapter 7 and also Chapter 9—while the hypothesis of external but hidden heresy constitutes one of the subdivisions which we introduce in the fifth opinion of Saint Robert Bellarmine—see our observations at position B.II.2 in the Synoptic Outline at the end of Chapter 7, and further on at chap. 12, sec. 3 (*Subdivision of This Opinion*).

791. It does not appear that Bouix gives due importance here to the principle that heresy brings about *ipso facto* the loss of any ecclesiastical jurisdiction whatsoever, at least *in radice* (in its root). We lay out this principle in Chapter 13.

792. Bouix, *Tractatus de papa*, 2:660–62.

Bouix expresses his thinking on the matter in a summary formula: "If the case of a pope privately a heretic were possible, one must judge that, despite this, Christ desired that this pope retain the supreme authority and that in no way might he be deprived of that authority by a General Council."[793]

Immediately after that, he declares in perhaps more emphatic terms, "As to Suárez and many others, it appears more *probable* to me that the pope, even as a private person, cannot fall into heresy. But in the hypothesis that he could become a heretic privately, I would deny absolutely that he would be deposed *ipso facto* or that any Council could depose him."[794]

*   *   *

Despite Bouix's great efforts to defend this third opinion, it seems that one ought to qualify it, with Saint Robert Bellarmine, as "very improbable." Indeed, it has against it the practically unanimous Tradition of the Church.[795] It does not harmonize with numerous texts of Sacred Scripture; it does not seem to give due importance to the extreme evil a heretical pope could do to the Church; and it is so much a minority opinion among theologians that Cardinal Camillo Mazzella, S.J. even affirms that, among those who admit the possibility of a heretical pope, no author denies or doubts that he would be removed from his charge *ipso facto*, or at least must be removed.[796]

---

793. Bouix, 2:666.
794. Bouix, 2:666. (Our emphasis.)
795. We remind the reader that, of 136 authors we consulted, only Bouix defends this opinion.
796. See Card. Camillo Mazzella, *De religione et ecclesia* (Rome: Ex Typographia Polyglotta, 1880), 817. In the same sense, Cardinal Billot wrote, "Once this is supposed [that a pope had become a heretic], all concede that the bond of communion [with] and subjection [to him] would be dissolved, based on the divine dispositions which order expressly that heretics be avoided (Tit. 3:10; 2 John 10; etc.)." Billot, *Tractatus de ecclesia*, 1:615. See also R. de M., *Institutiones iuris canonici* (Paris: Lecoffre, 1853), 1:265.

CHAPTER ELEVEN

Fourth Opinion: The Pope Heretic Only Loses the Papacy With an Act Declaratory of His Heresy

According to this fourth opinion, the pope never loses the papacy through his fall into heresy. Rather, for his deposition to be effective, there must be an act declaratory of his defection from the faith. As is obvious, such a declaration cannot be a judicial decision in the strict sense, given that the pope has no superior on Earth to judge him.[797] Instead, it would be a non-judicial declaration, on account of which Jesus Christ Himself would depose the pope.

The principal followers of this fourth opinion are Cajetan and Suárez.[798]

1. Defense of This Opinion by Suárez

After refuting the opinion according to which the heretical pope is automatically *deposed*,[799] Suárez defends his position in the following terms:

---

797. Therefore, this fourth opinion is absolutely not the same as Conciliarism—a theory condemned as heretical, according to which the Council would be superior to the pope, being able, therefore, to judge and depose him.

Among the possible solutions to the question of a heretical pope, we do not study the conciliarist opinion because, while it had many followers in the past, it is nevertheless manifestly unacceptable to Catholics, particularly after the definitions of the First Vatican Council.

798. We reemphasize that Suárez is a partisan of the first opinion, defending this fourth one only in the hypothesis—which he judges less probable—that the pope could fall into heresy—see the text supported by footnote 767. Cajetan, on the contrary, admits positively the possibility of the pope's defection from the faith (*De comparatio*, 112ff.), as was, moreover, a common opinion in his time.

799. *Deposition*: the use of the term *deposition* in a different sense than the common one has already become classical in this matter. For example, the aphorisms *Papa haereticus est depositus* ("the pope heretic is deposed") and *Papa haereticus non est depositus sed deponendus* ("the pope heretic is not deposed, but must be deposed") are commonplace. They express respectively the thesis of the automatic loss of the papacy and that of the loss after a declaration (see explanation in Journet, *L'Église*, 1:626).

As is evident, in this theological context, the term deposition cannot be understood in its ordinary sense, for thus one would fall into Conciliarism, that is, admitting that some human power—normally the Council—could strip the pope from his office. In the above-mentioned aphorisms and the faithful authors using the term *deposition* in this theological context, the word signifies only the loss of the papacy. That will be seen in the text of Suárez that we go on to cite.

It seems advisable to eliminate the term *deposition* from ongoing debates about the matter, for,

3. . . . In no case, even that of heresy, is the pontiff deprived of his dignity and power immediately by God Himself, before the judgment and sentence of man. This is the common opinion today: Cajetan (*De auctoritate papae*, c. 18 et 19); Soto (4, d. 22, quaest. 2, art. 2); Cano (4 *de locis*, c. ult. ad 12); Corduba (book 4, q. 11). Later, when discussing the penalties of heretics, we will list other authors, and in a general manner show that by divine law no one is deprived of dignity and ecclesiastical jurisdiction because of the crime of heresy. Now we will give an *a priori* argument: since such a deposition is a most grave penalty, one would only incur it *ipso facto* if it were expressed in divine law. However, we do not find any law establishing this, either generally, as far as heretics are concerned, or in particular as to bishops, nor in a very particular way insofar as the pope is concerned.[800] Neither does Tradition address this matter. Nor can the pope lose his dignity *ipso facto* through human law, for it would have to be established by an inferior, that is, by a Council, or by an equal, that is, by a previous pope. However, neither a Council nor a previous pope possesses such coercive power as to be able to punish a superior or equal.

4. . . . You will say that there could be a law interpreting Divine Law. However, this would be without foundation, for you do not quote any such Divine Law. Furthermore, until now, no law interpreting such a Divine Law has been laid down by the Councils or popes.

This is confirmed by the fact that such a law would harm the Church. By no means would one be able to believe that Christ had instituted it. The foregoing is proved: if the pope were a hidden heretic and had consequently fallen *ipso facto* from his office, all his acts would be invalid. You will say that this argument proves nothing insofar as a notorious and public heretic is concerned. But this is not true, for if the external but hidden heretic can still be the true pope, with equal right, he can continue being pope should that offense become known, as long as sentence has not been passed on him. This is how it is both because no one suffers a penalty if it is not *ipso facto* or by sentence,[801] and because even greater evils would arise by doing this. Indeed, doubts would arise about the degree of infamy necessary for him to lose his office. Schisms would arise because of this, and everything would become uncertain, especially if, after being known

---

in the civil plane, it indicates exclusively the act whereby someone removes another from an office. In so doing, we would defend more comfortably the traditional thesis against neo-conciliarists reappearing all around us.

800. This affirmation of Suárez seems baseless. Saint Paul (see Tit. 3:10) and Saint John (see 2 John 1:10–11) command us to avoid heretics. Now—asks Saint Robert Bellarmine when he answers Suárez—"How will we shun our head? How will we recede from a member to whom we are joined?" St. Robert Bellarmine, *On the Roman Pontiff*, book 2, chap. 30, 339. We cite this text in its entirety at chap. 11, sec. 2 (*Refutation of This Opinion by Saint Robert Bellarmine*).

801. The dilemma presented here by Suárez is undoubtedly valid since, evidently, no one incurs a penalty unless it is *ipso facto* or by sentence. Nevertheless, Suárez does not appear to perceive that, according to the fifth opinion, there is a fact that carries as a consequence the automatic loss of the papacy, that fact being a *complex offense*, for it involves, in addition to secret heresy, its public manifestation.

as a heretic, the pope should have maintained himself in possession of the papacy by force or other means and performed many papal acts.[802]

A second confirmation, which is of great importance, is as follows: If the pope's heresy became external but hidden, and he then turned back with true repentance, he would find himself in total perplexity. For if the heresy removed him from the office, then he ought absolutely to abandon the papacy, which is most serious and almost contrary to natural law, for it is to denounce oneself. However, he could not retain the bishopric [of Rome], for this would be intrinsically evil. This being the case, even the defenders of the contrary opinion confess that in this event, it would be licit to retain the diocese and that he would, therefore, be the true pope. This is the common opinion of the canonists and of the Gloss (c. *Nunc autem*, d. 21). From thence, one infers an evident argument against them: The pontifical office is not restored by God through penance, as grace is, for it is unheard of that he who is not the true pope be made pope by God without the election and ministry of men.[803]

Finally, the faith is not absolutely necessary for a man to be capable of spiritual and ecclesiastical jurisdiction and exercise true acts which demand this jurisdiction. The preceding is obvious, given that, as is taught in the treatises on penance and censures, in case of extreme necessity, a priest heretic may absolve, which is not possible without jurisdiction.[804]

5. . . . The heretical pope is not a member of the Church as far as the substance and form which constitute the members of the Church. However, he is the head as far as the office and action. This is not surprising since he is not the primary and principal head who acts by his own power but is, as it were, an instrument. He is the vicar of the principal head, who

---

802. As we see, the opinion attacked here by Suárez is the fifth opinion presented and subscribed to by St. Robert Bellarmine (see also the Synoptic Outline, position B.II.2, and Chapter 13).

Unquestionably, the concrete application of this opinion in the eventual case of a heretical pope could occasion the gravest confusions and afflictions for the Church. It seems, nevertheless, that, supposing the hypothesis of a heretical pope, these confusions and afflictions would follow inescapably, regardless of which opinion one adopted. Considering things only from the perspective of the schisms, confusions, and rivalries that could arise, we do not consider any of the opinions preferable to the rest. We shall take as an example only the position of Suárez: What divisions could not arise if some cardinals and bishops declared the pope a heretic while others supported him!

We believe, however, that this is not the perspective from which to address the question. It is not a question, fundamentally, of asking which is the solution that would best keep the "peace" Rather, one should ask which would best keep the faith and which would be more in accordance with the divine institution of the Church. From this viewpoint, as we will state in Chapter 13, we judge that there are solid reasons to embrace the fifth opinion, with St. Robert Bellarmine, Wernz and Vidal, and others.

803. Today, the thesis that he who is not the true pope can be "made pope by God without the election and ministry of men" does not sound so bad to the ears of many theologians, for St. Alphonsus Liguori admits, in principle, such an eventuality. He teaches that a pope intruder would become a true pope if peacefully accepted by the Church universally. This is a little-known and extremely delicate point of doctrine, which we analyze in chap. 14, sec. 2 (*The Hypothesis of a Dubious Pope*), item C.

804. See chap. 13, sec. 2 (*Incompatibility in Root*) on the *in radice* (in the root) but *not absolute* incompatibility existing between heresy and ecclesiastical jurisdictions.

can exercise his spiritual action over the members, even through a head of bronze. Analogously, sometimes he baptizes using heretics, sometimes he absolves, etc., as we have said.

6. . . . I affirm that if he is a heretic and incorrigible, the pope ceases to be pope as soon as a declared sentence of his crime is pronounced against him by the legitimate Church jurisdiction. This is the common position held by the doctors and can be concluded from the first Epistle of Pope St. Clement I, in which one reads that St. Peter taught that the heretical pope should be deposed. The reason is the following: It would be extremely harmful to the Church to have such a pastor and not be able to defend herself from so grave a danger. Furthermore, it would go against the Church's dignity to oblige her to remain subject to a heretical pope without being able to expel him from herself, for such as are the prince and the priest, so the people are accustomed to being. The reasons adduced in favor of the previous opinion (that of deposition *ipso facto*) confirm this, especially when it says that heresy "spreads like cancer," which is why heretics should be avoided as much as possible. This is, therefore, all the more so regarding the heretical pastor. However, how can such a situation be avoided unless he ceases to be the pastor?

7. . . . Concerning this conclusion, some explanations should be made. In the first place, who should pronounce such a sentence? Some say that it should be the cardinals. The Church could undoubtedly assign them this faculty, above all, if it were established with the consent and decision of the supreme pontiff, as it was done for the election. But throughout and up to the present, we have not read anywhere that such a judgment has been confided to them. For this reason, it must be affirmed that, of itself, it belongs to all the bishops of the Church. For since they are the ordinary pastors and pillars of the Church, one should consider that such a case concerns them. Since by Divine Law there is no reason to affirm that the matter interests more these bishops than those, and since by human law there is nothing established in the matter, it must needs be sustained that the matter should be referred to all of them, and even to the General Council. This is the common opinion of the doctors. One can see what Cardinal Albano posits regarding this point at length (*De cardinalibus*, q. 35, 1584 ed., 13:2).

8. Second doubt. . . . How can such a Council be called together legitimately when it is the pope who lawfully should convoke it? One answers, in the first place, that perhaps it would not be necessary for a General Council as such to meet. It might suffice if, in each region, there met provincial or national councils, convoked by the archbishops or primates, and that all arrived at the same conclusion. In the second place, if a General Council meets to define matters of faith or to lay down universal laws, it can only legitimately be convoked by the pope, but if it meets to deal with the matter of which we speak, which especially concerns the pope himself and is in some way opposed to him, the Council can legitimately

be convoked either by the College of Cardinals or by the agreement of the bishops. In addition, if the pontiff tries to prevent such a meeting, they should not obey him because he would be abusing his supreme power, acting against justice and the common good.

9. . . . From this arises a third doubt: By what right could the pope be judged by the assembly, being superior to it?[805] In this matter, Cajetan makes extraordinary efforts to avoid being forced to admit that the Church or a Council is above the pope in case of heresy. He concludes in the end that the Church and the Council are superior to the pope, not as a pope, but as a private person. This distinction, however, is unsatisfactory, for, with the same argument, one could say it belongs to the Church to judge or to punish the pope, not as pope, but as a private person; . . .

10. . . . Others affirm that, in the case of heresy, the Church is superior to the pope, but this is hard to admit, for Christ constituted the pope as the absolute supreme judge. The canons also affirm this principle in a general way and without distinctions. Finally, the Church cannot exercise any jurisdiction over the pope and, when electing him, does not confer the power upon him but designates the person upon whom Christ directly confers the power. Therefore, on deposing a heretical pope, the Church would not act as superior to him, but juridically, and, by the consent of Christ, she would declare him a heretic and, therefore, unworthy of pontifical honors.[806] He would be then *ipso facto*[807] and immediately deposed by Christ, and, once deposed, he would become inferior and punishable.[808]

---

805. Here is the principal objection which can be raised against this fourth opinion. As Suárez demonstrates, Cajetan does not meet it successfully. It seems that the solution presented by Suárez is also unsatisfactory, as we will explain in footnotes 806 next and 841.

806. Behold the central point, which appears weak, of Suárez's arguments. He admits that the Council, while inferior to the pope, would be able nevertheless to *juridically* declare him a heretic and deposed from the papacy. Things being so, the Council would be, in the true sense, *judging* the pope—and one cannot admit that it possesses this attribute even in the case of heresy in the person of the sovereign pontiff. It is not enough to say that the Council would not *depose* the pope but would only *judge* him, and Christ would depose him—for even this power to *judge* a pope does not exist.

On the other hand, the *juridical* declaration defended by the fourth opinion has nothing to do with a *non-judicial declaration*, which could be made by the Council or by anyone of the faithful, before or after the loss of the papacy by the heretical pope. Such a declaration, even though previous to the effective loss of office, *would not be an official judicial act* because of which the deposition would take place. Rather, it would only seek to warn Catholic opinion against the heresy of the chief pastor of the Church. All authors admit such a *non-judicial* declaration is legitimate (see Chapter 18).

807. One must not confuse the loss of the office *ipso facto*, which characterizes the fifth opinion, with this one that Suárez refers to here. In the fourth opinion, the *fact* is the declaration of the pope's heresy, whereas, in the fifth, the *fact* is the manifest heresy itself.

808. Suárez, *De fide*, disp. 10, sect. 6 nos. 3–10, 316–18.

2. Refutation of This Opinion by Saint Robert Bellarmine

Saint Robert Bellarmine, who did not approve of this fourth opinion, refutes it as follows:[809]

> The fourth opinion is of Cajetan. There he teaches that a manifestly heretical pope is not *ipso facto* deposed;[810] but can and ought to be deposed by the Church. Now in my judgment, such an opinion cannot be defended. For in the first place, that a manifest heretic would be *ipso facto* deposed, is proven from authority and reason. The authority is of St. Paul, who commands Titus, that after two censures, that is, after he appears manifestly pertinacious, a heretic is to be shunned; and he understands this before excommunication and sentence of a judge. Jerome comments on the same place, saying that other sinners, through a judgment of excommunication are excluded from the Church; heretics, however, leave by themselves and are cut from the body of Christ, but a pope who remains the pope cannot be shunned. How will we shun our head? How will we recede from a member to whom we are joined?
>
> Now in regard to reason this is indeed very certain. A non-Christian cannot in any way be pope, as Cajetan affirms in the same book, and the reason is because he cannot be the head of that which he is not a member, and he is not a member of the Church who is not a Christian. But a manifest heretic is not a Christian, as St. Cyprian and many other Fathers clearly teach. Therefore, a manifest heretic cannot be pope.
>
> Cajetan responds in a defense of the aforementioned treatise, chapter 25, and in the treatise itself chapter 22, that a heretic is not a Christian simply; but is relatively. For since two things make a Christian, faith and the character, a heretic loses the virtue of faith, but still retains the character; and for that reason, still adheres in some way to the Church, and has the capacity for jurisdiction. Hence, he is still pope, but must be deposed, because due to heresy and his final disposition he is disposed to not be pope; as such he is a man, not yet dead, but constituted *in extremis*.
>
> But on the contrary, since in the first place, were a heretic to remain joined with the Church in act by reason of the character, he could never be cut off and separated from her, because the character is indelible; yet everyone affirms that some can be cut off from the Church *de facto*. Consequently, the character does not cause a heretical man [to] be in the Church by act; rather, it is only a sign that he was in the Church, and that he ought to be in the Church. While the character impressed upon a sheep when it

---

809. In the text cited immediately below, St. Robert Bellarmine presents and refutes the principal reasons alleged by Cajetan in defense of this fourth opinion. We refer the reader wishing to know in greater detail Cajetan's position on the question of a heretical pope to his works *De comparatione auctoritatis papae et concilii* and *Apologia de comparata auctoritate papae et concilii*.
810. We repeat that the term *deposition* is used by St. Robert Bellarmine in the generic sense of loss of the papacy and not in the current usage of an act by which a human power deprives someone of an office.

was in the mountains does not cause it to be in the sheepfold; it indicates from which fold it fled, and to where it can be driven back again. This is also confirmed by St. Thomas, who says that those who do not have faith are not united to Christ in act, but only in potency, and there he speaks on internal union, not external, which is made through the confession of faith, and the visible Sacraments. Therefore, since the character pertains to what is internal and not external, according to St. Thomas, the character alone does not unite a man with Christ in act. Next, either faith is a necessary disposition as one for this purpose, that someone should be pope, or it is merely that he be a good pope. If the first, then after that disposition has been abolished through its opposite, which is heresy, soon after the pope ceases to be pope. For the form cannot be preserved without its necessary dispositions. If the second, then a pope cannot be deposed on account of heresy. On the other hand, in general, he ought to be deposed even on account of ignorance and wickedness, and other dispositions which are necessary to be a good pope; and besides Cajetan affirms that the pope cannot be deposed from a defect of dispositions that are not necessary as one, but merely necessary for one to be a good pope.

Cajetan responds that faith is a necessary disposition simply, but in part not in total, and hence with faith being absent the pope still remains pope, on account of another part of the disposition which is called the character, and that still remains.

But on the other hand, either the total disposition which is the character and faith is necessary as one unit, or it is not, and a partial disposition suffices. If the first, then without faith, the necessary disposition does not remain any longer as one, because the whole was necessary as one unit and now it is no longer total. If the second, then faith is not required to be good, and hence on account of his defect, a pope cannot be deposed. Thereupon, those things which have the final disposition to ruin, soon after cease to exist, without another external force, as is clear; therefore, even a heretical pope, without another disposition ceases to be pope *per se*.

Next, the holy Fathers teach in unison that not only are heretics outside the Church, but they even lack all ecclesiastical jurisdiction and dignity *ipso facto*. Cyprian says: "We say that all heretics and schismatics have not power and right." He also teaches that heretics returning to the Church must be received as laymen; even if beforehand they were priests or bishops in the Church. Optatus teaches that heretics and schismatics cannot hold the keys of the kingdom of heaven, nor loose or bind. Ambrose and Augustine teach the same, as does St. Jerome who says: "Bishops who were heretics cannot continue to be so; rather let them be constituted such who were received that were not heretics."

Pope Celestine I, in an epistle to John of Antioch, which is contained in Volume One of the Council of Ephesus, ch. 19, says: "If anyone who was either excommunicated or exiled by Bishop Nestorius, or any that followed him, from such a time as he began to preach such things, whether they be from the dignity of a bishop or clergy, it is manifest that he has endured and endures in our communion, nor do we judge him outside, because he could not remove anyone by a sentence, who himself had already shown that he must be removed." And in a letter to the clergy of Constantinople: "The authority of our see has sanctioned that the bishop, cleric or Christian by simple profession who had been deposed or excommunicated by Nestorius or his followers, after the latter began to preach heresy, shall not be considered deposed or excommunicated. For he who had defected from the faith with such preaching, cannot depose or remove anyone whatsoever.

Nicholas I confirms and repeats the same thing in his epistle to the Emperor Michael. Next, even St. Thomas teaches that schismatics soon lose all jurisdiction; and if they try to do something from jurisdiction, it is useless.

Nor does the response which some make avail, that these Fathers speak according to ancient laws, but now since the decree of the Council of Constance they do not lose jurisdiction, unless excommunicated by name, or if they strike clerics. I say this avails to nothing. For those Fathers, when they say that heretics lose jurisdiction, do not allege any human laws which maybe did not exist then on this matter; rather, they argued from the nature of heresy. Moreover, the Council of Constance does not speak except on the excommunicates, that is, on these who lose jurisdiction through a judgment of the Church. Yet heretics are outside the Church, even before excommunication, and deprived of all jurisdiction, for they are condemned by their own judgment, as the Apostle teaches to Titus; that is, they are cut from the body of the Church without excommunication, as Jerome expresses it.[811]

Next, what Cajetan says in the second place, that a heretical pope who is truly pope can be deposed by the Church, and from its authority, seems no less false than the first. For, if the Church deposes a pope against his will, certainly it is over the pope. Yet the same Cajetan defends the opposite in the very same treatise. But he answers: the Church, in the very matter, when it deposes the pope, does not have authority over the pope, but only on that union of the person with the pontificate. As the Church can join the pontificate to such a person, and still it is not said on that account to be above the pontiff; so it can separate the pontificate from such a person in the case of heresy, and still it will not be said to be above the pope.

---

811. According to Canon Law (1917 CIC), there is no deposition *latae sententiae*; therefore, heretic bishops and priests continue to enjoy their charges and jurisdiction until their superiors depose them. Would such a determination be contrary to the principles which St. Robert Bellarmine expounds in the passage cited here? In part, yes, for he does not admit in any way the permanence in jurisdiction of a manifest heretic. However, if we consider that the pope can sustain, for the sake of the good of the Church, the jurisdiction as a heretic, and if we see that the holder of jurisdiction loses it, *in radice* (in its roots) by the very fact of his fall into heresy, we ascertain that the affirmation of St. Robert Bellarmine is entirely defensible as long as the nuances in these two points are preserved. For a perfect comprehension of what has just been said, we must keep in mind what we observe in Chapter 13.

On the other hand, from the very fact that the pope deposes bishops, they deduce that the pope is above all bishops, and still the pope deposing a bishop does not destroy the episcopacy, but only separates it from that person. Secondly, for one to be deposed from the pontificate against his will is without a doubt a penalty; therefore, the Church deposing a pope against his will, without a doubt punished him; but to punish is for a superior and a judge. Thirdly, because according to Cajetan and the other Thomists, in reality they are the same; the whole and the parts are taken up together. Therefore, he who has so great an authority over the parts taken up together, such that he can also separate them, also has it over the whole, which arises from those parts.

Furthermore, the example of Cajetan does not avail on electors, who have the power of applying the pontificate to a certain person, and still do not have power over the pope. For while a thing is made, the action is exercised over the matter of the thing that is going to be, not over a composite which does not yet exist; but while a thing is destroyed, the action is exercised over a composite; as is certain from natural things. Therefore, when cardinals create the pontiff, they exercise their authority not over the pontiff, because he does not yet exist; but over the matter, that is, over the person whom they dispose in a certain measure through election, for him to receive the form of the pontificate from God. But if they depose the pope, they necessarily exercise authority over the composite, that is, over the person provided with pontifical dignity, which is to say, over the pontiff.[812]

---

812. St. Robert Bellarmine, *On the Roman Pontiff*, book 2, chap. 30, 339–43.

CHAPTER TWELVE

Fifth Opinion: Falling Into Manifest Heresy, the Pope Loses the Papacy *Ipso Facto*

This opinion is defended by numerous renowned theologians, such as Saint Robert Bellarmine, Sylvius, Pietro Ballerini, Wernz and Vidal, and Cardinal Billot.[813]

1. Defense of This Opinion by Saint Robert Bellarmine

After refuting the other opinions on this matter, Saint Robert Bellarmine presents his position in the following terms:

> Now the fifth true opinion, is that a pope who is a manifest heretic, ceases in himself to be pope and head, just as he ceases in himself to be a Christian and member of the body of the Church; whereby he can be judged and punished by the Church. This is the opinion of all the ancient Fathers, who teach that manifest heretics soon lose all jurisdiction, and namely St. Cyprian who speaks on Novatian, who was a pope [anti-pope] in schism with Cornelius: "He cannot hold the episcopacy; although he was a bishop first, he fell from the body of his fellow bishops and from the unity of the Church." There he means that Novatian, even if he was a true and legitimate pope still would have fallen from the pontificate by himself if he separated himself from the Church.
>
> The opinion of the learned men of our age is the same, as John Driedo teaches, that they who are cast out as excommunicates, or leave on their own and oppose the Church, are separated from it as heretics and schismatics. He adds in the same work that those who have departed from the Church maintain no spiritual power over those who are in the Church.

---

813. See St. Robert Bellarmine, *On the Roman Pontiff*, book 2, chap. 30, 343–44. See also Franciscus Sylvius, *Commentarium in totam II–II S. Thomae Aquinatis* (Antwerp: Verdussen, 1697) q. 39, a. 1; Ballerini, *De potestate ecclesiastica*, 104–105; Wernz and Vidal: *Ius canonicum*, 2:433ff.; Billot, *Tractatus de ecclesia*, 1:609–10.

Melchior Cano teaches the same thing when he says that heretics are not part of the Church, nor members, and he adds in the last Chapter, 12th argument, that someone cannot even be informed in thought, so as to be head and pope, who is not a member nor a part. He teaches the same thing when he says that secret heretics are still in the Church and are parts and members, so that a secretly heretical pope is still pope. Others teach the same, whom we cite in Book 1 of *de Ecclesia*.

The foundation of this opinion is that a manifest heretic is in no way a member of the Church; that is, neither in spirit nor in body, or by internal union nor external. For even wicked Catholics are united and are members in spirit by faith, and in body through the confession of faith and the participation of the visible Sacraments. Secret heretics are united and are members, but only by an external union; just as on the other hand, good catechumens are in the Church only by an internal union but not an external one; manifest heretics by no union, as has been proved.[814]

2. Defense of This Opinion by Father Pietro Ballerini

The explanation that Fr. Pietro Ballerini—an eminent eighteenth-century Italian theologian and one more defender of this fifth opinion—gives for his position seems very enlightening.

After observing that the Council would only be able to pass sentence over a heretical pope if he were already deposed, Father Ballerini ponders:

> A peril for the faith so imminent and among all the gravest, as this of a pontiff who defended heresy, even just privately, could not be tolerated for long. Why expect remedy, then, from a General Council whose convocation is difficult? Is it not true that confronted with such a danger for the faith, any subjects can, by fraternal correction, warn their superior, resist him to his face, refute him and, if necessary, summon him and press him to repent? The cardinals, who are his counselors, can do this, or the Roman clergy, or the Roman Synod, if, being gathered, they judge this opportune. For the words of Saint Paul to Titus hold for any person, even a private one: "A man that is a heretic, after the first and second admonition, avoid: Knowing that he, that is such an one, is subverted, and sinneth, being condemned by his own judgment" (Tit. 3:10–11). For the person who, admonished once or twice, does not repent but continues pertinacious in an opinion contrary to a manifest or public dogma, this person declares himself openly a heretic. He is unable, by any means, to be excused on account of this public pertinacity of heresy proper, which requires pertinacity. He reveals that, by his own will, he has turned away from the Catholic Faith and the Church. Thus, no declaration or sentence whatsoever is now needed from anyone to cut him off from the body of the

---

814. St. Robert Bellarmine, *On the Roman Pontiff*, book 2, chap. 30, 343–44.

Church. In this matter, Saint Jerome's argument, given in connection with Saint Paul's cited words, is very clear: "Therefore it is said that the heretic has condemned himself. Because the fornicator, adulterer, murderer, and other sinners are expelled from the Church by the priests. Heretics pronounce sentence against themselves, however, excluding themselves spontaneously from the Church. This exclusion is their condemnation by their own conscience." Therefore, the pope, who, after such a solemn and public warning by the cardinals, the Roman clergy, or even a Synod, maintained himself hardened in heresy and openly turned away from the Church, would have to be avoided following Saint Paul's command. So that he might not harm the rest, his heresy and contumacy would have to be publicly proclaimed so that all might be equally on guard regarding him. Thus, the sentence he pronounced against himself would be made known to the whole Church, making clear that, by his own will, he turned away and separated himself from the body of the Church, and that, in a certain way, he abdicated the papacy, which no one who does not belong to the Church holds or can hold. One sees then that in the case of a heresy, to which the pope subscribed privately, there would be an immediate and efficacious remedy without the convocation of the General Council. In this hypothesis, whatever would be done against him before the declaration of his contumacy and heresy to call him to reason, would be an obligation of charity, not of jurisdiction. Further, if, after his turning away from the Church had been made manifest, sentence were passed on him by the Council, it would be pronounced against one who was no longer pope nor superior to the Council.[815]

3. Subdivision of This Fifth Opinion

We think that this fifth opinion ought to be subdivided into three.[816]

1. Some authors affirm that the pope loses the papacy *ipso facto* when he exteriorizes his heresy.

2. Others maintain that the loss occurs when the heresy becomes known to a certain number of persons, even if small.

3. Others, finally, judge that the heretical pope only falls from the Roman See when his heresy becomes "notorious and publicly divulged."[817]

*   *   *

815. Ballerini, *De potestate ecclesiastica*, 104–5.
816. We indicate this subdivision in the observation at position B.II.2 of the Synoptic Outline. Suárez, for example, alludes to this threefold subdivision in *De legibus*, book 4, chap. 7, no. 6, 360.
817. "Notoriam et palam divulgatam." [Notorious and publicly divulged.] The expression is from Wernz and Vidal, *Ius canonicum*, 2:433, no. 453.

This divergence is connected to a centuries-old dispute, which still divides theologians today over the exact moment when a heretic ceases to be a member of the Church.[818] We do not judge it necessary to explain here, in detail, the peculiarities of the subdivisions of this fifth opinion. Moreover, it seems unnecessary to show precisely the position of every holder of this opinion—especially since many of them are unclear. We will make only brief observations about the thinking of Saint Robert Bellarmine and Wernz and Vidal.

*   *   *

Salvo meliori judicio (with due respect for a better opinion), it seems that Saint Robert Bellarmine did not make his thesis sufficiently clear about the moment when the heretical pope would *ipso facto* lose the papacy.

He says that this would occur when the heresy became "manifest," and he contrasts the term "manifest" with "hidden."[819] Now, hidden heresy can be internal (hidden *per se*) or external but unknown to anyone else (hidden *per accidens*). If one attributes to Saint Robert Bellarmine the first interpretation, then the pope would lose the papacy in the moment when he exteriorized his heresy, even if no one perceived it. If one attributes to him the second, then the papacy's loss would occur when other persons—perhaps just one—knew the fact.

Is there room for a third interpretation? Can one understand as *hidden* heresy what is already known to many but has not yet reached the wider public, has not yet become "notorious and publicly divulged"? Wernz and Vidal adopt such an interpretation. They even affirm unhesitatingly that, according to Saint Robert Bellarmine, the heretical pope would only be deposed when his defection from the faith became "notorious and publicly divulged."[820]

---

818. As noted, there is no absolute correspondence between the position assumed by each author regarding the moment a heretic is excluded from the Church and his opinion on the question of a heretical pope.
819. See St. Robert Bellarmine, *On the Roman Pontiff*, book 2, chap. 30. See also Bellarmine, *On the Church Militant*, in *On the Church*, book 3, chaps. 4–10.
820. We would exceed the limits of this exposition if we tried to analyze how fluctuating are the concepts of *hidden*, *manifest*, *public*, *notorious*, and so forth, even among the best authors. We mention just some references on this point: 1917 CIC, canons 2197; 2259, §2; 2275, §1; Billot, *Tractatus de ecclesia*, 2:608–9; Lercher, *Institutiones theologiae*, 1:233, no. 407; Hervé, *Manuale theologiae dogmaticae*, 1:448; Sipos, *Enchiridion iuris*, 774, item a, 810; item b, 833; Salaverri, *De ecclesia Christi* (no. 1047), 1:879; Lorenzo Miguélez Domínguez, Sabino Alonso Morán, Marcelino Cabreros de Antas, *Código de derecho canónico* (Madrid: B.A.C., 1957), commentary on can. 2197.

4. Evaluation of This Opinion

We refrain from presenting again the reasons which can be alleged against this fifth opinion. They were presented in previous pages.[821]

As we shall say in the next chapter, we believe that this fifth opinion is the true one. We believe further that Wernz and Vidal are correct when—interpreting Saint Robert Bellarmine—they say that a heretical pope loses the papacy *ipso facto* when his heresy becomes "notorious and publicly divulged."

---

821. See especially our quotation from Suárez—see chap. 11, sec. 1 (*Defense of This Opinion by Suárez*)—and Bouix—text supported by footnotes 792–94.

CHAPTER THIRTEEN

Defending the Fifth Opinion Enumerated by Saint Robert Bellarmine

Introduction

In the 1970 Portuguese text of this Chapter 13, we held the position of Saint Robert Bellarmine that the heretical pope would lose the papacy when his heresy became "manifest."[822] Since the Jesuit saint does not specify the degree of manifestation needed to trigger the loss of office, we did not delve into this matter but subscribed to the general statement, i.e., that the loss would occur when the heresy became manifest.

In the French 1975 edition, we sustained that the pope would only lose his office when the manifestation of his heresy reached a very special and broad degree of exteriorization, clarity, and knowledge by the faithful, that is, when his heresy became "notorious and publicly divulged," to use Wernz and Vidal's expression.

Now, more than forty years after the publications in Brazil and France, it seems that this Chapter 13 must be complemented by new observations in the light of what emerged during that timespan from debates on the subject and reflections suggested by developments within the Church. Thus, we now divide this Chapter 13 into three parts:

- Division A: This Chapter in the 1975 French Edition;

---

822. We refer to our study's Portuguese, French, and Italian versions with the abbreviations AXS.pt, AXS.fr, and AXS.it followed by the page numbers. The subject matter of this book being divided according to the five opinions enumerated by St. Robert Bellarmine (see AXS.pt, 3–4; AXS.fr, 218–19; AXS.it, 27–28), one sees that the hypothesis of a heretical pope involves three different questions:

Question 1: Can the pope become a heretic or already be one when elected?—the topic of the first opinion;

Question 2: If the pope can be heretical, should he lose the papacy?—the topic of the third opinion;

Question 3: If he loses his office, how does that happen?—the topic of the second opinion (for being a heretic, even if hidden), the fourth (by a declaration of the Church), and the fifth (*ipso facto*, upon manifesting his formal heresy).

- Division B: New Reasons Expounded in 2017;
- Division C: Synthesis of Our Position, Now Better Presented.

Division A: This Chapter in the 1975 French Edition

In the previous chapters, we commented on the arguments of the different schools. At this point, we intend to present an overview of our conclusions.

1. Possibility of a Heretical Pope

Neither in Scripture nor Tradition do we find any evidence to argue that a pope cannot fall into heresy.[823] On the contrary, numerous testimonies from Tradition favor the possibility of such a fall. We must, therefore, consider as theologically possible that a pope can pertinaciously fall into heresy and study its consequences in Church life.[824]

2. Incompatibility in Root

Note, however, that as such, and by the arguments we have adduced to demonstrate it, the thesis we sustain here does not identify with that expounded on by Saint Robert Bellarmine and taken up by Wernz and Vidal.[825]

Scripture and Tradition clearly teach that there is a profound, *root incompatibility* between the heretical condition and the possession of ecclesiastical jurisdiction[826] since a heretic ceases to be a member of the Church.[827]

This incompatibility is such that, normally, the condition of pertinacious heretic and the possession of an ecclesiastical jurisdiction cannot be harmonized. However, this incompatibility is not *absolute*, which means that falling into internal or even external heresy does not *ipso facto* entail, in all cases and immediately, the removal from an office with ecclesiastical jurisdiction.

---

823. See Chapter 8. We are referring to Tradition in the broad sense. It includes the Divine Tradition and the ecclesiastical one. We know it from the documents of the Councils, papal documents, writings of the Church Fathers, theological works, and so forth. See Pesch, *Praelectiones dogmaticae*, 1:564, 571.

824. In the definition of heresy, we recall that the term *pertinacity* has a different meaning than the common one. In common use, pertinacious means obstinate, persistent, lasting, and persevering. In theology and canon law, pertinacious is the heretic who, as Tanquerey teaches, denies or questions a truth of faith *scienter et volenter*, that is, fully aware that this truth is a dogma and with full adherence of the will. See Adolph Tanquerey, *Synopsis theologiae moralis et pastoralis* (Paris–Tournai–Rome: Desclée, 1948), 2:473. Hence, there can be pertinacity in a sin of heresy committed out of mere weakness.

825. See Chapter 12. About the exact terms with which St. Robert Bellarmine defends the fifth opinion, despite his preference for the first, see the end of Chapter 8 and the synoptic table of Chapter 7.

826. See the texts by St. Robert Bellarmine and Suárez, which we have reproduced in chap. 11, no. 2 (*Refutation of This Opinion by Saint Robert Bellarmine*), and Chapter 9.

827. On the moment a heretic ceases to be a member of the Church, see Chapter 9.

That is why we are speaking about root incompatibility.[828] Heresy cuts the very root and foundations of jurisdiction, that is, the faith and status of Church member. However, such incompatibility does not eliminate jurisdiction *ipso facto* and necessarily. As a tree can stay alive for a time after its roots have been cut, so too, frequently, albeit precariously, jurisdiction can remain in an officeholder who falls into heresy.[829]

The arguments of the various authors on this last point are decisive,[830] especially that presented by the 1917 *Code of Canon Law* in canon 2314, §1, arts. 1 and 2, and canon 2264.

> [Canon 2314, §1, arts. 1 and 2 states:] All apostates from the Christian faith and each and every heretic or schismatic:
>
> 1. Incur by that fact excommunication;
>
> 2. Unless they respect warnings, they are deprived of benefice, dignity, pension, office, or other duty that they have in the Church, they are declared infamous, and [if] clerics, with the warning being repeated, [they] are deposed....
>
> [Canon 2264, concerning the administration of sacraments and sacramentals in extraordinary cases, states:] Acts of jurisdiction, whether for the external forum or the internal forum, placed by one excommunicated are illicit; and if a condemnatory or declaratory sentence has been laid down, they are also invalid with due regard for the prescription of Canon 2261 §3.[831]

Therefore, the heretic does not *ipso facto* lose his benefits, duties, and the like but *must be* deprived of them. If he is a cleric, he is not deposed *ipso facto* but *must be* deposed. As long as this has not occurred, or as long as the heretic is not the object of a sentence of conviction or declaration under the terms of canon 2264,

---

828. The relationships between the root and the tree are used in theology and canon law to indicate certain special situations. On the subject, see Canons 1138–1141; Petrus da Bergamo, *In opera sancti Thomae Aquinatis index* (Alba-Rome: Paulinae, 1960), termine radix, p. 812; Suárez, *De fide*, disp. 21, sect. 2, no. 7, 540; Billot, *Tractatus de ecclesia*, 1:612; Lalande, "Raiz" in *Vocabulario tecnico*; Salaverri, *De ecclesia Christi*, 1:930; "Il Vaticano II come luogo teologico," *Renovatio* (1967), no. 2, 324.

829. As Suárez says in the text quoted in chap. 11, sec. 1 (*Defense of This Opinion by Suárez*), in this case, "the heretical pope is not a member of the Church as far as the substance and form which constitute the members of the Church. However, he is the head as far as the office and action." Suárez, *De fide*, disp. 10, sect. 6, no. 5, 317.

830. See, for example, the reasons given by Suárez (see Chapter 9) and St. Robert Bellarmine (see Chapter 12). However, we must observe that the argument of analogy often mentioned by Suárez and other authors does not seem valid: If the power of Holy Orders, which is more spiritual, is maintained in a heretic, so could ecclesiastical jurisdiction. No doubt, the power of jurisdiction is lower than that of Holy Orders and oriented to it. However, the power of Holy Orders is bound to an indelible character, which does not happen with the power of jurisdiction. On the other hand, the functions of government and magisterium, linked to the power of jurisdiction, confer on the latter a specific and intimate relationship with the preservation of the faith of the Catholic people, which does not happen with the power of Holy Orders to the same degree. It follows that it is impossible to base the argument on the analogy between these two powers.

831. 1917 CIC, cans. 2314, §1, arts. 1 and 2, can. 2264, pp. 735, 720.

his jurisdiction is valid, albeit he cannot exercise it legitimately. It is evident, therefore, that heresy, even external, does not eliminate jurisdiction necessarily and *ipso facto*.[832] However, given the *root incompatibility*, it is clear that any jurisdictional power in a heretic is retained only precariously, in a state of violence, and to the extent necessary for a precise and obvious reason dictated by the good of the Church or souls.

We thus reject the position that the pope would never lose his office (third opinion enumerated by St. Robert Bellarmine). Moreover, other important arguments from Tradition and natural reason counter this position.[833]

---

832. However, according to 1917 CIC canon 188, §4, any ecclesiastical office becomes *ipso facto* vacant, by tacit *resignation*, if the cleric has publicly *apostatized* from the Catholic faith. It should be noted that this paragraph concerns a *public* heretic, while the aforementioned Canons 2314 and 2264 establish that an *external but non-public* heretic does not lose his jurisdiction *ipso facto*. He loses it only when the *ab homine* penalties indicated in these two canons are applied. Maroto comments on 1917 CIC canon 188, §4: "If this [distancing from the Catholic faith] is not done *publicly*, he incurs another penalty, *deprivation ab homine*." Felipe Maroto, *Instituciones de derecho canonico* (Madrid: Editorial del Corazón de Maria, 1919), no. 684, 2:444n1.

We have no room for a more in-depth analysis of this fourth paragraph of 1917 CIC, canon 188. However, we will express our perplexity at the fact that when this chapter was being rewritten (July 1974), we were not aware of any study on the consequences of this fourth case of tacit resignation in regards to the current crisis in the Church. Here are some bibliographical indications for the study of 1917 CIC, canon 188, §4: Ludovicus Huguenin and Clemens Marc, *Expositio methodica juris canonici* (Lyon-Paris: Vitte, 1903), 393–94; Maroto, *Instituciones de derecho*, 2:443–44; Wernz and Vidal, *Ius canonicum*, 2:330–31; Ioannes Chelodi, *Ius de personis* (Trent: Tridentum, 1922), 232–33; Arthurus Vermeersch, S.J. and Joseph Creusen, S.J., *Epitome iuris canonici* (Malines-Rome: Dessain, vol. 1, 1949; vol. 2, 1940; vol. 3, 1946), 1:264; Sipos, *Enchiridion iuris*, 133; J. Brys, *Juris canonici compendium* (Bruges: Desclée, 1949), 1:266; Udalricus Beste, *Introductio in codicem* (Collegeville, Minn.: St. John's Abbey, 1946), 212; Pier Giovanni Caron, *La rinuncia all'officio eclesiastico* (Milan: Vita e Pensiero, 1946), passim; F. Claeys Bouuaert, *Traité de droit canonique* (Paris: Letouzey, 1954), 335; R. Naz, "Offices ecclésiastiques," in *Dictionnaire de droit canonique*, 1099–1100; Regatillo, *Institutiones iuris*, 1:269; Miguélez, Alonso, and Cabreros, *Código de derecho*, comments on Canon 188; Arturo Alonso Lobo, *Comentarios al código de derecho canónico* (Madrid: B.A.C., 1963), 1:482. An analysis of this bibliography shows that 1917 CIC canon 188, §4 provides important arguments in favor of the thesis that an eventually heretical pope loses his office *ipso facto* when his heresy becomes "notorious and publicly divulged." However, this argument is not decisive because the pope is above positive ecclesiastical law. It would be necessary to prove that the canonical provision in this fourth case of a tacit resignation is an expression of the Church's positive or natural divine law. In addition, it would be necessary to demonstrate that this possible positive or natural divine law applies to the particular case of the pope. Now, it is precisely in this regard that a multi-century dispute has divided the greatest theologians so that a first analysis of 1917 CIC canon 188 §4 reinforces the fifth opinion of St. Robert Bellarmine but does not prove it.

833. See Chapters 10 and 12.

3. The Jurisdiction of a Heretic

Cut at the root as it is, the jurisdiction of a heretic subsists only in the measure that a superior authority *sustains* it.[834] Thus, for the good of souls and upkeep of the Church's legal order, the pope *sustains* the jurisdiction of a non-publicly heretical bishop who has not yet been punished *ab homine* according to Canons 2264 and 2314, §1 and 2. Who can retain the pope in his jurisdiction if he falls into heresy? The Church? We do not believe so because the Church is not superior to the pope and, therefore, cannot keep him in his jurisdiction. The pope is not subject to ecclesiastical law. So, who can do it? Jesus Christ? Yes, to the extent that it is legitimate to attribute to Him the intention of *sustaining*, on a precarious basis, a heretical pope in his jurisdiction.

4. The Central Question

The central question is precisely this: Would there be circumstances in which one could or should say that Our Lord decides to *sustain*, at least for some time, a possibly heretical pope in his jurisdiction? Or would there be circumstances in which the good of the Church or souls would require, for a precise and evident reason, that a possibly heretical pope retain his jurisdiction? What would these circumstances be? We believe that we can answer these questions by analyzing, according to reason, certain aspects of the Church as a simultaneously visible and invisible society.

Since the Church is a visible and perfect society, the facts of its official and public life legally become real only when they are "known and publicly divulged."[835]

---

834. It is normally said that in certain cases provided by law, the jurisdiction of one who has none is supplemented by the pope or the Church. For example, as foreseen by 1917 CIC canon 209, in case of a common error, the Church supplements non-existent jurisdiction. However, the authors teach that the supplemented jurisdiction exists only as an *act*, not a *habit*. See Augustinus Lehmkuhl, S.J., *Theologia moralis* (Freiburg: Herder, 1888), 2:281, no. 387; Wernz and Vidal, *Ius canonicum*, 2:367–68; Vermeersch and Creusen, *Epitome iuris*, 1:278. In the hypothesis we are discussing, jurisdiction would exist as a *habit*, not just an *act*. To our knowledge, there is no technical term to qualify such a legal situation, so we say that the jurisdiction is *sustained* in the person of the heretic.

835. See Denz-Umb., Systematic index, art. II, a; Denz-Sch., Systematic index, art. G 4 a. It should not be forgotten that the Church, being a visible and perfect society, could nevertheless be numerically and geographically small. In the early days of its history, it consisted of just a handful of members and flourished only in small areas of the Mediterranean. Only later did it spread all over the Earth. It is theologically possible that, in times of crisis, the number of its members can become remarkably reduced.

To forget or deny this truth would cause serious damage to souls and the Church in general.[836] Thus, it would be absurd that an eventually heretical pope may lose his office before his heresy becomes public and notorious. On the other hand, it would be equally absurd for a heretical pope to retain his jurisdiction after this disclosure.

The only reason that could validly justify the maintenance of jurisdiction by a heretical pope would be the insufficiency of that public disclosure and notoriety.[837] However, when this reason ceases to exist, the loss of office by the heretical pope should automatically take place, as it necessarily derives from the profound incompatibility between heresy and jurisdiction extant in the Church—for the rest, an invisible society.

These considerations lead us to conclude, with Saint Robert Bellarmine, Wernz and Vidal, and many others, that the eventually heretical pope loses his office *ipso facto* when his heresy becomes "known and publicly divulged."[838] Moreover, this conclusion perfectly aligns with the doctrinal premises of Canons 2314, 2264,

---

836. We cannot conceive that the public and official life of a visible and perfect society occurs only with internal acts that are, therefore, impossible to verify in the social and visible order; or with external but hidden acts; or, still, with insufficiently disclosed external acts. It is easy to prove that these acts cannot be only internal or surreptitiously external. Suárez expounds on this principle in the text we reproduce in Chapter 9, point b (*On the Reasons Against This Second Opinion*). Domingo de Soto uses a particularly fortunate expression saying that if prelates were deposed for causes that could not be known externally, "all jurisdictions would become ambiguous and confused" (*omnes iuridictiones versarentur in ambiguo et in confuso*). *Commentarium fratris Dominici Soto Segobiensis (. . .) in quartam sententiam* (Salamanca: 1561), dist. 22, q. 2, a. 2, 1022. These arguments are also valid, *mutatis mutandis*, to show that acts of the public and official life of the Church must be known and publicly divulged. Failure to admit this principle would easily make jurisdictions ambiguous and confused, especially in times of crisis. The authors have often resorted to this principle to solve cases similar to that of the heretical pope. Thus, for example, they say that a pope's resignation takes place only at the moment when it is communicated to the Church. See Matthaeus Conte a Coronata, *Institutiones iuris canonici* (Turin: Marietti, 1928), 1:366. Explaining the ancient canonical provision according to which simony was a reason for annulling a papal election, they taught that this was only determined when it became public. See Wernz and Vidal: *Ius canonicum*, 2:402n56; Coronata, *Institutiones iuris*, 1:362n7.

837. The other reasons put forward over time in favor of the heretical pope retaining his jurisdiction seem inconsistent. Some are fundamentally erroneous, denying the incompatibility between jurisdiction and heresy (see Chapter 10). Others, insisting above all on the evils that would result from refusing to obey a heretical pope, actually minimize the evils that would result from the spread of heresy by the head of the Church. In this regard, see what we have expounded on in footnote 783.

838. As mentioned in footnote 817, the expression "*notoriam et palam divulgatam*" is found in Wernz and Vidal (*Ius canonicum*, 2:433, no. 453). In a different volume of this same work, the concept of notoriety is defined as follows: "Notorious is what is so certain, precisely because of the evidence of the thing, that it cannot be (materially) hidden with any subterfuge or (formally) excused with legal considerations. Therefore, a notorious crime is a criminal act that cannot be hidden by any subterfuge precisely because the evidence of things is highly certain, not only as a fact but also as a crime. For example, killing a man in the presence of several people or a large part of a community can be a notorious fact, but if there is any doubt whether the act was committed in legitimate self-defense, the crime is no longer notorious (it is materially, but not formally)." Wernz and Vidal, *Ius canonicum*, 7:46–47, no. 35. From this text, it follows that to lose the pontificate, the pope must be formally heretical and, therefore, must be manifestly pertinacious in adhering to a proposition opposed to the faith. As readily seen, the definition of notorious given by Wernz and Vidal could be more precise. On the other hand, one can also observe this same inaccuracy in other authors (see footnote 820). We hope to be able to delve deeper into this interesting question opportunely.

and 188.[839] Therefore, Jesus Christ would presumably *sustain* the jurisdiction of a heretical pope, on a precarious basis,[840] from the time of his fall into heresy until this heresy becomes "known and publicly divulged."[841]

Consequently, all acts of jurisdiction by the pope during this period will be valid. Even if he pronounces a dogmatic definition, it will be valid; in such case, the Holy Spirit will speak for him, as with Balaam's donkey.[842]

As mentioned, the thesis we sustain does not identify with that expounded by Saint Robert Bellarmine, followed by Wernz and Vidal.[843] Here are some points that differentiate the two theses:

1) Saint Robert and Wernz and Vidal do not propose the notions, which seem essential, of (a) *root but not absolute incompatibility* between heresy and jurisdiction; and (b) Our Lord's *sustaining* a heretical pope's jurisdiction while his heresy is not yet "notorious and publicly divulged."

2) Regarding the heretical pope, we do not link in an absolute way—as Saint Robert Bellarmine and Wernz and Vidal do—the effective loss of the papacy to the loss of Church membership.[844] We believe it is certain that a heretic

---

839. We have quoted canon 188 in footnote 832.

840. Here we consider only the case of the loss of papacy due to heresy. If we are not talking about the loss of the papacy for some other reason, it is not because we believe there are cases in which the notoriety and public divulgation can be dispensed with, but because we do not want to overextend the scope of our study, as it would oblige us to consider a casuistry unrelated to our subject. In the next chapter, we will show that what is said about the hypothesis of a heretical pope is also valid for a schismatic pope. We will also deal with similar cases.

841. In our view, these arguments eliminate the opinion that the pope would lose the papacy the moment he fell into internal heresy (the second opinion by St. Robert Bellarmine, see Chapter 9); in hidden external heresy (our first subdivision proposed to the fifth opinion of St. Robert Bellarmine, see Chapter 7); and in externally manifest but not "notorious and publicly divulged" heresy (our second subdivision on the fifth opinion of St. Robert Bellarmine, see Chapter 7). These arguments also eliminate the opinion that the pontificate is lost after a declaration (the fourth opinion by St. Robert Bellarmine, see Chapter 12). This latter opinion also seems unsustainable for another reason: As St. Robert Bellarmine has demonstrated in his argument against Cajetan—see chap. 11, sec. 2 (*Refutation of This Opinion by Saint Robert Bellarmine*)—this is not in accordance with the principle that the pope cannot be judged by any man. Thus, only our third subdivision proposed to the fifth opinion of St. Robert Bellarmine—see chap. 12, sec. 3 (*Subdivision of This Fifth Opinion*)—remains standing, and it is the position that we defend. To clearly support our criticism of the fourth opinion (deposition after a declaration), we must observe the following: There must be no shadow of Conciliarism in the principle that ecclesiastical bodies, such as the Council, may issue a declaration on the eventual cessation of the functions of a heretical pope since these bodies have no greater right than that enjoyed by every faithful Catholic. These bodies could be the first to make such a statement for reasons of convenience or courtesy, but this priority would not be a personal right, let alone an exclusive one.

842. See footnote 729. Laymann speaks in the same way. See Paulus Laymann, *Theologia moralis* (Venice: Maldura, 1700), book 11, tr. 1, chap. 7, no. 1, 146.

843. See Chapter 12. About the exact terms with which St. Robert Bellarmine defends the fifth opinion, despite his preference for the first, see the end of Chapter 8 and the synoptic table of Chapter 7.

844. See Chapter 12.

ceases to be a member of the Church before his heresy becomes "notorious and publicly divulged."[845]

5. Degree of Notoriety and Divulgation

What degree of notoriety and divulgation is required for a heretical pope to lose his office? To answer this question, we must first observe that there would be a certain degree of notoriety and divulgation with which, without any doubt, the loss of the papal office would have taken place. The problem would indeed be posed regarding the precise moment when the loss occurs. This question could be fully answered only by considering all of the concrete circumstances. In theory, the concepts of "notorious" and "publicly divulged" seem clear. Their concrete application would require the examination of a vast casuistry which we cannot cover here. For the time being, it suffices to recall an earlier observation we made:[846] One should not consider an opinion false simply because, in practice, it could give rise to very important dissensions.

6. Conclusion

Summing up, we believe, therefore, that a careful examination of the question of a heretical pope, using the theological elements we have at present, enables one to conclude that a heretical pope would lose his office the moment his heresy became "notorious and publicly divulged." We believe this opinion is not only *intrinsically probable* but *certain* since the reasons that can be adduced to support it seem entirely compelling. Moreover, we found no arguments convincing us of the opposite in the works we consulted.

In any event, other opinions remain *extrinsically probable* since they have important authors in their favor. Therefore, in the order of concrete action, it does not seem licit to opt for a determined position, wishing to impose it without further ado. This is the reason why, as we said at the beginning,[847] we invite specialists in the matter to restudy the issue. Only in this way will it be possible to reach a consensus among theologians, thus settling on one opinion as *theologically certain*.

---

845. Wernz and Vidal are unclear when studying the relationship between heresy and the condition of Church membership (see *Ius canonicum*, 1:197ff.). Let us say that their exposition on this subject is full of hesitation. On the other hand, it is already symptomatic that in a treatise as voluminous and detailed as their *Ius canonicum*, they should deal with so important an issue as this in a simple footnote.
846. See footnote 802.
847. See the Introduction to Part Two.

DIVISION B: NEW REASONS EXPOUNDED IN 2017

1. Theology as a Science and the Magisterium of the Church

The position of those for whom certainties about the theological question of the heretical pope will exist only when and if the Magisterium makes a pronouncement about it may seem laudable. Such a humble attitude would supposedly express confidence in the Church and a rejection of the Protestant principle that everyone may interpret Revelation as he wishes. However, this position tends to deny that theology can arrive at certainties. Now, to hold that even people who know theology could not reach certain conclusions based on theology would involve an abdication of reason.

Indeed, theology, or sacred doctrine, as the Scholastics called it, is a science,[848] and it is proper for every science, each in its own way, to reach certainties. Saint Thomas Aquinas writes:

> Since this science is partly speculative and partly practical, it transcends all others speculative and practical. Now one speculative science is said to be nobler than another, either by reason of its greater certitude, or by reason of the higher worth of its subject-matter. In both these respects this science surpasses other speculative sciences; in point of greater certitude, because other sciences derive their certitude from the natural light of human reason, which can err; whereas this derives its certitude from the light of divine knowledge, which cannot be misled; in point of the higher worth of its subject-matter because this science treats chiefly of those things which by their sublimity transcend human reason; while other sciences consider only those things which are within reason's grasp.[849]

From this perspective, we deal here with the theological hypothesis of a heretical pope and come to some conclusions that we hold as certain, particularly in points 2 to 9 below.

2. The Five Degrees of the Manifestation of Heresy

Saint Robert Bellarmine speaks of "manifest" heresy. In fact, such a manifestation has degrees. We believe one can distinguish five degrees of "manifestation":

1st **degree**: The simple manifestation of heresy by the one who embraces it;
2nd **degree**: When heresy becomes "notorious and publicly divulged," according to the expression of Wernz and Vidal;
3rd **degree**: When the papal heresy and the principle whereby a heretic loses the papacy become known to *tota Ecclesia* (the whole Church), to use

---

848. See St. Thomas Aquinas, *Summa Theologica,* I, q. 1, a. 2, c.
849. Aquinas, *Summa Theologica*, I, q. 1, a. 5, c.

Ballerini's expression.[850] It is our opinion that "the whole Church" says
more than "manifest" or "notorious and publicly divulged" and that
knowledge of the papal heresy and loss of the papacy should reach even
the capillaries of Catholic opinion down to the common faithful, whom
we would personify as a good and simple mother of a Catholic family;

4th degree: Can be reached at any level of this process when the pope,
admonished for his heresy as Saint Paul prescribes, does not recant but
remains adamant, becoming a formal, "manifest" heretic;

5th degree: This degree is attained when the still recalcitrant heretical pope
and "the whole Church" having become aware both of the facts and the
law, the heretical pope tacitly renounces the papacy. According to this
doctrine, no one deposes the pope. Rather, he does this himself through
his heresy. It is, therefore, "by his own will"[851] that he loses the condition
of being a member of the Catholic faithful and, consequently, the papal
office. According to Saint Paul, the heretic "condemns himself" (Tit.
3:11).[852] Such "tacit resignation" is objective, not subjective, that is,
it does not result from an express statement or an explicit resignation
but from the practice of an act incompatible with the papacy, namely,
embracing heresy. This case is similar to that of the father of a family
who practices an act incompatible with his paternal authority and
consequently loses it, even though he wants to keep it.

3. Some Observations on These Five Degrees

The degrees correspond to stages of manifestation. Each degree does not represent a
chronological instant but rather a stage in the procedure, and, therefore, it has a
beginning and end in time.

The first three degrees refer to the pope's material heresy. The formal character
of heresy will manifest itself only when the pope is admonished in the manner
indicated by Saint Paul (Tit. 3:10–11) and remains unwilling to respond to the
admonitions or to be quiet. The meaning of these first three degrees is that the
heresy affirmed by the pope is externalized in a restricted circle of his relationships
(1st degree), then makes the general news (2nd degree), and then attains the
whole Church (3rd degree), but so far only as a material heresy.

The 4th degree aims at making formal heresy manifest. Saint Paul's admonitions
are intended to call the pope back to the true faith and, if he remains obstinate,
to make his heresy formally manifested. Therefore, this degree represents the
externalization of the pope's full and unequivocal adherence to heresy. Its content
differs from the first three degrees, which deal only with the greater or lesser exte-

---

850. Pietro Ballerini, *De potestate ecclesiastica summorum pontificum et conciliorum generalium,*
edited by E.W. Westhoff, vol. 2 of *Opus de romano pontifice* (Monasterii Westphalorum: Sumptibus J.H. Deiters, 1847), part 1, chap. 9, sect. 2, no. 8, 125. See the note about Fr. Pietro Ballerini in
Prof. de Mattei's *Presentazione.*
851. Billot, *Tractatus de ecclesia*, 1:609. See sec. 6 (*The True Fifth Opinion of St. Robert Bellarmine*)
infra.
852. See sec. 6 (*The True Fifth Opinion of St. Robert Bellarmine*) *infra.*

riorization of material heresy. It begins with the first admonition and ends with the pope's eventual pertinacity in the face of the second when he becomes a formal heretic and should, therefore, be avoided.

The 5th degree is the quasi promulgatio of the loss of the papacy. In the fifth degree, there is a *quasi promulgatio* to the whole Church of the loss of office by the heretical pope. This loss of office has an analogy with law-making, to which having an assented-to and enrolled bill is essential.[853] At this stage, the law becomes clear: the heretical pope cannot keep the papacy; no Church body can judge him; by the attitude he took in the face of the admonitions, he excluded himself from the Church and, therefore, from the papal office. This was already present more or less explicitly in the first degree. However, the *full manifestation* of the extreme gravity of heresy and all the force of the law governing this matter only become patent in the fifth degree. Then it becomes clear to the whole Church that the loss of office is not the result of some spurious collusion but the externalization of the pope's formal heresy. It is the simple application of divine law to the facts established in the first four stages.

Saint Robert teaches that a heretic loses the papacy when his heresy becomes *manifest*. This is to be understood as a *full manifestation*, i.e., one that *imposes itself* on the acceptance of the *sana pars* (healthier, sounder part) of the Catholic faithful.

4. Objects of the *Quasi Promulgatio* and Enrollment of the Law

In the case of the law, an *ordinatio rationis* [ordinance of reason] is approved and enrolled. In the case of the heretical pope, the *quasi promulgatio* has as its object a canonical fact: the loss of the papacy. This canonical fact imposes itself because of the Church's visibility. The reasons for this loss must be made clear to the faithful to the extent that each can understand them, always respecting the texture of Catholic public opinion.[854] Being a visible and perfect society, the *quasi promulgatio* of fundamental facts in the Church's institutional life, such as the loss of office by a heretical pope, is of absolute necessity.

5. The Alternative-Successive Opinion of Saint Robert Bellarmine and Others

Having more than one object, the obligation, request, or opinion may be cumulative or alternative. In turn, alternatives can be simple or conditioned, and conditional ones can have numerous subspecies according to the nature of the condition to which they are subject, one of which is successiveness. A debtor may be required to deliver a horse *and* an ox (cumulative obligation) or to deliver a horse *or* an ox (alternative). In the latter case, he may be obliged to deliver one or the other indifferently (simple alternative), or he may be obliged to deliver a

---

853. See sec. 13 (*Would We Thus Fall Into Sedevacantism?*) *infra.*
854. See sec. 13 (*Would We Thus Fall Into Sedevacantism?*) *infra.*

horse *or* an ox, which will be specified according to certain criteria (conditioned alternative). This condition can be successive, that is, he must deliver this one, but if this one cannot be delivered for some objective reason, he must deliver the other (successive alternative).

Among the five opinions on the pope's fall into heresy, Saint Robert is in favor of the first, that the pope could not be a heretic, but he does not close the question in favor of that position. He declares it "probable," immediately stressing that "it is not certain."[855] Thus, he upholds the fifth opinion as a successive alternative, that is, he sees the first as probable, but, considering that the pope may fall into heresy, he states that among the second, fourth, and fifth, the last is the *true* one.[856] Therefore, one can and should say that from a successive-alternative perspective, the fifth opinion is that of Saint Robert Bellarmine.

For the sake of clarity, and in the face of doubts which have arisen, we make it clear that Saint Robert's alternative opinion corresponds to the following position: Among the five, he preferred the first; but since it could prove to be erroneous, from the remaining, he subscribed to the fifth.

The position of other authors who hold the first opinion only as probable, among whom are Suárez, Bouix, Bishop Zinelli in the First Vatican Council, and Salaverri, is somehow analogous to this.[857]

6. The True Fifth Opinion of Saint Robert Bellarmine

The position of Saint Robert Bellarmine has given rise to controversies. He maintains that the loss of the papacy occurs *ipso facto* by the very manifestation of the pope's formal heresy: "A pope who is a manifest heretic, ceases IN HIMSELF to be pope and head, just as he ceases IN HIMSELF to be a Christian and member of the body of the Church," that is, of the visible Church.[858] For he who is not a member cannot be the head. Nor can he be so in a stable and normal way because, with the sin of heresy, the pope ceases to be a member of the Mystical Body of Christ, the invisible Church, but remains a member of the visible Church until he manifests his defection in faith. During this period, the pope will have lost the papacy *in radice*[859] since heresy is incompatible with ecclesiastical jurisdiction. If these two can coexist in the same person for some time, it is because of the visibility of the Church, whose offices are acquired and lost only by external and public acts. Thus, until he manifests his formal heresy, the pope holds the papacy in a precarious way and in a state of violence, an anomalous situation to be corrected as soon as possible.

855. St. Robert Bellarmine, *On the Roman Pontiff*, book 2, chap. 30, 338. See AXS.fr, 241; AXS. it, 50.

856. See St. Robert Bellarmine, *On the Roman Pontiff*, book 2, chap. 30, 343. See AXS.fr, 266; AXS.it, 79.

857. See AXS.fr, 220–22, 240–41; AXS.it, 29–31, 50–51; Salaverri, *De ecclesia Christi*, 1:718.

858. St. Robert Bellarmine, *On the Roman Pontiff*, book 2, chap. 30, 343. See AXS.fr, 261; AXS. it, 73.

859. See AXS.fr, 266; AXS.it, 79; St. Robert Bellarmine, *On the Roman Pontiff*, book 2, chap. 30, 343–44.

For the Jesuit saint, no one deposes the pope. Rather, he leaves the visible Church himself in manifesting his heresy. Hence, he loses the papacy even if he remains in the apostolic palaces and tries to hold on to both his office and Church governance. This is an *abdication*, a *tacit resignation*, for reneging the Faith is incompatible with the papacy.

All other opinions on how a heretic loses the papacy presuppose at least one jurisdictional act by the imperfect Council (that is, a Council without the pope), the College of Cardinals, or some other ecclesiastical body. The only opinion of the classical doctors that does not resort to a jurisdictional pronouncement against the still reigning pope is the fifth opinion of Saint Robert Bellarmine, also adopted, complemented, and enriched on some points by Ballerini, Wernz and Vidal, Billot, and others.

Ballerini sees the warnings of Saint Paul as acts of fraternal correction, not jurisdiction, and, therefore, of charity, not justice. Speaking of *abdication* he points out that no one would depose the pope, but he would implicitly resign the position himself even if he intended to keep it.[860]

Wernz and Vidal state without hesitation that, according to Saint Robert, the heretical pope would lose his position only when his defection from the faith became "notorious and publicly divulged."[861] Since ecclesiastical law does not apply to the pope, it is clear that "public" and "notorious" are to be understood here in their current sense, also called *de facto*, and not in their technical-canonical sense.

Billot: "Admitting the hypothesis that the pope became *notoriously* heretical, it should be conceded, without hesitation, that he would *ipso facto* lose the pontifical power since *he would have voluntarily placed himself outside the body of the Church, becoming an unbeliever.*"[862]

Corroborating his thesis, Saint Robert invokes Saint Jerome, whose words Ballerini quotes verbatim: "Therefore, the heretic is said to have condemned himself: for the fornicator, the adulterer, the murderer, and other sinners are expelled from the Church by the priests; but heretics utter the sentence against themselves, spontaneously excluding themselves from the Church: this exclusion is their condemnation by their own conscience."[863]

7. Does a Heretical Pope Lose His Office?

Objection: Since the Church cannot legally establish the pope's heresy and *depose him*, the heretical pontiff would never lose his office.

I answer: Such an objection is valid against opinions in which an ecclesiastical body *judicially ascertains* the papal heresy or judges the pope; however, it

---

860. See AXS.fr, 268; AXS.it, 82–83. Ballerini, *De potestate ecclesiastica* (De Propaganda Fide edition), 104–5.
861. Wernz and Vidal, *Ius canonicum*, 2:517. See AXS.fr, 278; AXS.it, 83–85.
862. Billot, *Tractatus de ecclesia*, 1:609–10. See AXS.fr, 268–69; AXS.it, 82.
863. Ballerini, *De potestate ecclesiastica* (De Propaganda Fide edition), 104–5. See AXS.fr, 268–69; AXS.it, 82.

is not opposed to the fifth opinion, in which, according to the true position of Saint Robert Bellarmine, no one establishes the pope's heresy *judicially*. Instead, he tacitly resigns his office on his own, there being an eventual *legal confirmation* only by the imperfect Council when he has already lost the papacy. This objection marks well the position of theologians who, with specious distinctions, conclude that a heretical pope does not lose his office but continues indefinitely to poison the faithful. This position corresponds to the third opinion enumerated by Saint Robert, long abandoned, because it disregards the fact that heresy and jurisdiction are mutually incompatible.[864]

8. Cajetan, Suárez, and Saint Robert Bellarmine

After stating that no one, not even the Church, is above the pope, Cajetan proposed a solution to the question of the heretical pope that does not exclude the principle that no one can judge the supreme pontiff.[865] In the words of Suárez, "Cajetan makes extraordinary efforts to avoid being forced to admit that the Church or a Council is above the pope in case of heresy. He concludes in the end that the Church and the Council are superior to the pope, not as pope, but as a private person. This distinction, however, is unsatisfactory, for, with the same argument, one could say that it belongs to the Church to judge or punish the pope, not as pope, but as a private person."[866] Saint Robert strongly criticizes Cajetan's niceties.[867]

According to Suárez, once formal heresy is externalized, Our Lord *ipso facto* deposes the Roman pontiff, and then the imperfect Council declares this deposition before the visible Church. According to Saint Robert, not even Our Lord deposes the pope. Instead, the pope himself leaves the papacy by practicing an act incompatible with the same. Both sustain the *ipso facto* loss of office by the unequivocal exteriorization of formal heresy. The *ipso facto* is the same for both, but what follows after it varies. For Saint Robert Bellarmine, as mentioned, the loss of office occurs with the manifestation of heresy. For Suárez, there is still, after that, an act of Our Lord with the subsequent declaration by the Council. Therefore, he used the expression *ipso facto* improperly.

That is why we attribute to Suárez the fourth opinion listed by Saint Robert Bellarmine, not the fifth. According to Suárez, Our Lord deposes the pope by an act of His own, not manifested to men. Now, the visibility of the Church postulates that such deposition be manifested to the Church Militant, and here Suárez imagines a Conciliar act, which, in turn, would violate the principle that the pope is not subject to any ecclesiastical body.

We repeat: The position of Saint Robert Bellarmine is the only one relative to how the pope falls from office, which does not require the intervention of

---

864. AXS.fr, 246–52; AXS.it, 57–63.
865. AXS.fr, 253–60; AXS.it, 65–72.
866. Suárez, *De fide*, disp. 10, sect. 6, no. 9, 318. See AXS.fr, 259; AXS.it, 71.
867. See St. Robert Bellarmine, *On the Roman Pontiff*, book 2, chap. 30, 339–43; AXS.fr, 260–65; AXS.it, 73–78.

any ecclesiastical body. All others deserve Saint Robert's criticism of Cajetan by showing that any act of an official Church body in the removal of the pope would involve jurisdiction, that is, the judgment of the pope by the Church.

For Cajetan, the Church alone causes the pope's deposition; for Suárez, it is Christ and the Church; for Saint Robert Bellarmine, it is the pope himself, who, by making his heresy public and notorious, *ipso facto* leaves the Church, and, therefore, the papacy.

9. Three Theologically Certain Opinions

In the 1970 Brazilian edition of our study on the heretical pope, in the French edition of 1975, and the Italian one of 2016, we stated that for intrinsic theological reasons constituting the foundation of the fifth opinion, we considered it not only probable but certain. However, we did not insist on the "theologically certain" qualification for an extrinsic reason, namely, because authoritative authors do not adopt it.[868] That was also the thinking of Bishop Mayer, then-bishop of Campos, as expressed in a letter of January 25, 1974, when he sent our work to Paul VI asking him to indicate possible errors (which the pope never did) and expressly stating that he was attaching a study "authored by the lawyer Arnaldo Vidigal Xavier da Silveira, the contents of which I associate myself with."[869] Now, however, more than four centuries after the 1588 study by Saint Robert Bellarmine, we believe that it is necessary to consider as *theologically certain* the fifth opinion upheld by Saint Robert, according to which the loss of the papacy occurs when the pope's formal heresy becomes manifest before *tota Ecclesia*.[870] We affirm this based on these foundations:

—For its underlying intrinsic reasons;[871]

—Because extrinsic probability gives way to intrinsic certainty;

—Because, now, more than four centuries after the 1588 study by Saint Robert Bellarmine, the issue has matured, and today the fifth opinion can receive a better theological note;

—Because the fifth opinion is the only one of those addressing how a heretical pope would lose his office that does not require any ecclesiastical body to judge him and, therefore, be placed above him;[872]

—Because recently, many works of greater or lesser value have dealt with the question without solving it, either from some new perspective or in the sense of the fourth opinion, of Cajetan, showing, on the whole, that the fifth is certain;

---

868. AXS.pt, 40; AXS.fr, 281; AXS.it, 96–97.
869. Antonio de Castro Mayer, "Carta a Paulo VI" (Jan. 25, 1974), in "O Leão de Campos (VI): O bispo de Campos e o magistério de Paulo VI," FratresInUnum.com, June 27, 2010.
870. Question 3, indicated in footnote 822. See secs. 5 and 6 *supra*.
871. Chapter 12, AXS.pt, 32–35; AXS-fr., 266–71; AXS.it, 79–85.
872. See footnote 822, Question 3; and secs. 5 and 7 *supra*.

—Because sedevacantists, though with basic errors and unacceptable conclusions, have largely dealt with the matter, thereby somehow enriching the *status quaestionis* on the theological hypothesis of a heretical pope.

Likewise, we believe that Question 1, in footnote 822, should be considered settled. Accordingly, we suggest that this proposition be taken as *theologically certain*: *Only God can establish laws that apply to the pope; now then, in Revelation—Sacred Scripture and Tradition—there is nothing explicit on the impossibility of the pope falling into formal and notorious heresy; therefore, in dogmatic terms, nothing prevents the pope from becoming a heretic or being one when elected.*[873]

We also think that Question 2, in footnote 822,[874] must now be considered settled since the arguments of Saint Robert Bellarmine and others against the third opinion, which he enumerates, are cogent. Therefore, we propose that one consider as *theologically certain* that, *given the profound incompatibility between heresy and ecclesiastical jurisdiction, and, further, that the formal and notorious heretic ceases to be a member of the Church, the formal and notorious heretical pope should lose his office.*[875]

10. The Controversy's Pressures and Surprises

Having established the speculative principles on the theological hypothesis of a heretical pope, imposed with the adoption of the fifth opinion enumerated by Saint Robert Bellarmine, we now move onto prudential ground. Now one can ask, what is the result of all this? Is it not true that an eventual heretical pope will remain in office whether one adopts the opinion of Cajetan, Saint Robert, Suárez, or any other important theologian, and even if the whole rigorous procedure is followed, with admonitions and everything else? Can any of the opinions concretely solve the crisis? Is it not a vain effort, a mere empty academicism, to deal with this matter?

Because of these questions, it is not enough to say that the controversy will produce pressures and surprises about which little can be said in theory. It is not enough to try and predict maneuvers and strategies or set tactical guidelines to deal with a slippery and unpredictable reality. The real answer to these questions is to face the situation with a supernatural spirit so that the thick of battle does not cause those fighting the good fight to panic, but rather always to bear in mind the profound meaning of events. To this end, some theoretical and practical observations follow.

---

873. See footnote 822, Question 1.
874. See footnote 822, Question 2.
875. See AXS.fr, 273–75; AXS.it, 88–91.

11. What If the Heretical Pope Does Not Leave His Office?

Ballerini considers that once the pope has been admonished and his formal heresy is externalized, this will be reported to *tota Ecclesia*. Rightly so because, as he stresses even more than Wernz and Vidal, who speak only of a heresy "notoriously and publicly divulged," the fundamental facts in the life of a visible and perfect society must be known by its members, and the pope's identity is fundamental in the life of the Church. When the news of formal heresy reaches the whole Church, will the heretic have lost his office? Is he now an antipope, an intruder? Tending to respond positively to these questions, Ballerini believes that, at that point, the faithful will start avoiding the heretic, making it unfeasible for him to remain in office.

So one asks, "What if the faithful do not take that attitude and the heretic, now manifestly a formal heretic, remains in the apostolic palaces and in Church government with at least a tacit acceptance of this situation by the body of the Church?"

If the fervor of the faithful and the pressure brought on the heretic are very weak, everything will continue as before, and it will be impossible to predict what will happen in the heat of the struggle if there is one. In the face of his unequivocal manifestation of heresy, will one be able to say that he has ceased to be pope and that, therefore, his disciplinary and magisterial decisions are invalid? In the real world, the facts may not be as simple and clear as in a hypothetical analysis. Thus, the reality may lead to an extremely complex casuistry, with schisms, disorders of every kind, and other terrible events foreshadowed in the Passion of Our Lord. In any case, the resistance and commitment of the truly faithful will not have been in vain, for they will have valiantly contributed to the defense of the Faith.

12. Saint Alphonsus and a Lively and Ardent *Sensus Fidei*

Questions remain open about the actual loss of the papacy and the value of the decisions taken by the publicly avowed heretic. To confront them, it is essential to bear in mind the teaching of Saint Alphonsus Liguori, that he whom the whole Church accepts as pope is the true pope.[876] The theological reason for this principle lies in the promises of Our Lord to assist the Church and in the fact that, if one adhered to a false pope, the whole Church would be adhering to a false rule of faith, as Billot explains.[877]

Thus, the very removal of the formal and manifest heretical pope referred to in nos. 2, 3, and 5 above, and, therefore, the value of his decisions should be analyzed with special discernment.

We find it difficult to answer such questions in theory. Everything will depend greatly on the details of events, particularly to affirm or deny the universal acceptance of that man as pope.

---

876. AXS.pt, 50; AXS.fr, 297; AXS it, 115.
877. AXS.pt, 49–50; AXS.fr, 296; AXS.it, 114.

One truth, however, dominates the subject: Such perplexities will not exist if the *sensus fidei* of the people is alive and ardent. If, with the powerful support of leader souls,[878] Catholics understand the importance of faith in the life of the Church and the gravity of the evil of heresy; if they have fervor and a true supernatural commitment to bring the crisis to an end; if they confide in prayer and in the action to be carried out with Divine Grace, then their resistance and opposition will not be lackluster but certainly strong and victorious.

Can one expect that, with the kindness with which He governs the Church, Our Lord will not allow the crisis to reach such extremes? Yes, one can, even more since He said that He will always be with us and that His burden is light. However, He who allowed the Passion might also allow the Church to suffer similar torments. Indeed, He asked whether faith would still be found on the face of the Earth when He comes again at the end of time. At this point, both discouraging pessimism and foolish optimism are pernicious to the good fight.

13. Would We Thus Fall Into Sedevacantism?

Could the situation described in nos. 9 to 11 above lead to sedevacantism? *We answer: In no way whatsoever.* In the panorama that we imagine, the manifestation of the pope's formal heresy and the dogmatic-canonical principles governing the matter would have been brought to the knowledge of *tota Ecclesia*. The procedures[879] envisaged by Saint Paul, Saint Robert Bellarmine, and Ballerini would all have been effectuated. If the universal acceptance of the pope persisted, as Saint Alphonsus says, *the see would not be vacant.* One of the characteristics of sedevacantism is that ten, a hundred, or a thousand Catholics meet and proclaim the vacancy of the Apostolic See, disregarding the principle that in the Church, a visible and perfect society, leadership acquisition or loss and all other fundamental facts of its life must be known to the social body.[880] For this reason, already decisive as such, one sees that there is no risk that the fifth opinion of Saint Robert, such as we propose it, based mainly on Ballerini's explanations, could result in sedevacantism.

14. *Quasi Promulgatio*, *Sana Pars*, Clamor of the Faithful, Texture, Leaders and Followers, *Sensus Fidei*, Passive Infallibility of the Faithful

How would that *quasi promulgatio* take place? It would not be an official act of the imperfect Council or some other ecclesiastical body, nor would it be an unofficial and unique juridical act practiced by anyone at any given moment. It would be a comprehensive set of unofficial acts of varied natures practiced by private individuals or by civil or religious entities, which would eventually take to the Catholic people, through the language of the facts, not in jurisdictional terms,

---

878. See sec. 14 *infra*.
879. See sec. 5 *supra*.
880. See secs. 5 and 6 *supra*.

the news of the pope's formal heresy and the general lines of the law governing the matter. To lucidly influence the divulgation of the news and the law involved herein, it is necessary to clearly keep in mind the notions of *quasi promulgatio* of the pope's formal heresy, the *sana pars* of Catholics, the clamor of the faithful, the texture of Catholic public opinion, leaders and followers ('planet and satellite' faithful), and the *sensus fidei*.

If the Catholic people have a healthier, sounder part (*sana pars*), orthodox, fervent, and willing to fight for the Faith, *the clamor of the faithful* against heresy will rise vigorously even in the face of authorities. As history shows, this is what happened in the fourth-century Arian crisis, of which Cardinal Newman wrote that

> The Nicene dogma was maintained during the greater part of the 4th century,
> 1. not by the unswerving firmness of the Holy See, Councils, or bishops, but
> 2. by the "consensus fidelium."[881]

Likewise, one needs to bear in mind *the texture of Catholic public opinion* since the concern would not be to reach each believer directly and individually but to reach all the faithful through the *sui generis* and intimate texture of Catholic opinion, in which there is a rich and complex system of leaders and followers of opinion—*planet and satellite souls*. Catholic opinion has a diversified internal texture in which each believer is not an anonymous unit in a shapeless mass but fits into a hierarchical and cohesive system of reciprocal influences in which each has his proper place. There is also talk of a system of "stars, planets, and satellites." In his turn, Saint Thomas Aquinas distinguishes the "greater" Jews or princes, who knew the Law well, from the "minor" or "popular" ones, who hardly knew it and allowed themselves to be deceived and seduced by the learned during the Passion.[882]

In the organization of any civil movement, it is fundamental for people to be united by the same tendency, idea, and end. This also applies to a Catholic movement, but with a fundamental difference: In defense of the Faith or of a specific point of Catholic doctrine, convergence in the tendencies of the combatants must be born of a supernatural principle, i.e., grace. Thus, it is not only a matter of uniting souls in a certain direction but of nourishing their faith.

A Catholic movement in defense of the Faith will only have life and strength if it springs from the depth of souls inspired by the *sensus fidei*, which differs radically from natural tendencies. The *sensus fidei* is like a spiritual sense, which sees, appreciates, and judges all things in the light of the Faith. It is, as it were, the sensibility of a soul vivified by the gifts of the Holy Spirit, infused virtues,

---

881. **Translator's Note:** John Henry Cardinal Newman, *On Consulting the Faithful in Matters of Doctrine*, ed. John Coulson (Kansas City, Mo.: Sheed and Ward, 1961), 77.
882. See *Summa Theologica*, III, q. 47, a.5 and 6, c. See also *ST*, II–II, q. 2, a. 8, c.

actual graces—that make present and lively the truths revealed by Our Lord—and wisdom, the savory science of the Faith.

This *sensus fidei* transcends the contingencies of the moment, gives fervent souls firm doctrinal support, and guides their action in a line of orthodoxy and virtue that depends not only on external commands, but is born from the life of grace within each Catholic.

Without the *sensus fidei*, religious movements fall into the chaos of divergent and contradictory tendencies, losing the unity characteristic of things Catholic. The Marxist philosopher Antonio Gramsci said that the "evil" of the Church and its strength lies in that all its members, from St. Thomas Aquinas down to the simple believer, think the same way.[883] Indeed, this is about having the same *sensus fidei*, mentality, and worldview, having the mind shaped according to the truth revealed by Our Lord. It is in this context of living Faith that one speaks about the *passive infallibility of the faithful*, which is not a special grace to teach the truth—as is the *active infallibility of the hierarchy* (pope and bishops)—but consists of a special grace to accept without deviations the infallible teachings of the teaching Church.

Faced with a pope who has fallen into heresy, the normal reaction would be for the faithful people, terrified and with all the vigor of the faith, to rise against the errors being spread with a unity of action inexistent in any other movement.

Under the action of grace, Catholic campaigns enter a virtuous circle in which good attracts good. A Catholic thinker or man of action must pay attention to this phenomenon, aware that all virtues are related and that to exalt one is to exalt the others.

Catholics perplexed by the current crisis will not know what is happening and what they should do if they do not pay attention to their own *sensus fidei* and that of others, as well as to the inflows of grace. They must remember that Catholic struggle is governed by supernatural inspirations and motivations that consider but transcend the teachings of psychology, sociology, and other world sciences about the merely human movements of political campaigns and the like. "My eyes are ever toward the Lord" (Ps. 24:15) is the simple but beautiful and fruitful indication of the perspective in which a Catholic should always position himself to understand what is happening around him.

Division C: Synthesis of Our Position, Now Better Presented

Next, we synthesize our position in the face of the theological hypothesis of a heretical pope, graphically highlighting the terms and phrases that best characterize each proposition.

---

883. **Translator's Note:** "The strength of religions, and of the Catholic Church in particular, has lain, and still lies, in the fact that they feel very strongly the need for the doctrinal unity of the whole mass of the faithful and strive to ensure that the higher intellectual stratum does not get separated from the lower." Antonio Gramsci, "Notes for an Introduction and an Approach to the Study of Philosophy and the History of Culture," Note IV, in *An Antonio Gramsci Reader: Selected Writings, 1916–1935*, ed. David Forgacs (New York: Schocken Books, 1988), 330.

1. It is *theologically certain* that nothing in Revelation asserts that the pope will never fall into heresy. Therefore, in principle, *the pope may become a formal heretic* (see section 8 above).

2. The supreme pontiff may be a heretic as a private person. And he can also be one as *a public person* when teaching as a pope, albeit without fulfilling the conditions of infallibility (see Chapters 15 and 16).

3. It is *theologically certain* that by becoming a formal heretic or being one already when elected, the pope should lose his office since he is no longer a member of the visible Church and because there is a *profound incompatibility* between heresy and ecclesiastical jurisdiction (see section 8 above).

4. It is *theologically certain* that the *loss of office is not automatic*, nor does it take place by an act of an ecclesiastical body but *ipso facto*, that is, by the very fact of the *full manifestation* of heresy by the pope himself (see section 3 above).

5. The loss of office by the heretical pope, like other *fundamental facts* in the life of the Church, a visible and perfect society, must be clearly brought to the knowledge of the faithful (see section 3 above).

6. Since, as a visible society, the Church's official acts must also be visible, *the heretical pope continues in office* until the full external manifestation of his heresy. In this period, he will already have lost the papacy *in root* while keeping it precariously and in a state of violence, an anomalous situation to be corrected as soon as possible (see section 5 above).

7. To combat heresy, one should bear in mind the value of *prayer* and *penance* and the notions, among others, of the *quasi promulgatio* of the pope's formal heresy, the *sana pars* of Catholics, the *clamor* of the faithful, the *texture* of Catholic public opinion, *leading and follower souls* (planets and satellites), the *sensus fidei*, the *passive infallibility of the faithful*, the *full manifestation* of the pope's heresy (see section 13 above).

8. A heretical pope or one suspected of heresy will be *admonished twice* (Tit. 3:10–11) so that he confesses the true Faith or manifests his pertinacity by *responding or failing to respond*. These admonitions or warnings, made by cardinals, bishops, other ecclesiastics, or even laymen, all in their sole condition of faithful Catholics, will not be official or jurisdictional acts but private acts of fraternal correction or charity (see sections 3, 9, and 10 above).

9. If the pope is pertinacious in heresy, his defection in the Faith, the divine right applicable to the case and the loss of office will be announced to *tota Ecclesia*. This announcement will be made by ecclesiastics, in the capacity of simple faith-

ful, or even by laymen, and not by any official body of the Church (see section 10 above).

10. Saint Robert Bellarmine teaches that the heretical pope loses the papacy when his heresy becomes *manifest*. This is to be understood as a *full manifestation*, that is, one that *imposes itself* to acceptance by the *sana pars* of Catholics. If a block of Catholics considers the manifestation doubtful or insufficient, it is either because it is not full or *the block's members are not the true* sana pars. A clash will then become inevitable, with everything depending on the *sensus fidei* of Catholics and the movements of grace (see section 10 above).

11. For as long as he is *tolerated and accepted* by the universal Church, the heretic will be a *true pope*, and, in principle, his acts are valid (see section 11 above).

12. The loss of the papacy, therefore, *will not result from a deposition* by anyone but from an act of the pope himself, who, by becoming a formal and notorious heretic, *will have excluded himself* from the visible Church, thus *tacitly resigning* the papacy (see section 2, 5th degree above).

13. The Apostolic See being *vacant*, an ecclesiastical body such as the College of Cardinals or the imperfect Council *can legally declare* the loss of office by the heretic *who was pope* to render the fact official and make it unequivocally known by all. The Church may then proceed to the election of a new pope (see section 6 above).

CHAPTER FOURTEEN

The Schismatic Pope and the Dubious Pope

Along with the question of the heretical pope, theologians usually study various other extraordinary cases, which would create delicate juridical situations for the person of the pope in his relationship with the office of the papacy.

They address the hypotheses of a schismatic pope, a doubtful pope, a pope resigning, an incompetent pope, a scandalous pope, a demented pope, a pope exceedingly old but still master of himself, a pope imprisoned, the election of a person juridically incapable of the papacy, and so forth.

Obviously, we cannot examine all these hypotheses in the light of all circumstances. Such an analysis would be devoid of interest because, regarding several of the cases indicated, the Church teaches a well-known doctrine about which no one feels uncertain.

We shall say only a brief word about the hypotheses that are irrelevant to our theme. Afterward, we will study more deeply the two cases intimately related to the question before us: the cases of a schismatic pope and a doubtful pope.

*   *   *

Regarding a pope's right to resign, Canon 221 determines that "If it happens that the Roman pontiff resigns, for the validity of this resignation, acceptance by a cardinal or another is not necessary."[884]

*   *   *

Concerning the dementia hypothesis, Claeys Bouuaert teaches that the pope who definitively loses the use of his mental faculties ceases to be pope. He explains, "Having become incapable of performing a human act, the demented pope would consequently be incapable of exercising his jurisdiction. The help of a vicar could not supply this, given that infallibility and the primacy of jurisdiction cannot be delegated."[885]

---

884. 1917 CIC, can. 221, p 94. In the same sense, one may see Boniface VIII, c. *Quoniam, de Renunt.,* in 6; Suárez, *De fide,* disp. 10, sect. 6, no. 1, 315–16; Billot, *Tractatus de ecclesia,* 1:603–5; Coronata, *Institutiones iuris,* 1:366; Claeys Bouuaert, *Traité de droit,* 1:376; F. Claeys Bouuaert, "Pontife Romain," *Dictionnaire de droit canonique* (Paris: Letouzey, 1958), 27.
885. Claeys Bouuaert, *Traité de droit,* 1:376.

Almost all authors express the same opinion.[886] Some, however, say with Cappello that it is impossible to prove certain and perpetual dementia.[887] This last position is difficult to sustain today because of medical progress.

Writing on the various hypotheses we have indicated, Suárez teaches:

> 17. . . . Unless a true pope falls into perpetual insanity—in which hypothesis he is deposed by divine law from the papacy—he always remains in his office. He cannot be deprived of it, even though other troubles and calamities impede him from governing the Church fittingly. Under this conclusion, I include the many events that Cajetan, Torquemada, and Pighi discuss at length in the passages indicated above, and I agree with them entirely. Because perpetual insanity is equivalent to death insofar as the use of reason and liberty are concerned and, therefore, insofar as the capacity of jurisdiction and holding of an office. This is also demonstrated by the reasons presented in no. 10 above. Because if it were licit to imagine other cases in which the pope ought to be deposed—advanced senility, perpetual captivity and the like—this would create the occasion for schisms, and frequently the true pope would be justly or unjustly doubted. For this reason, it was absolutely necessary to block the way for seditions and disturbances in the Church regarding the true pope.[888]

*   *   *

It is fitting to say a specific word about the cases of the incompetent pope and the morally scandalous pope. In these hypotheses, the circumstances would eventually oblige the pope in conscience to resign his office. However, if he did not do it, by no means would he lose the papacy, nor could he be deposed. This is what the Tradition of the Church unanimously and dogmatically affirms.[889] As is obvious, the right or perhaps the duty to admonish the erring pope in his personal behavior could fall to the bishops, priests, or even the simple faithful.[890]

The hypothesis of the election to the papacy of a person legally incapable of holding the office is of interest when studying the problem of a doubtful pope, as we shall indicate ahead. For now, it suffices to repeat what the authors say: At present, there is no provision of ecclesiastical law regarding this matter. By divine law, the following classes of persons cannot be elected pope: women; persons who

---

886. See, for example, Wernz and Vidal, *Ius canonicum*, no. 452, 2:516; Guilelmus Wilmers, *De Christi ecclesia* (Ratisbonne–New York–Cincinnati: Pustet, 1897), 258; Chelodi, *Ius de personis*, 245n155; Guidus Cocchi, *Commentarium in codicem iuris canonici* Turin: Marietti, 1940), no. 155, 3:25; Vermeersch and Creusen, *Epitome iuris*, no. 340, 1:292.

887. Felice M. Cappello, *De curia romana* (Rome: n.p., 1913), 2:13–14, quoted by Coronata, *Institutiones iuris*, 1:366n7. On this point, one can consult also: Coronata, *Institutiones iuris*, 1:366; Sipos, *Enchiridion iuris*, 156n31. In another work, Cappello affirms that in the concrete order God will never permit it to happen that a pope become insane. See Felice M. Cappello, *Summa iuris canonici* (Rome: Universitas Gregoriana, 1945), 1:276n309.

888. Suárez, *De fide*, disp. 10, sect. 6, no. 17, 321.

889. See, for example, Suárez, *De fide*, disp. 10, sect. 6, nos. 14–18, 320–22; *De legibus*, book 4, chap. 7, nos. 3–5, 359; Bouix, *Tractatus de papa*, 2:640ff.; Billot, *Tractatus de ecclesia*, 1:605–6; Ballerini, *De potestate ecclesiastica* (De Propaganda Fide edition), 99.

890. On this matter, see Chapter 18.

do not have the use of reason, that is, young children and mentally ill persons; persons who are not members of the Church, that is, pagans, apostates, heretics,[891] and schismatics. Therefore, the election would be valid where the choice fell on a non-cardinal, or a lay male Catholic, even if married.[892]

1. The Hypothesis of a Schismatic Pope

In theory, the possibility of the pope falling into schism seems absurd. Is schism not some of the faithful breaking off from the pope? How can the pope break off with himself? *Ubi Petrus, ibi ecclesia*: Where Peter is, there is the Church.

Nevertheless, numerous authors of importance ponder the hypothesis.[893]

a. Suárez

Suárez explains it in the following terms:

> 2. . . . Schism may come about not only because of heresy but also without it, as when someone, retaining the faith, does not wish to maintain the unity of the Church in his actions and manner of practicing our religion. This may happen in two ways. First, by separating oneself from the head of the Church, as one reads in the chapter "Non Vos," 23, q. 5, where the Gloss says that schism consists in not having the pope as one's head. It does not consist in denying that the pope is the head of the Church, for this would be schism united to heresy, but either rashly denying some pope in particular or behaving regarding him as if he were not the head, for example, if someone tried to convoke a General Council without his authorization, or elect an anti-pope. This is the most common mode of schism.
>
> There could be a second kind of schism, where someone separated himself from the body of the Church by not wishing to communicate with it in the participation of the sacraments. Saint Epiphanius narrates an example of this (*Haeres.*, 68) regarding the sect of Melecius. Dissenting with his Patriarch, Peter of Alexandria, he separated himself from him in all the sacraments, and was accused of schism, there not existing between the two any divergence in matters of faith, as Epiphanius attests.

---

891. It is this aspect of the question—the election of a heretic—which will be of particular interest for the hypothesis of a doubtful pope, as we shall present in chap. 14, sec. 2 (*The Hypothesis of a Dubious Pope*), item D.

892. On the persons unqualified for the papacy by divine law, see other data in chap. 14 sec. 2 (*The Hypothesis of a Dubious Pope*), item D.

893. Among them we can cite: Juan de Torquemada, *Summa de ecclesia* (Venice: Tramezinus, 1561), book 2, chap. 102; book 4, chap. 11; Cajetan, *in II–II*, q. 39, a. 1; Franciscus Suárez, *De caritate*, in vol. 12 of *Opera omnia* (Paris: Vivès, 1858), disp. 12, sect. 1, no. 2, 733–34; sect. 2, no. 3, 737; Sylvius, *in totam II–II*, 39, I, 228–29; Adam Tanner, *De spe et caritate*, q. 6, dub. 2, quoted by Wernz and Vidal, *Ius canonicum*, 2:518; Van Laak, *Institutionum theologiae*, pars I, 506; Billot, *Tractatus de ecclesia*, 1:606; Wernz and Vidal, *Ius canonicum*, 2:518; Yves M.J. Congar, "Schisme," in *D.T.C.*, 14–1e.:1303, 1306; Journet, *L'Église*, 2:839–40; Hans Küng, *Structures de l'Église* (Paris: Desclée, 1964), 306ff.; Mondello, *La dottrina del Gaetano*, 182ff.

In this second mode, the pope could be schismatic if he did not want to have proper union and coordination with the whole body of the Church, as would be the case if he tried to excommunicate the whole Church or wanted to subvert all the ecclesiastical ceremonies founded on Apostolic tradition, as noted by Cajetan (*ad II–II*, q. 39) and more extensively, by Torquemada (1. 4, c.11).[894]

b. Cardinal Journet

On the same matter, Cardinal Journet writes:

1. The ancient theologians (Torquemada, Cajetan, Bañez) who thought, in agreement with the Decree of Gratian (part 1, dist. 15, c. 4), that the pope, infallible as Doctor of the Church, could nevertheless personally sin against faith and fall into heresy (see *L'Église du Verbe Incarné* 1:596), admitted with a greater reason that the pope could sin against charity, even in the measure that it constitutes the unity of the ecclesiastical communion, and thus fall into schism.[895]

According to what they have said, the unity of the Church subsists when the pope dies. Therefore, it could also subsist if a pope fell into schism (Cajetan, *II–II*, q. 39, a. 1, n VI).

They ask themselves, however, in what manner can the pope become schismatic? He can separate himself neither from the chief of the Church, i.e., himself, nor the Church, for where the pope is, there is the Church.

To this, Cajetan responds that the pope could break communion by ceasing to conduct himself as the spiritual chief of the Church, deciding, for example, to act as a mere temporal prince. To save his liberty, he would thus flee from the duties of his office; and if he did this with pertinacity, there would be schism.[896] As for the axiom "where the pope is, there is the Church," it holds when the pope conducts himself as pope and chief of

---

894. Suárez, *De caritate*, disp. 12, sect. 1, no. 2, 733–34. As we see, the hypothesis of a pope falling into schism, as conceived by the theologians who really studied the question, is logically possible, granted that it does not involve a contradiction. We do not understand how a canonist of incontestable authority, such as Fr. Cappello, could write, "Some also cite (among the cases of cessation of pontifical power) *schism* (of the pope), and they match it with heresy (see Wernz and Vidal, *Ius canonicum*, II, no. 616). But how can the pope become schismatic? For where he is, is not the (see Can. 1325, §2) true Church there also? This opinion, as others, must be considered antiquated." Cappello, *Summa iuris*, no. 276, vol. I, n21. A position analogous to that of Fr. Cappello is also adopted by Phillips, *Du droit ecclésiastique*, 1:178. In our view, the attitude taken by these authors leads one to think that they did not study the question *ex professo*.

895. In a footnote, Cardinal Journet observes: "This possibility is not universally admitted. Still, J.M. Congar says, 'Considered in a purely theoretical manner, it does not appear doubtful' (Congar, "Schisme," *D.T.C.*, 14–1e.:1306). It is taught by Suárez (*De caritate*, disp. 12, sect. 1, n 2, t. 12, 733)." Journet, *L'Église*, 2:839n6.

896. In a footnote, Cardinal Journet cites the Latin text itself of Cajetan, which we translate: "The person of the pope may refuse to submit himself to the papal office. . . . And if he did this with pertinacity of spirit, he would become schismatic by separating himself from the unity of the head. In effect, his person is bound, before God, by the laws of his office." Journet, 2:840n1.

the Church; otherwise, the Church is not in him, nor is he in the Church (Cajetan, *II–II*, q. 39, a. 1, no. 6).

2. Sometimes, it is said that the pope, being unable to disobey, has only one door to schism.[897] From the analyses we are carrying out, on the contrary, he can also sin against the ecclesiastical community in two ways: 1° By breaking the *unity of connection*, which would suppose on his part the will to avoid the action of grace as far as this is *sacramental*, and that which brings the unity of the Church into being; 2° breaking the *unity of direction*, which would happen if, according to Cajetan's penetrating analysis, he rebelled as a private person against the obligations of his office and refused to give to the Church (by trying to excommunicate the whole Church or simply by resolving, in a deliberate way, to live as a mere temporal prince) the spiritual *guidance* which she has the right to expect from him in the name of Someone greater than he, i.e., in the name of Christ and of God.[898]

c. Cardinal John de Torquemada

In analyzing the possibility of a schismatic pope, both the authors of past centuries and modern ones usually refer to a classic study of the matter: that of Cardinal John de Torquemada.[899]

One of the most illustrious fifteenth-century theologians, and a famous defender of papal prerogatives against the conciliarists, John de Torquemada, wrote authoritative treatises on the Church, as described by Hans Küng in the following terms: "The especially clear example, however, is the powerful and most influential champion of papal primacy in the fifteenth century, the Spanish Cardinal Juan de Torquemada. All the subsequent defenders of the primacy—from Domenico Jacobazzi and Cajetan, through Melchior Cano, Suárez, Gregory of Valencia, and Bellarmine, up to the theologians of the First Vatican Council—have drawn their arguments from him."[900]

Father Yves M.J. Congar observes that Torquemada's *Summa de ecclesia* is a treatise "of real and durable value."[901]

---

897. In a footnote, Cardinal Journet cites a topic of the text of Suárez, which we cite above, and comments: "According to Suárez, the pope, therefore, would not be able to sin against the unity of direction. But he presents as an example what we consider precisely as a sin against the unity of direction." Journet, 2:840n3.

898. Journet, 2:839–40.

899. We list here some relevant names among the expounders of the question of a schismatic pope who appeal to Torquemada's authority: Suárez, *De caritate,* disp. 12, sect. 1, no. 2, 734; Sylvius, *in totam II–II,* 39, 1; Küng, *Structures de l'Église,* 351ff; Journet, *L'Église,* 2:839; Congar, "Schisme," *D.T.C.,* 14–1e.:1306.

900. Hans Küng, *Structures of the Church,* trans. Salvator Attanasio (New York: Thomas Nelson & Sons, 1964), 303–4.

901. Congar, "Schisme," in *D.T.C.,* 14–1e.:1295. On the authority which John de Torquemada enjoys in this matter, see also Paul De Vooght, "Le conciliarisme aux conciles de Constance et de Bâle," in *Le concile et les conciles: Contribution à l'histoire de la vie conciliaire de l'église* (Namur, Belgium: Éditions Chevretogne—Éditions Cerf, 1960), 176; A. Michel, "Torquemada (Jean de)," in *D.T.C.,* 15–1e.:1235–39; Mondello, *La dottrina del Gaetano,* 44–45.

To demonstrate that "the pope can separate himself illegitimately from the unity of the Church and from obedience to the head of the Church, and, therefore, fall into schism," Cardinal Torquemada uses three arguments:

> 1. By disobedience, the pope can separate himself from Christ, the principal head of the Church, and regarding Whom the unity of the Church is primarily constituted. He can do this by disobeying the law of Christ[902] or by ordering something contrary to natural or divine law. In this way, he would separate himself from the body of the Church while it is subject to Christ by obedience. Thus, the pope could, without a doubt, fall into schism.

> 2. The pope can separate himself without any reasonable cause, just by pure self-will, from the body of the Church and the college of priests. He will do this if he does not observe what the Church Universal observes based on the Tradition of the Apostles, according to the chapter "Ecclesiasticarum," dil. 11, or if he did not observe what was universally commanded by the universal Councils or the authority of the Apostolic See, above all regarding divine worship; for example, not wishing to observe something from the Church's universal customs or the universal rite of the ecclesiastical cult. This would occur if he did not wish to celebrate with the sacred vestments, or in consecrated places, or with candles, or if he did not wish to make "the Sign of the Cross" like the other priests make it, or other similar things which have been decreed in a general way for perpetual utility, according to the Canons *Quae ad perpetuam, Violatores, Sunt quidam* and *Contra statuta* (25, q. 1). Departing in such a way, and with pertinacity, from the universal observance of the Church, the pope could fall into schism. The consequence is good, and the antecedent is not doubtful, for the pope, just as he could fall into heresy, could also disobey and pertinaciously cease to observe what was established for the common order in the Church. For this reason, Innocent says (c. *De consue.*) that one ought to obey the pope in everything, as long as he does not turn against the universal order of the Church, for in such a case, the pope must not be followed, unless there be reasonable cause for this.

> 3. Let us suppose that more than one person considers himself pope, and one of them is the true pope, but some consider it probably dubious.

---

902. Obviously, the sin of schism is not committed in just any act of disobedience, but only that which denies the very principle of authority in the Church, thus breaking the ecclesiastical unity. See Saint Thomas, *Summa Theologica*, II–II. 39, 1; Congar, "Schisme," *D.T.C.*, 14–1e.:1304. Such a conception is presupposed by Torquemada in the text cited. We make this observation because it might appear to the reader that the passage transcribed above grossly conflates "disobedience to the law of Christ" with schism—which would have the absurd consequence that, for any sin whatsoever, the pope would become schismatic. Torquemada is, moreover, one of the greatest defenders of the principle that a scandalous and immoral but not heretical or schismatic pope does not lose the papacy. See Torquemada, *Summa de ecclesia*, book 2, chap. 101.

Let us also suppose that this true pope conducted himself with such negligence and obstinacy in pursuing unity within the Church that he failed to do everything he could to reestablish unity. In this hypothesis, the pope would be considered a fomenter of schism, according to the arguments of many, even in our days, in connection with Benedict XIII and Gregory XII.[903]

d. A Schismatic Pope Would Lose the Papacy

Generally, the authors admitting the possibility of a schismatic pope do not hesitate to affirm that, in such an event, as with the heretical pope, the pope loses his office. The reason is evident: Schismatics are excluded from the Church, like heretics.[904]

In this matter, Suárez is an exception, sustaining that the schismatic pope is not deprived of, nor can he be deprived of, his office.[905] His opinion, however, does not merit particular attention since it is based on the Suárezian thesis, today abandoned by all,[906] that schismatics, even public ones, continue to be members of the Church.

Consequently, we can conclude with Cajetan that the Church is in the pope "when the pope conducts himself as pope and chief of the Church; otherwise, the Church is not in him, nor is he in the Church."[907]

Moreover, it is opportune to recall that "he who is pertinacious in schism is practically indistinguishable from a heretic";[908] that "no schism fails to think up some heresy to justify its separation from the Church";[909] that schism constitutes a disposition for heresy;[910] and that the schismatic, according to Canon Law and natural law, is suspect of heresy.[911]

---

903. Torquemada, part 1, book 4, chap. 11, 369 v.
904. Apostates are also excluded from the Church. An apostate pope would wholly abandon the Christian religion—for example, becoming a Muslim or Buddhist. The hypothesis, though fantastical, is mentioned in passing by some authors, such as Billot, *Tractatus de ecclesia*, 1:606. and Franciscus Schmalzgrueber, *Ius ecclesiasticum universum* (Rome: Typ. Rev. Cam. Apostolicae, 1843), part 1, dissert. proem., 8, no. 316, 1:132.
905. Suárez, *De caritate*, disp. 12, sect. 2, no. 3, 737.
906. See Congar, "Schisme," in *D.T.C.*, 14–1e.:1306–7.
907. Cajetan, *in II–II*, 39, 1, ad 6. The same thesis, that the schismatic pope loses the pontificate, is defended by: Torquemada, *Summa de ecclesia*, book 2, chap. 102, 341 v." book 4, chap. 11, 369–70; Sylvius, *in totam II–II*, 39, 1, concl. 2, 229; Tanner, *De spe*, q. 6. dub 2 (quoted by Wernz and Vidal, *Ius canonicum*, 2:518); Billot, *Tractatus de ecclesia*, 1:606; Wernz and Vidal, *Ius canonicum*, 2:518; Congar, "Schisme," in *D.T.C.*, 14–1e.:1306; Journet, *L'Église*, 2:839–40; Küng, *Structures de l'Église*, 306ff.; Mondello, *La dottrina del Gaetano*, 182–84, 189.
908. Ballerini, *De potestate ecclesiastica*, chap. 6, sect. 5, no. 14.
909. St. Jerome, *Expositio in epistola ad Titum*, 3:11, *P.L.*, 26:598. See Sylvius, *in totam II–II*, 39, 1, ad 3, 228.
910. This position is subscribed to by Sts. Jerome, Augustine, and Raymond of Penafort. See Congar, "Schisme," *D.T.C.*, 14–1e.:1269.
911. See Congar, *D.T.C.*, 14–1e.:1305.

2. The Hypothesis of a Dubious Pope

Among the authors of treatises in general, the hypothesis of a dubious pope is related especially to a pope whose *election* was doubtful. When the election is certain, the doubts that can appear are reduced to the other extraordinary cases enumerated above.[912] Indeed, any doubt surfacing after a valid election can only arise—with or without foundation—in the event of the pope falling into heresy, showing signs of insanity, lapsing into schism, and the like.

Such being the case, we shall especially analyze here the eventuality of a dubious election. We shall also consider some determined cases of doubt arising from a possible heresy in the person of the pope.

a. A Dubious Pope Is a Null Pope

In this respect, Wilmers writes:

> If the election of a pope has become so doubtful that it is impossible to know with certainty who the true pontiff is, he whose election was dubious must resign, according to the majority of authors, so that new elections can be held. If he does not resign, the Church or the bishops can declare that he is not pope since his election was doubtful. This is based on the principle that "a dubious pope is a null pope." Indeed, he whose authority is uncertain cannot require one to obey him for the same reason that men are not obliged to obey a law that has not been promulgated.[913]

Some authors disagree with this way of thinking and deny such an interpretation of the axiom "a dubious pope is a null pope" (*papa dubius, papa nullus*). It does not seem, however, that such theologians have framed the question in its proper terms. They merely sustain what no one denies, namely, that no earthly authority can depose a legitimate pope, even if he is considered dubious by many.[914]

What such authors do not seem to take into account is what Wilmers commented when refuting Phillips, another adversary of the principle "a dubious pope is a null pope": "He seems to confuse an election that is legitimate before God with an election that can be and is indeed known by men as legitimate. It is

912. See beginning of Chapter 14.
913. Wilmers, *De Christi ecclesia*, 258. See also St. Robert Bellarmine, *On Councils,* in *On the Church*, book 2, chap. 19, ad 3 arg. Gerson, 220–22; Suárez, *De fide*, disp. 10, sect. 6, n. 19; *De caritate*, disp. 12, sect. 1, no. 11, 736; Sylvius, *in totam II–II*, 39, 1, 228; Ferraris, "Papa," *Prompta bibl.*, nos. 69–70, 1846; St. Alphonsus Liguori, *Verità della fede*, vol. 8 in *Opera de S. Alfonso Maria de Liguori* (Turin: Pier Giacinto Marietti, 1887), 8:720; St. Alphonsus Liguori, *Oeuvres dogmatiques*, trans. Vidal-Delalle-Bousquet (Paris: Parent-Desbarres, 1836), 17:bis, p. 11; Pesch, *Compendium theologiae*, 1:208; Mazzella, *De religione*, 747; Billot, *Tractatus de ecclesia*, 1:612–13; Wernz and Vidal, *Ius canonicum*, 2:520–21; Wilmers, *De Christi ecclesia*, 258–59; Coronata, *Institutiones iuris*, 1:367.
914. Bouix, a partisan of this opinion, writes: "We shall prove that, as a remedy for the case under study, Christ did not institute any authority with power over the true and legitimate pope." Bouix, *Tractatus de papa*, 2:673.

not enough that the election be legitimate before God; it is necessary that it also be known as legitimate and not subject to serious doubt. Analogously, it is not enough for a law to have been approved; it must also be promulgated."[915]

Above all, this controversy revolves around the questions the Council of Constance raised. We think it unnecessary to treat this matter at length here since it is not our purpose to focus on historical problems.

b. Declaration by a Council

Whose responsibility is it to declare that the dubious pope is not the true pope? Our forefathers in the Faith attributed this mission to the bishops united in Council. Saint Robert Bellarmine, for example, wrote:

> A doubtful pope is held for no pope, and so to have power in that case is not to have power against the pope. . . .
> . . . For, even if the Council without a pope cannot define new doctrines of faith, still it can judge in a time of schism who is the true pope and prove to be a true shepherd for the Church when there is not one, or there is a doubtful one.[916]

* * *

The apostolic constitution *Vacante sede* (December 25, 1904) and the 1917 Code of Canon Law modified some norms for the pope's election. After these documents came into effect, certain authors continued to sustain that it pertained to the bishops gathered in Council to decide the validity of the election of a dubious pope.[917] Other authors, however, believe that this attribute is currently the bailiwick of the College of Cardinals. Among the latter is found Coronata, who explains his viewpoint as follows:

> If the doubt, therefore, is antecedent, because the legitimacy of the election was always doubted, [the authors commonly] attribute to the Ecumenical Council the power to make a judgment about this legitimacy. This position, however, does not appear correct, at least according to the Law in force, for two hypotheses are then possible. Either the election is objectively and truly doubtful according to the thinking of the whole Church, and, in this case, the pope is null even without the judgment of any Council, for the election was not made in a legitimate manner (Can. 219), or the objective doubt is not so probable and universal but is of more difficult solution according to the thinking of the learned and prudent. In this [latter] case, the judgment which will resolve the doubt does not

---

915. Wilmers, *De Christi ecclesia*, 258n1.
916. St. Robert Bellarmine, *On Councils* in *On the Church*, book 2, chap. 19, 221–22. On this passage of St. Robert Bellarmine, see Wilmers, *De Christi ecclesia*, 258–59; Pesch, *Compendium theologiae*, 1:208.
917. For example, Wernz and Vidal, *Ius canonicum*, 2:521.

belong to the Ecumenical Council, which cannot be conceived without the pope (see Canons 222 and 229) and to which this power has not been attributed by anyone whatsoever in a manner one can prove. It is within the competency of the College of Cardinals, however, to which the Constitution *Vacante sede* expressly conceded the right to interpret the laws covering the pope's election (nos. 3–4). Furthermore, in this same Constitution (no. 19) and Canon 229, any continuation or new reunion of an Ecumenical Council—and, it would seem *a fortiori*, its convocation—is absolutely prohibited during a vacancy in the Apostolic See.[918]

*   *   *

What should one think of this dispute? We believe that the partisans of judgment by the Council would not oppose what Coronata says. They hypothesize that the cardinals had not reached a definitive solution to the doubt. In that case, "the Church would always have the right to know with certainty who is her true chief," as Suárez, a follower of judgment by the Council, observes.[919] Such circumstances would destroy the arguments of Coronata, for ecclesiastical law cannot prevent the bishops from asserting their divine right to ascertain with certainty who is the true pope.

Can one prove that the right to pronounce on such a question belongs to the bishops? Coronata denies it. It seems, however, that Suárez would base this right on the fact that the bishops are "the ordinary pastors and pillars of the Church."[920] The argument he presents to defend the thesis of the declaration of papal heresy by the Council is what we judge, by analogy, to be applicable in the case of a dubious pope.[921]

---

918. Coronata, *Institutiones iuris*, no. 317, 1:367–68.
919. Suárez, *De fide*, disp. 10, sect. 6, no. 19, 322.
920. Suárez, no. 7, 318.
921. Cf. Suárez, nos. 7 and 19.

c. Pacific and Universal Acceptance

Concerning a doubtful pope, it is necessary to clarify here that the peaceful acceptance of a pope by the whole Church is "a sign and an infallible effect of a valid election."[922]

This is the common teaching of the authors.[923]

Simultaneously analyzing aspects of the questions of a heretical pope and a dubious pope, Cardinal Billot expounds on this principle in the following terms:

> Finally, whatever you still think about the possibility or impossibility of the above hypothesis (of a heretical pope), at least one point must be considered absolutely incontrovertible and placed firmly above any doubt whatever: the adhesion of the Universal Church will always, in itself, be an infallible sign of the legitimacy of a specific pope, and, therefore, also of the existence of all the conditions required for legitimacy itself. It is not necessary to look far for the proof of this, but we find it immediately in the promise and the infallible providence of Christ: "The gates of Hell shall not prevail against it," and "Behold I shall be with you all days." For the adhesion of the Church to a false pope would be the same as its adhesion to a false rule of faith, seeing that the pope is the living rule of faith that the Church must follow and which, in fact, she always follows. As will become even clearer by what we shall say later, God can permit that, at times, a vacancy in the Apostolic See to last for a long time.
>
> He can also permit doubt to arise about the legitimacy of this or that election. God cannot, however, permit the whole Church to accept as pope one who is not so, truly and legitimately.
>
> Therefore, from the moment the pope is accepted by the Church and united with her as the head to the body, it is no longer permitted to raise doubts about a possible defect of election or a possible lack of any condition whatsoever necessary for legitimacy. This is because the above adhesion of the Church heals all defects in the election at the root, infallibly proving the existence of all required conditions.
>
> Let this be said in passing against those who, trying to justify certain attempts at schism made in the time of Alexander VI, allege that its promoter broadcast that he had most certain proofs, which he would reveal to a General Council, of Alexander's heresy. Putting aside other reasons with which one could easily refute such an opinion, it suffices to remember one: It is certain that when Savonarola was writing his letters to the

---

922. Wernz and Vidal, *Ius canonicum*, 2:520n171. The expression "infallible effect" does not indicate here an effect that infallibly follows from its cause. It indicates something which, if it occurs, can only have been produced by such a cause, of which, therefore, it is, beyond a shadow of a doubt, an effect—i.e., an "infallible effect." See an explanation of this specific point in Suárez, *De fide*, disp. 10, sect. 5, no. 8, 315.

923. See, for example, Suárez, *De fide*, disp. 10, sect. 5, especially nos. 6–8, 314–15; Ferraris, "Papa," *Prompta bibl.*, 1846, no. 69; St. Alphonsus Liguori, *Verità della fede*, chap. 8, no. 9, 8:720; Bouix, *Tractatus de papa*, 2:683ff.; Wernz and Vidal, *Ius canonicum*, 2:520–21; Billot, *Tractatus de ecclesia*, 1:612–13; Journet, *L'Église*, 1:624.

princes, all of Christendom adhered to Alexander VI and obeyed him as the true pope. For this reason, Alexander VI was not a false pope but a legitimate one. Therefore, he was not a heretic, at least in the sense that being a heretic takes away one's Church membership and, consequently, deprives one, by the very nature of things, of the papal power and any other ordinary jurisdiction.[924]

On this same *sanatio in radice* (healing at the root) through the pope's acceptance by the entire Church, Saint Alphonsus Liguori writes, in less heated but perhaps even more incisive terms, "It matters naught that in past centuries some pope was illegitimately elected or took possession of the papacy by fraud. It suffices that he was accepted as pope afterward by the whole Church since, through such acceptance, he would have become the true pope. If, however, during a certain time he had not been truly and universally accepted by the Church, during that time the pontifical see would have been vacant, as it is vacant on the death of a pontiff."[925]

d. The Election of a Person Who Cannot Be Pope

The designation as pope of a person who cannot hold the papal office would constitute a special case of dubious election. It is a common opinion[926] that the election of a woman, a child, a demented person, or someone who was not a member of the Church (an unbaptized person, a heretic, apostate, schismatic) would be invalid by divine law.

Among these causes of invalidity, it seems necessary to distinguish the ones that admit a *sanatio in radice* from those that do not. A woman could not become pope under any hypothesis, but that absolute bar would not apply to a demented person, who could be cured; a child, who could grow; an unbaptized person, who could convert.

That said, we ask, "In the hypothesis of invalidity that admits of *sanatio in radice*, would the eventual acceptance by the whole Church of an invalidly elected pope remedy the defects in his election?"

A full answer to the question would require a detailed analysis of each case of invalidity. This would exceed the objectives we have set for ourselves.

Such being the case, we shall only consider the hypothesis most relevant to the perspective in which we place ourselves: the election of a heretic to the papacy. What would happen if a notorious heretic were elected pope and assumed the papal office without anyone challenging his election?

At first sight, the answer to this question is, *in theory*, very simple: Since God cannot permit the whole Church to err about who is her chief, the pope whom the

---

924. Billot, *Tractatus de ecclesia*, 1:612–13.
925. St. Alphonsus Liguori, *Verità della fede*, chap. 8, no. 9, 8:720.
926. See Joannes B. Ferreres, *Institutiones canonicae* (Barcelona: Subirona, 1917), 1:132; Coronata, *Institutiones iuris*, 1:360; Schmalzgrueber, *Ius ecclesiasticum*, part II, 1:376, no. 99; Cajetan, *De auctoriatate papae et concilii*, chap. 26, no. 382, 167–68.

entire Church peacefully accepts is the true pope.[927] It would be the duty of theologians, based on this clear *theoretical* principle, to resolve the *concrete* question which would then be put: Either proving that, in reality, the pope had not been a formal and notorious heretic at the moment of election; showing that he had converted afterward; verifying that the acceptance by the Church had not been pacific and universal; or presenting any other plausible explanation.

A more careful examination of the question would reveal, however, that, even on purely *theoretical* grounds, an important difficulty arises, which would consist in determining, with precision, the characteristics of the pacific and universal acceptance by the Church standard. For such acceptance to have been pacific and universal, would it suffice that no cardinal had contested the election? Would it be enough that in a Council, for example, the near totality of the bishops had signed the documents, recognizing in this way, at least implicitly, that the pope is the true one? Would it be enough that no voice, or practically no voice, had publicly sounded the alarm? Or, on the contrary, would a certain very generalized—though not always well-defined—distrust be sufficient to destroy the seemingly pacific and universal character of the pope's acceptance? Furthermore, if this distrust became a suspicion in numerous minds, a positive doubt in many, a certainty in some, would the pacific and universal acceptance subsist? In addition, if such distrusts, suspicions, doubts, and certainties cropped up with some frequency in conversations or private papers, or now and again in published writings, could one still classify as pacific and universal the acceptance of a pope who was already a heretic when elected by the Sacred College?

*   *   *

It is not in the nature of the present work to try to respond to questions such as these. We only wish to formulate them here, asking those who are learned in the matter to clarify them.

---

927. See chap. 14, sec. 2 (*The Hypothesis of a Dubious Pope*), item C.

CHAPTER FIFTEEN

Can There Be Error in Documents of the Magisterium?

Sacred theology furnishes many reasons for defending the thesis that, in principle, there can be errors in Magisterium documents that do not fulfill the conditions of infallibility.[928] They are so numerous and weighty that it suffices to highlight some of them to give the reader an overview of the matter.

1. Possibility of Error in Episcopal Documents

We must first note that Church Magisterium comes from the pope and bishops. They alone are authorized to speak officially in the Church's name as authentic interpreters of Revelation. Priests and theologians do not enjoy the privilege of infallibility under any circumstances, not even when they teach with a canonical mission received from a pope or bishop.

Also, when the bishops speak, individually or jointly, they can err, except when they solemnly define a dogma with the supreme pontiff, either in or outside a Council.

That bishops are never infallible in their pronouncements without the supreme pontiff is an unquestionable point in Church doctrine.[929]

In his *Pastoral Letter on Problems of the Modern Apostolate*, Bishop Mayer writes, "The papal magisterium being infallible, and that of each bishop, even though official, fallible, the possibility that one or other bishop fall into error is within the limits of human frailty. History records some of these eventualities."[930]

Here, then, a conclusion imposes itself: When clear reasons show that a bishop, some bishops acting together, or even the whole episcopate of a country or part of the world have fallen into error, nothing can compel a member of the faithful to embrace this error by alleging that it is not licit for him to disagree with

---

928. In substance, this chapter reproduces the essay we published in *Catolicismo*, no. 223, translated and published within Xavier da Silveira, *Can Documents of the Magisterium*, chap. 6, 103ff.
929. See Second Vatican Council, dogmatic constitution *Lumen gentium*, no. 25.
930. Mayer, "Problemas do apostolado moderno," 115. On the possibility of bishops and even entire episcopates falling into error and even heresy, a point admitted by all Catholic authors, see Pesch, *Praelectiones dogmaticae*, 1:259–61; Hurter, *Theologiae dogmaticae*, 1:263; d'Herbigny, *Theologica de ecclesia*, 2:309; Hervé, *Manuale theologiae dogmaticae*, 1:485; Salaverri, *De ecclesia Christi*, 1:682.

those whom Our Lord placed at the head of His flock. It will be licit, a duty even, for him to disagree with such episcopal teachings. According to the circumstances, such disagreement could even be expressed publicly.[931]

2. A First Vatican Council Definition

Moving from episcopal documents to papal ones, we shall start with seeing that, in principle, there can also be some error in these, even in matters of faith and morals.

This follows from the very definition of papal infallibility by the First Vatican Council, which established the four *conditions* under which the pope is infallible. Thus, it is easy to understand that, *in principle*, when such conditions are not fulfilled, there can be error in a papal document.[932]

In other words, we could say that the simple fact that Magisterium documents are divided into infallible and non-infallible ones leaves open, in theory, the possibility of error in any of the non-infallible ones. This conclusion is imposed based on the metaphysical principle expounded on by Saint Thomas Aquinas: *Quod possible est non esse, quandoque non est*—"that which is possible not to be, at some time is not."[933]

If, in theory, there can be error in a papal document because it does not fulfill the four conditions of infallibility, then the same thing must be said regarding conciliar documents that do not fulfill the same conditions. In other words, when a Council does not intend to define dogmas, then, strictly speaking, it can fall into error. This conclusion flows from the symmetry between papal infallibility and that of the Church, as the First Vatican Council stressed.[934]

3. Suspension of Internal Assent

Also favoring the thesis that, in principle, there can be error even in papal and conciliar documents is the argument—explained by some of the most renowned theologians—that, in very special cases, a Catholic may suspend his assent to a decision of the Magisterium.

As such, even when not infallible, papal decisions call for the external respectful silence (*silentium obsequiosum*) and the internal assent of the faithful. Pius XII declared this truth incisively: "Nor must it be thought that what is expounded in encyclical letters does not of itself demand consent, since in writing such letters the popes do not exercise the supreme power of their teaching authority. For these

---

931. See Chapter 18.
932. The First Vatican Council teaches that the pope is infallible "when he speaks *ex cathedra*, that is, when in discharge of the office of Pastor and Doctor of all Christians, by virtue of his supreme apostolic authority, he defines a doctrine regarding faith or morals to be held by the Universal Church." Cardinal Henry Edward Manning, *The Vatican Council and Its Definitions: A Pastoral Letter to the Clergy* (New York: D. & J. Sadlier, 1871), 62–63. See Denz.-Sch., 3074; Second Vatican Council, *Lumen gentium*, no. 25.
933. St. Thomas Aquinas, *Summa theologica*, I, q. 2, art. 3.
934. See Denz.-Sch., 3074.

matters are taught with the ordinary teaching authority, of which it is true to say, 'He who heareth you, heareth me' (Luke 10:16)."[935]

However, when there is "a precise opposition between an encyclical text and the other testimonies of Tradition,"[936] it would be licit for one of the faithful who is learned and has carefully studied the question to suspend or deny his assent to the papal document.

This doctrine is found among theologians of great authority. Let us quote some of them:

A. FRANCISCUS DIEKAMP

These non-infallible acts of papal magisterium do not oblige one to believe and do not demand an absolute and definitive submission. But it behooves one to adhere to such decisions with religious and internal assent since they constitute acts of the supreme Magisterium of the Church and are founded upon solid natural and supernatural reasons. The obligation to adhere to them can only begin to terminate in cases where, and this only occurs very rarely, a man fit to judge such a question, after a repeated and very diligent analysis of all the arguments, arrives at the conviction that an error has been introduced into the decision.[937]

B. CHRISTIANUS PESCH

One must assent to the decrees of the Roman Congregations, so long as it does not become positively clear that they have erred. Since the Congregations, per se, do not furnish an absolutely certain argument in favor of a given doctrine, one may, or even must, investigate the reasons for that doctrine. Thus, either it will come to pass that such a doctrine will be gradually accepted in the whole Church, attaining the condition of infallibility in this way, or the error will be detected little by little. Because since the religious assent referred to is not based on a metaphysical certainty, but only on a moral and general one, it does not exclude all suspicion of error. For this reason, as soon as sufficient motives for doubt arise, the assent will be prudently suspended. Nevertheless, so long as such motives for doubt do not arise, the authority of the Congregations is sufficient to oblige one to assent. . . .

The same principles apply without difficulty to the declarations that the supreme pontiff makes without engaging his supreme authority, as well as the decisions of the other ecclesiastical superiors who are not infallible.[938]

C. BENEDICTUS MERKELBACH

When the Church does not teach with infallible authority, the proposed doctrine is not irreformable. For this reason, if *per accidens*, in a hypothesis

---

935. Pius XII, *Humani generis*, no. 20.
936. Paul Nau, *Une source doctrinale: Les encycliques* (Paris: Éditions du Cèdre, 1952), 34.
937. Diekamp and Hoffman, *Theologiae dogmaticae manuale*, 1:72.
938. Pesch, *Praelectiones dogmaticae*, no. 521, 1:314–15.

which is, however, *very rare*, after a very careful examination of the matter, it appears to someone that there exist very grave reasons contrary to the doctrine thus proposed, it will be licit, without falling into temerity, to suspend *internal* assent.[939]

D. HUGO HURTER

If *grave* and solid reasons, above all *theological* ones, present themselves to the mind of one of the faithful, against [decisions of the authentic Magisterium, either episcopal or pontifical], it will be licit for him to fear error, assent conditionally, or even suspend assent.[940]

E. SISTO CARTECHINI

[In the hypothesis of non-infallible decisions,] the inferior must give his internal assent, except when he has evidence that the thing commanded is illicit. . . .

If some learned and studious person has very grave reasons to suspend his assent, he can do so without temerity or sin.[941]

In such cases, the counsel frequently given to the faithful is that they "suspend judgment" on the matter. If this "suspension of judgment" implies an abstention on the part of the faithful from taking any attitude regarding the papal teaching in question, it represents only one of the licit positions in the hypothesis under consideration. Indeed, the "suspension of internal assent" that theologians speak of has a broader sense than the mere "suspension of judgment" in everyday language. Depending on the case, the right of "suspending internal assent" includes the right to fear that there is error in a Magisterium document, to doubt the teaching contained therein, or even to reject it.

4. Some Do Not Admit the Suspension of Internal Assent

It is possible to object to the thesis we are defending since not all authors admit this suspension of internal assent. Such is the case of Choupin,[942] Pègues,[943] and Salaverri.[944]

---

939. Benedictus Henricus Merkelbach, *Summa theologiae moralis* (Paris: Desclée, 1931), 1:601.
940. Hurter, *Theologiae dogmaticae*, 1:492.
941. Cartechini, *Dall'opinione*, 153–54. The following authors express the same opinion: Pesch, *Compendium theologiae*, 1:238–39; Lercher, *Institutiones theologiae*, 1:297–98; J. Forget, "Congrégations Romaines," in *D.T.C.*, 3–1e.:1108–11; Josephus Mors, *Institutiones theologiae fundamentalis* (Petrópolis: Vozes, 1943), 2:187; J. Aertnys, C.SS.R., and C.A. Damen, C.SS.R., *Theologia moralis* (Turin: Marietti, 1950), 1:270; Marcelino Zalba, S.J., *Theologiae moralis compendium* (Madrid: B.A.C., 1958), 2:30n21.
942. See Lucien Choupin, *Valeur des décisions doctrinales et disciplinaires du Saint-Siège* (Paris: Beauchesne, 1928), 53ff., 88ff.; Lucien Choupin, "Motu proprio *Praestantia* de S.S. Pie X," *Études* 114 (Jan. 5, 1908), 119ff.; Lucien Choupin, "Le décret du Saint-Office: Sa valeur juridique," *Études* 112 (Aug. 5, 1907), 415–16.
943. See Thomas-M. Pègues, O.P., "L'autorité des encycliques pontificales d'après Saint Thomas," *Revue Thomiste* 12 (Paris—Nov.-Dec. 1904), 531.
944. See Salaverri, *De ecclesia Christi*, 1:725–26.

However, even these authors do not deny the possibility of error in documents of the Magisterium: "Since the decision does not come guaranteed by infallibility, the possibility of error is not excluded."[945]

They merely sustain that the pope's great religious authority, the scientific value of his advisers, and everything else surrounding the non-infallible documents counsel one against suspending internal assent, even when a studious person has serious reasons to admit that the papal decision contains error.

There is no reason for us to analyze the position of these theologians in more detail here. For now, it suffices to show, as we have done, that even they admit the possibility of error in documents of the ordinary Magisterium.

As far as their thesis is concerned, according to which it is never permitted to suspend internal assent,[946] we do not believe that these authors have directly considered the hypothesis grouping all of the following factors together in a single case:

1. real life circumstances oblige a member of the faithful, in conscience, to take an attitude about a problem;

2. he has evidence that there is, in this respect, a precise opposition between the teaching of the ordinary Magisterium and the other testimonies of Tradition in this regard;

3. the infallible decision ending debate on the question has not been pronounced yet.

In the doctrinally admissible hypothesis where these three factors come together, it does not seem that any theologian could condemn the suspension of internal assent to the non-infallible decision. To condemn it would be an unnatural, even violent, act, for it would oblige one to believe, contrary to the very evidence, in something which is not guaranteed by the infallibility of the Church.

5. Some Deny the Possibility of Error in Non-infallible Documents

Some prestigious authors who oppose the thesis that there can be error in documents of the ordinary pontifical or conciliar Magisterium raise yet another objection. According to Cardinals Franzelin and Billot, even non-infallible documents are guaranteed against error through the assistance of the Holy Spirit.[947]

Thus, the thesis we are defending could seem at least uncertain. One would ask: "Would it not be more consonant with the eminently hierarchical and even monarchical spirit of the organization of the Church to adopt the opinion of these eminent theologians? Would it not be more in accordance with the condition of

---

945. Choupin, *Valeur*, 54; See Pègues, "L'autorité," 531; Salaverri, *De ecclesia Christi*, 1:722.
946. See our essay "What is the Doctrinal Authority of the Pontifical and Conciliar Documents?" *Catolicismo*, no. 202 (Oct. 1967), p. 7.
947. See Franzelin, *Tractatus de divina*, 116–20; Billot, *Tractatus de ecclesia*, 1:428–34.

sons of the Church to admit that, even in pronouncements that are not *ex cathedra,* it would be absurd for error to occur?"

An exhaustive analysis of this question would lead us far beyond the objectives of the present work. For this reason, we would only like to show that, all things considered, even Cardinals Franzelin and Billot and the theologians who subscribe to their position admit the possibility of error in the non-infallible documents.

They start with the presupposition that the documents of the Holy See either teach an infallible doctrine or declare that a determined opinion is safe or not safe: "In these declarations, though the *truth* of the doctrine is not *infallible*—given the hypothesis that there is no intention of using the power of the keys—there is an *infallible* assurance, in that it is *safe* for all to embrace it, and it is not safe to reject it, nor can this be done without violation of the due submission to the Magisterium established by God."[948]

Therefore, these authors sustain that, in the non-infallible pronouncements, the Magisterium does not commit itself with an affirmation of the truth of the doctrine it proposes but sustains only that, in the present circumstances, such doctrine does not offer any danger to the faith.

Such theologians recognize clearly that the teaching contained in these documents can be false: "The doctrine in favor of which there is a solid probability that it is not opposed to the rule of faith, *may perhaps be theologically false on the speculative plane,* that is, if it were taken concerning the norm of faith objectively considered."[949]

It becomes clear, therefore, that even these authors admit the possibility of error regarding the *doctrine* contained in documents of the ordinary Magisterium.

What should we think about the theory that non-infallible pronouncements only aim to declare that a doctrine is safe or not? Such theory does not seem to agree with the terms of most of the Holy See documents. In some, it is clear that it is only a question of the safety or danger of a certain doctrine, but in many others—in the encyclicals, for example—the intention of presenting teachings as *certain,* not merely safe, is manifest.

Moreover, generally speaking, authors have abandoned this theory.[950]

We do not have room here to analyze the above position of Cardinals Franzelin and Billot minutely. We only wish to point out that, even according to them, in principle, the possibility of doctrinal error in documents of the ordinary Magisterium is not excluded.

---

948. Franzelin, *Tractatus de divina,* 116–20.
949. Billot, *Tractatus de ecclesia,* 1:430. (Our emphasis.)
950. See Hervé, *Manuale theologiae dogmaticae,* 1:513; Cartechini, *Dall'opinione,* passim; Salaverri, *De ecclesia Christi,* 1:726; Journet, *L'Église,* 1:455–56, who, when appealing to the opinion of Cardinal Franzelin, gives to the words of the former Gregoriana professor an interpretation that modifies his thinking entirely.

6. Conclusion

From everything presented, one may infer that, in principle, the existence of errors in non-infallible documents of the Magisterium is not impossible, even in the pontifical and conciliar Magisterium.

Without a doubt, such errors cannot be sustained for a long time in the Holy Church, to the point of exposing upright souls to the dilemma of accepting the false teaching or breaking with Her. For, if it were so, then Hell would have prevailed against the Church. However, it is possible, in principle, that for some time, above all in periods of crisis and great heresies, some error can be found in documents of the Magisterium.

Clearly, we do not make such observations with any destructive purpose. We do not seek to lay the foundations for some heretic to make "contestations," with which progressives seek, at every moment, to undermine the principle of authority in the Church.

What we do seek, by making evident the possibility of error in non-infallible documents, is to help clarify the problems of conscience and the studies of many anti-progressives who, because they are unaware of such a possibility, frequently feel perplexed.

CHAPTER SIXTEEN

Can There Be Heresy in Documents of the Pontifical or Conciliar Magisterium?

In the previous chapter, we demonstrated that, in principle, it is possible for there to be some form of error in official non-infallible documents of the Magisterium, be they episcopal, conciliar, or pontifical.

Here we must continue our investigations into the matter, asking ourselves if, in principle, beyond just error, there could be heresy in such documents.

To simplify the handling of the matter, we will address it directly at its thorniest point. In principle, can one admit the existence of heresy in an official pontifical document, though not an infallible one, or do the Catholic teachers who do not reject the hypothesis of a heretical pope only suggest the possibility of his fall into heresy as a *private person*?

We said that by addressing the question directly at its thorniest point, we would be able to resolve it in the simplest way. Indeed, if the hypothesis of a pope teaching some heresy in an official document of the Magisterium is not to be excluded in principle, then, with equal reason, there could be heresy in a non-infallible conciliar document[951] and, further, in official pronouncements of bishops—something which all admit and history does not permit us to doubt.

1. A Hasty Answer

A superficial examination of the passages in which the great theologians discuss the problem of a heretical pope would lead a hasty reader to give, immediately and peremptorily, a negative answer to the question we present.

---

951. The hypothesis of there being some heresy in a non-infallible conciliar document is not to be confounded with the hypothesis that all the bishops or the entire Church fall into heresy. Indeed, adhesion to a document that does not fulfill all the conditions that would make it infallible would not be imposed absolutely on bishops who had rejected it in a conciliar session, nor on bishops who had been absent from that session, nor on the priests and faithful of the entire world. As is evident, the fall of the whole Catholic world into heresy is impossible, for that would completely contradict the divine promises of assistance to the Holy Church.

All the authors whom we know to have studied the hypothesis of a heretical pope formulate the question only regarding a pope's eventual heresy *as a private person*. Such being the case, it appears inevitable to conclude that it is theologically impossible to find heresy in an official pontifical document, that is, in a pope's teaching *as a public person*.

We cite below some texts that illustrate well the terms in which the theologians usually formulate the question.

The chapter in which Saint Robert Bellarmine expounds his opinion on the possibility of a heretical pope is titled "On the Pope as a Particular Person." The great Jesuit doctor formulates his opinion as follows: "It is probable and may piously be believed that not only as 'pope' can the supreme pontiff not err, but he cannot be a heretic even as a particular [private] person by pertinaciously believing something false against the Faith."[952]

Suárez writes, "Though many may hold with verisimilitude [that the pope can fall into heresy], to me, however, in a few words, it appears more pious and probable to affirm that the pope, as a private person, can err by ignorance, but not contumaciously."[953]

De Soto taught, "Though some masters of our time sustain that the pope cannot be a heretic in any way, the common opinion is the opposite. For though he might not be able to err as pope—that is, he could not define an error as an article of faith because the Holy Spirit will not permit it—nevertheless, as a private person, he can err in faith, just as he can commit other sins since he is not impeccable."[954]

According to the Jesuit moralist Paul Laymann (d. 1625), the pope, as a person, might be able to fall into heresy, even notoriously, for which he would merit to be deposed by the Church, or rather, declared to be separated from her. However, while affirming that the pope as a private person might be able to become a heretic and, therefore, cease to be a true member of the Church, Laymann believed that as long as the Church tolerated and publicly recognized him as the universal pastor, he would enjoy papal power, so that all his decrees would have no less force and authority than if he were truly faithful.[955]

The canonist Bouix expounds his thinking in the following terms:[956]

> In the first place, therefore, we have said that the papal heresy we are discussing here does not constitute an evil so grave that it necessarily obliges one to think that Christ would desire the deposition of such a pope. We are discussing here *private* heresy exclusively, that is, professed by the pontiff not as Pastor of the Church and in his papal acts and decrees, but only as a private teacher and limited to his personal sayings and writings. Now, since the pope always teaches the true faith when he defines and pronounces as

---

952. St. Robert Bellarmine, *On the Roman Pontiff*, book 4, chap. 6, 532.
953. Suárez, *De fide*, disp. 10, sect. 6, no. 11, 319.
954. De Soto, *Commentarium ... in quartam*, dist. 22, q. 2, a. 2, 1021.
955. See Laymann, *Theologia moralis*, book 2, tract. 1, chap. 7, 145–46.
956. Other Bouix texts in the same line are found in his *Tractatus de papa*, 2:653, 665n1.

pontiff, the faithful are sufficiently secure, even though it be known, at the same time, that the pope himself adheres privately to some heresy. All will easily understand that an opinion defended by the pope as a private teacher would be completely lacking in authority and that he would only have to be obeyed when he defined and imposed truths of faith officially and with his pontifical authority.[957]

The neo-scholastic canonist Matthaeus Conte a Coronata, O.M.C., studying the various cases in which the pope loses the papacy, observes that one of them is falling into notorious heresy. He writes:

> Some authors deny the *supposition*, that is, that there could be a heretical Roman pontiff.
>
> However, it cannot be proven that the Roman pontiff, as a private doctor, could not become a heretic.[958]

*   *   *

It would be useless to multiply citations. Theologians are unanimous in presenting the problem in this manner. The doubt being raised refers exclusively to the possibility of heresy in the pope *as a private person.*

We believe, however, that whoever believed that he saw in these quotations a decisive argument supporting the thesis that the Catholic Tradition has always excluded the possibility of heresy in a document of the pontifical Magisterium would be erring.

This is what one verifies, *salvo meliori judicio,* by a more detailed analysis of the matter.

2. A Forgotten Hypothesis

The reading of some of the texts we have just presented, together with those we shall present shortly, reveals a curious and unexpected fact: In studying the question of a heretical pope, both ancient and modern scholars have considered only two kinds of papal acts: infallible pronouncements and private ones. The official but non-infallible documents seem not to exist.

Note de Soto's argument: The pope cannot err as pope, that is, in defining an article of faith, because the Holy Spirit will not permit it. He can err as a private person, though. The great Dominican did not consider the third hypothesis, namely, that of the pope who makes a pronouncement as pope, but *without defining* an article of faith.

See also what was argued by Bouix. The heresy of the head of the Church would not be so grave because it would be restricted to his private person. At the same time, one must obey him without fear of error "when he defined and

---

957. Bouix, *Tractatus de papa,* 2:670.
958. Coronata, *Institutiones iuris,* 1:367.

imposed truths of faith officially and with his pontifical authority." Bouix did not consider the third hypothesis: a heretical pope pronouncing "officially and with his pontifical authority" but without "defining and imposing truths of faith."

The same silence about this third hypothesis occurs in the texts below that discuss the question of the heretical pope and papal infallibility. Cardinal Camillo Mazzella wrote, "It is one thing that the pope cannot teach a heresy when speaking *ex cathedra* (defined by the First Vatican Council). It is another that he cannot fall into heresy, that is, become a heretic as a private person. On this last question, the Council said nothing, and the theologians and canonists are not in agreement among themselves in this regard."[959]

Further on, the silence of Cardinal Camillo Mazzella about the abovementioned third hypothesis becomes even stranger: "The pope can teach in two ways. First, in what he has in common with all other private teachers, for example, publishing books or theological commentaries, as other theologians do. Second, when he teaches the whole Church as the supreme and authentic teacher. In his capacity as a private teacher, he does not enjoy any pontifical authority, much less infallibility. . . . However, as the supreme and authentic teacher, he is infallible."[960]

In discussing pontifical infallibility, the Jesuit theologian Horatio Mazzella wrote, "Due to the gift of infallibility, the pope cannot fall into heresy when he speaks *ex cathedra*. This was defined in the [First] Vatican Council. Theologians dispute, however, whether he can become a true heretic as a private person, adhering publicly[961] and pertinaciously to an error against the faith. As is evident, we treat (in this chapter on infallibility) of the pontiff who speaks *ex cathedra*, and not as a private person."[962]

The words of Dominicus M. Prümmer, O.P.: "It is the common opinion of the authors that for certain and notorious heresy the pope loses his power, but they rightly doubt whether this can occur. Supposing that the pope falls into heresy as *a private man* (for as pope, being infallible, he cannot err in the faith), the divine authors developed various opinions to explain how he would be deprived of power. Still, none of them is more than probable."[963]

Saying that one of the conditions for the pope to be infallible is that he speak as a public person, the manual of dogmatic theology of the Capuchins Iragui and Abarzuza indicates what the concept of *public person* excludes: "Not then as bishop of a particular church, or as Patriarch of the West; in a word, not as a private person who converses familiarly about common things, exhorts the people in sermons, publishes scientific books, etc."[964]

---

959. Mazzella, *De religione*, no. 1045, p. 817.
960. Mazzella, no. 1048, p. 819.
961. Note that adhering "publicly" to an error against the Faith does not signify here adhering as a public person, but rather as a private person, in a document which, however, comes to the knowledge of the public.
962. Horatius Mazzella, *Praelectiones scholastico-dogmaticae* (Turin: Libreria Editrice Internazionale, 1915), 1:545.
963. Prümmer, *Manuale iuris canonici* (Freiburg: Herder, 1933), 131.
964. Iragui and Abarzuza, *Manuale theologiae dogmaticae*, 1:429.

The Second Vatican Council's dogmatic constitution *Lumen gentium* also explains pontifical infallibility. It counterposes the pope as a private person with the pope who uses his infallibility. Though the Council shortly before had discussed official non-infallible pontifical pronouncements, the silence in this text about the third hypothesis is noteworthy:

> Therefore, his definitions [those of the pope], of themselves, and not from the consent of the Church, are justly styled irreformable since they are pronounced with the assistance of the Holy Spirit, promised to him in blessed Peter, and, therefore, they need no approval of others, nor do they allow an appeal to any other judgment. For then, the Roman Pontiff is not pronouncing judgment as a private person but as the supreme teacher of the universal Church, in whom the charism of infallibility of the Church itself is individually present, he is expounding or defending a doctrine of Catholic faith.[965]

3. A Noted Gap

Undoubtedly, one could not admit that theologians, in general, have purely and simply left out the existence of official non-infallible pontifical documents. Nor is this our affirmation. We sustain that, regarding the concept of "private person," there is a certain imprecision in theological writings and that such imprecision is responsible for the apparent exclusion, in the authors discussing the problem of the possibility of heresy in non-infallible documents of the papal Magisterium.

To make our position clear, we make three observations:

1. First, it is necessary to reaffirm that even the writings containing the noted gap admit somewhere the existence of official non-infallible pontifical documents.[966]

2. Second, note that numerous documents and treatises recognize, directly or indirectly, that it is possible, in principle, to have heresy in some non-infallible pronouncement of the papal Magisterium.

Regarding the letters of Pope Honorius I to the Patriarch Sergius, for example—letters whose official character no one contests—it is common among theologians to find the explanation, presented even before the examination of their contents, that they do not compromise the privilege of infallibility because they are not *ex cathedra* documents. Now, such an explanation would be inoperative if it were impossible to have any heresy in official non-infallible pontifical

---

965. Second Vatican Council, *Lumen gentium*, no. 25.
966. See, for example, *Lumen gentium*, no. 25; Laymann, *Theologia moralis*, book 2, tract 1, chap. 7, 146; Mazzella, *De religione*, 819; Mazzella, *Praelectiones*, 1:551–52.

documents. An analogous explanation is given in the other cases, which history records, of papal pronouncements suspected of heresy.[967]

Moreover, regarding the letters of Pope Honorius I, it must be observed that Pope Adrian II, and with him, the Roman Synod and the Eighth Ecumenical Council, admitted that they contained heresy. As Saint Robert Bellarmine observes,[968] it is true that Pope Adrian II was probably mistaken in his evaluation of the concrete case. It is nevertheless certain that he and the mentioned assemblies judged it possible for the letters to contain heresy.[969]

3. Third, it is very important to observe that theologians have already pointed out the imprecision with which many use the expression "private teacher." Below we give some examples worthy of note.

Immediately after showing that the pope can make a pronouncement without involving his infallibility, Palmieri writes, "In this hypothesis, one who speaks of him as a 'private teacher' does not speak with sufficient propriety, for, while he does not speak with the plenitude of his authority, he speaks however with authority; for this reason, when he makes a pronouncement in this form, the Roman pontiff cannot be lowered to the category of any private teacher who has no authority."[970]

In the *Dictionnaire de théologie catholique* article "Infaillibilité du pape," Dublanchy shows that there are non-infallible pontifical teachings to which the faithful must, however, morally adhere.[971] Refuting one possible objection against the principle that there exist many official but non-infallible pontifical pronouncements, he writes:

> It is true that in the sixteenth and following centuries, many theologians frequently give to understand that the pope speaks as a *private doctor* when he does not teach *infallibly as pontiff.* (See Bellarmine, *On the Roman Pontiff*, book 4, chap. 22;[972] Bañez, *Commentaria in II–II*, q. 1, a.10, dub. 2, Venice: 1602, 127).[973] But if one examines all those assertions carefully—they frequently contradict one another on account of totally opposing assertions—it is easy to see that they are answers given in passing to certain historical objections. There was never an intention to

---

967. In this regard, see Diekamp and Hoffman, *Theologiae dogmaticae manuale*, 2:270–71; d'Herbigny, *Theologica de ecclesia*, 2:319; Hurter, *Theologiae dogmaticae*, 1:422; Lercher, *Institutiones theologiae*, 1:294; Mazzella. *Praelectiones*, 1:552; Tanquerey, *Synopsis theologiae dogmaticae*, 1:599; Hervé, *Manuale theologiae dogmaticae*, 1:481; Iragui and Abarzuza, *Manuale theologiae dogmaticae*, 1:440–41; Ludwig Ott, *Fundamentals of Catholic Dogma* (St. Louis: B. Herder Book Co., 1954), 287; Salaverri, *De ecclesia Christi*, 1:666, 717.
968. See text supported by footnote 765.
969. See chap. 8, sec. 2 (*Arguments Contrary to This Opinion*), B. a.
970. Palmieri, *Tractatus de romano pontifice*, 632.
971. See Dublanchy, "Infaillibilité du pape," in *D.T.C.*, 7–2e.:1709ff.
972. We believe there is a mistake in the indication of chap. 22, which does not discuss this matter. What Dublanchy references is found in chaps. 6 and 7.
973. Please note that both the text cited from St. Robert Bellarmine (given the mistake pointed out in our previous note) and that of Bañez deal with the question of the heretical pope.

establish thereby a doctrine generally applicable to all cases not involving pontifical infallibility.[974]

How can one explain such imprecision in the concept of "private doctor' in theologians of such authority? We believe that the explanation is to be found in that only since the nineteenth century have the official non-infallible pronouncements of the pope become the object of more profound studies.[975] Before that, the matter was undoubtedly discussed, but not very explicitly and clearly. For this reason, some less than appropriate expressions were used,[976] which the more recent authors have still not defined exactly, nor even duly corrected.

4. A Hypothesis Which Still Stands

Considering the reasons presented, we do not see how to exclude, in principle, the hypothesis of heresy in an official document of the pontifical or conciliar Magisterium that does not include the conditions that would make it infallible.

Consequently, should a heresy be found in an official non-infallible pontifical or conciliar document, one would not have to conclude that the Holy Spirit had failed His Church. Nor would the absurdity of the hypothesis oblige one to find, at whatever the cost, a non-heretical interpretation of the text indicated as being opposed to the faith. Nor would one apply the celebrated rule of Saint Ignatius in these circumstances: "We ought always to hold that the white which I see is black if the Hierarchical Church so decides it."[977]

In conclusion, the admirable Ignatian principle represents a complete expression of faith in the infallibility of the Magisterium. Whoever attributed to this saying, however, a significance that Catholic doctrine does not justify—interpreting it, for example, in the sense that one must accept always and unconditionally, even against the evidence, each non-infallible teaching of the ecclesiastical Magisterium—would be wanting in the very "*sentire cum ecclesia* [thinking with the Church]."

---

974. Dublanchy, "Infaillibilité du pape," in *D.T.C.*, 7–2e.:1710.
975. "This non-infallible doctrinal authority (of the supreme pontiff) was affirmed particularly in the second half of the nineteenth century." Dublanchy, 7–2e.:1710.
976. Other imprecise terms used in treating this subject are *dogma, heresy, define, solemn definition, extraordinary Magisterium,* and *anathema.* See Xavier da Silveira, "What Is the Authority of the Documents of the Pontifical and Conciliar Magisterium?" "Not Only Heresy Can Be Condemned by the Ecclesiastical Authority," and "Can a Catholic Reject *Humanae Vitae?*" *Catolicismo,* nos. 202, 203, and 212–214, respectively Oct. 1967, Nov. 1967, and Aug.-Oct. 1968.
977. Elder Mullan, S.J., trans., *The Spiritual Exercises of St. Ignatius of Loyola* (New York: P.J. Kenedy & Sons, 1914), rule no. 13 (for thinking with the Church).

Chapter Seventeen

Acts, Gestures, Attitudes, and Omissions Can Characterize a Heretic

In his encyclical *Pascendi Dominici gregis*, Saint Pius X said that the modernists were the most dangerous enemies of the Church because they hid in her very bosom and never confessed their heresy clearly.[978]

It would, therefore, be highly censurable for one of the faithful to believe that only declared enemies of the Bride of Christ should be combatted. To sustain that a person becomes unassailable merely by declaring himself a Catholic, however absurd his words or actions might be, is to establish absolute impunity for wolves in sheep's clothing who infiltrate the flock. This attitude would also deprive people in good faith of the warnings and clarifications that could forewarn them against error or even extricate them from it when already deceived by its tricks.

"The ally that he [the devil] manages to plant inside the ranks of the faithful," Bishop Mayer teaches, "is his most precious weapon in the fight."[979] This is why, since its foundation in 1951, *Catolicismo* has constantly alerted its readers both against the Church's declared enemies—communists, socialists, divorce advocates, and the like—and her disguised ones.

1. Wolves Inside the Fold

Anyone worried at the sight of wolves in sheep's clothing roaming freely among the flock finds himself in a difficult position. He is often misunderstood and viewed as one obsessed with policing—as a narrow-minded person prone to seeing heresy in everything.

---

978. See St. Pius X, *Pascendi*, no. 3. This chapter reproduces an essay published in *Catolicismo*, no. 204 (Dec. 1967), when the 1917 CIC of Saint Pius X and Benedict XV was still in effect. John Paul II published the new Code in 1983 with major changes based on the Second Vatican Council. Endowed with a true *sensus fidei*, a faithful Catholic easily sees that the dogmatic principles underlying the 1917 rules cannot but remain untouched and untouchable. This essay, and six others on the same topic, were published in the already referenced book *Can Documents of the Magisterium of the Church Contain Errors?* published by the American TFP in 2015.
979. Mayer, "Problemas do apostolado moderno," 27.

For that reason, *Catolicismo* has not only fought against internal adversaries, but always striven to show that this is a legitimate, advisable, and even necessary combat. To wage this struggle is to act in the best Church tradition, to obey the recommendations of the holy popes, imitate the saints, and heed Our Lord's warning: "Beware of false prophets, who come to you in the clothing of sheep, but inwardly they are ravening wolves" (Matt. 7:15).

In this chapter, we do not wish to repeat the many arguments that *Catolicismo* has given over the last seventeen years, upholding the thesis that it is licit and even necessary to warn people against enemies inside the Church. We will not demonstrate again that such action is recommended by the popes, that it is not opposed to charity, does not have a morbid negativist character, and so on.

We want only to deal with a very specific point, but one of paramount importance: to define precisely the enemy within the Church. The question we ask is this: "For a Catholic to become a heretic or one suspected of heresy, is it necessary for him to defend propositions opposed to the faith with written or spoken words, or can the ensemble of a person's attitudes, way of being, acting, and behaving, characterize a heretic even if he says or writes nothing formally opposed to the faith?"

In short: Can someone fall into heresy by his acts?

The speculative and practical importance of this question is obvious. In the theoretical plane, one should remember that, according to Canon Law, a heretic who externally manifests his heresy is *ipso facto* excommunicated and excluded from the Church. Thus, the possibility for someone to fall into heresy merely by practicing certain acts profoundly affects the study of the Mystical Body of Christ and many other parts of sacred theology.

However, we start the analysis by noting that not every act irreconcilable with a dogma must be interpreted as revealing a heretical mentality. Indeed, out of weakness or malice, a sinner who believes in Hell can behave as if he did not. He wants to enjoy life, hopes to convert before dying, or simply does not want to make an effort to overcome his bad habits. Does such behavior make him a heretic? Absolutely not. An act or an ensemble of actions reveals a heretical *animus* only when—all surrounding circumstances having been considered first—they unequivocally indicate that the person, in addition to acting in discrepancy with some dogma, knowingly denies or questions that dogma.[980]

In the practical realm, it is obvious that if simple acts can characterize a heretic, the number of those excommunicated is greater than it might appear at first sight.

Furthermore, once it is proven that it is possible to fall into heresy by practicing certain acts, the combat against disguised wolves gains new amplitude and momentum.

The common notion in Catholic circles is that a principle of the faith can only be denied with words. This erroneous idea makes many fearful people feel insecure combatting this or that internal Church enemy. They believe they are attacking a brother in the faith, a member of the Mystical Body of Christ. Even if they admit

---

980. On the concept of heresy, see Chapter 8.

a given attitude is tactically erroneous or harmful to the interests of Religion, such people hesitate to denounce a fellow Catholic. If we can show them that, in this or that case, they are not confronting a fellow Catholic but a heretic, we will have helped them overcome a thousand unjustified hesitations and mental reluctances.

The problem becomes even graver because "The promoters of such errors are very frequently persons of exemplary personal conduct. . . . Because of this, far from serving the cause of good principles, they, on the contrary, further facilitate the spread of evil by giving these doctrines a disinterested and purely speculative character."[981]

Huge devastation wreaked upon the flock of Christ would have been avoided if the wolves had been called wolves from the beginning, that is, if their sheep's clothing had been ripped off from them early on, revealing a heretic's coarse, hairy, and repelling skin.

Take, for example, a university student who professes to be a Catholic. He actively works with so-called peasant, student, and worker advocacy movements. Long allied to Communists in those movements, he is used to having them by his side. He does not claim to be a Marxist and even says he is a staunch enemy of every form of atheism, but he looks at Socialism, even extreme Socialism, with sympathy. For his support of "advanced" social reforms, he has even had some scuffles with the police—whom he calls reactionary and "sellouts" to capitalists and colonialism. He receives Communion daily but believes that the childish practices of the "Constantinian Church" should be eliminated from the pious practices of adult Catholics enlightened by the "Church of Vatican Two." For this reason, he smiles scornfully when he hears of the Sacred Heart of Jesus, the virginity of Mary Most Holy, devotion to the saints, transubstantiation, Hell, and so forth. He never attacks any dogma directly because he knows it would be a disservice to his cause, but he does not talk about them and does not like to hear about them.

So we ask: Could one affirm that this young man is a heretic?

2. Internal and External Heresy

To answer this question, we must first note that, for juridical purposes, there is an enormous difference between internal and external heresy. In other words, between the sin of heresy committed in the secret of one's conscience and that which is externally manifested, thus constituting heresy in the canonical sense.

Indeed, being a visible society, the Church can only juridically punish visibly manifest sins. A sin that never leaves the inner conscience is truly sin and will be punished by God. The Church can forgive it at the tribunal of Confession. If the sin is not manifested in the visible world, however, it cannot be the object of ecclesiastical censures or punishments.

---

981. Plinio Corrêa de Oliveira, *In Defense of Catholic Action* (Spring Grove, Penn.: The American Society for the Defense of Tradition, Family, Property—TFP, 2006), 110.

A man succumbs to temptation against the faith and, for example, denies in his mind the dogma of the eternity of Hell. He tells no one. Undoubtedly, he has committed a mortal sin of heresy, but he is not excommunicated or excluded from the Church. That will only happen after he exteriorizes the heresy.

Now, it is a generally accepted thesis among theologians that heresy can be exteriorized not merely by words but also by gestures, attitudes, signs, and omissions, thus incurring canonical penalties.

This affirmation by theologians is based on an obvious and very simple argument. Canonically, a person becomes a heretic when he exteriorly manifests his interior heresy. Now, thoughts can be manifested not only with words but also with gestures, attitudes, and signs.

Indeed, a mere nod of the head, a hand gesture, or a facial expression can unequivocally indicate a thought. On a broader front, taking a political stand, keeping silent or taking a public attitude toward an authority can indicate, depending on the circumstances, that the person holds such and such ideas.

3. That Heresy Can Be Manifested by Acts Is Generally Accepted

Before examining some collateral though fundamentally important problems raised by this thesis, we want to show that there is nothing new or original in what we have just stated. On the contrary, as we said, it is an undisputed point among theologians. However, since there is a widespread misbelief that a heretic is only someone who enunciates a heresy with written or spoken words, we want to extend our arguments by citing some quotations from highly renowned theologians:

> —According to the general rule, for something to constitute external heresy and incur censure, it is necessary and sufficient to manifest the internal heresy through some external sign. These signs are usually classified in two kinds: words and acts. Words include signs with the head, hands, or anything else, such as sign language. Acts also include omissions of some external action. Indeed, sometimes an omission is just as much a manifestation of internal heresy as a positive act, which is why heretics are often discovered by the very fact that they do not do what Catholics do.[982]
> —External heresy is that which is manifested by external signs (words, signs, acts, or the omission thereof).[983]
> —External heresy is an error against the faith manifested by word or another external sign.[984]

---

982. See Joannes de Lugo, S.J., *Tractatus de virtute fidei divinae*, vol. 2 of *Disputationes scholasticæ et morales* (Paris: Vivès, 1868), disp. 23, sect. 2, no. 11.
983. See Merkelbach, *Summa theologiae moralis*, 1:570.
984. See Dominicus Prümmer, O.P., *Manuale theologiae moralis* (Freiburg: Herder, 1940), 1:365.

—To incur such excommunication [*latæ sententiæ*, especially reserved to the pope], heresy must be manifested externally by a word, writing, or act after being conceived internally.[985]

—[External heresy] adds to internal heresy a sufficient external manifestation, expressed by words, signs, or actions that are conclusive.[986]

—The external manifestation of heresy can occur in any way, through signs, writings, words, and actions, as long as it becomes sufficiently clear that it is a true and proper adhesion, and, moreover, a formal one, that is, fully intended.[987]

—To incur excommunication, the heresy conceived interiorly must be manifested externally by some sign—word, action, or writing—even though no one is present or hears it.[988]

—It matters little [for someone to incur excommunication] that he manifests the heresy alone or before others; that he does it by *word*, *writing*, or an *action*, as long as he is aware of the heresy implicit in the act.[989]

—Internal heresy is the one conceived only mentally and not manifested by any external sign. External heresy is displayed through outward signs: words, writings, actions, denials, and the like.[990]

—External heresy is manifested by omissions, words, or other perceptible signs.[991]

—Heretics, that is, Christians who pertinaciously deny or call into question, not only internally or externally, but at the same time internally and externally, through some sign—words, acts, or writings—truths of the faith that are proposed by the Church [incur excommunication].[992]

—For there to be an offense, apostasy, heresy, or schism must be manifested exteriorly through acts or words.[993]

---

985. See A. Tanquerey, *Synopsis theologiæ moralis et pastoralis* (Paris: Desclée, 1948), 2:475.

986. See Wernz and Vidal, *Ius canonicum*, 2:444.

987. See Luciano de Bruyne, "Eresia," in *E.C.*, 5:490.

988. See Noldin, Schmitt, and Heinzel, *Summa theologiæ moralis*, 1:48.

989. See Eduardus Genicot and Ioseph Salmans, S.J., *Institutiones theologiae moralis* (Bruges: Desclée, 1951), 2:647.

990. See Antonius Peinador, *Cursus brevior theologiae moralis* (Madrid: Coculsa, tomus 2, vol. 1, 1950; tomus 2, vol. 2, 1954), book 2, 1:103.

991. See Zalba, *Theologiæ moralis*, 2:28.

992. See Thomas A. Iorio, S.J., *Theologia moralis* (Naples: D'Auria, 1960), 2:258.

993. See Miguélez, Alonso, and Cabreros, *Código de derecho*, 845. The same thesis is found in the following authors: Suárez, *De fide*, disp. 19, sect. 4, nos. 4–5; disp. 21, sect. 2, no. 8; Anacletus Reiffenstuel, *Theologia moralis* (Venice: Bortoli, 1704), tract. 4, dist. 4, q. 3, no. 26; Schmalzgrueber, *Ius ecclesiasticum*, (1845), book 5, vol. 10, pars 1, tit. 7, no. 98; Josephus D'Annibale, *In constitutionem apostolicæ sedis commentarii* (Reate: Salvatore Trinchi, 1880), no. 31; Lehmkuhl, *Theologia moralis*, 2:656; Mattaeus Conte a Coronata, O.M.C., *Institutiones juris canonici* (Turin: Marietti, 1935), 4:280; Cappello, *Summa iuris* (1955), 3; Ioannes Ferreres, S.J. and Alfredus Mondria, S.J., *Compendium theologiæ moralis* (Barcelona: Eugenius Subirana, 1953), 2:743; Wernz and Vidal, *Ius canonicum*, 7:445, 449–50; A. Michel, "Hérésie, hérétique," *D.T.C.*, 6–2e:2242–43; Noldin, Schmitt, and Heinzel, *Summa theologiae moralis*, 2:26; Brys, *Juris canonici*, 2:502; Antonius M. Arregui, S.J., *Summarium theologiæ moralis* (Bilbao: El Mensajero del Corazón de Jesús, 1952), 78; Peinador, *Cursus brevior*, book 2, 1:74; Sipos, *Enchiridion juris*, 608; Zalba, *Theologiæ moralis*, 2:973.

4. No Small Difficulties

As we have said in passing, the difficulties raised by the thesis that someone can become a heretic by practicing certain acts are not small.

Let us examine some of them.

A. Can an Action Have an Unequivocal Meaning?

1. An act, attitude, gesture, or omission can always have more than one meaning. Moreover, they may result from coercion, weakening mental faculties, and other factors. Does one not risk committing grave injustice in affirming that someone incurs the delict of heresy and is thus excommunicated and excluded from the Church for having acted in a certain way?

The answer is obvious. There is no question that there are ambiguous acts susceptible to more than one interpretation. One who practices such acts does not become a heretic. Depending on the circumstances, he may become suspected of heresy. It is equally evident, however, that there are unequivocal actions or sets of actions. That is, they are unsusceptible to more than one interpretation.

As for the possibility of coercion, of course, it exists. However, it exists not only when practicing acts but also when uttering or writing words. Legal science has elaborated minutely detailed and wise rules of procedure over the centuries to avoid mistaken judgments regarding actions motivated by coercion, fear, ignorance, error, and so forth. Such cautious rules are also rigorously adopted in Canon Law. In the case we are examining, heresy by acts, canon law sees a crime only when it becomes certain that the one committing it is fully aware of what he is doing and, therefore, is pertinacious in his condemnable attitude and heretical *animus*.

Therefore, one must not rush to judgment about actions whose nature indicates a heretical mind, but one cannot deny that, in many cases, ideas are unequivocally manifested through actions.

An important observation imposes itself here. When we say that we must not rush to judgment about someone's ambiguous actions, are we thereby affirming that a Catholic must never be suspicious of his neighbor and that every suspicion is a rash judgment?

Absolutely not. Prof. Corrêa de Oliveira thoroughly analyzed rash judgment in highly-acclaimed articles published in *Legionário* in 1941.[994] After proving that perspicacity is an indispensable virtue for men in all walks of life, he shows that Our Lord practiced it and recommended it insistently. Insufficient indications to make an unfavorable judgment about someone can, nevertheless, constitute sufficient evidence to raise suspicion. Raising a suspicion is often a duty. A company director has a real moral obligation to his partners to be suspicious of a worker he sees behaving strangely. A father must be suspicious of his son who shows signs of a grave spiritual crisis, for only then can he fulfill his fatherly duties.

---

994. See Plinio Corrêa de Oliveira, "Juizo temerário," *Legionário*, nos. 475–477, Oct. 19, Oct. 26, and Nov. 2, 1941.

Furthermore, a favorable judgment can be unfounded and, therefore, rash. It can even gravely harm the interests of third parties. A company director who trusted his clerk without reason or a father whose excessive indulgence led him to form a better idea of his son than he deserved—both have made favorable rash judgments and are thus unable to fulfill their duty.

Applying these considerations to our topic, we must say that there is nothing rash about viewing someone as suspected of heresy when there are grounds for this. On the contrary, it would be rash not to do so. And, above all, it would be rash to sustain that, out of principle, one should never raise a suspicion of heresy. That would favor the attack on the flock by wolves in sheep's clothing.

B. Can Actions Manifest Pertinacity?

2. How does one prove pertinacity in someone who says nothing contrary to the faith? Does pertinacity not require an obstinacy that can only be manifested through words?

In answer to this objection, words and actions alike are apt to characterize a pertinacious mind unequivocally. Just as benevolence, prudence, enthusiasm, hatred, and pride can be manifested through facial expressions or in a gesture or succession of gestures, so too can pertinacity.

In addition, note that in the definition of heresy, the word *pertinacity* has a different meaning than in everyday use. In common usage, as defined in any dictionary, 'pertinacious' means doggedly tenacious, unyieldingly persistent, and stubbornly unshakable. This is also the meaning of the word in Latin.

If this meaning of pertinacity were essential to the sin of heresy, it would exist only in cases of a refined malice, perhaps frequent but difficult to prove. It could be ascertained only after long observation and would never be committed in a moment of weakness, for example, in a fit of rage.

Now then, moralists and canonists unanimously affirm that the Code of Canon Law[995] does not use the word in this sense. As Tanquerey teaches, a pertinacious person denies or calls into question a truth of the faith *scienter et volenter*, that is, fully aware that that truth is a dogma and with the full adhesion of his will. "For *pertinacity* to exist," he adds, "it is not necessary for the person to be warned several times and persevere in his obstinacy for a long time, but it suffices for him to deny, *consciously and voluntarily* [sciens ac volens] his assent to a truth proposed in a sufficient way, whether he does so out of pride, from the pleasure of contradicting, or from any other cause."[996] It suffices for him to deny it *brevi mora*, that is, in an instant, a very brief time,[997] for, in this case, pertinacity "does not mean

---

995. See canon 1325, § 2.
996. Tanquerey, *Synopsis theologiæ moralis*, 2:473.
997. See Adolphe Tanquerey, *Brevior synopsis theologiæ moralis*, (Paris-Tournai-Rome: Desclée, 1946), 95.

duration in time but the perversity of the reason."[998] And pertinacity can exist in a sin of heresy committed out of mere weakness.[999]

C. Is an Admonition Necessary in the Case of Heresy Manifested by Acts?

3. Saint Paul commands that a heretic be admonished once or twice before being avoided (see Tit. 3:10). How can one then claim that someone becomes a heretic by merely practicing certain actions?

When canonists affirm that one can incur the sin of heresy by practicing acts, they are not saying or insinuating that the conditions required in the case of heresy by words are not required in the case of heresy by actions. Therefore, in principle, an admonition is necessary for both hypotheses.

We say "in principle" because the rule enunciated by Saint Paul admits an important exception. Authors teach that the admonition required by the Apostle of the Gentiles is aimed at making it clear to the sinner that he is denying a truth of the faith, which cannot be denied under any pretext whatsoever. The Church is always keenly concerned about avoiding mistakes in ascertaining the heretical *animus*.

Now there are cases when such mistakes cannot occur. There are cases when the heretic obviously knows that the truth he is denying or questioning is a truth of the faith. For example, one cannot admit that a theology scholar does not know that the virginity of Our Lady is a dogma.

On the other hand, in a conversation or lecture, even a theologian can inadvertently utter an improper expression that would be heretical as such. Strictly speaking, it is possible to admit that an error might even creep into a book he had written after long reflection, without his perceiving it, but if the central thesis of the book is manifestly heretical, it is no longer possible to admit any mistake, oversight, or neglect. Admonition would be superfluous.

Quoting great authors of his time, de Lugo expounds on this important question:

> In the external forum, a previous admonition and reprimand are not always
> required to punish someone as heretical and pertinacious; nor is such
> requirement always admitted in the practice of the Holy Office. For if
> it can be ascertained in some other way, given the defendant's qualities,

---

998. Zalba, *Theologiae moralis*, 2:28n9.
999. See Thomas de Vio (Cajetan), O.P., *Commentaria in summam sancti Thommæ II–II*, book 2, pt. 2, q. 11, a. 2, quoted by Peinador, *Cursus brevior*, book 2, 1:99.

About the canonical meaning of *pertinacity*, see also: St. Thomas Aquinas, *Summa Theologica*, book 2, pt. 2, q. 11, a. 2, a. 3; St. Thomas Aquinas, "*Super epistolam ad Titum lectura*," in *Super epistolas S. Pauli lectura* (Turin-Rome: Marietti, 1953), no. 102; Wernz and Vidal, *Ius canonicum*, 7:449–50; Merkelbach, *Summa theologiae moralis*, 1:569; Prümmer, *Theologiae moralis*, 1:364; Noldin, Schmitt, and Heinzel, *Summa theologiae moralis*, 2:25; Henry J. Davis, S.J., *Moral and Pastoral Theology* (London: Sheed and Ward, 1945), 2:292; Peinador, *Cursus brevior*, book 2, 1:99; Regatillo, *Institutiones iuris*, 2:142; Journet, *L'Église*, 2:709.

obvious doctrinal knowledge, and other circumstances, that he could not be unaware that his doctrine was opposed to the Church's, by this very fact, he will be considered a heretic. . . .

158. The reason for this is clear, for external admonition can only serve to make the person in error aware of the opposition between his error and the doctrine of the Church. If he knows the subject much more through books and conciliar definitions than he could through the words of his admonisher, there is no reason to require another admonition for him to become pertinacious against the Church.[1000]

Someone could object that such doctrine is found in treatises but has not been accepted by the Code of Canon Law, which in Canon 2233, §2 definitely establishes that the defendant must be admonished and reprimanded before censure is imposed.

The objection is flawed because that canon applies only to censures *ferendæ sententiæ*, that is, those meted out by the superior or the ecclesiastical judge. When a censure is *latæ sententiæ*, that is, when the defendant incurs it automatically by the very fact that he has committed a certain delict, the admonition is unnecessary. In such cases, as a beautiful juridical formula puts it, *lex interpellat pro homine*—the law interpellates in man's place.[1001]

Now, the excommunication weighing upon the heretic is *latæ sententiæ* (Can. 2314, §1). Therefore, the present Code of Canon Law has also accepted the principle that admonition is not always necessary to characterize pertinacity.

5. Acts That, Canonically, Involve a Suspicion of Heresy

The study of heresy manifested by acts requires an analysis of the legal concept of the suspicion of heresy.

Indeed, the Code of Canon Law enumerates many acts whose nature raises a suspicion that the one practicing them is a heretic. They are not, therefore, unequivocal acts. Normally, only a heretic would do them, but strictly speaking, they can be explained by causes other than heresy.

Before looking into how the Church proceeds in such cases to ascertain whether or not a person is a heretic, let us analyze the crimes that, according to Canon Law, create a suspicion of heresy:

(1) To marry with the explicit or implicit agreement that all children, or some of them, will be raised outside the Catholic Church (Can. 2319, §1, no. 2). The reason is obvious. If, in a mixed marriage, the Catholic spouse agrees that his children will be raised, for example, in the Protestant religion, it is because he

---

1000. de Lugo, *De virtute fidei*, disp. 20, sect. 4, nos. 157–58, 569. See Antonius Diana, *Resolutiones morales* (Venice: Franc. Baba, 1635), par. 4, tract. 7, resol. 36; Vermeersch and Creusen, *Epitome iuris*, 3:245; Noldin, Schmitt, and Heinzel, *Summa theologiae moralis*, 2:21; Regatillo, *Institutiones iuris*, 2:508.
1001. See Pietro Palazzini, "Censura. C. Penale Medicinale," in *E.C.*, 3:1298.

probably deems Protestantism a valid form of praising God. It is heresy to believe that the Catholic Church is not the only true church.

(2) To knowingly deliver one's children to non-Catholic ministers to "baptize" them (Can. 2319, §1, no. 3).

(3) To knowingly deliver one's own or the children in one's custody to be raised or educated in a non-Catholic religion (Can. 2319, no. 4).

(4) To throw away the consecrated species or keep them for an evil purpose (Can. 2320). It is very much to be suspected that one who commits such crimes does not believe in the Real Presence or that he may deny other dogmas by the hatred he has for the Sacred Species.

(5) To remain obstinately with the stain of excommunication for a year (Can. 2340, § 1). He who acts this way does not believe in the jurisdictional power of the ecclesiastical authorities or denies other dogmas.

(6) Out of simony and knowingly, to confer or receive Holy Orders, or to administer or receive other Sacraments. The Code emphasizes that suspicion of heresy in this hypothesis can also fall upon a person elevated to the episcopal condition (Can. 2371). Commercialization of the Sacraments reveals such scorn for everything that is most sacred in the Church that it is to be feared that one who practices it believes in no dogma whatsoever.

(7) Spontaneously and knowingly to help the propagation of heresy in any way (Can. 2316).

(8) To actively attend the religious services of non-Catholics or to take part in them, except by a merely passive presence, when necessary because of the civil post one occupies or social reasons, for a grave reason, and as long as there is no danger of scandal (Can. 2316). The Ecumenical Directory *Ad totam ecclesiam*, published by the Secretariat for the Union of Christians on May 14, 1967, expanded enormously the cases of *communicatio in sacris* authorized by the Holy See. Thus, many acts, which until recently created a canonical suspicion of heresy, no longer do so. It remains true, however, that under Canon 2316, those who participate in the religious services of non-Catholics in circumstances that characterize disrespect for the laws in force become canonically suspect of heresy. The reason for this canon is clear: To participate unjustifiably in non-Catholic religious ceremonies is to lend credence to the idea that they are pleasing to God.

(9) To appeal to a universal Council against laws, decrees, or orders of the supreme pontiff, regardless of the appellant's rank, station, or condition, even if he is a king, bishop, or cardinal (Can. 2332). Anyone who appealed to a Council

against a papal decision would implicitly admit the Council's superiority over the pope, which is a heretical thesis.[1002]

6. Canonical Measures Against One Suspected of Heresy

How does the Church ascertain whether one suspected of heresy is indeed a heretic? Canon 2315 stipulates that,

> One suspected of heresy who, having been warned, does not remove the cause of suspicion is prohibited from legitimate acts [certain juridical acts defined by Canon 2256 §2 as to be a godparent in a Baptism or the sponsor for Confirmation, to vote in ecclesiastical elections, to administer ecclesiastical assets, etc.]; if he is a cleric, moreover, the warning having been repeated without effect, he is suspended from things divine [that is, forbidden to celebrate Holy Mass and exercise the other acts of worship proper to the clergy]; but if within six months from contracting the penalty, the one suspected of heresy does not completely amend himself, let him be considered as a heretic and liable to the penalties for heretics.[1003]

Note, therefore, how the Church is prudent and patient regarding such persons. In addition to the admonition, which must be repeated in the case of a priest, she gives six months for recanting or eventual clarifications before applying penalties proper to heretics. Even such penalties do not apply automatically but must be applied by the bishop, who eventually may have reasons for not carrying them out.

However, in addition to being prudent and patient, the Church is also just, and justice demands forcefulness. Once certain thresholds are crossed, the Church must cut off the gangrened member who has already excommunicated and excluded himself from her ranks and who, moreover, poses a threat to the faith of others.

In the spirit of the Church, censures must be imposed with sobriety and great circumspection, but also with severity and rigor, when necessary.[1004]

The cases of suspicion of heresy listed above are those contemplated in the Code of Canon Law. However, as the theologians observe, there are also non-canonical cases of suspicion of heresy.

"A suspicion of heresy is created," say Wernz and Vidal,

> by working magic, casting spells, or making divinations; in cases of severe abuse of the Sacraments, such as the delict of soliciting during Confession,

---

1002. Regarding canonical cases of suspicion of heresy, see Wernz and Vidal, *Ius canonicum*, 7:451–52; Tanquerey, *Brevior synopsis*, 386; Vermeersch and Creusen, *Epitome iuris*, 3:316; Cappello, *Summa iuris*, 3:552ff.; Ferreres and Mondria, *Compendium theologiae*, 2:743 Sipos, *Enchiridion iuris*, 609; Regatillo, *Institutiones iuris*, 2:573; Iorio, *Theologia moralis*, 2:253ff., 260ff.
1003. 1917 CIC, can. 2315, p. 736.
1004. See 1917 CIC canons 2214, §2, 2241, §2; Wernz and Vidal, *Ius canonicum*, 7:180ff.; Vermeersch and Creusen, *Epitome iuris*, 3:236–37, 259; Regatillo, *Institutiones iuris*, 2:500–501. 523.

violating the secret of Confession, fraudulent administration of the Sacraments by a person who is not an ordained priest; in delicts against the ecclesiastical authority that raise a well-founded suspicion that the defendant has erroneous ideas, not about the person exercising it, but about authority as such, as happens with those who give their names to sects that openly or covertly plot machinations against the Church or civil society.... These cases, which in the old Law [that is, the Canon law that preceded the 1917 Pio-Benedictine Code of Canon Law] were brought by the Doctors, continue by their own nature [ex natura rei] to provide grounds for the suspicion of heresy; but the juridical suspicion exists only in the cases stated in the Law [they are the nine cases listed above].[1005]

We call the reader's attention to this distinction between canonical and non-canonical cases of suspicion of heresy. Insofar as the former is concerned, the Code itself foresees the hypothesis, defines, and punishes it. As for the latter, there is no direct reference to ecclesiastical laws, but the very nature of the act raises the suspicion that the one who practices it is a heretic, at least in his soul. For example, a person who dabbles in magic probably denies some dogma, though the Code does not deal with this.

Thus, we ask ourselves: Do the numerous acts that by their very nature raise a suspicion of heresy but which are not contemplated in the present Code of Canon Law remain unpunished? This question is of capital importance, all the more so since many authors, when dealing with the canonical delict of suspicion of heresy, emphasize that this juridical figure includes only cases expressly defined in the law.[1006]

Should one perhaps sustain that the Church, as a good and benign Mother, punishes only the nine cases indicated above and leaves the rest of the field wide open to the action of her bad children?

7. Other Actions Connected With Heresy Not Contemplated in the Code

Before answering the question, let us complete the context within which it must be analyzed, for there are several other categories of acts connected with heresy that were punished by the old Law and no longer figure in the Code, at least explicitly. These acts are: to believe in a heretic, and favor, receive, and defend him.[1007]

1005. Wernz and Vidal, *Ius canonicum*, 7:451–52. In the same sense, see D'Annibale, *In constitutionem*, no. 31.

1006. See Cappello, *Summa iuris*, 3:553; Vermeersch and Creusen, *Epitome iuris*, 3:316; Brys, *Juris canonici*. 2:504; Zalba, *Theologiae moralis*, 2:30; Iorio, *Theologia moralis*, 2:260.

1007. About these delicts, see Suárez, *De fide*, disp. 24, sect. 1; de Lugo, *De virtute fidei*, disp. 25, sect. 1; Schmalzgrueber, *Ius ecclesiasticum*, book 5, 10: nos. 91ff.; Josephus D'Annibale, *Summula theologiae moralis* (Milan: Ex Typ. S. Josephi, 1882), par. 2, 8; Wernz and Vidal, *Ius canonicum*, 7:450ff.; Michel, "Hérésie, hérétique," in *D.T.C.*, 6–2e.:2244.

A. BELIEVERS: THOSE WHO BELIEVE OR ARE DISPOSED TO BELIEVE A HERETIC

Believers *(credentes)*—that is, those who believe a heretic or give him credit—"are those who accept in bad faith, by a judgment of the intellect, at least one heretical doctrine proposed by the heretic, though not belonging to any given sect."[1008] This delict is of little interest to our study because "believers do not essentially differ from heretics and are, therefore, covered by the delict of heresy if the other circumstances are not missing."[1009] Indeed, he who accepts a heretical doctrine is a heretic. This distinction between believers and heretics affiliated with some sect should serve only to make it very clear that both are excommunicated, though the latter incur special penalties contemplated in Canon 2314, §1, 3.

However, as Suárez observes, the concept of believers should also extend to: "Those who, though still not assenting to the errors, nonetheless listen to the heretics with a disposition such that they are ready to give them credit if their reasons or arguments are pleasing to them."[1010]

Further on, Suárez adds that persons who attend many times, with regularity, meetings of heretical sects must be seen as "believers." Thus, we face another clear case of a delict connected with heresy committed not by words but by actions.

B. FAVORERS OF HERESY

Favorers *(fautores)* of heresy "are those who, by some act or omission, do heretics a favor that helps to promote the heretical doctrine."[1011] Note that, for the delict of favoring heresy to occur, a favor must be rendered to the heretic as a heretic. Evidently, a physician who provides medical care to an indigent Protestant is not thereby a favorer of heresy. The same observation is valid, *mutatis mutandis*, for receivers and defenders of heretics, whom we will discuss ahead.

Concerning the favoring of heresy by omission, de Lugo writes:

> They favor the heretic who, by their office, are obliged to arrest, punish, or expel him and yet neglect these duties. For example, the judges to whom a bishop or inquisitors resort, or to whom they deliver a heretic to be punished; and also the Inquisitors and ecclesiastical prelates themselves, if they neglect what they are obliged to do by their office and thus favor heresy. The same should be said of the other ministers and officials of the Holy Office and even of the private person on whom this office is imposed by those who have the power to impose it; and also of the witnesses who, obliged to tell the truth when legitimately interrogated, hide it to favor a heretic.[1012]

1008. Wernz and Vidal, *Ius canonicum*, 7:450.
1009. Wernz and Vidal, 7:450.
1010. Suárez, *De fide*, disp. 24, sect. 1, no. 3, 586. The same doctrine is taught, among others, by de Lugo, *De virtute fidei*, disp. 25, sect. 1, no. 3, and Schmalzgrueber, *Jus ecclesiasticum*, book 5, 9: no. 92.
1011. Wernz and Vidal, *Ius canonicum*, 7:450.
1012. De Lugo, *De virtute fidei*, disp. 25, sect. 1, no. 6, 690. In the same sense, see Suárez, *De fide*, disp. 24, sect. 1, no. 6; Schmalzgrueber, *Jus ecclesiasticum*, book 5, 9:no. 94.

C. Receivers: Those Who Receive Heretics

"Receivers *(receptoribus)* are those who hide or lodge heretics in their own or someone else's house to free them from a judicial probe and the penalties they would deserve."[1013] De Lugo notes that for a delict to take place, "It suffices to receive a heretic only once, as all authors affirm, similarly to what happens with receivers and defenders of heretics. This censure [for being a receiver] covers not only those who receive and hide a heretic in their own home so that he will not be caught but also the judges and princes who receive them in their own towns or provinces so that, under their protection, they will be free to remain in the sect to which they belong."[1014]

D. Defenders of Heretics

Defenders *(defensores)* "are those who do not internally adhere to the heretical doctrine, but despite that defend it in word or writing against those who attack it. They are also those who protect, by force or other unjust means, the persons of heretics against a legitimate persecution carried out on account of the heresy."[1015]

E. Anachronistic Texts?

Some of the texts we have just quoted regarding believers, favorers, receivers, and defenders of heretics may appear entirely anachronistic and obsolete under current Church practices. We have brought them up, however, for two reasons.

First, they make it clear that numerous Catholics, even today, fall into sins connected with heresy. Today, as in the past, some listen to heretics with a disposition to believe them; some do them favors that redound in the promotion of heresy; others, while in official functions that oblige them to punish heretics, fail to do so, and so forth.

Second, a theoretical study about heresy could not be limited to analyzing the present-day situation. The malice of our times has led the Church to tolerate, in her legislation, behaviors that do not correspond to the ideal order aspired to and fought for by the Church and her children. The above-quoted texts show how far-reaching is the obligation to persecute heretics in an entirely Catholic society, and this by the very nature of things. These were the principles in force in the Middle Ages, of which Pope Leo XIII, in the encyclical *Immortale Dei*, said:

> There was a time when the philosophy of the Gospel governed the states. In that epoch, the influence of Christian wisdom and its divine virtue permeated the laws, institutions, and customs of the peoples, all categories and all relations of civil society. Then the religion instituted by Jesus Christ, solidly established in the degree of dignity due to it, flourished everywhere thanks to the favor of princes and the legitimate protection of magistrates. Then Priesthood and Empire were united in a happy concord and by the friendly interchange of good offices. So organized, civil society gave fruits superior

---

1013. Wernz and Vidal, *Ius canonicum*, 7:450–51.
1014. De Lugo, *De virtute fidei*, disp. 25, sect. 1, no. 4, 689.
1015. Wernz and Vidal, *Ius canonicum*, 7:451.

to all expectations, whose memory subsists and will subsist, registered as it is in innumerable documents that no artifice of the adversaries can destroy or obscure.[1016]

8. Canonical Impunity for So Many Heresy-Related Sins?

At this point, we can repeat the question we asked earlier: Are the numerous heresy-related sins not contemplated in the Code left unpunished by current Canon Law?

The answer must be: absolutely not.

Indeed, we could affirm, *a priori*, that practices so harmful to the Faith could not remain unpunished. To leave the ecclesiastical authority unarmed before such practices would be to install the wolf inside the flock of Christ.

It is well known that in the civil and ecclesiastical orders, positive law neither should nor can punish all condemnable acts. For example, seeking to repress by law everything they deem evil, socialists set up an unnatural juridical regime, one incomparably more unjust than the injustices they sought—or claimed to seek—to eliminate.

However, there are certain crimes that the law cannot fail to punish because they are fundamentally contrary to the social order. If left unpunished, such crimes would become so widespread as to threaten the very existence of society. Thus, civil laws cannot fail to punish homicide, attempted homicide, injury to someone's bodily integrity, and the like.

Likewise, the delicts connected with heresy that we have analyzed above are such that Canon Law could not fail to punish them in one way or another.

How could anyone imagine that those suspected of heresy could poison the minds of the faithful with scandalous acts while the ecclesiastical authority is left without any means to repress them? How can one imagine promoters of heresy having full citizenship rights in the Holy Church? How can they inoculate the deadly virus into the Mystical Body of Christ without any measure being taken against them?

A priori—we repeat—one can affirm that Canon Law does repress delinquent acts connected with heresy. Indeed, legal means are found in the Code to punish such acts. We will indicate some of those means without attempting to exhaust the question.

Many of the acts referred to above are undoubtedly covered by canon 2316. It states that "whoever in any manner willingly and knowingly helps in the promulgation of heresy . . . is suspected of heresy."[1017] Thus, the person who committed the delinquent act will be treated as one suspected of heresy according to canon 2315, which we have analyzed.

1016. Leo XIII, encyclical *Immortale Dei* (on the Christian constitution of States), (Nov. 1, 1885), no. 9 (Latin), no 21 (English). (Our translation.)
1017. 1917 CIC, can. 2316, p. 736.

Some authors judge that this is the situation of all receivers, defenders, and favorers of heretics in the present Code.[1018] As for believers, they either fit into this same category or are directly heretics, as we have seen.

This question could be seen as settled were it not for two facts: Some canonists exclude delicts by omission from canon 2316;[1019] others affirm that, as a general rule, receivers, defenders, and favorers of heretics are not covered by this canon but by others.

Thus, Sipos considers them covered by canon 2209, §7,[1020] which punishes the act of praising the delict committed, participating in its fruits, hiding the perpetrator, and so forth and reserves for canon 2316 only the specific hypotheses of helping to propagate heresy.

Wernz and Vidal place them under the several paragraphs of canon 2209,[1021] not just under the seventh. The other paragraphs deal with the notions of complicity, inducement to commit a delict, cooperating with its consummation, condoning it by negligence in exercising one's office, and so forth.

On the other hand, many authors leave open the possibility of including all heresy-connected delicts in canon 2315 itself, which punishes the suspicion of heresy. Indeed, such canonists consider that the delict of suspicion is committed not only in the nine cases defined by law as we have seen above but also in others whose very nature suggests that those who practice them deny some dogma.[1022]

Finally, we should note that even in the absurd hypothesis of the absence of any law to punish heresy-connected delicts, there would still be a canonical way open to punish them: the legal concept of heresy itself.

Indeed canon 2314, §1 states that heretics incur excommunication *ipso facto*. As we have seen, it is possible to fall into heresy by the spoken or written word and by actions. By the very nature of things, therefore, and not only by canonical disposition, someone who commits a delict connected with heresy becomes one who is suspected of heresy. Also, by the very nature of things, a suspect must be treated like one.

What would happen, then, if no law punished the said delicts? When a suspicion of heresy arises, the bishop, superior, or even a concerned friend could contact the suspect—and depending on the case, they should ask him to remove the cause for suspicion. If necessary, they would make a second admonition, following the precept of Saint Paul.

Depending on the circumstances, he could still be given some time to recant. Finally, if everything turned out to be useless, he would be characterized as a heretic, thus incurring the penalties established in canon 2314, §1.

We repeat, therefore, that it would be absurd to imagine a Canon Law in which heresy-related sins would be left unpunished, thus leaving the gates of the

---

1018. See Michel, "Hérésie, hérétique," in *D.T.C.*, 6–2e.:2244.
1019. See Vermeersch and Creusen, *Epitome iuris*, 3:317.
1020. See Sipos, *Enchiridion iuris*, 608.
1021. See Wernz and Vidal, *Ius canonicum*, 7:451.
1022. See Sipos, *Enchiridion iuris*, 609; Regatillo, *Institutiones iuris*, 2:573. Those who do not admit this possibility are Vermeersch and Creusen, *Epitome iuris*, 3:316; Cappello, *Summa iuris*, 3:553; Brys, *Juris canonici*, 2:504; Zalba, *Theologiae moralis*, 2:30; Iorio, *Theologia moralis*, 2:260.

sheep pen wide open to voracious wolves, as long as they presented themselves in sheep's clothing. As for knowing which sins must be covered by this or that Canon, the existing disagreement among authors indicates that there is more than one juridical way to punish a heresy-related delict. There is no lack of laws; on the contrary, they are so abundant as to create perplexity among canonists.

9. Diffused Heresy

In a recent pastoral letter, Bishop Mayer warned his flock against diffused heresy, "which, without becoming concrete in explicit propositions, is subjacent and operative in the common way of being of men today, and infiltrates Catholic circles through society."[1023]

Earlier, Archbishop Sigaud had alerted his faithful to diffused Communism, which "is by far a greater danger than direct Communism."[1024]

In our era of so many declared heresies, the disguised and diffused ones constitute the gravest threats to Christian civilization and the faith of every Catholic. We have sought to help combat them by showing that someone can fall into external heresy not only with words but also with gestures, signs, attitudes, and omissions.

1023. Antonio de Castro Mayer, "Considerações a propósito da aplicação dos documentos promulgados pelo Concílio Ecumênico Vaticano II," in *Por um cristianismo autêntico* (São Paulo: Editôra Vera Cruz, 1966), 20.
1024. Geraldo de Proença Sigaud, *Carta pastoral sobre a seita comunista: Seus erros, sua ação revolucionária, e os deveres dos católicos na hora presente*, 2nd ed. (São Paulo: Editora Vera Cruz, 1963), 123.

Chapter Eighteen

Public Resistance to Decisions of Ecclesiastical Authority

The Church teaches that, in the face of an erroneous decision of the ecclesiastical authority, it can happen that it will not only be licit for the enlightened Catholic to deny his assent to this decision but also, in certain extreme cases, to oppose them, even publicly. Moreover, such opposition may constitute a true obligation.[1025]

1. Bishops and Lower Ecclesiastical Authorities

In taking up this matter, we prefer not to add our voice to those of the great saints and theologians approved in the Holy Church. To them shall we leave the charge of teaching us, not only the extension of the theses they defend but also the arguments on which these are grounded. Thus, in this and the next sections, we shall limit ourselves to repeating what some have said.

We shall not occupy ourselves, except in passing, with the principle that it is licit to resist, even publicly, those bishops and lower ecclesiastical authorities who, by their evil doctrine, scandalous life, or iniquitous decrees, endanger the faith and the salvation of souls. Among theologians, there is no doubt regarding this matter. So many are the examples of saints in Church history who have raised their voices against evil shepherds that the difficulty would rather consist in selecting from among the many proofs of the legitimacy of such a procedure.

Let us, therefore, consider some texts on the legitimacy of public resistance to episcopal authority:

A. Dom Prosper Guéranger

Writing about Saint Cyril of Alexandria, the outstanding adversary of Nestorianism, Dom Guéranger, abbot of Solesmes, teaches, "When the shepherd becomes a wolf, the first duty of the flock is to defend itself. It is usual and regular, no doubt, for doctrine to descend from the bishops to the faithful, and those who are subject

---

1025. In substance, this chapter reproduces the essay published in *Catolicismo*, no. 224 (Aug. 1969), pp. 2–3. See Xavier da Silveira, *Can Documents of the Magisterium of the Church Contain Errors?* chap. 7, 127–46.

in the faith are not to judge their superiors. But in the treasure of Revelation, there are essential doctrines which all Christians, by the very fact of their title as such, are bound to know and defend."[1026]

B. Jean Marie Hervé

Analyzing the various factors that contribute to making dogmas ever more explicit over the centuries, Hervé praises the opposition mounted by the Catholic faithful against Nestorius, the heretical patriarch of Constantinople. "By an instinct of the Holy Spirit, the faithful may be led to a better understanding and belief regarding what increases piety and worship, favoring in this way the progress of dogma. Indeed, the murmuring of the faithful against Nestorius was a great help toward the definition of the Divine Maternity of the Most Holy Virgin."[1027]

C. Bishop Antonio de Castro Mayer

The illustrious bishop of Campos recently published a document in which he recalled the traditional doctrine on the right of resistance to iniquitous ecclesiastical authorities. It was in a letter of approbation of the magnificent *Vademecum of the Faithful Catholic* in which four hundred priests from various countries, combating Progressivism, explained the principles of the true Catholic Faith and invited the faithful to oppose the new heresy which today invades the entire world. The bishop of Campos declared the *Vademecum* most opportune and added, "Let no one come and say to us that it is not for the faithful . . . to pass judgment on what is happening in the Church; that it is for them only to follow with docility the orientation given by the ministers of the Lord. This is not true. Church history eulogizes the attitude of the faithful of Constantinople who opposed the heresy of their Patriarch Nestorius."[1028]

Afterward, Bishop Mayer cites the text of Dom Guéranger, which we reproduce above.

2. "I Resisted Him to His Face Because He Was in the Wrong"[1029]

In extreme cases, would it be legitimate to resist even the pope's decisions?

In answering this question, we shall transcribe only documents related to *public* resistance because, if in certain circumstances this is legitimate, with a greater reason, it would be legitimate to oppose a papal decision privately. We are aware of no author who has ever raised any doubt about the right of such private resistance. This can be done in two ways: Manifesting to the Holy See the existing objections against the document, or through what is called "fraternal correction,"

1026. Abbot Guéranger, "Feast of Saint Cyril of Alexandria (Feb. 9)," in *The Liturgical Year*, trans. Laurence Shepherd, 4th ed. (Great Falls, Mont.: St. Bonaventure Publications, 2000), 4:379–80.
1027. Hervé, *Manuale theologiae dogmaticae*, 3:305.
1028. Mayer, Letter of Approval for *Vademecum do Católico Fiel*.
1029. James A. Kleist, S.J. and Joseph L. Lilly, C.M. trans., *The New Testament: Rendered From the Original Greek With Explanatory Notes* (Milwaukee: The Bruce Publishing Company, 1954), Gal. 2:11, p. 475.

that is, using an observation made in private, with the object of obtaining the amendment of the fault committed.[1030]

Let us pass on to the texts which admit public resistance in very special cases:

a. Saint Thomas Aquinas

The Angelic Doctor teaches, in several of his works, that in extreme cases, it is licit to resist a papal decision publicly, as Saint Paul resisted Saint Peter to his face: "If the faith were endangered, a subject ought to rebuke his prelate even publicly. Hence Paul, who was Peter's subject, rebuked him in public on account of the imminent danger of scandal concerning faith, and, as the gloss of Augustine says on Galatians 2:11, 'Peter gave an example to superiors, that if at any time they should happen to stray from the straight path, they should not disdain to be reproved by their subjects.'"[1031]

In his commentary on the Epistle to the Galatians, studying the episode in which Saint Paul resisted Saint Peter to his face, Saint Thomas writes, "The occasion of the rebuke was not slight, but just and useful, namely, the danger to the Gospel teaching. . . . The manner of the rebuke was fitting, i.e., public and plain. Hence he says, *I said to Cephas*, i.e., to Peter, *before them all*, because that dissimulation posed a danger to all. 'Them that sin, reprove before all' (1 Tim. 5:20). This is to be understood of public sins and not of private ones, in which the procedures of fraternal charity ought to be observed."[1032]

Saint Thomas observed further that the referenced scriptural passage contains instructions both for superiors and subjects: "Therefore from the foregoing, we have an example: prelates, indeed, an example of humility, that they not disdain corrections from those who are lower and subject to them; subjects have an example of zeal and freedom, that they fear not to correct their prelates particularly if their crime is public and verges upon danger to the multitude."[1033]

b. Franciscus de Vitoria

The eminent sixteenth-century Dominican theologian writes:

> In the same work in which he defends the superiority of the pope over the Council, Cajetan says in chap. 27: "Then, one must resist to his face a pope who publicly destroys the Church, for example, not wishing to confer ecclesiastical benefices except for money or in exchange for services;

1030. On private resistance to decisions of the pope or the Roman Congregations, one may consult: St. Thomas Aquinas, *Commentum in IV librum sententiarum Petri Lombardi*, vol. 10 in *Opera omnia* (Paris: Vivès, 1889), dist. 19, q 2, a. 2; *Summa Theologica*, II–II, 33, 4; Francisco Suárez, *Defensio fidei catholicæ et apostolicæ contra errores anglicanæ sectæ*, in vol. 24 of *Opera omnia* (Paris: Vivès, 1859), book 4, chap. 6, lies. 14–18; Pesch, *Praelectiones dogmaticae*, 1:314–15; Bouix, *Tractatus de papa*, 2:635ff.; Hurter, *Theologiae dogmaticae*, 1:491–92; Peinador, *Cursus brevior*, tom. 2, 1:286–87; Salaverri, *De ecclesia Christi*, 1:725–26.
1031. St. Thomas Aquinas, *Summa Theologica*, II–II, q. 33, art. 4.
1032. St. Thomas Aquinas, *Commentary on St. Paul's Epistle to the Galatians*, trans. F.R. Larcher, O.P. (Albany, N.Y.: Magi Books, Inc. 1966), ad 2:11.
1033. Aquinas, *Commentary on Galatians*, 46.

and one must deny, with all obedience and respect, the possession of such benefices to those who have bought them."

And Sylvester (Prierias), at the word *papa*, §4, asks: "What must one do when the pope, by his evil customs, destroys the Church?" And in §15: "What must one do if the pope wishes, without cause, to abrogate positive Law?" To this, he responds: "He would certainly sin; one should not permit him to carry on like this, nor should one obey him in what is evil, but should resist him with a courteous rebuke."

Therefore, if he wished to hand over all the treasure of the Church or the patrimony of Saint Peter to his family, if he wished to destroy the Church or other similar things, one should not permit him to act this way. Rather, one would be obliged to resist him. The reason for this is that he does not have power to destroy; it being clear, therefore, that if he does, it is licit to resist him.

Hence, it follows that if the pope, by his orders and acts, destroys the Church, one can resist him and impede the execution of his commands. . . .

A second proof of the thesis: According to natural law, it is licit to repel violence with violence. Now, with such orders and dispensations, the pope does violence because he acts against the law, as was proven above. Then, it is licit to resist him. As Cajetan observes, we do not affirm all this in the sense that someone has the right to be the judge of the pope or have authority over him, but rather in the sense that it is licit to defend oneself. Anyone has the right to resist an unjust act, to try to impede it, and defend himself.[1034]

C. FRANCISCUS SUÁREZ

"If [the pope] lays down an order contrary to right customs, one does not have to obey him; if he tries to do something manifestly opposed to justice and the common good, it would be licit to resist him; if he attacks by force, he could be repelled by force, with the moderation characteristic of a just defense (*cum moderamine inculpatæ tutelæ*)."[1035]

D. SAINT ROBERT BELLARMINE

"Just as it would be lawful to resist a pontiff invading a body, so it is lawful to resist him invading souls or disturbing a state, and much more if he should endeavor to destroy the Church. I say, it is lawful to resist him, by not doing what he commands, and by blocking him, lest he should carry out his will; still, it is not lawful to judge or punish or even depose him, because he is nothing other than a superior."[1036]

1034. Franciscus de Vitoria, O.P., *Obras de Francisco de Vitoria* (Madrid: B.A.C., 1960), 486–87.

1035. Suárez, *De fide*, disp. 10, sect. 6, no. 16, 321.

1036. St. Robert Bellarmine, *On the Roman Pontiff*, book 2, chap. 29, 336.

E. CORNELIUS À LAPIDE

The illustrious exegete shows that, according to Saints Augustine, Ambrose, Bede, Anselm, and many other Fathers, the resistance of Saint Paul to Saint Peter was public "in order that the public scandal caused by him [Saint Peter] might be removed by a public rebuke."[1037]

After analyzing the various theological and exegetical questions raised by the attitude assumed by Saint Paul, Cornelius à Lapide writes:

> Superiors may, in the interests of truth, be corrected by their inferiors. Augustine (*Epist. 19*), Cyprian, Gregory, and S[aint] Thomas lay down this proposition in maintaining also that Peter, as the superior, was corrected by his inferior. . . Gregory says (*Homil. 18 in Ezech.*): "Peter kept silence, that the first in dignity might be first in humility;" and Augustine says the same (*Epist. 19 ad Hieronymum*): "Peter gave to those who should follow him a rare and holy example of humility under correction by inferiors, as Paul did of bold resistance in defense of truth to subordinates against their superiors, charity being always preserved."[1038]

F. FRANCISCUS X. WERNZ AND PETRUS VIDAL

Citing Suárez, Wernz and Vidal in their work *Ius canonicum* admit that, in extreme cases, it is licit to resist a bad pope: "The just means to be employed against a bad pope are, according to Suárez (*Defensio fidei catholicae*, book 4, chap. 6, nos. 17–18), the more abundant help of the grace of God, the special protection of one's guardian angel, the prayer of the Church universal, admonition, or fraternal correction in secret or even in public, as well as legitimate defense against aggression, whether it be physical or moral."[1039]

G. ANTONIUS PEINADOR

The more recent authors adopt as their own the assertions of the classical authors regarding the matter we are analyzing. Thus it is that Peinador, citing large sections from Saint Thomas, writes:

> "A subject also can be obliged to the fraternal correction of his superior." (*S. Theol.*, II–II, 33, 4), for the superior can also be spiritually needy, and there is nothing to prevent him from being liberated from such need by one of his subjects. Nevertheless, "in a correction by which subjects reprehend their prelates, it behooves them to act appropriately, that is, not with insolence and asperity, but with meekness and reverence" (*S. Theol.*, ibid). Therefore, in general, the superior must always be admonished privately. "Keep in mind, however, that, when there is a proximate danger for the

---

1037. Cornelius à Lapide, *II Corinthians and Galatians*, vol. 8 in *The Great Commentary of Cornelius à Lapide*, trans. and ed. W. F. Cobb (Edinburgh: John Grant, 1908), 243.
1038. à Lapide, *II Corinthians and Galatians*, 247.
1039. Wernz and Vidal, *Ius canonicum*, 2:436.

faith, prelates must be censured, even publicly, by their subjects" (*S. Theol.*, II–II, 33, 4, 2).[1040]

3. A Superficial Divergence

As we see, the authors who declare that it is licit in extraordinary cases to oppose, even publicly, some erroneous decisions of the ecclesiastical authority and the Roman See itself are numerous and of great importance. If we add the historical examples of saints who proceeded this way, we shall conclude that this is a thesis accepted without discussion in the Holy Church.

However, according to some, there is a fact that takes away from this thesis its undisputed character. In both dogmatic and moral theology works, it is frequent—even common—to find the opinion that it is *never* licit for one of the faithful to break his *respectful silence* ("*silentium obsequiosum*") regarding a papal document, even when there is evidence that it contains some error.

We have previously taken up the delicate question of breaking this respectful silence.[1041] To set out the fundamental points of the problem, we shall summarize quickly what we wrote:

1. A Magisterium document is only infallible when it fulfills the four conditions made explicit by the First Vatican Council.[1042]

2. Documents that do not fulfill those conditions are not infallible and can, therefore, in principle, and in rare cases, contain some error.

3. The hypothesis that a learned person could, after carefully examining a particular document of the non-infallible Magisterium, come upon evidence that there is some error in it is not, therefore, to be excluded, in principle.

4. In this case, it will be necessary to proceed with circumspection and humility, using all reasonable means to clear up the question, the most salient of these being representations to the magisterial body that issued the document.

1040. Peinador, *Cursus brevior*, tom. 2, 1:287. To delve deeper into this matter, see also: Saint Thomas Aquinas, *Commentum in IV librum*, d. 19, q. 2, a. 2, ql. 3, sol. et ad 1; Suárez, *De legibus*, book 9, chap. 20, nos. 19–29; Suárez, *Defensio fidei catholicae*, book 4, chap. 6, nos. 14–18; Reiffenstuel, *Theologia moralis*, tract. 4, dist. 6, q. 5, nos. 51–54, 162–63; Joseph Mayol, *Præambula ad decalogum*, in *Theologiae cursus completus* (Paris: Migne, 1858), tom. 13, q. 3, a. 4, col. 918; Joannes Petrus Gury and Antonius Ballerini, *Compendium theologiae moralis* (Rome: Civiltà Cattolica, 1866), 1:222–27; Mazzella, *De religione*, 747–48; Teófilo Urdañoz, *Relecciones teológicas: edición crítica del texto latino, versión española, introducción general e introducciones con el estudio de su doctrina teológico-jurídica* in *Obras de Francisco de Vitoria* (Madrid: B.A.C., 1960), 426–29.
1041. See Xavier da Silveira, *Can Documents of the Magisterium*, chap. 6, 103ff, which we reproduce substantially in Chapter 15 of the present study.
1042. See Xavier da Silveira, chap. 1, subtitle "What Is an 'Ex Cathedra' Pontifical Pronouncement?" 10ff.

5. If the evidence of error persists after all advisable means have been used, it would be licit to suspend, regarding this point, the *internal* assent which the document demands.

Here, the question which now occupies us presents itself: Would it be licit also, at least in extreme cases, to refuse *external* submission to the pontifical declaration, that is, the so-called *respectful silence*? In other words: Would it, in any circumstances, be licit to oppose *externally*, perhaps even *publicly*, a document of the Roman Magisterium?

It is in answer to this question that the authors seemingly differ.

On the one hand, great theologians, such as those cited above, admit, in principle, that, in certain circumstances, one of the faithful has the right and even the obligation to resist Peter to his face, so to speak. On the other, eminent theologians *seem to sustain* that under absolutely no hypothesis would it be licit to break the so-called *respectful silence*.

However, before proposing the solution which we believe reconciles the opinions of the two camps, we would like to place before the eyes of the reader some characteristic texts which *appear* to completely bar the way for any breach of the *respectful silence*.

4. Respectful Silence Appears to Be Required Always

A. *Antonius Straub*

Straub expounds on the question as follows:

> It can happen, *per accidens*, that . . . to someone the decree appears to be certainly false or opposed to an argument so solid . . . that the force of this argument will not be in any way annulled by the weight of the sacred authority. . . . In the first hypothesis, *it would be licit to dissent*. In the second, *it would be licit to doubt* or even to hold as probable an opinion that disagrees with the sacred decree. However, because of the reverence due to sacred authority, IT WOULD NEVER BE LICIT TO CONTRADICT IT PUBLICLY . . . BUT THAT SILENCE which is called *respectful* WOULD HAVE TO BE MAINTAINED.[1043]

B. *Benedictus Merkelbach*

In the *Summa theologiæ moralis*, Merkelbach closes his examination of the matter as follows: "If *per accidens*, in a case which however would be *most rare*, after a very careful examination, it appears to someone that there exist very grave arguments against a doctrine proposed in this way, it would be licit, without rashness, to

---

1043. Straub, *De ecclesia*, 2:968; See Salaverri, *De ecclesia Christi*, 1:725.

suspend *internal* assent. *Externally*, however, THE RESPECTFUL SILENCE WOULD BE OBLIGATORY because of the reverence owed to the Church."[1044]

C. *JOSEPHUS MORS*

Father Mors defines "respectful silence" in the following way: "It is external and reverential submission to ecclesiastical authority. It consists in saying nothing [publicly] against its decrees. Such silence is demanded by the respect owed to ecclesiastical authority and for the good of the Church, EVEN WHEN THE CONTRARY WERE TRULY EVIDENT."[1045]

After expounding on the traditional doctrine of the assent due to the documents of the Magisterium, Father Mors concludes: "However, if there were truly evident arguments against the decrees, the obligation of internal assent would cease; BUT EVEN THEN, THE OBLIGATION OF SILENCE WOULD CONTINUE TO EXIST. Such a case, however, would not occur easily."[1046]

D. *MARCELINO ZALBA*

"*Per accidens*, internal assent could be denied if the error [in a teaching of a Roman Congregation] were known with certainty; in the same way, it would be licit to doubt when there were truly solid reasons to do so. But in both cases, IT BEHOOVES ONE TO MAINTAIN A RESPECTFUL EXTERNAL SILENCE."[1047]

5. Two Enlightening Examples

Would there be a true contradiction between the opinion of theologians who defend the lawfulness, in very rare cases, of publicly resisting papal decisions and those who declare that it is always illicit to break the *respectful silence*? Are these two orientations different, and do they really and effectively divide the authors?

We do not believe so. A pondered analysis of the question will show that it is easy to harmonize the two opinions—which, therefore, as we see it, are only contradictory in appearance.

Indeed, it is frequent in theology, above all in moral theology—and our case is more of the moral order than the dogmatic one—to encounter affirmations that are general, decisive, and absolute but do not have the universal strength they seem to have. The author resolves the question in principle, abstracting from the rich casuistry that could bring greater precision to the proposed solution. Or, to resolve a concrete case, he presents his conclusion in abstract and general terms, which can lead one to believe—contrary to his own most intimate opinion—that the enunciated opinion admits no exception.

1044. Merkelbach, *Summa theologiae moralis*, 1:601.
1045. Mors, *Institutiones theologiae*, 2:187.
1046. Mors, 2:187.
1047. Zalba, *Theologiae moralis*, 2:30n21. The following also express the same opinion: Tanquerey, *Synopsis theologiae dogmaticae*, 1:640; Choupin, *Valeur*, 91; Cartechini, *Dall'opinione*, 154.

Two examples will make it easier to understand this fact. On the one hand, let us take the putative condemnation of private property by Church Fathers and medieval authors. On the other, Saint Thomas Aquinas and ancient theologians generally prohibited interest on loans.

A. Seeming Condemnation of Private Property

Saint Ambrose wrote, "Nature has poured forth all things for all men for common use. God has ordered all things to be produced so that there should be food in common to all, and that the earth should be a common possession for all."[1048]

In addition, various Church Fathers and the *Corpus juris canonici* declared that it is not licit for anyone to say, "this is mine," because nature made all things for all.[1049]

Such affirmations, so general and absolute, do not, however, have the universal force they would seem to have. In other passages, the Fathers who formulated them affirm clearly the legitimacy of private property.[1050] In the texts under consideration, the Fathers above either thought to combat an excessive attachment to material goods; to affirm the principle that, in case of extreme necessity, the common destination of the goods takes precedence over the right of ownership; or sought to emphasize other principles of Catholic doctrine about the limits of the right of property.

However, what is certain is that their affirmations contrary to the individual possession of material goods do not have the absolute force that a less informed reader could attribute to them.[1051]

B. Seeming Condemnation of Any and Every Loan at Interest

Another very enlightening example of this phenomenon is the condemnation of loans at interest by ancient theologians. Saint Thomas, for example, writes peremptorily: "Wherefore if he exacts more for the usufruct of a thing which has no other use but the consumption of its substance, he exacts a price of something non-existent: and so his exaction [interest] is unjust."[1052] The absolute character of the assertion appears to indicate that, for the Angelic Doctor, lending at interest would be immoral in any situation.

Now, a careful analysis of the writings of Saint Thomas and ancient theologians generally shows that they prohibited interest because they considered money

---

1048. St. Ambrose, *On the Duties of the Clergy*, in *St. Ambrose: Select Works and Letters*, vol. 10 of *A Select Library of Nicene and Post-Nicene Fathers of the Christian Church*, trans. H. de Romestin (New York: The Christian Literature Company, 1896), book 1, chap. 28, no. 132, 23.

1049. See Victor Cathrein, *Philosophia moralis* (Barcelona: Herder, 1945), no. 457.

1050. See Cathrein, *Philosophia moralis*, no. 457; M.B. Schwalm, "Communisme," in *D.T.C.*, 3–1e.:579ff.; Teófilo Urdañoz, *Comentario a la "Suma teológica" de San Tomás de Aquino*, in *Suma Teologica* (Madrid: B.A.C., 1956), 8:480.

1051. See Cathrein, *Philosophia moralis*, no. 457; Schwalm, "Communisme," *D.T.C.*, 3–1e.:585–86; Peinador, *Cursus brevior*, tom. 2, vol. 1, §264n27; Urdañoz, *Comentario a la Suma teológica*, 8:479–81.

1052. St. Thomas Aquinas, *Summa Theologica*, II–II, q. 78, art. 1.

a simple instrument destined for facilitating exchanges. In modern economics, however, the function of money has increased tremendously. In addition to facilitating exchanges, it has come to represent the goods themselves for which it can be exchanged at any moment: "He who is the owner of money," writes Cathrein, "possesses, not formally, but *equivalently*, all that in concrete can be acquired with that money."[1053]

That being the case, today's loans at interest are fundamentally different from what they were in the Middle Ages, equivalent in a certain way to rents and leases. Thus, the moralists do not hesitate to declare that Saint Thomas, despite his absolute affirmations to the contrary, would not condemn interest in an economic order such as ours today.[1054]

6. Resolving an Apparent Disagreement

Accordingly, we invite the reader to carefully review the passages quoted above or any others in which theologians declare it always illicit to break the *respectful silence*. The text and context of such passages make it clear they only established a general principle valid for ordinary cases. They did not consider rare and extraordinary admissible hypotheses rather pertaining to casuistry, as those Saint Thomas Aquinas and the other authors cited had in mind. For example, they did not consider:

1. The case of an error that endangers the faith of the Christian people (as was the case, Saint Thomas explained, in the episode in which Saint Paul resisted Saint Peter to his face).

2. The case of an error that amounts to an aggression against souls (in the expression of Saint Robert Bellarmine).

* * *

In other words, the passages declaring that every breaking of the respectful silence is prohibited show their authors considered only the case of someone who diverges from a point in the magisterial document in *sede doctrinaria*, that is, strictly in the realm of theological speculation. They do not thereby intend to declare that, when solving a concrete case of conscience afflicting one of the faithful in the practical order, it would always be illicit to act publicly contrary to a decision of the Magisterium.

If these authors were faced with "a proximate danger for the faith" (see Saint Thomas), we can believe with all assurance that they, too, following in the footsteps of the Angel of the Schools and Saint Paul, would authorize a public resistance.

1053. Cathrein, *Philosophia moralis*, no. 498, 348.
1054. See Cathrein, 344–51; Tanquerey, *Synopsis theologiae moralis*, 3:445–48; Henri du Passage, "Usure: La doctrine a partir du XVIe. siècle," in *D.T.C.*, 15–2e.:2372–90; Peinador, *Cursus brevior*, tom. 2, 2:266ff.; Urdánoz, *Comentario a la Suma teológica*, 8:688.

If they were faced with an aggression against souls (see Saint Robert Bellarmine); a "public scandal" (see Cornelius à Lapide) in a doctrinal matter; a pope who had "departed from the right path" (see Saint Augustine) by his erroneous and ambiguous teachings; or "a public crime" which redounded in peril for the faith of many (see Saint Thomas), how could they deny the right of resistance and, if necessary, public resistance?

* * *

In our opinion, the explanation, which could occur to some, that the above disagreement among authors would be resolved by a distinction between disciplinary and doctrinal decisions, would be absolutely insufficient and even erroneous. According to this explanation, it would be licit to resist the former but not the latter. Such an explanation appears erroneous for two main reasons:

1. The arguments presented by the first group of authors we cited hold for both doctrinal and disciplinary decisions. For example, the first and the second can occasion a "proximate danger for the faith" on which Saint Thomas based his reasoning. The arguments of the second group also hold for both doctrinal and disciplinary decisions. For example, if the "respect due to sacred authority" (Straub) requires an absolute silence in the presence of erroneous doctrinal decisions, why does it not require it in the face of unjust disciplinary decrees?

2. Once the possibility of doctrinal error in documents of the Magisterium is admitted—a possibility which, in principle, one does not see how to exclude[1055]—it is unquestionable that in the doctrinal order, too, there would be room for very grave cases of conscience, which would make the resistance of one of the faithful licit or even obligatory. To sustain the contrary would be to ignore or deny the fundamental role of the faith in Christian life.

1055. See our essay "Pode haver êrro em documentos do magistério?" (*Catolicismo*, no. 223, July 1969), reproduced in its essential features as Chapter 15 of the present work.

CONCLUSION

The New Mass and the Catholic Conscience

Given the considerations which have been presented, one is forced to conclude that the New Mass cannot be accepted either in its 1969 or 1970 versions.

We make this observation with the greatest regret, knowing full well the consequences that flow therefrom, but we make it also with full conviction. It is unnecessary to list again all the reasons that have led us to this conclusion. However, we wish to emphasize one that, in our opinion, has not been duly focused on in previous debates about the *Ordo* of Paul VI. That is, the principle that a formal break with the customs founded on the Apostolic Tradition, above all in matters of worship, involves schism.[1056] Now, a liturgy tending to desacralization has no basis in Tradition. On the contrary, it constitutes a formal and violent break with all the rules that have oriented Catholic worship until the present.

* * *

Considering specifically the modifications introduced in 1970 in the New Mass, we must make the following observations:

(1) The intention to eliminate the very widespread uneasiness caused by the absolute silence of the 1969 text regarding the fundamental terms of the traditional exposition of Eucharistic doctrine, namely, *transubstantiation, Real Presence* and *propitiation,* is obvious, above all in the foreword. It is licit to ask to what extent the introduced corrections and additions removed the grounds for that uneasiness.

The foreword was so sparing in using those words that one could almost call it reluctant. It introduced only those expressions indispensable to prevent one from saying that those words were still *absent* from the 1970 *Institutio*. However, one could not affirm that they appear here expressing their respective concepts in such a manner as to avoid any equivocation, as the very nature of these matters and the good of souls would postulate.

This situation in which the terms thus introduced appear in the text of the *Institutio*, which one could in a certain sense call a state of violence, inevitably

---

1056. See chap. 14, sec. 1 (*The Hypothesis of a Schismatic Pope*).

suggests that they are there as a concession. A concession made in the degree that it was indispensable and, as it were, unwillingly, revealing the note of instability inherent to all states of violence and all concessions in which the heart does not join.

(2) The 1970 corrections were not complete. On the contrary, in addition to leaving intact many passages susceptible to fundamentally grave reservations, they introduced even new and inadmissible ambiguities concerning the notions of the priesthood of the faithful, the Real Presence, and so forth. Among the passages which would have had to be corrected and were not, we wish to indicate here, by way of example, those referring to uttering the words of the Consecration aloud, as if their very nature required it;[1057] the ambiguities about the notion of *presence*;[1058] the "presidential character" of the Eucharistic Prayer;[1059] the relations between the "liturgy of the word" and the "eucharistic liturgy."[1060]

(3) The fact that substantial corrections in the *Ordo* proper have not been made is especially grave. We especially call the reader's attention to the fact that the dispositions that marked a profound and violent rupture with the ritual tradition of the Catholic liturgy continue unaltered.

(4) Once it was determined to make so many modifications in the *Institutio*— altering several dozen items—it becomes incomprehensible that such reform has been unsatisfactory. Abstracting from persons and considering the matter only on the scientific plane, one can foresee that future historians will compare the 1970 *retreat* to what is common to all heresies through the ages: Confronted and refuted by Catholics, they recede from Arianism to semi-Arianism, from Pelagianism to semi-Pelagianism, from Protestantism to Jansenism, and so forth.[1061]

(5) It remains impossible to accept the New Mass even after the introduced modifications. There is more. A serene, objective, and scientific analysis of the facts reveals that the 1970 reform made the errors less evident without, however, eliminating them. Thus, the doctrinal deviations and ambiguities of the texts became more subtle and, therefore, more dangerous. Herein lies a new and stronger reason preventing faithful Catholics from accepting the new *Ordo missae*.

1057. See chap. 1, sec. 5 (*The President of the Assembly*), item C, commentary on no. 12 of the *Institutio*, and the commentary on the rubric which introduces the narration of the Last Supper— see the section surrounding footnote 217.

1058. See chap. 1, sec. 1 (*The 1969* Institutio *and the Dogma of Transubstantiation*).

1059. See chap. 1, sec. 5 (*The President of the Assembly*), item B, commentary on no. 10 of the *Institutio*.

1060. See chap. 1, sec. 7 (*A Tendency to Make the "Liturgy of the Word" Equal to the "Eucharistic Liturgy"*).

1061. See our observation regarding this in chap. 2, sec. 2 (*Second Answer: The Contradictory Character of All Heresies*). See especially what M. Jugie wrote about Monothelitism: "It is the chameleon heresy *par excellence*. In the measure in which it was unmasked and met resistance, it retreated and made concessions so that its point of arrival was in perfect contradiction with its point of departure." Jugie, "Monothélisme," in *D.T.C.*, 10–2e.:2307.

*   *   *

To avoid misunderstandings that could falsify our position, it is necessary to clarify that the reservations we have expressed concerning various topics of the New Mass are not all of the same importance. In our study, we have always sought to express the sense and the exact scope of each observation we made. Taken in their ensemble, however, these observations converge in one direction so that the new texts of the Mass overall merit even graver reservations than each part considered on its own.

*   *   *

We declare anew that we do not assume this position motivated by a spirit of contestation. We do not question in any way the principle of authority in the Holy Church, but we do ask ourselves, *in what measure, according to the purest Catholic doctrine, does the very principle of authority oblige us to accept or reject the new liturgy of the Mass?* Grounded in these presuppositions, we are forced to conclude that, for the love of the Church and the Faith received from our forefathers, we are obliged to say, *non possumus*.

Finally, we must consider one last reason being alleged in defense of the New Mass. It is a question of the speeches in which Paul VI is supposed to have affirmed the traditional doctrine about the Eucharist. Many think that the *Institutio* and *Ordo* should be interpreted in the light of these papal pronouncements. However, based on the principles of sound hermeneutics,[1062] we do not see how anyone can sustain that such pronouncements have changed the picture presented in Part One of this study. Indeed, the traditional-sounding assertions appearing in recent allocutions of Paul VI are juxtaposed to the *Institutio* and *Ordo* as parallel affirmations. They do not correct what must be considered with reservation.[1063] On the contrary, they create new motives for perplexity.[1064]

*   *   *

We beseech the Most Holy Virgin that She assist her children amid the tremendous storms bringing incalculable harm to souls in our days, and solemnly beg her to hasten the day when her Immaculate Heart will triumph. On that day, Holy Mother Church will appear more radiant than ever, and the papacy, the unshakable rock of Truth, will illuminate all nations with a new brilliance.

1062. See chap. 2, sec. 1 (*First Answer: A Rule of Hermeneutics*).
1063. See chap. 2, sec. 4 (*Conclusion*).
1064. See chap. 2, sec. 1 (*First Answer: A Rule of Hermeneutics*).

Appendix

A Brief Study of Theological Deviations in *Desiderio Desideravi*

by José Antonio Ureta

The Need for Careful Examination

Up to now, comments in traditionalist circles on the apostolic letter *Desiderio desideravi* have been limited to lamenting its repetition that the Mass of Paul VI is the only form of the Roman rite and to denying that the new ordinary of the Mass is a faithful translation of the wishes for reform expressed by the Council Fathers in the constitution *Sacrosanctum concilium*.

No theological critique of the principles Pope Francis developed in his meditation on the liturgy has reached my hands. I see with concern that some articles, while condemning the two failures mentioned above of *Desiderio desideravi*, imply that positive results would be achieved if the pope's principles and some of his comments were implemented in parishes. "In fact, much of Pope Francis's liturgical advice could be read as a rallying cry for liturgical traditionalism," writes a prominent traditionalist leader. After quoting excerpts from the apostolic letter on the richness of symbolic language, he adds, "If diocesan liturgists took these statements to heart, we would see a worldwide transformation of the Catholic liturgy, in a traditional direction."[1065]

For their part, biformalist priests of the Versailles diocese who direct the *Padreblog* affirm, "Many elements of the letter have in common the fact that they are neither specific to the missal of 1962 nor the 1970 one." They conclude, "What is best in the missal of Saint Pius V will naturally find its place in the liturgical development the Holy Father has requested."[1066]

1065. Joseph Shaw, "Pope Francis' Liturgical Longing," OnePeterFive.com, July 5, 2022. In this Brief Study, for clarity and the reader's convenience, because some of the quotations use *italic* for emphasis, I will always use boldface to show my emphases.
1066. Les prêtres du Padreblog, "Au-delà des querelles liturgiques, le pape nous fait contempler le souffle qui doit habiter toute liturgie," *La Croix*, July 6, 2022.

The chaplain of the traditional Mass I regularly attend (belonging to an Ecclesia Dei community) seems to agree. At the end of a recent sermon, he suggested one should get over *Desiderio desideravi*'s unsavory number 31 and take advantage of the European summer vacation to nourish oneself spiritually by reading the papal document.

Worried that this welcoming stance might spread in traditionalist circles, I intend to show the doctrinal deviations that underpin Pope Francis's meditations on the liturgy. Such deviations result from the new theological orientation assumed by the constitution *Sacrosanctum concilium* of Vatican II. I compare the vision of the liturgy taught in the last pre-conciliar document on the subject, that is, Pius XII's encyclical *Mediator Dei*, with the one contained in *Desiderio desideravi*. I will conclude that the latter deserves at least the criticism Cardinal Giovanni Colombo made of *Gaudium et spes*: "That text has all the right words; it is the accents that are wrong."[1067] Unfortunately, readers will gather more wrong accents than right words from the pope's recent apostolic letter.

The comparison between Pius XII's vision and that of Pope Francis will focus on four specific points: (1) the purpose of liturgical worship, (2) the Paschal mystery as the center of the celebration, (3) the memorial character of the Holy Mass, and finally, (4) the presidency of the liturgical assembly. All four of these points are tightly interrelated, as readers shall see thanks to the sterling candor of the Jesuit liturgist Fr. Juan Manuel Martín-Moreno, an unsurpassed guide to the thinking of the current liturgical intelligentsia who stand behind *Desiderio desideravi*.

1. An Imbalanced Account of Worship

Liturgy's Primary Purpose: Paying Homage to the Triune God

Mediator Dei clearly establishes that Catholic worship has two main purposes that intersect and support each other: the glory of God and the sanctification of souls. Its primary purpose is to pay homage to the Creator.

Pius XII explains that "It is unquestionably the fundamental duty of man to orientate his person and his life towards God," acknowledging His supreme majesty and giving "due worship to the One True God by practicing the virtue of religion." He recalls that the Church does so by continuing the priestly function of Jesus Christ (nos. 2 and 3), and concludes with this definition: "The sacred liturgy is, consequently, the public worship which our Redeemer as Head of the Church renders to the Father, as well as the worship which the community of the faithful renders to its Founder, and through Him to the heavenly Father. It is, in short, the worship rendered by the Mystical Body of Christ in the entirety of its Head and members."[1068]

1067. Inos Biffi, "Riletture conciliari," www.Chiesa.Espressonline.it, Apr. 15, 2011.
1068. Pius XII, *Mediator Dei*, nos. 13, 20.

Even the liturgy's secondary end (in fact, primary from another point of view) of sanctifying souls has the glory of God as its ultimate end: "Such is the nature and the object of the sacred liturgy: it treats of the Mass, the sacraments, the divine office; it aims at uniting our souls with Christ and sanctifying them through the divine Redeemer in order that Christ be honored and, through Him and in Him, the most Holy Trinity, *Glory be to the Father and to the Son and to the Holy Ghost.*"[1069]

This relationship between the glorification of God and the sanctification of souls in the liturgy was reversed due to the influence of theologians in the so-called Liturgical Movement. Their ideas were collected in *Sacrosanctum concilium.*

The Systematic Inversion of the Ends of Worship

In his *Apuntes de liturgia* [Notes on Liturgy] for the course he taught at the Pontifical University of Comillas (of the Society of Jesus) from 2003–2004, Jesuit theologian Fr. Juan Manuel Martín-Moreno explains it pedagogically:

> A double dimension to the liturgical act has always been recognized. On the one hand, its objective is glorifying God (ascensional or anabatic dimension), and on the other hand, the salvation and sanctification of men (descensional or katabatic dimension)....
>
> Liturgical theology before Vatican II started from the concept of worship conceived anabatically. The liturgy was primarily glorifying God, fulfilling the Church's obligation as a perfect society to render public worship to God, thereby attracting His blessings.
>
> Conversely, for Vatican II, the descending dimension prevails. The divine Trinity is manifested in the Incarnation and Pasch of Christ. The Father delivering his Son to the world in the Incarnation, and his Spirit in the fullness of Easter, communicates his Trinitarian communion to us as a gift. This double gift of the Word and the Spirit is given to us in the liturgical service for our liberation and sanctification....
>
> The anabatic conception of the liturgy focuses on man's service to God, while the katabatic conception focuses on the service offered by God to man. The criticism of worship, understood as man's service to God, is based on the fact that God does not need these services from man....
>
> If the liturgy were basically worship, it would be superfluous. But if the liturgy is how man can enter into the possession of God's salvation, how salvific action becomes truly present here and now for man, then it is clear that man still needs the liturgy.[1070]

In reality, the katabatic dimension *also* has the anabatic purpose of leading men to God and making them glorify Him. I note that the view that "the liturgy...

1069. Pius XII, no. 171.
1070. Juan Manuel Martín-Moreno, *Apuntes de liturgia*, Academia.edu, 48–49.

would be superfluous" if it were "basically worship" would, in effect, wipe out most of the content of traditional Christian rites, Eastern and Western, as if the Catholic Church had been in error about the nature of divine worship for most of her history.

Pope Francis Follows This Inversion

In *Desiderio desideravi*, Pope Francis almost exclusively emphasizes this primarily katabatic conception of the liturgy while leaving in the shadow the glorification of God, which is its primordial element for Pius XII.

His meditation begins with the opening words of the Last Supper's account: "I have earnestly desired to eat this Passover with you." Such words, he stresses, give us "the surprising possibility of intuiting the depth of the love of the persons of the Most Holy Trinity for us." "The world still does not know it, but everyone is *invited to the supper of the wedding of the Lamb* (Rev. 19:9)," the pope adds. However, "Before our response to his invitation—well before!—there is his desire for us. We may not even be aware of it, but every time we go to Mass, the first reason is that we are drawn there by his desire for us." The liturgy, then, is above all the place of the encounter with Christ, because it "guarantees for us the possibility of such an encounter."[1071]

Here, the liturgy's katabatic and descending meaning—entering into possession of salvation—is very well highlighted. But the fact that the first priestly function of Christ is to worship the Eternal Father in union with His Mystical Body, highlighted by Pius XII in the already cited text, was entirely omitted. This one-sidedness is reiterated in another paragraph dealing specifically with the ascending anabatic aspect, that is, the glorification of the divinity by the assembled faithful. The following text insinuates that the glory of God is secondary insofar as it adds nothing to what He already possesses in Heaven. In contrast, His presence on earth and the spiritual transformation that it produces is what counts:

> The liturgy gives glory to God not because we can add something to the beauty of the inaccessible light within which God dwells (see 1 Tim. 6:16). Nor can we add to the perfection of the angelic song which resounds eternally through the heavenly places. The liturgy gives glory to God because it allows us—here, on earth—to see God in the celebration of the mysteries, and in seeing Him to draw life from his Passover. We, who were dead through our sins and have been made [to] be alive again with Christ—we are the glory of God.[1072]

These words are correct because man truly gives God a merely "accidental" glory. However, God Himself wanted to receive it from man when creating him. However, due to their one-sidedness, the accents lead the faithful to a mistaken

---

1071. Pope Francis, apostolic letter *Desiderio desideravi* (June 29, 2022), nos. 2, 5, 6, and 11, Vatican.va.
1072. Pope Francis, *Desiderio desideravi*, no. 43.

position that easily degenerates into the cult of the golden calf, "a feast that the community gives itself, a festival of self-affirmation," an attitude denounced by then-Cardinal Joseph Ratzinger.[1073]

2. Decentering the Mass From the Redemptive Passion

The Paschal Mystery as the Center of the Celebration

In the encyclical *Mediator Dei*, Pius XII underlines the centrality of the Passion in the life of Our Lord Jesus Christ and our Redemption:

> In the sacred liturgy, the whole Christ is proposed to us in all the circumstances of His life, as the Word of the eternal Father, as born of the Virgin Mother of God, as He who teaches us truth, heals the sick, consoles the afflicted, who endures suffering and who dies; finally, as He who rose triumphantly from the dead and who, reigning in the glory of heaven, sends us the Holy Paraclete and who abides in His Church forever; "Jesus Christ, yesterday and today, and the same forever." Besides, the liturgy shows us Christ not only as a model to be imitated but as a master to whom we should listen readily, a Shepherd whom we should follow, Author of our salvation, the Source of our holiness and the Head of the Mystical Body whose members we are, living by His very life.
>
> [However,] **since His bitter sufferings constitute the principal mystery of our redemption, it is only fitting that the Catholic faith should give it the greatest prominence. This mystery is the very center of divine worship** since the Mass represents and renews it every day and since all the sacraments are most closely united with the cross.[1074]

Later, Pius XII refers to the purposes of the Eucharistic sacrifice (adoration, thanksgiving, propitiation and impetration). When describing the third purpose, Pope Pacelli once again highlights the role of the Passion and Death of the divine Redeemer, summarizing in a few lines the doctrine of Saint Anselm on the vicarious atonement of Jesus Christ on the cross: "The third end proposed is that of expiation, propitiation, and reconciliation. **Certainly, no one was better fitted to make satisfaction to Almighty God for all the sins of men than was Christ. Therefore, He desired to be immolated upon the cross 'as a propitiation for our sins,** not for ours only but also for those of the whole world' (1 John 2:2)."[1075]

When describing the fruit of the divine sacrifice, he reiterates that traditional teaching by quoting Saint Augustine:

1073. "The Pope on Community Worship and the Golden Calf," *New Liturgical Movement*, Mar. 30, 2008.
1074. Pius XII, *Mediator Dei*, nos. 163–64.
1075. Pius XII, no. 73.

For the merits of this sacrifice, since they are altogether boundless and immeasurable, know no limits; for they are meant for all men of every time and place. This follows from the fact that in this sacrifice, the God-Man is the priest and victim; that His immolation was entirely perfect, as was His obedience to the will of His eternal Father; and also that He suffered death as the Head of the human race: "See how we were bought: Christ hangs upon the cross, **see at what a price He makes His purchase . . . He sheds His blood, He buys with His blood, He buys with the blood of the Spotless Lamb,** He buys with the blood of God's only Son. **He who buys is Christ; the price is His blood; the possession bought is the world** (St. Augustine, In psalm. 147; *P.L.*, 37, 1925)."[1076]

Reinterpreting the Redemption Through the Resurrection

This insistence on the centrality of the sacrifice of the cross for the Redemption of the human race was a response to the lucubrations of the Liturgical Movement's most radical theologians. Already at that time, they placed it in the shadows, by emphasizing the triumph and Resurrection of Christ and in His present glorious state.

Once again, the Jesuit Fr. Martín-Moreno will serve as a guide to clarify the change of accent introduced by the innovators:

> Western theology is freeing itself from this Anselmian redemption model, which has negatively affected the liturgy. In reality, salvation has been an initiative of the Father, who already loved us when we were still sinners (Rom. 5:10). It was the Father's initiative to send us his Savior Son as the head of a new Humanity. Jesus did not die because he sought death, nor because the Father demanded it of him. The Father did not send him to die but to live. The Father's action is not to kill his Son but to resurrect him, accepting his loving offering. . . .
>
> . . . The cruel way in which Jesus suffered his death is not the consequence of an unavoidable destiny set by God the Father, but rather the consequence of the cruelty of men who could not tolerate the presence of the Just One in their midst. . . .
>
> When we say that Jesus died "for our sins," we mean that he died because sinful humanity could not help but kill him. He died because we were sinners. If we had been just, we would never have killed him, and Jesus would not have suffered that death. It is not the Father who wants the death of Jesus on the cross, but sinful humanity. . . .
>
> Jesus dies because he was faithful to the line of conduct that had been marked out for him, showing us the true face of the Father. In this sense, we can say that he died for the fulfillment of the will of God. . . .

1076. Pius XII, no. 76.

Because he died in the fulfillment of his mission and assumed our
human nature to the ultimate consequences by dying a death similar to
ours, that is why the Father resurrected the humanity of Jesus. With this,
the door of resurrection and eternal life was also opened for all of us. . . .
Our salvation is the effect of his incarnation, life, death, resurrection and
the gift of his Spirit.[1077]

It could not be clearer: the door of resurrection and eternal life was opened to
us, not so much because of the Precious Blood shed on the cross, but because the
Father resurrected the humanity of Jesus.

This paradigm change, which Fr. Martín-Moreno described pedagogically,
ceased to be mere speculation of theologians and began to be taught by some
bishops even before the beginning of the first conciliar session when the preliminary outline of the constitution on the liturgy was being prepared. The original
title of the chapter on the Eucharist, approved on August 10, 1961, was *De sacro
sancto Missae* **sacrificio**. In the November 15 session of the same year, however, it
became *De sacro sancto Eucharistiae* **mysterio**.[1078]

How This View Entered the Liturgy Constitution

As they began debating the liturgy schema—the only one that was not rejected
outright at the council due to its intentionally moderate innovative character,
which enabled it to be accepted and amended[1079]—Bishop Henri Jenny, then
auxiliary bishop of Cambrai and member of the preparatory commission on the
liturgy (later, a member of the Consilium that elaborated the new Mass), observed
that it was missing an essential thing: a doctrine on the mystery of the liturgy. A
sub-commission was then established. It drafted the first chapter of *Sacrosanctum
concilium*,[1080] whose content became the doctrinal core not only of that conciliar
constitution but also of Paul VI's liturgical reform and the whole post-conciliar
magisterium on the liturgy. That first chapter of *Sacrosanctum concilium* dilutes
the centrality of the death on the cross into the whole "paschal mystery": "The
wonderful works of God among the people of the Old Testament were but a
prelude to the work of Christ the Lord in redeeming mankind and giving perfect
glory to God. **He achieved His task principally by the paschal mystery of His
blessed passion, resurrection from the dead, and the glorious ascension,**
whereby 'dying, he destroyed our death and, rising, he restored our life.' For it was
from the side of Christ as He slept the sleep of death upon the cross that there
came forth 'the wondrous sacrament of the whole Church.'"[1081]

1077. Martín-Moreno, *Apuntes*, 44–45.
1078. See Patrick Prétot, "La place de la constitution sur la liturgie dans l'herméneutique de Vatican II," *Recherches de Science Religieuse* 101 (2013/1), 16.
1079. See Peter Kwasniewski, "*Sacrosanctum Concilium*: The Ultimate Trojan Horse," *Crisis
Magazine*, June 21, 2021.
1080. See "Présentation de *Sacrosanctum concilium*," Fraternités Monastiques de Jérusalem
– Montreal.
1081. Second Vatican Council, constitution *Sacrosanctum concilium*, no. 5.

There is no doubt that the expression *paschale sacramentum* ("paschal mystery") frequently occurs in the texts of the Church Fathers and the prayers of the traditional missal. In all of them, however, the expression was understood within the traditional conception of the Redemption as a ransom operated mainly by the Blood shed in the Savior's Passion and Death. See, for example, the Good Friday prayer: "Remember, Lord, thy deeds and mercy, and sanctify thy servants over whom thou dost watch eternally, and for whom **Christ thy Son inaugurated this Paschal mystery by the shedding of his blood**" (*per suum cruorem, instituit paschale mysterium*)."[1082]

Nevertheless, in its modern meaning, the paschal mystery came to be understood primarily as the full revelation of the Father's love, expressed above all in the Resurrection of Jesus: "When we switch from redemption to the paschal mystery, the emphasis shifts completely. Whoever speaks of redemption thinks first of the Passion and then of the Resurrection as a sequel. He who speaks of paschal mystery thinks first of the risen Christ,"[1083] wrote the Dominican Aimon-Marie Roguet in a famous article published by the Parisian magazine *Maison-Dieu*, a bulwark of the Liturgical Movement.

Pope Francis Downplays Christ's Redemptive Death

This one-sided emphasis on Easter to the detriment of the Passion (contrary to the traditional balance) informs *Desiderio desideravi* entirely. The words "Redemption," "Redeemer," and "redeem," which evoke liberation from sin through the payment of a debt, were not used a single time in the document. It always uses "salvation," which does not have that connotation. It preferentially associates it with Easter, cited no less than 29 times, while the Resurrection is mentioned 14 times, and the Lord's death is evoked only six times.

The text's very definition of liturgy suffers from this bias. For Pope Francis, it is "the priesthood of Christ, revealed to us and given **in his Paschal Mystery**, rendered present and active by means of signs addressed to the senses (water, oil, bread, wine, gestures, words), so that the Spirit, **plunging us into the paschal mystery**, might transform every dimension of our life, conforming us more and more to Christ."[1084]

Regarding respect for the rubrics, Pope Francis says it is necessary not to deprive the assembly of its due, "namely, the **paschal mystery** celebrated according to the ritual that the Church sets down." He says it should arouse the astonishment of participants, described as "marveling at the fact that the salvific plan of God has been revealed in the **paschal deed** of Jesus (see Eph. 1:3–14), and the power of this **paschal deed** continues to reach us in the celebration of the 'mysteries,' of the sacraments."[1085] Later, he affirms, "The action of the celebra-

---

1082. Philip Caraman and James Walsh, arrs. and eds., *The Fulton J. Sheen Sunday Missal* (New York: Hawthorn Books, Inc., 1961), 207.
1083. Dominique Greiner, "La revue 'La Maison-Dieu,' la liturgie au cœur," *La Croix*, Nov. 29, 2020.
1084. Pope Francis, *Desiderio desideravi*, no. 21.
1085. Pope Francis, nos. 23, 25.

tion is the place in which, by means of memorial, **the Paschal mystery is made present** so that the baptized, through their participation, can experience it in their own lives."[1086]

This change of emphasis poses the risk that what remains of the Faith in Catholics can be deformed in two ways. On the one hand, they can be led to think that the work of salvation should be attributed more to the Father and the Holy Spirit than to Jesus, the Incarnate Word and son of Mary, who shed his Precious Blood for our sins. On the other hand, they could be led to think that Jesus Christ is not exactly the Redeemer but rather the "place" in which God saves us since the Father's love is revealed to us in Christ's Passover. In their pious practices, the faithful might also be led to underrate all traditional devotions that encourage them to atone for their sins and those of humanity. It might also induce them to claim that they are saved by faith alone in God's salvific plan, without having to "complete in [their] flesh what is lacking in the sufferings of Christ" (Col. 1:24). Alternatively, and worse, to believe in universal salvation because of God's unbreakable Covenant with the human race.

3. From the Sacrifice of Calvary to a Memorial of Presence

The Holy Mass as a True and Proper Sacrifice

When dealing with the Eucharistic sacrifice, *Mediator Dei* reiterates the teaching of the Council of Trent that the Holy Mass is a proper and true sacrifice and not just a memorial of the Passion or the Last Supper:

> Christ the Lord, "Eternal Priest according to the order of Melchisedech," (Ps. 59:4) "loving His own who were of the world" (John 13:1), "at the last supper, on the night He was betrayed, wishing to leave His beloved Spouse, the Church, a visible sacrifice such as the nature of men requires, that would re-present the bloody sacrifice offered once on the cross, and perpetuate its memory to the end of time, and whose salutary virtue might be applied in remitting those sins which we daily commit, . . . offered His body and blood under the species of bread and wine to God the Father, and under the same species allowed the apostles, whom he at that time constituted the priests of the New Testament, to partake thereof; commanding them and their successors in the priesthood to make the same offering (Council of Trent, 22, 1).
>
> **The august sacrifice of the altar, then, is no mere empty commemoration of the passion and death of Jesus Christ, but a true and proper act of sacrifice**, whereby the High Priest by an unbloody immolation offers Himself a most acceptable victim to the Eternal Father, **as He did upon the cross**. "It is one and the same victim; the same person now offers it by the

ministry of His priests, who then offered Himself on the cross, the manner of offering alone being different (Council of Trent, 22, 2)."[1087]

The reason for the latter is that, given the present glorious state of Christ's human nature, the shedding of blood is now impossible. Thus, His sacrifice is manifested outwardly by the separation of the Eucharistic species under which He is present, symbolizing the bloody separation of His Body and Blood. "Thus the commemorative representation of His death, which actually took place on Calvary, is repeated in every sacrifice of the altar, seeing that Jesus Christ is symbolically shown by separate symbols to be in a state of victimhood."[1088]

Reformers Shift Emphasis to the "Memorial"

This traditional presentation was not to the taste of the innovators, who began to put the accent on the commemoration (although without the *nuda commemoratio* connotation of the Protestant reformers). Rather, they gave it the meaning of an objective and real memorial that "re-presents" what happened historically and effectively communicates it here and now.

From this new perspective, R. Gerardi explains, "the memorial [celebration] expresses the reality of the event, the 'objective updating' and presence of what is commemorated. **It is not that it repeats itself since the event was set historically once and for all** (*ephápax*), but it is present. The act of Christ makes its effect felt here and now, committing those who remember it. **The sacrifice of Christ was historically performed only once: the Eucharist is his memorial** (in the fullest sense of the word), a living presence of grace."[1089]

The Jesuit mentioned above, Fr. Martín-Moreno, explains why it is not a question of multiple reiterations of the unique sacrifice of Christ:

> It is not that the time of salvation repeats itself here and now, but rather that **man here and now enters again and again into communication with a permanent presence that is beyond elapsed time.** . . .
>
> . . . In the liturgy, the point of intersection of time and eternity is reached. There, **the participant becomes a contemporary of biblical events.** Man becomes a contemporary witness to what happened then. Christ is born at Christmas, [and] rises at Easter.
>
> Is anamnesis man's work or God's? It is man who commemorates, but as a human act, his action of remembering cannot transcend time; it cannot enter the time tunnel to return to the past. **The divine action alone, transcending time, brings the mysteries to our here and now.** That is why the liturgy is the action of God before being an action of man.[1090]

1087. Pius XII, *Mediator Dei*, nos. 67–68.
1088. Pius XII, no. 70.
1089. R. Gerardi, "Memorial," in *Diccionario Teológico Enciclopédico*.
1090. Martín-Moreno, *Apuntes*, 47.

The path had been opened by the pioneering theses of then-Father Charles Journet (later made a cardinal by Paul VI) and the French philosopher Jacques Maritain, for whom the real presence of Jesus Christ would double as a kind of real presence of His sacrifice.[1091]

This theological option in favor of the memorial, which omits that the Mass is a bloodless *renewal* of the sacrifice of Calvary and affirms that the latter only *becomes present* during the celebration, offers a weak interpretation of the dogma of faith proclaimed by the Council of Trent. According to this dogma, *each Mass is "a proper and true sacrifice"* performed in sacramental form because transubstantiation causes the Divine Victim's Body and Blood to be truly present and symbolically separated.[1092]

Pope Francis Opts for an Extreme Memorializing Concept

Desiderio desideravi clearly and insistently adopts this theological option of the Mass as a memorial that has the sacrificial aspect only secondarily to the extent that it is a commemoration. Already at the beginning, describing the Last Supper the Lord wanted to eat with the apostles, Pope Francis says:

> He knows that he is the Lamb of that Passover meal; he knows that he *is* the Passover. This is the absolute newness, the absolute originality, of that Supper, the only truly new thing in history, which renders that Supper unique and for this reason "the Last Supper," **unrepeatable**. Nonetheless, his infinite desire to re-establish that communion with us that was and remains his original design, will not be satisfied until every man and woman, *from every tribe, tongue, people and nation* (Rev. 5:9), shall have eaten his Body and drunk his Blood. And for this reason **that same Supper will be made present in the celebration of the Eucharist until he returns again**.[1093]

Incidentally, note that, in the document's first paragraph describing the Mass, in addition to the theory of the one unrepeatable action, the pope affirms that the Mass is a representation of the *Supper* and not of the sacrifice on Calvary *per se*. This is reminiscent of the original (defective and subsequently changed) Protestant-leaning definition of the Mass in the General Instruction on the Roman Missal, to which Cardinals Ottaviani and Bacci objected so forcefully in their *Short Critical Study*. It is also noteworthy that this paragraph suggests that every man and woman should or shall eat of the Eucharist. This suggests a soteriological universalism and fits in with Pope Francis's pragmatic support of all Christians

---

1091. See Philippe-Marie Margelidon O.P., "La théologie du sacrifice eucharistique chez Jacques Maritain," *Revue Thomiste* (Jan.-Mar. 2015), 101–147.
1092. See Claude Barthe, *La Messe de Vatican II—dossier historique* (Versailles: Via Romana, 2018), 181.
1093. Pope Francis, *Desiderio desideravi*, no. 4.

receiving the Eucharist, whether Catholic or not, in the state of grace or not, living or not by the Ten Commandments.

Returning to the main theme: *Desiderio desideravi* has some references to the sacrifice of Jesus on the cross, but at no point does it say that, at each Mass, that sacrifice is renewed in a bloodless way. On the contrary, in number 7, Pope Francis starts by saying that "the content of the bread broken is the cross of Jesus, his sacrifice of obedience out of love for the Father." He then goes on to say that, after participating in the Last Supper's ritual anticipation of his death, the apostles could have understood what He meant by "'body offered,' 'blood poured out.' It is this of which we make memorial in every Eucharist."[1094] That would have been the most appropriate time to teach that the Mass is not only a memorial but also an unbloody renewal of the sacrifice of Calvary, sacramentally represented in the separation of the Eucharistic species. Pope Francis chose to omit that truth of the Faith and refer only to the memorial.

A few paragraphs later, the document insists that the liturgy is not a memorial of the apostles' remembrances but a true encounter with the Risen One—an idea repeated nine times throughout the document. He continues:

> The liturgy guarantees for us the possibility of such an encounter. For us a vague memory of the Last Supper would do no good. **We need to be present at that Supper,** to be able to hear his voice, to eat his Body and to drink his Blood. We need Him. In the Eucharist and in all the sacraments we are guaranteed the possibility of encountering the Lord Jesus and of having the power of his Paschal Mystery reach us. The salvific power of the sacrifice of Jesus, his every word, his every gesture, glance, and feeling reaches us through the celebration of the sacraments.[1095]

Again, note that the emphasis is placed on participation in the Supper and not on being spiritually united to Jesus. He offers himself to the Father in sacrifice at each Mass, an aspect which was entirely omitted.

Mass as Remembering the "Gift" Jesus Gave at the Last Supper?

When speaking of the correct understanding of the dynamism of the Liturgy, Pope Francis uses words already quoted in the previous section, which make it clear that, for him, the sacrificial character of the Mass results from the commemoration of the Passover of Jesus. He states, "The action of the celebration is the place in which, **by means of memorial, the Paschal Mystery is made present** so that the baptized, through their participation, can experience it in their own lives."[1096]

Later, this idea becomes more explicit when referring to the central nucleus of the Mass: "In the Eucharistic prayer—in which also all of the baptized participate by listening *with reverence and in silence* and intervening with the acclamations

---

1094. Pope Francis, no. 7.
1095. Pope Francis, no. 11.
1096. Pope Francis, no. 49.

(*Institutio generalis missalis romani*, nos. 78–79)—the one presiding has the strength, *in the name of the whole holy people*, **to remember before the Father the offering of his Son in the Last Supper, so that that immense gift might be rendered newly present** on the altar."[1097]

The text not only completely omits Christ's offering during the Passion (of which the Supper was a ritual anticipation) and avoids saying that the sacrifice is renewed, but even leaves out the very word "sacrifice" by calling it an "immense gift."

Add to all of the above the fact that nowhere in *Desiderio desideravi* are found the expressions "transubstantiation," "Real Presence," or analogous formulations indicating that "the Eucharistic Food contains, as all are aware, 'truly, really and substantially the Body and Blood together with soul and divinity of our Lord Jesus Christ,'" as Pius XII says, citing the Council of Trent (sess. 13, can. 1).[1098] Nor does it contain anything resembling *Mediator Dei*'s exhortation that pastors should not allow the faithful to neglect "the adoration of the august Sacrament and visits to our Lord in the tabernacles" nor allow "churches [to] be closed during the hours not appointed for public functions"—a viewpoint defended by some "who are deceived under the pretext of restoring the liturgy or who idly claim that only liturgical rites are of any real value and dignity."[1099]

These unilateral actions are responsible for the disastrous loss (or at least the serious dilution) of faith in the Real Presence of Our Lord Jesus Christ under the Eucharistic species, confirmed by opinion polls in several countries. The most expressive is by the Pew Research Center, which found that "just one-third of U.S. Catholics agree with their church that Eucharist is [the] body, blood of Christ."[1100]

4. From Priests of Sacrifice to Presidents Over Assemblies

The Unique Role of the Priest in the Mass

In *Mediator Dei*, Pius XII explicitly teaches: "Only to the apostles, and thenceforth to those on whom their successors have imposed hands, is granted the power of the priesthood, in virtue of which they represent the person of Jesus Christ before their people, acting at the same time as representatives of their people before God." However, he adds, in the Holy Mass "**the priest acts for the people only because he represents Jesus Christ, who is Head of all His members and offers Himself in their stead.** Hence, he goes to the altar as the minister of Christ, inferior to Christ but superior to the people (see Saint Robert Bellarmine, *On the Mass*, bk. 2, ch. 4). **The people, on the other hand, since they in no sense**

1097. Pope Francis, no. 60.
1098. Pius XII, *Mediator Dei*, no. 129.
1099. Pius XII, no. 176.
1100. Gregory A. Smith, "Just One-Third of U.S. Catholics Agree With Their Church That Eucharist Is Body, Blood of Christ," PewResearch.org, Aug. 5, 2019.

represent the divine Redeemer and are not mediator between themselves and God, can in no way possess the sacerdotal power."[1101]

The rites and prayers of the Eucharistic sacrifice "show no less clearly that the oblation of the Victim is made by the priests in company with the people," since "by the waters of baptism, as by common right, Christians are made members of the Mystical Body of Christ the Priest, and by the 'character' which is imprinted on their souls, they are appointed to give worship to God. Thus they participate, according to their condition, in the priesthood of Christ."[1102]

How do people participate in the acts of Christ's priesthood? "Now the faithful participate in the oblation, understood in this limited sense, after their own fashion and in a twofold manner, namely, because they not only offer the sacrifice by the hands of the priest, but also, to a certain extent, in union with him. It is by reason of this participation that the offering made by the people is also included in liturgical worship."[1103]

Nevertheless, Pius XII feels compelled to reiterate, "the fact, however, that the faithful participate in the Eucharistic sacrifice does not mean that they also are endowed with priestly power." This insistence is justified because even then, in 1947, some liturgists believed "that the command by which Christ gave power to His apostles at the Last Supper to do what He Himself had done, applies directly to the entire Christian Church." Pius XII asserts, "They look on the Eucharistic sacrifice as a 'concelebration.'"[1104]

Against this error, *Mediator Dei* taught, "The unbloody immolation at the words of consecration, when Christ is made present upon the altar in the state of a victim, **is performed by the priest and by him alone, as the representative of Christ** and not as the representative of the faithful."[1105]

> [These] offer the sacrifice by the hands of the priest from the fact that the minister at the altar, in offering a sacrifice in the name of all His members, represents Christ, the Head of the Mystical Body. Hence the whole Church can rightly be said to offer up the victim through Christ. But the conclusion that the people offer the sacrifice with the priest himself is not based on the fact that, being members of the Church no less than the priest himself, they perform a visible liturgical rite; for this is the privilege only of the minister who has been divinely appointed to this office: rather it is based on the fact that the people unite their hearts in praise, impetration, expiation and thanksgiving with prayers or intention of the priest, even of the High Priest himself, so that in the one and same offering of the victim and according to a visible sacerdotal rite they may be presented to God the Father.[1106]

1101. Pius XII, *Mediator Dei*, nos. 40, 84.
1102. Pius XII, nos. 87, 88.
1103. Pius XII, no. 92.
1104. Pius XII, nos. 82, 83.
1105. Pius XII, no. 92.
1106. Pius XII, no. 93.

Pius XII draws a logical conclusion by explaining that private Masses without the participation of the people cannot be condemned, nor the simultaneous celebration of several private Masses on different altars, on the false pretext of "the social character of the Eucharistic sacrifice." The reason is that the holy sacrifice of the Mass "necessarily and of its very nature, has always and everywhere the character of a public and social act, inasmuch as he who offers it acts in the name of Christ and of the faithful, whose Head is the divine Redeemer, and he offers it to God for the holy Catholic Church, and for the living and the dead." Hence, "it is in no wise required that the people ratify what the sacred minister has done."[1107]

Furthermore, "although it is most desirable that the people should also approach the holy table, this is not required for the integrity of the sacrifice." Therefore, the view of those who "consider the general communion of all present as the culminating point of the whole celebration" should be rejected.[1108]

The Reformers Reject Sacerdotalism in Favor of a "Communal Celebrant"

Egalitarian reformers naturally found this hierarchical distinction between the celebrant and the faithful unbearable—a distinction was made clear by the communion rail, which separated the sanctuary (reserved for the ministers of the altar) from the nave (where the faithful remained). To reduce it as much as possible, they resorted to the stratagem of "rediscovering" the "liturgical assembly." In a lengthy but extremely revealing passage, the Jesuit liturgist Fr. Martín-Moreno explains:

> Pre-conciliar liturgy was perfectly visible in the ecclesiology that started from the division between clergy and laity. The choirs of canons were located in the privileged part of the cathedrals, isolated from the others by grills. The sanctuary was located on the heights, separated from the faithful by a grandiose staircase. This way, they highlighted his mediating function by having the priest located up there, halfway between heaven and earth.
>
> However, *Lumen gentium* starts by considering the People of God before speaking of the different ministries in the Church. The ecclesiology of communion[1109] that Vatican II embraced will be reflected in the great importance the assembly acquires in the liturgy. This is perhaps one of the most emblematic features of the liturgical reform.
>
> **The mediating role between God and men is no longer played by the priest** but by the assembly, within which the priest exercises his function. We do not oppose priest to assembly just as we do not oppose head to body.

1107. Pius XII, no. 96.
1108. Pius XII, nos. 112, 114.
1109. Allow us a little detour to highlight the vagueness of the concept of "ecclesiology of communion," found on all lips after the 1985 Extraordinary Synod of Bishops' unsuccessful attempt to resolve the conflict between the traditional concept of the Church-perfect-and-hierarchical-society and the egalitarian Church-People-of-God, of the Basic Christian Communities. Fr. Juan Manuel Martín-Moreno is perhaps right to include such a concept within his vision of the liturgical assembly.

The head is also part of the body. There is no body without a head. There is no assembly without ministries.

Nevertheless, **there are [also] no ministries without an assembly**. The ultimate origin of the ministry is not the assembly but Christ. However, as Borobio says, "the ministry does not originate apart from or without the community." The minister does not receive his mandate directly from Christ, as did the apostles or Paul.

The assembly is the translation of *qhl*, which in Greek is translated as *ekklesia* or *synagoge*. These words designate the convocation, the act of gathering, and the gathered community. *Qahal* is the general assembly of the people. In its semantic evolution, it has designated the call, the levy, the meeting, the gathered community, and the Church. *Ecclesia* is not just Church, but Church convened and gathered in a specific place and at a precise time to celebrate the mysteries of worship. . . .

It is this Church or assembly, which includes the bishop, priests, and deacons, **which directly and formally participates in the priesthood of Christ**. The gathered assembly is the reflection and expression of the Church. In it, the Church is incarnated and made visible; in it and through it, it is projected to the world, especially in the local Church, which celebrates, presided over by the bishop. The council does not want thereby to exclude the existence of other manifestations of the Church. The liturgy is the most visible expression of the Church but not the only one. The Church also manifests itself in the charitable action of Christians and many other ways.

As said, the foundation of this participation is found in the common priesthood of the faithful. In the Eucharist, the people offer the gifts together with the president. In SC 48, it is said that the faithful should "learn to offer themselves by offering the immaculate host not only by the hands of the priest but together with him." On this point, *Sacrosanctum concilium* **goes beyond *Mediator Dei*, which used the expression** *quodammodo*, 'in a way.' The council suppressed this expression.

From thence arises the awareness that liturgical actions are not private but have a community character (SC 26). It is necessary to return to the body of the Church what had always been its heritage; **the assembly must recover the leading role it had lost due to abusive clericalism**. . . .

This insistence on the community character of the celebration motivates the recovery of concelebration, which has contributed to de-privatizing the Mass and highlighting the unity of the priesthood and the Eucharistic sacrifice (SC 57). From this perspective, **it is incomprehensible today that in the pre-conciliar liturgy, different simultaneous liturgies could be celebrated in the same church** and that some faithful attended one and others another.

Therefore, **today we can no longer speak of an assembly that attends Mass but of an assembly that celebrates Mass. The bishop or priest who presides over the celebration can no longer be called the "celebrant"**—

because they are *all* celebrants—but rather the "president." This, which was already hinted at in SC 26, is expressly stated in the GIRM [*General Instruction of the Roman Missal*] nos. 1 and 7. The popular expression "hearing Mass" has been banned forever. . . .

This communion ecclesiology influences even the smallest details of the liturgical reform. It greatly influences the architecture of post-conciliar churches, where the sanctuary is barely raised above the assembly so that all can see its actions. The grills and the communion rails have been eliminated. The center of the church is the altar, not the tabernacle, which has now been moved to a side chapel. The layout of the nave is no longer rectilinear, like a tram, but semicircular, so the faithful see each other better and feel part of one another. Side altars attached to the naves have been removed. The choir located at the back of the church has disappeared. The singing ministry cannot be situated outside the assembly but as part of it.[1110]

Reducing Priest to President, Elevating Laity to Concelebrants

Desiderio desideravi emphasizes that the celebrant is the entire assembly and reduces the minister of the altar to the condition of the president while omitting entirely that he alone performs the bloodless immolation of the Eucharistic sacrifice *in persona Christi*.

In the original Spanish version [of *Desiderio desideravi*], the word "priest"—which precisely defines the one who performs and offers the sacrifice—appears only three times,[1111] two of which only refer to an ordained cleric. However, the expression "presbyter"—that in its Greek and Latin origin means only "the oldest," the "dean"—is used 15 times. Whereas "presidency" and the verb to preside (or its conjugations) appear 14 times, the expression "celebrant" appears only once, with the insinuation that it applies to the entire assembly: "Let us always remember that it is the Church, the Body of Christ, that is the celebrating subject and not just the priest." Later on, he affirms it explicitly: "The priest also is formed by his **presiding in the celebrating assembly.**"[1112]

The document recognizes that the priestly office "is not primarily a duty assigned to him by the community but is rather a consequence of the outpouring of the Holy Spirit received in ordination which equips him for such a task." Nevertheless, when defining that task, he does not say it is the priestly task of sacramentally sacrificing the Victim. Rather it is the task of presiding over assemblies: "The priest lives his characteristic participation in the celebration in virtue

---

1110. Martín-Moreno, *Apuntes*, 61–63. (Our emphasis.)
1111. This is not the case in the English version, because the word "presbyter" never became common among English-speaking Catholics to refer to priests. It is only used as an adjective in expressions like "presbyteral ministry," "presbyteral council," and so forth.
1112. Pope Francis, *Desiderio desideravi*, nos. 36, 56.

of the gift received in the sacrament of Holy Orders, and this is expressed precisely in presiding."[1113]

In the following paragraph, he offers an exclusively katabatic and descending interpretation of the priest's mediating mission while omitting that he offers the sacrifice to God on behalf of the whole Church:

> For this service to be well done—indeed, with art!—it is of fundamental importance that the priest have a keen awareness of being, through God's mercy, a particular presence of the risen Lord. The ordained minister is himself one of the types of presence of the Lord which render the Christian assembly unique, different from any other assembly (see *Sacrosanctum concilium*, no. 7). This fact gives "sacramental" weight (in the broad sense) to all the gestures and words of the one presiding. The assembly has the right to be able to feel in those gestures and words the desire that the Lord has, today as at the Last Supper, to eat the Passover with us.[1114]

Individuality Merged Into the Collectivity

On the other hand, this almost total immersion of the ordained minister in the "assembly" is attested to by the fact that the latter term is mentioned 18 times, highlighting its celebratory function and collective character. This often makes it difficult for each member of the faithful to render God a truly interior worship by personally offering himself to the Christ-Victim, in intimate union with Him:

> I think of all the gestures and words that belong to the assembly: gathering, careful walking in procession, being seated, standing, kneeling, singing, being in silence, acclamations, looking, listening. There are many ways in which the assembly, *as one body* (Ne 8:1) participates in the celebration. Everybody doing together the same gesture, everyone speaking together in one voice—this transmits to each individual the energy of the entire assembly. It is a uniformity that not only does not deaden but, on the contrary, educates individual believers to discover the authentic uniqueness of their personalities not in individualistic attitudes but in the awareness of being one body.[1115]

How much more reasonable is this recommendation of Pius XII:

> So varied and diverse are men's talents and characters that it is impossible for all to be moved and attracted to the same extent by community prayers, hymns and liturgical services. Moreover, the needs and inclinations of all are not the same, nor are they always constant in the same individual. Who, then, would say, on account of such a prejudice, that all these Christians

---

1113. Pope Francis, no. 56.
1114. Pope Francis, no. 57.
1115. Pope Francis, no. 51.

> cannot participate in the Mass nor share its fruits? On the contrary, they
> can adopt some other method which proves easier for certain people; for
> instance, they can lovingly meditate on the mysteries of Jesus Christ or
> perform other exercises of piety or recite prayers which, though they differ
> from the sacred rites, are still essentially in harmony with them.[1116]

It would be necessary to ask whether the diminished attendance at Sunday Mass after the liturgical reform is not largely because of the displeasure of many faithful at the "assemblyist" and collectivist character with which the new rite was celebrated in most parishes, leaving no room for individual piety.

Above all, one would have to ask if the vertiginous drop in seminary enrollments is not because some of those who may sense a vocation are disappointed seeing the image of an ordained minister reduced to "assembly president," not matching the traditional image of the priesthood, in which personal sacrifice finds its model and fulfillment in the sacrificial reality of the Holy Mass.

5. The Mass "of Another Faith"?

An Uncomfortable Question

In the four aspects analyzed in the preceding parts—(1) the purpose of liturgical worship, (2) the Paschal mystery as the center of the celebration, (3) the memorial character of the Holy Mass, and finally, (4) the presidency of the liturgical assembly—it has become quite clear that *Desiderio desideravi*'s vision of the liturgy is one-sided. Although its words, considered individually, may seem fair to the point of deserving praise from some traditionalists (even highly educated ones), it only succeeds in stressing the wrong syllables. What seems to be emphasized are the theories and preferences of modern liturgists, not the Church's traditional doctrine.

A detailed analysis shows that, ultimately, the apostolic letter presents the Church's sacramental life, particularly the rite of Holy Mass. This presentation does not seem to harmonize, as a whole, with the principles and pastoral advice of the last great liturgical encyclical before the Second Vatican Council, *Mediator Dei* of Pope Pius XII.

I must, therefore, ask an uncomfortable question: Do these two very different ritual forms express the same Faith?

The answer from most advanced innovators is clear. They openly say these are two incompatible liturgical stances corresponding to two incompatible dogmatic stances. One is the Faith that permeates the traditional rite; the other is the faith that permeates the new rite. That is why the Jesuit I quoted, Fr. Martín-Moreno, so vehemently insists that the "new Mass" definitively supplants (and, it must be said, repudiates) the theological orientation and stance of the old Mass.

1116. Pius XII, *Mediator Dei*, no. 108.

Yesterday's Mass "Can No Longer Be the Norm" for Today's Faith

In February, 2022, halfway between the controversial motu proprio *Traditionis custodes* and the latest apostolic letter, *Desiderio desideravi*, a couple who are directors at the self-proclaimed Catholic Conference of the Francophone Baptized published an eloquent article in the newspaper *La Croix*. Taking advantage of the fact that, in French, the old Mass is sometimes referred to as *la messe d'autrefois* (from times past) and that the expressions *autrefois* and *autre foi* (another faith or a different faith) are pronounced the same, they conveyed their opinion with a pun: "*La fin des messes d'autre 'foi', une chance pour le Christ!*" (The end of Masses of another faith, a chance for Christ!).

Aline and Alain Weidert's article has the merit of calling things by their name and being logical in its conclusions. Here are some long selected excerpts that speak for themselves:

> Without discernment, the spirit of the liturgy of another "faith," its theology, the norms of yesterday's prayer and Mass (the *lex orandi* of the past), can no longer continue to be the norms of today's faith, or its content (our *lex credendi*). One's reluctance [in the face of disputes] might dictate that we should not think too much about this content so as not to destabilize the Church further.
>
> Quite the contrary! A faith that would still derive from yesterday's *lex orandi*, which made Catholicism the religion of a perverse god who causes his son to die to appease his wrath, a religion of perpetual *mea culpa* and reparation, would lead to a counter-testimony of faith, to a disastrous image of Christ. Proof if any: the still too frequent activation of indulgences, linked among other things to sacrifices and redemptions for sins.
>
> Unfortunately, our [traditional] Masses are always imbued with a strong "expiatory" sacrificial character, having a "propitiatory" purpose to annihilate sins (mentioned 20 times), to bring about our salvation and save souls from divine vengeance. "*Propitiation*," which Ecclesia Dei communities defend tooth and nail together with their priest-sacrificers, who are formed to use the words *the Holy Sacrifice of the Mass*, a true immolation. . . .
>
> We must continue to emerge from this submerged part of the Tridentine Mass, a historical drift curiously passed over in silence (taboo?) in current debates. Since Vatican II, we have made much progress in recovering the initial datum of a positive Eucharist, a "*Do this in memory of me!*" where all are invited to be a daily Sacrament of the Covenant: "Just as this water mixes with wine for the sacrament of the Covenant, may we be united to the divinity of Him who took our humanity." Sacrament of the Covenant, a new concept in this prayer since Vatican II. . . .
>
> . . . If we want to be able to offer a tasty Christian faith and practice in the future, we must venture, *by reflection and formation*, to discover an as yet unexplored (untapped) font of salvation opened by Jesus, not first by his death against ("on account of") sins but by his existence as Covenant. "For His humanity, united with the person of the Word, was the

instrument of our salvation" (Vatican II, *Sacrosanctum concilium, no.* 51. The choice is clear! It is not between different religious sensitivities and aesthetics but between endless sacrifices to erase sins and Eucharists [*sic*] that seal the Covenant/Christ.[1117]

At least here, things are said clearly and without semantic detours!

Suppose the magnetic needle of *Desiderio desideravi* was placed between the two visions of the liturgy and the Mass described by the Weiderts. In that case, I fear the needle would quickly jump to the "Covenant" pole. Indeed, the proof is already at hand: The same Weidert couple just published a new article in *La Croix* filled with excitement over *Desiderio desideravi*.[1118]

The Perennial Faith and the New Theology Are Incompatible

At any rate, the goals Pope Francis set for himself with the publication of his latest apostolic letter, that is, that Catholics should "abandon [their] polemics" and that the beauty of the Christian celebration is "not to be spoiled by a superficial and foreshortened understanding of its value or, worse yet, by its being exploited in service of some ideological vision," are far from achieved.[1119]

The pope explains why: "It would be trivial to read the tensions, unfortunately present around the celebration, as a simple divergence between different tastes concerning a particular ritual form."[1120] Precisely. Modernist firebrands consider the rite of St. Pius V as the Mass "of another faith" mainly for theological reasons. Likewise, it is for theological reasons that traditionalists consider that the rite of Paul VI departs from the traditional teachings on the Mass on essential points. In the name of the perennial faith, they do not and cannot accept that the new rite is "the unique expression of the *lex orandi* of the Roman Rite," as *Traditionis custodes* claims and *Desiderio desideravi* reiterates.[1121]

I believe the shot missed the mark if the recent apostolic letter sought to give a theological foundation to that claim. Its unilateral nature only confirms the conviction of the traditionalist flock that the new *lex orandi* does not correspond to the *lex credendi* the Church received in deposit. Furthermore, the argument Pope Francis invokes as an *ultima ratio*, that traditionalists must accept the new Mass because it corresponds to the teachings of the Second Vatican Council, is unlikely to change their minds precisely because the Constitution *Sacrosanctum concilium* itself, the subsequent liturgical magisterium, and *Desiderio desideravi* all deserve the same theological objections.

In any case, here is an invitation to theologians and liturgiologists to address the subject and to analyze, more profoundly and scientifically, the contribution

---

1117. Aline and Alain Weidert, "La fin des messes d'autre 'foi', une chance pour le Christ!" *La Croix,* Feb. 10, 2022.

1118. See Aline and Alain Weidert, "Avec François, l'urgence d'une formation pour et par la liturgie," *La Croix,* Jul. 8, 2022.

1119. Pope Francis, *Desiderio desideravi*, nos. 65, 16.

1120. Pope Francis, no. 31.

1121. Pope Francis, no. 31.

Desiderio desideravi has made to the ongoing debate. Far from burying the hatchet, it seems to have opened a new battlefront.

Bibliography

A

Abarzuza, O.F.M.Cap., Franciscus X. de. Vols. 2–4 of *Manuale theologiae dogmaticae*. Madrid-Buenos Aires: Studium, 1956–1957.

Adrian II. Allocutio 3 lecta in Concilio VIII Act. 7, 4:471–72. In *Histoire des conciles* by Hefele and Leclercq. Paris: Letouzey et Ané, 1911; and 619–20 in *Tractatus de ecclesia Christi* by Louis Billot.

Aertnys, C.SS.R., J. and C.A. Damen, C.SS.R. 2 vols. *Theologia moralis*. Turin: Marietti, 1950.

Aldama, S.J., Joseph A. de. *On the Sacrament of Christian Unity or On the Most Holy Eucharist*. Treatise 3 of *On the Sacraments in General*. Vol. 4 of *Sacrae theologiae summa*. Translated by Kenneth Baker, S.J., 231–412. [Saddle River, N.J.:] Keep the Faith, Inc., 2015.

Alonso Lobo, Arturo. Vol. 1 of *Comentarios al código de derecho canónico*. Madrid: B.A.C., 1963.

Alphonsus Liguori, Saint. *Oeuvres dogmatiques*, trans. Vidal-Delalle-Bousquet. Paris: Parent-Desbarres, 1836.

———. *Verità della Fede*. Vol. 8 in *Opera de S. Alfonso Maria de Liguori*. Turin: Pier Giacinto Marietti, 1887.

Ambrose, Saint. *On the Duties of the Clergy*. In *St. Ambrose: Select Works and Letters*. Vol. 10 of *A Select Library of Nicene and Post-Nicene Fathers of the Christian Church*. Translated by H. de Romestin. New York: The Christian Literature Company, 1896. Accessed June 24, 2022. https://www.google.com/books/edition/A_Select_Library_of_Nicene_and_Post_Nice/vILYAAAAMAAJ?hl=en&gbpv=1.

Andrieu, Michel. *Immixtio et consecratio: La consécration par contact dans les documents liturgiques de moyen âge*. Paris: Picard, 1924.

Anonymous (un groupe de canonistes). "Consultation, témoignage et voeu sur le nouvel *Ordo missae*." *La Pensée Catholique* (Paris) no. 122 (1969), 44–47. Accessed July 1, 2022. http://salve-regina.com/index.php?title=Consultation,_t%C3%A9moignage_et_voeu_sur_le_nouvel_ordo.

Arregui, S.J., Antonius M. *Summarium theologiae moralis*. Bilbao: El Mensajero del Corazón de Jesús, 1952.

Augustine, Saint. "Letter 55." In *Letters 1–99*, 215–36. Vol. 1 in *The Works of Saint Augustine: A Translation for the 21st Century.* Edited by John E. Rotelle, O.S.A. Translated by Roland Teske, S.J. Hyde Park, N.Y.: New City Press, 2001. Accessed June 4, 2022. https://wesleyscholar.com /wp-content/uploads/2019/04/Augustine-Letters-1-99.pdf.

———. "Sermon 293." In *Sermons 273–305A*, 148–58. Vol. 8 in *The Works of Saint Augustine: A Translation for the 21ˢᵗ Century.* Edited by John E. Rotelle, O.S.A. Translated by Edmund Hill, O.P. Hyde Park, N.Y.: New City Press, 1994. Accessed June 4, 2022. https://wesleyscholar.com /wp-content/uploads/2019/04/Augustine-Sermons-273-305.pdf.

B

Ballerinius, Petrus. *De potestate ecclesiastica summorum pontificum et conciliorum generalium.* First edition. Rome: Typis S. Congr. de Propaganda Fidei, 1850.

———. *De potestate ecclesiastica summorum pontificum et conciliorum generalium.* Edited by E.W. Westhoff. Vol. 2 of *Opus de romano pontifice.* Monasterii Westphalorum: Sumptibus J.H. Deiters, 1847. Accessed June 30, 2022. https://archive.org/details/ra546170800balluoft/mode/2up.

Bañez, Domingo. *Commentaria in II–II.* Venice, 1602. Quoted in Dublanchy, "Infaillibilité du pape," *D.T.C.*, 7–2e.:1710, 1716.

Baronius, Card. Caesar. Vol. 18 of "Annales ecclesiastici," cum critica historico-chronologica P. Antonii Pagii O.M.C. Lucca: Venturini, 1776.

Barthe, Claude. *La Messe de Vatican II—dossier historique.* Versailles: Via Romana, 2018.

Bäumer, R. "Honorius I." In *Lexikon für theologie und kirche*, 5:474–75. Freiburg: Verlag Herder, 1960. Accessed June 17, 2022. https://archive .org/details/lexikonfrtheolog0005unse_j6k7/mode/2up.

Beauchamp, Philippe. "La nouvelle messe est-elle obligatoire?" *Cices—Bulletin du Cercle d'Information Civique et Sociale* (Paris), no. 104 (May 31, 1970), 1–2.

Benedict XIV. *De servorum Dei beatificatione, et sanctorum canonizatione.* In Vol. 1 of *Opera omnia* by *Benedicti XIV.* Venice: Remondini, 1767.

Bergamo, Petrus da. Editio fotot. *In opera sancti Thomae Aquinatis index seu tabula aurea.* Alba-Rome: Pauline, 1960.

Beste, O.S.B., Udalricus. *Introductio in codicem.* Collegeville, Minn.: St. John's Abbey, 1946.

Biffi, Inos. "Riletture conciliari." www.Chiesa.Espressonline.it, Apr. 15, 2011. http://chiesa.espresso.repubblica.it/articolo/1347506.html.

Billot, S.J., Louis. Vol. 1 of *De ecclesiae sacramentis.* Rome: Ex Typographia Pontificia in Instituto Pii IX, 1914. Accessed June 4, 2022. https://archive.org/details/deecclesiaesacra01bill/mode/2up.

———. *De credibilitate ecclesiae, et de intima ejus constitutione.* Vol. 1 of *Tractatus de ecclesia Christi.* Rome: Gregoriana, 1921.

Bossuet, Jacques-Benigne. *Explication de quelques difficultés sur les prières de la messe a un nouveau catholique.* In vol. 13 of *Oeuvres complètes de Bossuet.* Paris: Même Maison de Commerce, 1841. Accessed July 1, 2022. https://archive.org/details/explicationdequ00bossgoog/mode/1up.

Bouix, Marie Dominique. *Tractatus de jure liturgico.* Paris: Ruffet, 1873.

———. Vol. 2. *Tractatus de papa.* Paris: Lecoffre, 1869. Accessed July 28, 2022. https://archive.org/details/bub_gb_4gt1bEGHSZsC/page/n1/mode/2up.

Bruno of Segni, Saint. "S. Brunonis episcopi Signiensis epistolae." *P.L.*, 165:1139: Letter to the bishops and cardinals.

———. "S. Brunonis episcopi Signiensis epistolae." *P.L.*, 165:1139: Letter to the bishop of Oporto.

———. Letter to Paschal II. *P.L.*, 163:463.

Brys, J. Vol. 1 of *Juris canonici compendium.* Bruges: Desclée, 1947.

Bugnini, Annibale. "De editione missalis romani instaurati." *Notitiae* 54 (May 1970), 161–68. Accessed July 27, 2022. http://www.cultodivino.va/content/cultodivino/it/rivista-notitiae/indici-annate/1970/54.html.

———. "Exposição na II Conferência Geral do Episcopado Latino-Americano, em Medellin." *Revista Eclesiástica Brasileira* 28 (1968).

———. "Les travaux de la XIIeme session plenière de la comission pour la réforme de la liturgie." *L'Osservatore Romano,* weekly edition in French, Nov. 28, 1969, 12.

C

Cajetan, Thomas de Vio. *Commentaria in summam sancti Thommæ II–II*, book 2, pt. 2, q. 11, a. 2, quoted by Peinador, *Cursus brevior*, book 2, 1:99.

———. *De comparatione auctoritatis papae et concilii: Cum apologia eiusdem tractatus.* Vol. 1 of *Scripta theologica.* Edited by Vincentius M. Iacobus Pollet. Rome: Institutum Angelicum, 1936. Accessed June 30, 2022. http://www.obrascatolicas.com/livros/Teologia/d-Cajetanus%20OP-%20De%20Comparatione%20Auctoritatis%20Papae%20et%20Concilii%20Cum%20Apologia%20Eiusdem%20Tractatus.pdf.

———. *Le pape et le concile—Tractatus de comparatione auctoritatis papæ et concilii cum apologia ejusdem.* Translated and annotated by Fr. Jean-Michel Gleize, S.S.P.X. Condé-et-Poireau: *Courrier de Rome*, 2014.

Callewaert, Camillus. "De offerenda et oblatione in missa." *Periodica de Re Morali, Canonica, Liturgica* 33 (1944) 61–94.

———. *De sacra liturgia universim.* Vol 1 of *Liturgicae institutiones.* Bruges: Beyaert, 1944.

Cano, O.P., Melchior. *De locis theologicis.* In *Opera.* Venice: Bassani, 1776.

———. *De locis theologicis.* Translated by Juan Belda Plans. Madrid: B.A.C., 2006.

Cappello, S.J., Felice M. *De curia romana.* Rome: 1913, 13–15. Quoted by Coronata, *Institutiones iuris canonici,* 1:366.

———. Vol. 1 of *Summa iuris canonici.* Rome: Universitas Gregoriana, 1945.

Caraman, Philip and James Walsh, arrs. and eds. *The Fulton J. Sheen Sunday Missal.* New York: Hawthorn Books, Inc., 1961.

Caron, Pier Giovanni. *La rinuncia all'officio eclesiastico.* Milan: Vita e Pensiero, 1946.

Carreyre, J. "Jansénisme." In *D.T.C.,* 8–1e.:318–529. Accessed May 27, 2022. https://archive.org/details/dictionnairedethv8pt1vaca/page/158/mode/2up.

Cartechini, S.J., Sisto. *Dall'opinione al domma.* Rome: La Civiltà Cattolica, 1953.

Catherine of Siena, Saint. "Letter 196, to Gregory XI." In *Saint Catherine of Siena As Seen in Her Letters.* Translated and edited by Vida Dutton Scudder. New York: J.M. Dent and E.P. Dutton, 1905. Accessed May 29, 2022. https://archive.org/details/SaintCatherineOfSienaAsSeenInHerLetters/mode/2up.

Cathrein, S.J., Victor. *Philosophia moralis.* Barcelona: Herder, 1945.

Celestine I, Saint. On the *Indiculus,* erroneously attributed to Saint Celestine; see Prosper of Aquitaine.

Centre National de Pastorale Liturgique. French translation of the foreword to the *Institutio generalis missalis romani. La Documentation Catholique,* June 21, 1970, 568.

Chelodi, Ioannes. *Ius de personis.* Trent: Tridentum, 1922.

Choupin, S.J., Lucien. "Le décret du Saint-Office: Sa valeur juridique." *Études* 112 (Aug. 5, 1907), 413–17.

———. "Motu proprio *Praestantia* de S.S. Pie X." *Études* 114 (Jan. 5, 1908), 116–26.

———. *Valeur des décisions doctrinales et disciplinaires du Saint-Siège.* Paris: Beauchesne, 1928.

Claeys Bouuaert, F. Vol. 1. *Traité de droit canonique,* Paris: Letouzey, 1954.

———. "Pontife romain." In *Dictionnaire de droit canonique.* Paris: Letouzey, 1958.

Clark, S.J., Francis. *Adiumenta ad tractatum de SS. eucharistiae sacramento.* Rome: Gregorian University, 1966.

Cocchi, C.M., Guidus. Vol. 3. *Commentarium in codicem iuris canonici.* Turin: Marietti, 1940.

Congregation for Divine Worship and the Discipline of the Sacraments. "Presentazione del nuovo messale romano: Intervento del Cardinale Jorge Arturo Medina Estévez." Vatican.va, Mar. 18, 2002. https://www.vatican .va/roman_curia/congregations/ccdds/documents/rc_con_ccdds_doc _20020327_card-medina-estevez_it.html.

Congar, Yves M.J. "Schisme." In *D.T.C.,* 14–1e.:1286–314. Accessed May 25, 2022. https://archive.org/details/dictionnairedet14vacauoft/page/n653 /mode/2up.

Consilium ad Exsequendam Constitutionem de Sacra Liturgia. "Decima sessio plenaria 'Consilii.'" *Notitiae* 40 (May-June 1968), 180–84. Accessed July 27, 2022. http://www.cultodivino.va/content/cultodivino/it /rivista-notitiae/indici-annate/1968/40.html.

———. *Institutio generalis missalis romani.* In *Ordo missæ,* Editio Typica. Vatican: Typis Polyglottis Vaticanis: 1969.

———. *Missale romanum.* Vatican: Typis Polyglottis Vaticanis, 1970.

———. "Instruction for the Translation of the Liturgical Texts for Celebration With the People" (Jan. 25, 1969). *Notitiae,* no. 44, 3–12.

Coronata, O.M.C., Mathaeus Conte a. Vol. 1 of *Institutiones iuris canonici.* Turin: Marietti, 1928. Accessed June 26, 2022. https://archive.org /details/institutionesiur0001cont/mode/2up.

———. Vol. 4 of *Institutiones iuris canonici.* Turin: Marietti, 1935.

Corrêa de Oliveira, Plinio. *In Defense of Catholic Action.* Translated by American TFP. Spring Grove, Penn.: The American Society for the Defense of Tradition, Family, and Property, 2006.

———. "Juizo temerário," *Legionário,* nos. 475–477, Oct. 19, Oct. 26, and Nov. 2, 1941. Accessed July 3, 2022. https://pliniocorreadeoliveira.info /LEG_411019_juizo_temerario01.htm#.YsHn__3MKUk.

———. *Revolution and Counter-Revolution.* Third English Edition. York, Penn.: The American Society for the Defense of Tradition, Family, and Property, 1993.

———. *Revolution and Counter-Revolution* (digital). https://archive.org /details/rcr_20220702/mode/2up.

———. *Unperceived Ideological Transshipment and Dialogue.* Accessed May 8, 2022. https://www.tfp.org/unperceived-ideological-transshipment-and -dialogue/.

Council of Carthage, Sixteenth, (or Fifteenth). Denz.-Sch., 222–230; Denz.-Umb., 101–108.

Council of Constantinople, Third (Sixth Ecumenical). Session 13: Condemnation of the Monothelites and Pope Honorius I. Denz.-Sch., 550–552.

Council of Florence (Twelfth Ecumenical). *Decretum pro Armeniis.* Denz.-Sch., 1310–1328.

Council of Trent. *Canons and Decrees of the Council of Trent.* Translated by J. Schroeder, O.P. St. Louis: B. Herder Book Co., 1941. Accessed May 28, 2022. https://archive.org/details/canonsdecreesofc0000coun/mode/2up.

———. Session 22: Decree on the Most Holy Sacrifice of the Mass. Denz.-Sch., 1738–1759.

———. Session 23: Doctrine on the Sacrament of Orders. Denz.-Sch., 1763–1778; Denz.-Umb., 956a–968.

———. Session 25: Decree on the invocation, veneration and relics of the Saints and on Sacred Images. Denz.-Sch., 1821–1825; Denz.-Umb., 984–988.

Courrier de Rome. "La Messe polyvalente de Paul VI: L'instruction Bugnini, une pause tactique" (Paris), no. 56 (Nov. 10, 1969).

———. "La nouvelle ordonnance de la messe: Vers une messe oecumenique" (Paris), no. 49 (June 25, 1969).

Cristiani, L. *Du luthéranisme au protestantisme.* Paris: Bloud, 1911.

Cunha Alvarenga. "Pedras e serpentes para as almas que pedem pão." *Catolicismo,* no. 231 (Mar. 1970), 5. Accessed June 28, 2022. https://catolicismo.com.br/Acervo/Num/0231/P04-05.html.

D

D'Annibale, Josephus. *In constitutionem apostolicæ sedis commentarii.* Reate: Salvatore Trinchi, 1880.

———. *Summula theologiae moralis.* Milan: Ex Typ. S. Josephi, 1882.

Davis, S.J., Henry J. *Moral and Pastoral Theology.* London: Sheed and Ward, 1945.

de Bruyne, Luciano. "Eresia." In *E.C.*, 5:487–93. Accessed July 3, 2022. https://archive.org/details/enciclopedia-cattolica-vol.-5/page/n311/mode/2up.

De Lugo, S.J., Joannes. *Tractatus de eucharistia.* Vol. 4 of *Disputationes scholasticae et morales.* Paris: Vivès, 1869.

———. *Tractatus de virtute fidei divinae.* Vol. 2 of *Disputationes scholasticae et morales.* Paris: Vivès, 1868.

de M., R. Vol. 1. *Institutiones iuris canonici.* Paris: Lecoffre, 1853.

de Mattei, Roberto. *The Second Vatican Council: An Unwritten Story.* Translated by Patrick T. Brannan, S.J., Michael J. Miller, and Kenneth D. Whitehead. Edited by Michael J. Miller. Fitzwilliam, N.H.: Loreto Publications, 2012.

De Nantes, Abbé Georges. "L'interdit jeté sur la sainte messe romaine." *La Contre-réforme catholique au XXe siècle* (Saint-Parres-les-Vaudes, France), no. 33 (June 1970), 3–14.

Denzinger, Henricus. *Enchiridion symbolorum.* Edited by Adolfus Schoenmetzer, S.J. Accessed May 30, 2022. http://www.clerus.org /bibliaclerusonline/en/lt.htm#c.

———. *Enchiridion symbolorum.* Edited by Johannes Baptista Umberg. Barcelona: Herder, 1946.

———. *The Sources of Catholic Dogma.* Edited by Karl Rahner, S.J. Translated by Roy J. Deferrari. St. Louis: B. Herder Book Co., 1957. Accessed May 30, 2022. https://archive.org/details/sourcesofcatholi00denz/mode/1up.

———. *Compendium of Creeds, Definitions, and Declarations on Matters of Faith and Morals.* Edited by Peter Hünermann. English edition edited by Robert Fastiggi and Anne Englund Nash. 43rd edition. San Francisco: Ignatius Press, 2012.

de Soto, O.P., Domingo. *Commentarium fratris Dominici Soto Segobiensis (..) in quartum sententiarum.* Salamanca, 1561.

———. *In quartum sententiarum.* Venice: H. Zenarius, 1584.

De Vooght, O.S.B., Paul. "Le conciliarisme aux conciles de Constance et de Bâle." In *Le concile et les conciles: Contribution à l'histoire de la vie conciliaire de l'église,* 143–82. Namur (Belgium): Éditions Chevretogne— Éditions Cerf, 1960.

d'Herbigny, S.J., Michel. Vol. 2 of *Theologica de ecclesia.* Paris: Beauchesne, 1921.

Diana, Antonius. *Resolutiones morales.* Venice: Franc. Baba, 1635.

Diekamp, Franciscus, and Adolphus M. Hoffmann. *Theologiae dogmaticae manuale.* Paris–Tournai–Rome: Desclée, vol. 1, 1933; vol. 2, 1933; vol. 4, 1934.

di Napoli, Giovanni. "Terza edizione italiana del messale romano: Dono e *kairos* per riscoprire il linguagio, la forza e la grazia del celebrare." *Rassegna di Teologia* 61 (2020): 357–75. https://www.rassegnaditeologia.it /focus320.pdf.

Diocese de Campos, Diocesan Chancery. Special bulletin of September 1, 1970. On the celebration of the Mass in Latin. Signed by Fr. Henrique Conrado Fischer, Chancellor. *Catolicismo,* no. 237 (Sept. 1970), 7.

Dominicus a Sanctissima Trinitate. *Tractatus de summo pontifice romano.* Vol. 10 of "Bilbioth. Pontif." p. 496. Quoted by Benedict XIV, *De servorum Dei beatificatione,* book 1, chap. 42, no. 16, p. 143.

Dublanchy, E. "Église." In *D.T.C.*, 4:2108–224. Accessed May 25, 2022. https://archive.org/details/dictionnairedeth04vacauoft/page/1054 /mode/2up.

———. "Infaillibilité du pape." In *D.T.C.*, 7–2e.:1638–717. Accessed May 27, 2022. https://archive.org/details/dictionnairedethv7pt2vaca/page/190 /mode/2up.

Dumas, O.S.B., Antoine. "Pour mieux comprendre les textes liturgiques du missel romain." *Notitiae*, no. 54 (May 1970), 194–213.

Du Passage, Henri. "Usure: La doctrine a partir du XVIe siècle." In *D.T.C.*, 15–2e.:2372–90. Accessed May 27, 2022. https://archive.org/details /dictionnairedetv15pt2vaca/page/418/mode/1up.

F

Facchini, Tarcisio. *Il papato principio di unità e Pietro Ballerini di Verona.* Padua: Il Messaggero di S. Antonio, 1950.

Ferraris, F. Lucius. "Papa." In vol. 5 of *Prompta bibliotheca.* Paris: Migne, 1865.

Ferreres, S.J., Joannes B. Vol. 1 of *Institutiones canonicae.* Barcelona: Subirona, 1917.

———, and Alfredus Mondria, S.J., *Compendium theologiæ moralis.* Barcelona: Eugenius Subirana, 1953.

Fischer, Henrique Conrado. "Missa em latim." *Catolicismo*, no. 237, (Sept. 1970), 8. Accessed June 28, 2022. https://catolicismo.com.br/Acervo /Num/0237/P08.html.

Foley, Edward, Nathan D. Mitchell, and Joanne M. Pierce, eds. *A Commentary on the General Instruction of the Roman Missal.* Collegeville, Minn.: Liturgical Press, 2007. Accessed June 29, 2022. The introduction and first four chapters are available at https://litpress.org/Products /GetSample/6017/9780814660171.

Forget, J. "Congrégations romaines." In *D.T.C.*, 3–1e.:1103–19. Accessed May 25, 2022. https://archive.org/details/dictionnairedet03vaca/page/552 /mode/2up.

Fortescue, Adrien. *La messe.* Paris: Lethielleux, 1921.

Foulquié, Paul, and Raymond Saint-Jean. "Epochè," "Parenthèses," "Reduction phénoménologique." *Dictionnaire de la langue philosophique.* Paris: Presses Universitaires de France, 1962.

Francis, Pope. Apostolic letter *Desiderio desideravi* (June 29, 2022). Vatican.va. https://www.vatican.va/content/francesco/en/apost_letters /documents/20220629-lettera-ap-desiderio-desideravi.html.

Franzelin, S.J., Card. Joannes Baptista. *Tractatus de divina traditione et scriptura.* Rome-Turin: Marietti, 1870. Accessed June 4, 2022. https://play.google .com/books/reader?id=beZUAAAAcAAJ&pg=GBS.PA1&hl=en.

Fraternités Monastiques de Jérusalem – Montreal. "Présentation de Sacrosanctum concilium." Accessed Aug. 19, 2022. http://www.fraternites-jerusalem.ca/wordpress_sdssm/wp-content /uploads/2013/04/Présentation-Sacrosanctum-Concilium.pdf.

G

Garrido Bonaño, O.S.B., Manuel and Augusto Pascual. *Curso de liturgia romana.* Madrid: B.A.C., 1961.

Gelineau, Joseph. *Demain la liturgie: Essai sur l'évolution des assemblées chrétiennes.* Paris: Les Éditions du Cerf, 1977.

Genicot, S.J., Eduardus and Ioseph Salmans, S.J. Vol. 2 of *Institutiones theologiae moralis.* Bruges: Desclée, 1951.

Gerardi, R. "Memorial." In *Diccionario Teológico Enciclopédico.*

Gihr, Nicholas. Vol. 1. *Le saint sacrifice de la messe.* Paris: Lethielleux, 1901.

Goupil, S.J., Auguste-Alexis. *L'Église: Insititution, constitution, pouvoir.* Vol. 3 of *Une théologie en français.* Laval, Mayenne: Goupil, 1946.

Gramsci, Antonio. "Notes for an Introduction and an Approach to the Study of Philosophy and the History of Culture." In *An Antonio Gramsci Reader: Selected Writings, 1916–1935,* edited by David Forgacs, 324–43. New York: Schocken Books, 1988. Accessed June 18, 2022. https://archive .org/details/antoniogramscire0000gram/mode/2up.

Granero, J.M. Review of *O valor teológico da liturgia*, by Fr. Manuel Pinto. *Razon y Fé* 149 (1954), 284.

Gratian. *Decretum.* In *Corpus iuris canonici.* Accessed July 28, 2022. https://geschichte.digitale-sammlungen.de//decretum-gratiani/online /angebot.

Grausem, J.P. "Zaccaria, François-Antoine." In *D.T.C.*, 15–2e.:3643–48. Accessed May 25, 2022. https://archive.org/details /dictionnairedetv15pt2vaca/page/1054/mode/2up.

Graviers, Abbé des. "La messe tridentine est-elle morte?" *Courrier de Rome* (Jan. 1974).

Greiner, Dominique. "La revue 'La Maison-Dieu,' la liturgie au cœur." *La Croix,* Nov. 29, 2020. https://www.la-croix.com/Culture/revue-Maison-Dieu -liturgie-coeur-2020-11-29-1201127197.

Guéranger, O.S.B., Dom Prosper. *Institutions liturgiques.* Vol. 1. Paris: Débécourt, 1840. Accessed May 8, 2022. https://archive.org/details /institutionslitu01gu/mode/2up.

———. "Feast of Saint Cyril of Alexandria (Feb. 9)." In vol. 4 of *Liturgical Year*. Translated by Laurence Shepherd. Fourth edition. Great Falls, Mont.: St. Bonaventure Publications, 2000.

———. *Nouvelle défense des institutions liturgiques—II partie: Deuxième lettre* à *monseigneur l'évêque d'Orléans*. Le Mans: Fleuriot, 1846.

Gury, S.J., Joannes Petrus, and Antonius Ballerini, S.J. Vol. 1 of *Compendium theologiae moralis*. Rome: Civiltà Cattolica, 1866.

H

Haegy, Joseph. Vol. 1. Revised 11th edition. *Manuel de liturgie et cérémonial selon le rite romain*. Paris: Librairie Victor Lecoffre, 1922. Accessed June 5, 2022. https://babel.hathitrust.org/cgi/pt?id=uc1.$b193878&view=1up &seq=1&skin=2021.

Häring, Bernard. *Marriage in the Modern World*. Translated by Geoffrey Stevens. Westminster, Md.: The Newman Press, 1966. Accessed June 1, 2022. https://archive.org/details/marriageinmodern0000hari_w3j0 /mode/2up.

Hedde, R. and E. Amann. "Pélagianisme." In *D.T.C.*, 12–1e.:675–715. Accessed May 25, 2022. https://archive.org/details/dictionnairedet12pt1vaca /page/338/mode/2up.

Hefele, Charles-Joseph and Dom H. Leclercq. Vols. 4 and 5. *Histoire des conciles*. Paris: Letouzey et Ané, 1911–1912. Accessed June 26, 2022. https://archive .org/details/histoiredesconci51hefele/page/n3/mode/2up.

Hervé, J.M. *De revelatione christiana—De ecclesia Christi—De fontibus revelationis*. Vol. 1 of *Manuale theologiae dogmaticae*. Paris: Berche et Pagis, 1952. Accessed June 4, 2022. https://archive.org/details /manualetheologia00herv/mode/2up.

———. *De gratia Christi—De virtutibus theologicis—De sacramentis in genere, baptismo et confirmatione*. Vol. 3 of *Manuale theologiae dogmaticae*. Paris: Berche et Pagis, 1953. Accessed June 4, 2022. https://archive.org/details /manualetheologia03herv/mode/2up.

Hoger Katechetisch Instltunt. *O novo catecismo*. São Paulo: Herder, 1969.

Hoornaert, Eduardo. "A indissolubilidade do matrimônio na reflexão católica após Trento." *Revista Eclesiástica Brasileira* 28 (1968): 99–109.

Horn, E.T. "Liturgy." In *The Lutheran Cyclopedia*, edited by Henry Eyster Jacobs and John A.W. Haas, 278–83. New York: Charles Scribner's Sons, 1911. Accessed May 10, 2022. https://archive.org/details/cu31924029466533 /page/278/mode/1up.

Howell, Clifford, trans. *Apostolic Constitution (Missale romanum) of Pope Paul VI and General Instruction on the Roman Missal*. London: Catholic Truth Society, 1973.

Huguenin, Ludovicus, and Clemens Marc, C.SS.R. *Expositio methodica juris canonici.* Lyon-Paris: Vitte, 1903.

Hurter, S.J., Hugo. 3 vols. *Theologiae dogmaticae compendium.* Innsbruck, Austria: Wagneriana, 1883.

I

Ignatius of Loyola, Saint. *The Spiritual Exercises of St. Ignatius of Loyola.* Translated by Elder Mullan, S.J. New York: P.J. Kenedy & Sons, 1914.

Innocent III. "Sermo II in consecratione pontificis maximi." *P.L.*, 217:653–60. Accessed June 28, 2022. https://patristica.net/latina/#t217.

———. "Sermo IV in consecratione pontificis." *P.L.*, 217:666–72. Accessed June 28, 2022. https://patristica.net/latina/#t217.

Innocent X. Constitutioni *Cum occasione* (May 31, 1653—which condemned errors of Jansen). Denz.-Sch., 2001-2007.

International Commission on English in the Liturgy. *The Sacramentary, Volume One—Sundays and Feasts.* Washington, D.C.: International Commission on English in the Liturgy, 1998. Accessed June 22, 2022. https://www.tarsus.ie/resources/Liturgy/ICEL_Roman_Missal _Volume_1A.pdf.

Iorio, S.J., Thomas A. *Theologia moralis.* Naples: D'Auria, 1960.

Iragui, O.F.M. Cap., Serapius de. *Theologia fundamentalis.* Vol. 1 of *Manuale theologiae dogmaticae,* by Serapius de Iragui and Franciscus X. de Abarzuza. Madrid: Studium, 1959. Accessed June 4, 2022. https://www.europeana.eu/en/item/444/doai _BCCCAP0000000000C0000000000546_HTML. (Vols. 2, 3, and 4 of this title are by Franciscus X. de Abarzuza.)

Isnard, O.S.B., Clemente José Carlos. "Presentation" of the new *Ordo missae.* In *Presbiteral.* Petrópolis: Vozes, 1969. Also in *Liturgia da Missa.* São Paulo: Edições Paulinas, 1969.

Ivo of Chartres, Saint. "Epistola 233." *P.L.*, 162:235–36. Accessed June 28, 2022. https://archive.org/details/patrologiaecurs18unkngoog/page /n122/mode/2up.

———. "Epistola 236." (Of Saint Ivo of Chartres and other bishops to the archbishop of Lyon.) *P.L.*, 162:238–42. Accessed June 28, 2022. https://archive.org/details/patrologiaecurs18unkngoog/page/n122 /mode/2up.

———. *Decretum*, part 5, chap. 23. *P.L.*, 161:329–30. Accessed June 28, 2022. http://books.google.com/books?id=KPUUAAAAQAAJ.

J

Jacobs, Charles M. "The Ministry and the Sacraments." In *The Ministry and the Sacraments: Report of the Theological Commission Appointed by the Continuation Committee of the Faith and Order Movement,* edited by Roderic Dunkerley: 138–45. London: Student Christian Movement Press, 1937. Accessed May 17, 2022. https://archive.org/details /ministrysacramen0000worl/page/n7/mode/2up.

Jerome, Saint. *Expos. in epist. ad Titum,* c. III, v. 11. *P.L.,* 26:598. Accessed June 23, 2022.

John XXIII. Christmas Radio Message (Dec. 22, 1960). Accessed May 29, 2022. https://www.vatican.va/content/john-xxiii/es/messages/pont _messages/1960/documents/hf_j-xxiii_mes_19601222_natale.html.

Journet, Charles. 2 vols. *L'Église du Verbe Incarné.* Second revised edition. Bruges: Desclée de Brouwer, 1962.

Juergens, S.M., Sylvester P. *The New Marian Missal for Daily Mass.* New York: Regina Press, 1963.

Jugie, M. "Monothélisme." In *D.T.C.,* 10–2e.:2307–23. Accessed May 25, 2022. https://archive.org/details/dictionnairedet10vaca/page/502/mode/2up.

Jungmann, S. J., José A. *El sacrificio de la misa: tratado histórico-litúrgico.* Madrid: B.A.C., 1951.

K

Kleist, S.J., James A. and Joseph L. Lilly, C.M. trans. *The New Testament: Rendered From the Original Greek With Explanatory Notes.* Milwaukee: The Bruce Publishing Company, 1954. Accessed July 4, 2022. https://archive.org/details/newtestamentrend0000unse_o4i9 /mode/2up.

Kloppenburg, O.F.M., Boaventura. *Concílio Vaticano II.* 5 vols. Petrópolis, R.J.: Editora Vozes, Ltda. 1962–1966. Accessed May 8, 2022. https://drive .google.com/file/d/1WBmLhkJa5bquj_MCQj3ZxMCkfZVZgOM2 /view.

Küng, Hans. *Structures de l'Église.* Paris: Desclée, 1964.

———. *Structures of the Church.* Translated by Salvator Attanasio. New York: Thomas Nelson & Sons, 1964. Accessed June 17, 2022. https://archive .org/details/structuresofchur00kung/mode/2up.

Kwasniewski, Peter. "*Sacrosanctum Concilium*: The Ultimate Trojan Horse." *Crisis Magazine,* June 21, 2021. https://www.crisismagazine.com/2021 /sacrosanctum-concilium-the-ultimate-trojan-horse.

L

La Civiltà Cattolica. Review of *O valor teológico da liturgia*, by Fr. Manuel Pinto. Oct. 3, 1953, 581.

Lalande, Andre. "Parentesis." "Raiz." In *Vocabulario tecnico y critico de la filosofia.* Buenos Aires: El Ateneo, 1953.

Lapide, S.J., Cornelius à. *St. Matthew's Gospel–Chaps. 10 to 21.* Vol. 2 in *The Great Commentary of Cornelius à Lapide.* Translated by Thomas W. Mossman. Third Edition. London: John Hodges, 1887. Accessed June 21, 2022. https://archive.org/details/thegreatcomment02lapiuoft /mode/2up.

———. *St. Matthew's Gospel–Chapters 22 to 28.* Vol. 3 of *The Great Commentary of Cornelius à Lapide.* Translated by Thomas W. Mossman. Third Edition. London: John Hodges, 1887. Accessed June 13, 2022. https://www. ecatholic2000.com/lapide/untitled-170.shtml.

———. *II Corinthians and Galatians.* Vol. 8 in *The Great Commentary of Cornelius à Lapide.* Translated and edited by W.F. Cobb. Edinburgh: John Grant, 1908. Accessed June 21, 2022. https://archive.org/details /cu31924092350648/mode/2up.

Laymann, S.J., Paulus. *Theologia moralis.* Venice: Maldura, 1700.

Le Bachelet, X. "Arianisme." In *D.T.C.*, 1–2e.:1779–863. Accessed May 25, 2022. https://archive.org/details/dictionnairedeth01vaca/page/140 /mode/2up.

———. "Immaculée Conception." In *D.T.C.*, 7–1e.:845–1218. Accessed May 28, 2022. https://archive.org/details/dictionnairedethv7pt1vaca/page/2 /mode/2up.

Lefebvre, O.S.B., Dom Gaspar (of the Abbey of Snt. André). *Daily Missal With Vespers for Sundays & Feasts.* St. Paul, Minn.: The E.M. Lohmann Co., 1925. Accessed June 1, 2022. https://archive.ccwatershed.org/media /pdfs/21/02/16/05-35-23_0.pdf.

Lehmkuhl, S.J., Augustinus. 2 vols. *Theologia moralis.* Freiburg: Herder, 1888.

Leo the Great (I), Saint. "Epistola 129," chap. 2., 192–93. Accessed June 28, 2022. http://www.documentacatholicaomnia.eu/01p/0440-0461,_SS _Leo_I._Magnus,_Epistolae_[Schaff],_EN.pdf.

Leo II, Saint. "Letter *Cum diversa sint.*" (To the bishops of Spain.) Denz.-Sch., 561.

———. "Letter *Cum unus exstet.*" (To Erwig, king of Spain.) Denz.-Sch., 561

———. Ep. *Regi regum ad Constantinum IV imp.* Confirmation of the decisions of the Third Council of Constantinople (Sixth Ecumenical), which condemned the Monothelites and Pope Honorius I. Denz.-Sch., 561–563.

Leo XIII. Encyclical *Immortale Dei* (Nov. 1, 1885). On the Christian Constitution of States. Accessed Nov. 27, 2015. https://www.vatican.va /content/leo-xiii/la/encyclicals/documents/hf_l-xiii_enc_01111885 _immortale-dei.html.

Lepin, M. *L'idée du sacrifice de la messe d'après les théologiens.* Paris: G. Beauchesne, 1916.

Lercher, S.J., Ludovicus. *Institutiones theologiae dogmaticae.* Barcelona: Herder, vol. 1, 1951; vol. 4-2-1, 1948.

Lesegretain, Claire. "Le missel de Paul VI fête ses trente ans." *La Croix,* Apr. 28, 1999, 19.

Les prêtres du Padreblog. "Au-delà des querelles liturgiques, le pape nous fait contempler le souffle qui doit habiter toute liturgie." *La Croix,* July 6, 2022. https://www.la-croix.com/Debats/Au-dela-querelles-liturgiques -pape-nous-fait-contempler-souffle-doit-habitertoute-liturgie-2022-07-06 -1201223716.

Lynch, J.S.M. *The Rite of Ordination According to the Roman Pontifical.* Second revised edition. New York: The Cathedral Library Association, 1892. Accessed June 6, 2022. https://archive.org/details /ritusordinationu00cath/mode/2up.

M

Manning, Cardinal Henry Edward. *The Vatican Council and Its Definitions: A Pastoral Letter to the Clergy.* New York: D. & J. Sadlier, 1871. Accessed June 21, 2022. https://archive.org/details /TheVaticanCouncilAndItsDefinitions/mode/2up.

Mansi, Joannes Dominicus. Vol. 16 of *Sacrorum conciliorum nova et amplissima collectio.* Venice: Antonium Zatta, 1771. Accessed June 23, 2022. http://patristica.net/mansi.

———. Vol. 52 of *Sacrorum conciliorum nova et amplissima collectio.* Arnheim: Société Nouvelle d'Édition de la Collection Mansi, 1927. Accessed June 23, 2022. http://patristica.net/mansi.

Margelidon, O.P., Philippe-Marie. "La théologie du sacrifice eucharistique chez Jacques Maritain." *Revue Thomiste* (Jan.-Mar. 2015), 101–47.

Maroto, Felipe. *Instituciones de derecho canonico.* Madrid: Editorial del Corazón de Maria, 1919.

Martin, Victor. "Comment s'est formée la doctrine de la supériorité du concile sur le pape." *Revue des Sciences Religieuses,* no. 2 (1937), 121–43. Accessed June 21, 2022. https://www.persee.fr/docAsPDF/scir_0035-2217_1937 _num_17_2_1722.pdf.

———. Vol. 2. *Les origines du gallicanisme.* Paris: Bloud & Gay, 1939.

Martín-Moreno, Juan Manuel. *Apuntes de liturgia.* Academia.edu. Accessed Aug. 19, 2022. https://www.academia.edu/34752512/Apuntes _de_Liturgia.doc.

Martín Patino, José María, A. Pardo, A. Iniesta, and P. Farnes. *Nuevas normas de la misa: Ordenación general del misal romano.* Madrid: B.A.C., 1969.

Matthaeucci, O.F.M., Agostino. *Controversiae fidei de ecclesia,* VII. Quoted by Marie Dominique Bouix. *Tractatus de papa,* 2:658.

Mayer, Antonio de Castro, "Carta a Paulo VI" (Jan. 25, 1974). "O leão de Campos (VI): O bispo de Campos e o magistério de Paulo VI." FratresInUnum.com, June 27, 2010. https://fratresinunum.com/2010 /06/27/o-leao-de-campos-vi-o-bispo-de-campos-e-o-magisterio-de -paulo-vi/.

———. "Carta pastoral sobre o santo sacrifício da missa" (Sept. 12, 1969). In *Por um cristianismo autêntico,* 329–53. São Paulo: Editora Vera Cruz, 1971. Accessed June 1, 2022. https://archive.org/details/porum -cristianismo-autentico/mode/1up.

———. "Carta pastoral sobre problemas do apostolado moderno" (Jan. 6, 1953). In *Por um cristianismo autêntico,* 17–118. São Paulo: Editora Vera Cruz, 1971. Accessed June 1, 2022. https://archive.org/details/porum -cristianismo-autentico/mode/1up.

———. "Considerações a propósito da aplicação dos documentos promulgados pelo Concílio Ecumênico Vaticano II." São Paulo: Editôra Vera Cruz, 1966.

———. Letter of Approval for *Vademecum do católico fiel.* São Paulo, 1969.

Mayol, O.P., Joseph. "Praeambula ad decalogum." In *Theologiae cursus completus.* Paris: Migne, 1858, 13:730–1106.

Mazzella, Card. Camillus. *De religione et ecclesia.* Rome: Ex Typographia Polyglotta, 1880.

Mazzella, Horatius. Vol. 1 of *Praelectiones scholastico-dogmaticae.* Turin: Libreria Editrice Internazionale, 1915.

Merkelbach, O.P., Benedictus Henricus. Vol. 1 of *Summa theologiae moralis.* Paris: Desclée, 1931.

Michel, A. "Hérésie, hérétique." In *D.T.C.,* 6–2e.:2208–57. Accessed May 28, 2022. https://archive.org/details/dictionnairedetv6pt2vaca/page/484 /mode/2up.

———. "Torquemada, (Jean de)." In *D.T.C.,* 15–1e.:1235–39. Accessed May 28, 2022. https://archive.org/details/dictionnairedetv15pt1vaca /page/622/mode/2up.

Migne, Jacques Paul. *Patrologiae cursus completus: Series latina.* Accessed June 23, 2022. https://patristica.net/latina/.

Miguélez Domínguez, Lorenzo, Sabino Alonso Morán, O.P., Marcelino Cabreros de Anta, C.M.F. *Código de derecho canónico.* Madrid: B.A.C., 1957.

Mondello, Victorio. *La dottrina del Gaetano sul romano pontefice.* Messina: Pontificia Universitas Gregoriana, 1965.

Mors, S.J., Iosephus. Vol. 2 of *Institutiones theologiae fundamentalis.* Petrópolis: Vozes, 1943.

Moynihan, James M. *Papal Immunity and Liability.* Rome: Gregorian University Press, 1961.

Mullan, S.J., Elder. trans., *The Spiritual Exercises of St. Ignatius of Loyola.* New York: P.J. Kenedy & Sons, 1914.

N

Nau, O.S.B., Dom Paul. *Une source doctrinale: Les encycliques.* Paris: Éditions du Cèdre, 1952.

New Liturgical Movement. "The Pope on Community Worship and the Golden Calf." NewLiturgicalMovement.org, Mar. 30, 2008. https://www .newliturgicalmovement.org/2008/03/pope-on-community-worship -and-golden.html.

Newman, John Henry Cardinal. *On Consulting the Faithful in Matters of Doctrine.* Edited by John Coulson. Kansas City, Mo.: Sheed and Ward, 1961. Accessed June 18, 2022. https://archive.org/details /onconsultingfait00john/mode/2up.

Nicholas I, Saint. "Epistula ad Michaelem imperatorem." *P.L.,* 119:940.

Noldin, S.J., H., A. Schmitt, S.J., and G. Heinzel, S.J. 2 vols. *Summa theologiae moralis.* Innsbruck: Rauch, 1962.

Notitiae. "Variationes in 'Institutionem generalem missalis romani' inductae." No. 54 (May 1970), 177–90. Accessed July 27, 2022. http://www.cultodivino.va/content/cultodivino/it/rivista-notitiae /indici-annate/1970/54.html.

O

Oppenheim, O.S.B., Philippus. *Principia theologiae liturgicae.* Vol. 7 of *Institutiones systematico-historicae in sacram liturgiam.* Turin: Marietti, 1947. Accessed May 20, 2022. https://isidore.co/misc/Res%20 pro%20Deo/ITOPL_OCR-layer-only/11a.%20Liturgy/Principia%20 theologiae%20liturgiae%20-%20Institutiones%20VII-%20Oppenheim _OCR.pdf.

Ott, Ludwig. *Fundamentals of Catholic Dogma.* St. Louis: B. Herder Book Co., 1954. Accessed May 20, 2022. https://archive.org/details /fundamentalsofca0000ottl/mode/1up.

P

Palazzini, Pietro. "Censura. C. Penale Medicinale." In *E.C.*, 3:1296–301. Accessed July 3, 2022. https://archive.org/details/enciclopedia-cattolica -vol.-3/page/n755/mode/2up.

Palmieri, S.J., Dominicus. *Tractatus de romano pontifice.* Rome: Ex Typographia Polyglotta, 1877.

Paquier, J. "Luther." In *D.T.C.*, 9–1e.:1146–335. Accessed May 15, 2022. https://archive.org/details/dictionnairedet09vaca/page/573/mode/1up.

Paul VI. Allocution to the Students of the Pontifical Lombard Seminary (Dec. 7, 1968). Accessed May 29, 2022. https://www.vatican.va/content/paul -vi/it/speeches/1968/december/documents/hf_p-vi_spe_19681207 _seminario-lombardo.html.

———. Apostolic Constitution *Missale romanum* (Apr. 3, 1969). https://www .vatican.va/content/paul-vi/en/apost_constitutions/documents /hf_p-vi_apc_19690403_missale-romanum.html.

———. Encyclical *Mysterium fidei* (Sept. 3, 1965). https://www.vatican.va /content/paul-vi/en/encyclicals/documents/hf_p-vi_enc_03091965 _mysterium.html.

———. General audience (Nov. 19, 1969). Accessed June 13, 2022. https://www.vatican.va/content/paul-vi/it/audiences/1969/documents /hf_p-vi_aud_19691119.html.

———. General audience (Nov. 26, 1969). in *L'Osservatore Romano*, weekly edition in French, Dec. 5, 1969, p. 12. Accessed June 12, 2022. https://www.vatican.va/content/paul-vi/it/audiences/1969/documents /hf_p-vi_aud_19691126.html.

———. Instruction of October 20, 1969, on the gradual execution of the apostolic constitution *Missale romanum* of the Sacred Congregation for Divine Worship. In *Sedoc*, vol. 2, fasc. 6 (Dec. 1969), 749–52.

Pègues, O.P., Thomas-M. "L'autorité des encycliques pontificales d'après Saint Thomas." *Revue Thomiste* 12 (Paris, Nov.-Dec. 1904), 513–32. Accessed June 28, 2022. https://gallica.bnf.fr/ark:/12148/bpt6k5401635j/f519 .item.

Peinador, C.M.F., Antonius. *Cursus brevior theologiae moralis.* Madrid: Coculsa, tomus 2, vol. 1, 1950; tomus 2, vol. 2, 1954.

Penido, M. Teixeira-Leite. *O mistério dos sacramentos.* Petrópolis: Vozes, 1961.

Pesch, S.J., Christian. Vol. 1 of *Compendium theologiae dogmaticae.* Freiburg: B. Herder, 1921.

———. *Praelectiones dogmaticae*. Freiburg: Herder, vol. 1, 1898; vol. 6, 1900; vol. 9, 1899.

Peters, Edward N., trans. and ed. *The 1917 or Pio-Benedictine Code of Canon Law in English Translation with Extensive Scholarly Apparatus*. San Francisco: Ignatius Press, 2001.

Peter the Lombard. *IV sententiarum*. In St. Thomas Aquinas. "In IV sententiarum."

Phillips, Georges. Vol. 1. *Du droit ecclésiastique*. Paris: Lecoffre, 1885.

Pighi, Albert. *Hierarchiae ecclesiasticae assertio*. Cologne, 1538. Quoted by Dublanchy. "Infaillibilité du pape." *D.T.C.*, 7–2e.:1715.

Pinto, S.J., Manuel. *O valor teológico da liturgia*. Braga: Cruz, 1952. Accessed May 20, 2022. http://www.obrascatolicas.com/livros/Liturgia/O%20 VALOR%20TEOLOGICO%20DA%20LITURGIA%20PADRE%20 MANUEL%20PINTO%20SJ.pdf.

Pius VI. Bull *Auctorem fidei* (Aug. 28, 1794). On the errors of the Synod of Pistoia. Denz.-Sch., 2600–2700; Denz.-Umb., 1501–1599.

Pius IX. Brief *Eximiam tuam*, to the Archbishop of Cologne (June 15, 1857). In Denz.-Sch., 2828–2831.

———. Bull *Ineffabilis Deus* (Dec. 8, 1854). In *The Bull 'Ineffabilis' in Four Languages; on The Immaculate Conception of the Most Blessed Virgin Mary*, edited and translated by Ulick J. Bourke, 4–83. Dublin: John Mullany, 1868. Accessed June 12, 2022. https://archive .org/details/bullineffabilisi00cath/mode/2up.

Pius X, Saint. Apostolic constitution *Vacante sede apostolica* (Dec. 25, 1904).

———. Encyclical *Pascendi Dominici gregis* (Sept. 8, 1907). https://www .vatican.va/content/pius-x/en/encyclicals/documents/hf_p-x_enc _19070908_pascendi-dominici-gregis.html.

Pius XI. Apostolic constitution *Divini cultus* (Dec. 20, 1928). On the Liturgy, Gregorian Chant, and Sacred Music. Accessed June 5, 2022. https://www .vatican.va/content/pius-xi/la/apost_constitutions/documents/hf _p-xi_apc_19281220_divini-cultus-sanctitatem.html.

———. Bull *Inter multiplices* (Dec. 6, 1924). In *Missale bracarense*. Rome: Typis Polyglottis Vaticanis, 1924. Accessed June 5, 2022. https:// almabracarense.files.wordpress.com/2018/12/bullkalend.pdf.

Pius XII. "Allocution to the Participants in the International Congress on Pastoral Liturgy" (Sept. 22, 1956). Accessed May 29, 2022. https://www.vatican.va/content/pius-xii/fr/speeches/1956 /documents/hf_p-xii_spe_19560922_liturgia-pastorale.html.

———. "Allocution of November 1, 1954, on the occasion of the proclamation of the Feast of the Royalty of Our Lady." https://www.vatican.va/content/pius-xii/it/speeches/1954/documents /hf_p-xii_spe_19541101_maria-regina.html.

———. Apostolic constitution *Sacramentum ordinis* (Nov. 30, 1947). On the Sacrament of Holy Orders. Accessed June 12, 2022. https://www.papalencyclicals.net/pius12/p12sacrao.htm.

———. Encyclical *Humani generis*, on some erroneous doctrines. Accessed July 2, 2022. https://www.vatican.va/content/pius-xii/en/encyclicals /documents/hf_p-xii_enc_12081950_humani-generis.html.

———. Encyclical *Mediator Dei* (Nov. 20, 1947). Accessed May 15, 2022. https://www.vatican.va/content/pius-xii/en/encyclicals/documents /hf_p-xii_enc_20111947_mediator-dei.html.

(———.) Instruction of the Holy Office on Sacred Art, July 30, 1952. A.A.S., 1952, 542–46.

(———.) Instruction of February 20, 1950, which modifies the rubrics of the *Pontificale romanum*. Sacred Congregation of Rites. A.A.S., 1950, 448–55.

Pozo, S.J., Candido. *El credo del pueblo de Dios.* Madrid: B.A.C., 1968.

Prétot, Patrick. "La place de la constitution sur la liturgie dans l'herméneutique de Vatican II." *Recherches de Science Religieuse* 101 (2013/1). https://www .cairn.info/revue-recherches-de-science-religieuse-2013-1-page-13.htm.

Prosper of Aquitaine. (To whom the *Indiculus de gratia Dei* is attributed nowadays.) Denz.-Sch., 238–249, Denz.-Umb., 129–142.

Prümmer, O.P., Dominicus M. *Manuale iuris canonici.* Freiburg: Herder, 1933.

———. Vol. 1. *Manuale theologiae moralis.* Freiburg: Herder, 1940.

R

Ratzinger, Joseph. "L'intrépidité d'un vrai témoin." Introduction to *La réforme liturgique en question*, by Klaus Gamber, 6–8. Translated by Simone Wallon. Le Barroux, France: Éditions Sainte-Madeleine, 1992.

Reed, Luther D. *The Lutheran Liturgy: A Study of the Common Liturgy of the Lutheran Church in America.* Revised edition. Philadelphia: Fortress Press, 1947. Accessed Feb. 15, 2022. https://archive.org/details /lutheranliturgys0000reed/page/n5/mode/2up.

Regatillo, S.J., Eduardus F. 2 vols. *Institutiones iuris canonici.* Santander: Sal Terrae, 1961.

Reiffenstuel, O.F.M., Anacletus. *Theologia moralis.* Venice: Bortoli, 1704.

Renovatio. "Il Vaticano II come luogo teologico." *Renovatio* (1967), no. 2, 323–26.

Renwart, S.J., L. Review of *O valor teológico da liturgia*, by Fr. Manuel Pinto. *Nouvelle Revue Théologique* 87 (1955), 421.

Revista Eclesiástica Brasileira. Review of *O valor teológico da liturgia*, by Fr. Manuel Pinto. *Revista Eclesiástica Brasileira* 13 (1953), 812–13.

Rilliet, Jean. *Zwingli: Third Man of the Reformation.* Translated by Harold Knight. Philadelphia: The Westminster Press, 1964. Accessed May 16, 2022. https://archive.org/details/zwinglithirdmano0000rill/mode/1up.

Rivière, J. "La messe durant la période de la Réforme et du Concile de Trente." In *D.T.C.,* 10–1e.:1085–142. Accessed May 16, 2022. https://archive.org /details/dictionnairedeth10vacauoft/mode/1up.

Robert Bellarmine, Saint. *On Councils; On the Church Militant; On the Marks of the Church.* Vol. 1 of *De controversiis: On the Church.* Translated by Ryan Grant. Post Falls, Id.: Mediatrix Press, 2017.

———. *On the Most Holy Sacrifice of the Mass.* Translated by Ryan Grant. Post Falls, Id.: Mediatrix Press, 2020.

———. *On the Roman Pontiff.* Vol. 2 of *De controversiis.* Translated by Ryan Grant. Second edition. Post Falls, Id.: Mediatrix Press, 2017. Reprinted with permission.

———. Opinion on the definition of the Immaculate Conception read before the Sacred Congregation of the Holy Office in the presence of the sovereign pontiff. Quoted in Oppenheim, *Institutiones systematico,* 7:107 and Pinto, *O valor teológico,* 297. Both scholars cite "Dogmatischer wert der liturgie," in *Katholik* (1857), 510.

Rohrbacher, René-François. Vol. 15. *Histoire universelle de l'Église catholique.* Paris: Gaume Frères, 1844.

S

Salaverri, S.J., Ioachim. *De ecclesia Christi.* Vol. 1. *Sacrae theologiae summa.* Madrid: B.A.C., 1958.

Sancto Thomas, Iohannes a. *De auctoritate summi pontificis.* Quebec: Université de Laval, 1947.

Schall, James V. "On Heretical Popes." *The Catholic Thing,* Nov. 11, 2014. https://www.thecatholicthing.org/2014/11/11/on-heretical-popes-3/.

Schillebeeckx, O.P., Edward. "Transubstantiation, Transfinalization and Transignification." In *Living Bread, Saving Cup,* edited by R. Kevin Seasoltz, 175–89. Collegeville, Minn.: The Liturgical Press, 1982. Accessed May 30, 2022. https://archive.org/details/livingbreadsavin 00seas/mode/1up.

Schmalzgrueber, S.J., Franciscus. Vol. 1. *Ius ecclesiasticum universum.* Rome: Typ. Rev. Cam. Apostolicae, 1843.

Schwalm, M.B. "Communisme." In *D.T.C.,* 3–1e.:574–96. Accessed May 25, 2022. https://archive.org/details/dictionnairedet03vaca/page/286 /mode/2up.

Secretariado Nacional de Liturgia da C.N.B.B., arr. *Ordinário da missa: De acôrdo com a edição típica do "Ordo missae."* Petrópolis: Vozes, 1969.

Shaw, Joseph. "Pope Francis' Liturgical Longing." OnePeterFive.com, July 5, 2022. https://onepeterfive.com/pope-francis-liturgical-longing/.

Sigaud, Geraldo de Proença. *Carta pastoral sobre a seita comunista: Seus erros, sua ação revolucionária, e os deveres dos católicos na hora presente.* Second edition. São Paulo: Editora Vera Cruz, 1963. Accessed June 21, 2022. https://issuu.com/nestor87/docs/catecismo_anticomunista_pastoral _dom_sigaud_1963.

Sipos, Stephanus. *Enchiridion iuris canonici.* Orbis Catholicus. Rome: Herder, 1954.

Siscoe, Robert J. "Can the Church Depose an Heretical Pope?" *The Remnant,* Nov. 18, 2014, https://remnantnewspaper.com/web/index.php/articles /item/1284-can-the-church-%20depose-an-heretical-pope.

Sixtus V. "Apostolic constitution *Immensa aeterni Dei* (Jan. 22, 1587)." In vol. 2 of *Bullarium Romanum.* Cherubinorum edition, 463–68. Rome: Ex Typographia Rev. Camerae Apostolicae, 1638.

Smith, Gregory A. "Just One-Third of U.S. Catholics Agree With Their Church That Eucharist Is Body, Blood of Christ." PewResearch.org, Aug. 5, 2019. https://www.pewresearch.org/fact-tank/2019/08/05/transubstantiation -eucharist-u-s-catholics/.

Solá, S.J., Franciscus a P. *De sacramentis vitae socialis Christianae seu de sacramentis ordinis et matrimonii.* In *Sacrae theologiae summa.* Madrid: B.A.C., 1962.

Straub, S.J., Antonius. Vol. 2. *De ecclesia Christi.* Innsbruck: Rauch-Pustet, 1912.

Suárez, S.J., Franciscus. *De caritate.* In vol. 12 of *Opera omnia.* Paris: Vivès, 1858. Accessed June 13, 2022. https://archive.org/details /rpfranciscisuare12suar/mode/2up.

———. *Defensio fidei catholicae et apostolicae contra errores anglicanae sectae* In vol. 24 of *Opera omnia.* Paris: Vivès, 1859. Accessed June 13, 2022. https:// archive.org/details/rpfranciscisuare24suar/mode/2up.

———. *De fide theologica.* In vol. 12 of *Opera omnia.* Paris: Vivès, 1858. Accessed June 13, 2022. https://archive.org/details /rpfranciscisuare12suar/mode/2up.

———. *De legibus.* In vol. 5 of *Opera omnia.* Paris: Vivès, 1856. Accessed June 13, 2022. https://archive.org/details/rpfranciscisuare05suar/mode/2up.

———. *In tertiam partem D. Thomae.* In vol. 21 of *Opera omnia.* Paris: Vivès, 1877.

———. *De religione.* In vol. 15 of *Opera omnia.* Paris: Vivès, 1859. Accessed June 13, 2022. https://archive.org/details/rpfranciscisuare 15suar/mode/2up.

Sylvius, Franciscus. *Commentarium in totam II–II S. Thomae Aquinatis.* Antwerp: Verdussen, 1697.

T

Tanner, S.J., Adam. *De spe et caritate.* Quoted in Wernz and Vidal, *Ius canonicum,* 2:518.

Tanquerey, Adolphe. Vol. 1. *Synopsis theologiae dogmaticae.* Paris–Tournai–Rome: Desclée, 1959.

———. *Synopsis theologiae moralis et pastoralis.* Paris–Tournai–Rome: Desclée, 1948.

———. *Brevior synopsis theologiae moralis et pastoralis.* Paris–Tournai–Rome: Desclée, 1946.

Thomas Aquinas, Saint. *Commentary on the First Epistle to the Corinthians.* Translated by Fr. Fabian Larcher, O.P. Accessed June 4, 2022. https://isidore.co/aquinas/english/SS1Cor.htm#116.

———. *Commentary on St. Paul's Epistle to the Galatians.* Translated by F.R. Larcher, O.P. Albany, N.Y.: Magi Books, Inc. 1966. Html format by Joseph Kenny, O.P. Accessed June 21, 2022. https://isidore.co/aquinas/english/SSGalatians.htm#23.

———. *Commentum in IV librum sententiarum magistri Petri Lombardi.* Vol. 10 of *Opera omnia.* Paris: Vivès, 1889.

———. "*Super epistolam ad Titum lectura.*" In *Super epistolas S. Pauli lectura.* Turin-Rome: Marietti, 1953.

———. *The Summa Theologica.* Translated by Fathers of the English Dominican Province. Accessed June 4, 2022. http://www.documentacatholicaomnia.eu/03d/1225-1274,_Thomas _Aquinas,_Summa_Theologiae_%5B1%5D,_EN.pdf.

Torquemada, Juan de. *Summa de ecclesia.* Venice: Tramezinus, 1561. Accessed July 28, 2022. https://archive.org/details/bub_gb_GWP6pAt-ctEC /mode/2up.

U

Urdañoz, Teófilo. *Relecciones teológicas: Edición crítica del texto latino, versión española, introducción general e introducciones con el estudio de su doctrina teológico-jurídica.* In *Obras de Francisco de Vitoria.* Madrid: B.A.C., 1960.

———. *Comentario a la Suma teológica de San Tomás de Aquino.* Vol 8 of *Summa theologica.* Madrid: B.A.C., 1956.

V

Vacant, Jean Michel Alfred, Eugène Mangenot, and Émile Amann, eds. *Dictionnaire de théologie catholique [D.T.C.].* 30 vols. Paris: Letouzey et Ané, 1902–1950.

Vacca, Salvatore. *Prima sedes a nemine iudicatur : Genesi e sviluppo storico dell'assioma fino al Decreto di Graziano.* Rome: Pontificia Università Gregoriana, 1993.

Vagaggini, O.S.B., Cipriano. "O nôvo *Ordo missae* e a ortodoxia." *Revista Eclesiástica Brasileira* 30 (1970), 93–101.

———. *Theological Dimensions of the Liturgy: A General Treatise on the Theology of the Liturgy.* Translated by Leonard J. Doyle and W.A. Jurgens (from the fourth Italian edition). Collegeville, Minn.: The Liturgical Press, 1976. Accessed May 24, 2022. https://archive.org/details /theologicaldimen0000vaga/mode/2up.

Van Laak, S.J., H. Pars I. *Institutionum theologiae fundamentalis repetitorium.* Rome: Gregorian, 1921.

Van Noort, G. *Christ's Church.* Vol. 2 of *Dogmatic Theology.* Translated and revised by John J. Castelot and William R. Murphy. Westminster, Md.: The Newman Press, 1959. Accessed June 14, 2022. https://archive.org /details/vannoortvol2christchurch/mode/2up.

———. *Tractatus de ecclesia Christi.* Bussum, Netherlands: Brand, 1954.

Vasquez, S.J., Gabriel. *Disputationibus de eucharistia, & missae sacrificio.* Vol. 3 of *Commentariorum ac disputationum in tertiam partem sancti Thomae.* London: Pillehote, 1620.

Vatican Council, First. Dogmatic constitution *Dei Filius.* (On the Catholic Faith.) In Denz.-Sch., 3000–3045.

———. Dogmatic constitution *Pastor aeternus.* (On the Church.) In Denz.-Sch., 3050–3075.

Vatican Council, Second. Constitution *Sacrosanctum concilium* (Dec. 4, 1963). On the Sacred Liturgy. Accessed June 6, 2022. https://www.vatican.va/archive/hist_councils/ii_vatican_council /documents/vat-ii_const_19631204_sacrosanctum-concilium_en.html.

———. Dogmatic constitution *Lumen gentium* (Nov. 21, 1964). On the Church. Accessed June 6, 2022. https://www.vatican.va/archive/hist_councils/ii_vatican_council/ documents/vat-ii_const_19641121_lumen-gentium_en.html.

Veloso, A. Review of *O valor teológico da liturgia,* by Fr. Manuel Pinto. *Brotéria* 56 (1953), 240.

Vermeersch, S.J., Arthurus, and Joseph Creusen, S.J. *Epitome iuris canonici.* Malines-Rome: Dessain, vol. 1, 1949; vol. 2, 1940; vol. 3, 1946.

Vitoria, O.P., Franciscus de. *Obras de Francisco de Vitoria.* Madrid: B.A.C., 1960.

W

Weidert, Aline and Alain. "Avec François, l'urgence d'une formation pour et par la liturgie." *La Croix,* Jul. 8, 2022. https://www.la-croix.com/Debats /Francois-lurgence-dune-formation-liturgie-2022-07-08-1201224067.

———. "La fin des messes d'autre 'foi', une chance pour le Christ!" *La Croix,* Feb. 10, 2022. https://www.la-croix.com/Debats/fin-messes-dautre-foi -chance-Christ-2022-02-10-1201199636.

Wernz, S.J., Franciscus Xavier, and Petrus Vidal S.J. *Ius canonicum.* Rome: Gregoriana, vol. 1, 1938; vol. 2, 1923; vol. 7, 1937.

Wilmers, S.J., Guilelmus. *De Christi ecclesia.* Ratisbonne–New York– Cincinnati: Pustet, 1897.

Wood, Jacob W. "Can a Pope be a Heretic?" *Crisis Magazine,* Mar. 4, 2015. https://www.crisismagazine.com/2015/can-pope-heretic.

X

Xavier da Silveira, Arnaldo Vidigal. "A infalibilidade das leis eclesiásticas." São Paulo: self-published, Jan. 1971.

———. "Atos, gestos, atitudes e omissões podem caracterizar o herege." ("Acts, Gestures, Attitudes and Omissions Can Characterize the Heretic.") *Catolicismo,* no. 204 (Dec. 1967), 4–6. Accessed June 29, 2022. https://catolicismo.com.br/Acervo/Num/0204/P04-05.html.

———. *Can a Pope Be . . . a Heretic? The Theological Hypothesis of a Heretical Pope.* Porto: Caminhos Romanos, 2018.

———. *Can Documents of the Magisterium of the Church Contain Errors? Can the Catholic Faithful Resist Them?* Translated by John R. Spann and José Aloisio A. Schelini. Spring Grove, Penn.: The American Society for the Defense of Tradition, Family, and Property, 2015.

———. *Considerações sobre o* Ordo missae *de Paulo VI.* São Paulo: self-published, June 1970.

———. *Ipotesi teologica di un papa eretico.* Chieti: Edizioni Solfanelli, 2016.

———. *La nouvelle messe de Paul VI: Qu'en penser?* Chiré-en-Montreuil, France: Diffusion de la Pensée Française, 1975.

———. "Modificações introduzidas no Ordo de 1969." São Paulo: self-published, Aug. 1970.

———. "Não só a heresia pode ser condenada pela autoridade eclesiástica." ("Not Only Heresy Can Be Condemned By Ecclesiastical Authority.") *Catolicismo*, no. 203 (Nov. 1967), 4–6. Accessed June 29, 2022. https://catolicismo.com.br/Acervo/Num/0203/P04-05.html.

———. "Pode haver êrro em documentos do magisterio?" ("Can There Be Error in Documents of the Magisterium?") *Catolicismo*, no. 223 (July 1969), 7–9. Accessed June 29, 2022. https://catolicismo.com.br/Acervo/Num/0223/P06-07.html.

———. "Pode um católico rejeitar a *Humanae Vitae?*" ("Can a Catholic Reject *Humanae Vitae?*") *Catolicismo*, nos. 212/214 (Aug.-Oct. 1968), 19. Accessed June 29, 2022. https://catolicismo.com.br/Acervo/Num/0212-214/P18-19.html.

———. "Qual a autoridade doutrinária dos documentos pontifícios e conciliares?" ("What Is the Doctrinal Authority of Pontifical and Conciliar Documents?") *Catolicismo*, no. 202 (Oct. 1967), 4–5. Accessed June 29, 2022. https://catolicismo.com.br/Acervo/Num/0202/P04-05.html.

———. "Resistência publica a decisões da autoridade eclesiástica." ("Public Resistance to Decisions of Ecclesiastical Authority") *Catolicismo*, no. 224 (Aug. 1969), 2–3. Accessed June 29, 2022. https://catolicismo.com.br/Acervo/Num/0224/P02-03.html.

———. "Respondendo a objeções de um imaginário leitor progressista." ("Answering the Objections of an Imaginary Progressivist Reader.") *Catolicismo*, no. 206 (Feb. 1968), 2–3. Accessed June 29, 2022. https://catolicismo.com.br/Acervo/Num/0206/P02-03.html.

Z

Zaccaria, S.J., Franciscus Antonius. *De usu librorum liturgicorum in rebus theologicis.* In *Theologiae cursus completus*, 5:207–310. Paris: J.P. Migne, 1860.

Zalba, S.J., Marcelino. 2 vols. *Theologiae moralis compendium.* Madrid: E.A.C., 1958.

*   *   *

Liturgia da Missa. São Paulo: Edições Paulinas, 1969.

Liturgia Luterana. Publication authorized by the "Evangelical Lutheran Church of Brazil." Porto Alegre: Casa Publicadora Concordia.

New . . . Saint Joseph Sunday Missal: Prayerbook and Hymnal for 1972. New York: Catholic Book Publishing, Co. 1972.

Notitiae. Semi-official organ of the Consilium Pontificium ad Exsequendam Constitutionem de Sacra Liturgia.

O novo Ordo missae. Fourth edition. Petrópolis: Vozes, 1969.

Ordinario de la misa. Madrid: Various publishers, 1969.

Ordo missae, 1969 edition. Editio typica, Typis Polyglottis Vaticanis, 1969.

Ordo missae, 1970 edition. In *Missale Romanum,* Typis Polyglottis Vaticanis, 1970.

Presbiteral. Petrópolis: Vozes, 1969.

Index

For a Different Index Please Go To

www.issuu.com/crusademagazine/docs/two_timely_issues_index
OR
www.archive.org/details/two-timely-issues-index

W—

Weidert, Aline and Alain, 318–19

Wernz, Franciscus Xavier. *See also* Notorious and publicly divulged

on acts connected with heresy, 277–78, 280

on a dubious pope, 243n917

on external heresy, 269

on fifth opinion, 171, 199n802, 207, 210–11, 218, 225

on incompatibility between heresy and jurisdiction, 213, 219, 220n845, 221

on legitimacy of universally accepted pope, 245

on legitimate resistance to ecclesiastical authority, 287

on notoriety, 218n838

on papal infallibility in universal laws, 123

on a schismatic pope, 238n894

on suspicion of heresy, 275–76

William of Ockham, 158

Wilmers, Guilelmus, 242–43

Wine, 66–67. *See also* Bread

Women, and the *Novus Ordo,* xvii–xviii, 67, 87n339

Wood, Jacob W., 156

Word. *See* Liturgy

X—

Xavier da Silveira, Arnaldo Vidigal, xiv, xvi, xviii, 2n17, 32n122, 78n311, 155–56, 160–62

mentioned in letter to Paul VI, 227

Z—

Zaccaria, Francisco Antonio, 126, 139

Zalba, Marcelino, 269n991, 290

Zinelli, Federico Maria, 184, 224

Zoghby, Elias, 41

Zosimus, St., 35

Zwingli, Ulrich, 57, 90, 96–97, 108–9, 113

FOR A DIFFERENT INDEX PLEASE GO TO

www.issuu.com/crusademagazine/docs/two_timely_issues_index

OR

www.archive.org/details/two-timely-issues-index

www.ingramcontent.com/pod-product-compliance
Lightning Source LLC
Chambersburg PA
CBHW060854120626
46553CB00001B/86